Laughs, Lies & American Justice

East End Eddie Doherty

Foreword by Jim Craig
US Olympic Gold Medal Hockey Champion

Laughs, Lies & American Justice
©2023 East End Eddie Doherty. All rights reserved.

Any reproduction of any part of this publication without the written permission of the author, his agent or representative, with the exception of short excerpts for the purpose of reviews, is strictly prohibited and in violation of the law.

Written & published by Eddie Doherty,
Big Ditch Productions in association with Ballyjamesduff Entertainment,
Mattapoisett, Massachusetts
eastendeddie789@yahoo.com

Legal: Attorney Melissa Nasson
617-966-4499, melissa@literary-lawyer.com

Imprint by Lulu Press, Inc.

ISBN 978-1-312-28243-8
Library of Congress Control Number: 2023910916

This book was written, edited and printed
in the greatest country on the face of the earth -
the United States of America.

His Excellency, Governor A. Paul Cellucci once said, "The most dangerous place for a woman in Massachusetts is in her own home."
A percentage of the proceeds from the sale of this book will be donated by the author to Jane Doe Inc. in an effort to help combat the horrors of domestic violence.

Dedication

To our daughters Kaitlin M. Wirth & Christine E. Ehlers. They bring love and happiness to our family every day along with husbands Jon & Dan as well as grandchildren Adalyn, Joe, Lucy, Rose and Molly.

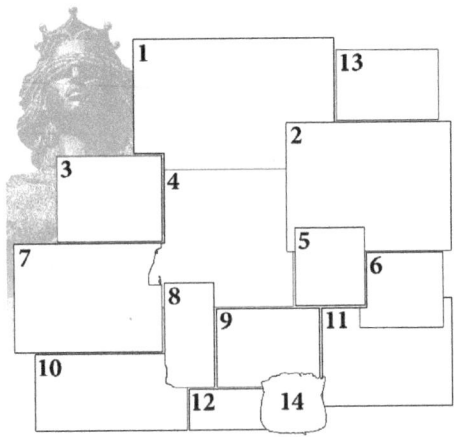

1. author taking oath of office from His Excellency, Governor A. Paul Cellucci
2. L-R Irish Taoiseach Bertie Ahern, author, United States Senator Edward M. Kennedy (Allan Goodrich photo, JFK Library)
3. PR King George K. Regan Jr. & author at Regan's Marina Bay home (David Hayman photo)
4. WDC Law Day L-R author, First Justice Emogene Johnson Smith, District Courts Chief Justice Paul C. Dawley
5. L-R Attleboro Police Detective Lieutenant Arthur J. Brillon & Massachusetts State Police Captain Robert A. Enos (Art Brillon photo)
6. Superior Court Judge William F. Sullivan at University of Notre Dame (Jim Sabitus photo)
7. L-R Massachusetts State Police Troopers Paul Landry & Michael Crosby holding evidence from rest area shootout; note 9mm bullet hole in license plate (photo courtesy of Massachusetts State Police Museum & Learning Center and retired Trooper Paul Landry)
8. author's wife Joanne, AKA J. Do, in Bermuda
9. Attorney Glen Hannington & author after delicious lunch at Vel's Restaurant in West Wareham (Judy A. Bump photo)
10. L-R author, J. Do, Attorney Tracy L. Wilson & husband Register of Probate, now Norfolk County Sheriff Patrick W. McDermott
11. WDC Law Day L-R Boston Police Officer Jennifer J. Penton, now MSP Trooper Penton, United States Attorney Carmen M. Ortiz, now a partner with the law firm Anderson & Kreiger LLP, J. Do, author
12. greyhound
13. thoroughbred race horse
14. fishing gear owned by John T. Brady, author's great-grandfather

Table of Contents

Message From a Distinguished Writer 2
About the Author 3
Foreword 4
Acknowledgements 6
Introduction 7
   1. The Jewelry City 9
   2. My Mother & My Wife - nobody worked a room better 11
   3. Courthouses 27
   4. "Gruffy" 133
   5. Law Enforcement 146
   6. Breaking News 209
   7. Family 229
   8. Grandkids 269
   9. Politics 273
   10. Race Tracks & more 292
   11. Canal Rats, et al 314
   12. Epilogue 332
Index 333

Message From a Distinguished Writer

"Eddie Doherty is as good a storyteller as he is a fisherman, and that is saying something. In fact, he lured me into this memoir with no trouble at all, and soon I was hooked. Strongly recommended."

- Ted Widmer, former White House speech writer for President Bill Clinton

About the Author

Eddie Doherty fished the East End of the Cape Cod Canal so often that other fishermen started calling him East End Eddie, thus a nickname became a pen name. Doherty is a graduate of Dominican Academy, Attleboro High School and the University of South Florida. He worked for almost 37 years in the Massachusetts Court system where he became the youngest Assistant Clerk-Magistrate in the state at age 25 for the Attleboro District Court before being appointed eighteen years later to the lifetime position of Clerk-Magistrate of the Wrentham District Court by His Excellency, A. Paul Cellucci, Governor of the Commonwealth. He was honored to be chosen as the recipient of the Amicus Curiae Award by the Norfolk County Bar Association, founded in 1797. He heard evidence on everything from speeding to murder, but now in retirement is hearing the sound of his grandchildren giggle and of striped bass breaking the surface of the ocean.

The author has fished the warm currents of the Gulf of Mexico as well as the powerful Atlantic surf pounding the rugged coast of Maine. He has surf cast along the striper coast all the way down to the clear tropical inlets of the Florida Keys. His cousins in Ireland took him from Ballyjamesduff to the River Shannon where he wet a line in the same water that had sustained his ancestors with fish during the potato famine long ago. He has been privileged to have fished Sakonnet with Charley Soares, Chappaquiddick with Janet Messineo and the Cape Cod Canal with State Representative Patrick Kearney.

Doherty is the author of *SEVEN MILES AFTER SUNDOWN* Surfcasting for Striped Bass along the World Famous Cape Cod Canal which was announced as the #1 New Release in Fishing on Amazon and was chosen as an Award-Winning Finalist at the 2019 International Book Awards in Los Angeles. He wrote a weekly column for *The Falmouth Enterprise* and has been published in *Cape Cod Magazine, On The Water, The Fisherman, Cape Cod Times, The Boston Globe, The Sun Chronicle, Cape Cod Life, Coastal Angler Magazine* and the *Congressional Record*. Doherty films a weekly Canal Report video for subscribers of *The Fisherman* and a monthly cable Surfcasting Report for Bourne TV. He is a member of the Canal Sportsman's Club, fished in the Stan Gibbs Cape Cod Canal Fisherman's Classic, and his striped bass entry won the shore division in his first Buzzards Bay Anglers Club Fall Derby. He lives close to the Cape Cod Canal in Mattapoisett with his wife Joanne who is affectionately known as J. Do.

They were lucky to be blessed with the birth of five healthy grandchildren to enjoy during retirement. His colleagues knew that he would be spending time teaching his young grandkids to fish for striped bass so on his last day on the job they presented him with many generous gifts including a nice shirt that is embroidered with a slogan coined by future Clerk-Magistrate & Judge Michelle L. Kelley, RETIREMENT - STRIPERS & DIAPERS!

Foreword
by
Jim Craig, US Olympic Hockey Gold Medal Champion

Throughout my entire career, in both the athletic and business industries, I have been guided by my moral compass: **"Family first, do the right thing, never jeopardize your integrity."** This compass led me through my hockey years to ultimately win Olympic Gold with my 1980 teammates, and beyond to build the business I currently own and operate, Gold Medal Strategies. With Gold Medal Strategies, I serve as a Motivational Speaker and Corporate Consultant, and have been fortunate to meet incredible people along my journey who align with my moral compass, and to learn more from them that I can teach.

When Ed came to me in 2016 and asked me to speak at Law Day Ceremony at the Wrentham District Court, I was immediately impressed by the way he carried himself and felt the synergy with our values. We share the same love for our country, mine first expressed through my representation at the Olympic Games, and Ed's represented through the way he has served our country as a Clerk-Magistrate, and for the work he has done for the veterans of our nation. I was further impressed by Ed's creation of the Christmas Card writing campaign, Court Cards for Combat, where school kids and adults would get cards to him to deliver overseas to our troops. Our collective patriotism is rampant, and I now serve as a board member for the Special Operations Warrior Foundation, committing to the education and future of the families of our veterans as well.

Both Ed and I have homes in Mattapoisett, MA, a place we call one of the "best kept secrets," as it affords you peace, tranquility, and opportunity to spend time with friends and family. When I met Ed, I was also able to meet his wife, Joanne (J. Do) and learn about their two married daughters and five grandchildren, and immediately recognized our shared love for this special place. One note (amongst many) that struck me about Ed is he had found a particular remote fishing hole nearby in Mattapoisett, and typically you don't share these locations with anyone else, to keep them for yourself – but Ed shared the location with me, because that's the type of person he is – the type who shares everything and wants the best for everyone.

A few years ago, my New Year's Resolution was to go back to all of my mentors and say "thank you," for the time, advice and kindness they had shared with me. I began to live by the saying, "It's nice to be important, but it's more important to be nice," and Ed is a person who has never forgotten that. He has been mentored by many, but mentored even more, with the way he carried himself through his profession – always remembering there is a difference between a bad guy, and a good guy who made a bad mistake. He finds humor everywhere, as I am sure you will learn through his stories, and he truly plays his role in making this world a better place.

Through Ed's hard work, mentorship and love for his country, he is now able to leave a legacy for his wife, J. Do, his two children, and do what I believe is the most important thing in life: be a grandfather. What you will learn from this book is that being a good human who cares about their country and its people is what makes Ed and his stories that he has chosen to share with you so special.

Enjoy the read, and remember: always be a good person, give more than you receive, stay true to your moral compass, and that the impossible becomes possible when you **believe.**

Jim Craig
1980 Olympic Gold Medalist
Founder, President & CEO of Gold Medal Strategies

Jim Craig

Acknowledgements

The following people are gratefully acknowledged for their valued assistance in the production of this book:

Attleboro Public Library Reference Department; Attleboro Police retired Detective Lieutenant Arthur J. Brillon; Pawtucket Police retired Detective Gene Champagne; Mike Connell; Jim Craig, US Olympic Gold Medal Hockey Champion; The Honorable Francis T. Crimmins Jr., former Stoughton District Court First Justice; The Honorable Kevan J. Cunningham, retired Regional Administrative Justice; Franklin Auto Body Owner Dick DeMarzi; Heather Douglas, Staples Supervisor; North Attleborough Police retired Detective Michael J. Elliott; Karen Fisher, WCVB Channel 5 Media Relations Specialist; FBI retired Special Agent John Gamel; Peter M. Gay, *Sun Chronicle* Columnist & Executive Director of North Attleborough Community Television; North Attleborough Police retired Chief Michael P. Gould Sr.; *Sun Chronicle* Columnist Bill Gouveia; Diana Gray, Foxborough Administrative Secretary, Planning, Zoning & Conservation; Massachusetts State Police retired Lieutenant Colonel Ronald J. Guilmette; Massachusetts State Police retired Lieutenant Herb Harding; Donald P. Hart, Nantucket District Court Clerk-Magistrate; Lesley J. Hazeldine, Wrentham District Court First Assistant Clerk-Magistrate; Mattapoisett Town Clerk Catherine Heuberger; James Hill, JFK Library; Brian J. "Gruffy" Kearney, Natick District Court Clerk-Magistrate; The Honorable Michelle L. Kelley, Associate Justice of the District Court; United States Senator Paul G. Kirk Jr.; Paige Kley, US District Court Public Realm Director; Massachusetts State Police retired Trooper Paul Landry; Darcy H. Lee, author of *GHOSTS OF PLYMOUTH, MASSACHUSETTS*; National Baseball Hall of Fame Reference Services Manager Cassidy Lent; *Sun Chronicle* Reporter David Linton; Sally A. Bruno Linton, Attleboro District Court retired Operations Supervisor; Francesca Lombardo, Lombardo's Creative Marketing Director; Attorney Paul F. Lorincz; Greyhound Hall of Fame Director Kathy Lounsbury; Henry Maxim, greyhound writer; Rhode Island House of Representatives Clerk Francis P. "Frank" McCabe; Joseph Case High School Principal Brian McCann; The Honorable Brian R. Merrick, Orleans District Court retired First Justice; Principal Clerk Samantha Mills, Taunton Building Department; Town of Franklin Appraiser Peter Mooney; website publisher Steve Ole Olson; Abby Murphy, Boston Red Sox Director of Baseball Communications & Media Relations; April Pascucci, MLIS, Reference Librarian, State Library of Massachusetts; Alessandro Pizzi, Wrentham District Court retired Chief Probation Officer; Kristin M. Ryan, Program Manager IV, Division of Administrative Services, Massachusetts State Police; bestselling author Casey Sherman; Michelle Skaar, Reference Librarian, Mattapoisett Free Public Library; *Sun Chronicle* Photo Editor Mark Stockwell; Brian V. Sullivan, Lynn District Court retired Clerk-Magistrate; Robert A. "Ted" Tomasone, Somerville District Court retired Clerk-Magistrate; Jeff Twiss, Vice President of Media Services/Alumni Relations, Boston Celtics; Kathryn Waxman, Director of Internal Sales & New Product Development, Gold Medal Strategies; The Honorable Phillip L. Weiner, International Judge; Kaitlin M. Wirth, Photo Technician; Lisa Witkus, King Philip Regional School District Executive Assistant; Joshua Wolloff, King Philip Regional Middle School Band Director.

Introduction

I grew up in Attleboro, Massachusetts after our family moved from Taunton when I was seven years old. This book is a compilation of mostly unrelated short stories, brief observations and anecdotes detailing multiple events that I was party to, witnessed, read in police reports or heard about mostly during my nearly thirty seven years of service in the Massachusetts court system. It was my privilege to work at the Attleboro District Court (ADC) from 1980 until leaving for the Wrentham District Court (WDC) in 1998 where I spent the last half of my career until retiring in 2016. I got to know many hardworking, honest court employees, attorneys and police officers who did their best every day to fulfill the valid expectations of those noble professions.

There are also stories included that have nothing to do with the courts that I hope you will find interesting or humorous. I wish that I had written down more of the particulars of certain circumstances over the years as my memory is far from perfect, but I have tried to be scrupulous in relating authentic details to the best of my ability and attempted to credit sources where research and recollection allowed. My third grade Nun, Sister Mary Alice would gasp in disbelief if she knew that I am sometimes being introduced as an author!

The book is divided into twelve chapters. I have tried to focus on positive aspects of personal interactions and included stories where it seemed to make the most sense, but many could have been listed in more than one chapter. My young grandchildren will eventually grow up to hear everything in this world and there is some profanity on these pages, but since there is at least one word that I don't want my grandkids to see coming from my keyboard - F*** has been substituted for the real thing.

I have tried to remember funny aspects of criminal and civil matters even when the humor was generated from a serious case. For example, there is nothing funny about the sometime tragic results of drunk driving, but the vast majority of cases don't end in tragedy. The recognition of humor should not be taken to be disrespectful to victims of crime as making victims whole was always my main objective. As long as feelings aren't hurt - laughter is the best medicine!

Clerk-magistrates and assistant clerk-magistrates use the preponderance of evidence standard for Civil Motor Vehicle Infraction hearings and only issue a criminal complaint after a finding of probable cause. In general, after a determination of culpability I would quite often give people a break on speeding tickets and other nonviolent offenses, but usually not on serious cases, especially where victims had been physically harmed. You will hear some say that there are too many people in jail in our country, even for serious violent offenses, but when an 82-year old lady in a Bind Over Hearing is testifying on the witness stand that she recited her prayers while holding her rosary beads over her head as she was being brutally raped by the smirking 22-year old male seated in the courtroom to my left, you begin to wonder about just what is a fair sentence. I have always had an abiding respect for the views of others, but many of the people opposed to long sentences would change their minds if they had followed me around to courtrooms and police stations for a few weeks.

Whenever a judge or clerk-magistrate is mentioned on these pages I have also included the appointing authority. The inclusion is not intended to define judicial philosophy, political alignment or any other consequential matter. I just believe that identification with the appointing governor becomes an integral part of the clerk-magistrate's or judge's life and that they should be forever linked together.

I listened to testimony from victims, plaintiffs, defendants, respondents, uniformed police officers, detectives and other witnesses while hearing small claims cases, civil motor vehicle infraction hearings, arrest & search warrant requests, criminal show cause hearings and more. I would have to make a decision on these cases based primarily on the credibility of each witness and the veracity of the testimony. Most people were truthful, but many were not. When it came to telling a lie, some of our litigants made George Santos look like George Washington! A Cape Cod attorney smiled and told me one time that it seems as though I make my living listening to people lie to me. We both had a good laugh about such a unique job description!

The immortal Lou Gehrig eventually succumbed to the disease that still carries his name. I have always admired his strength, tenacity, courage and optimism in the face of terrible adversity. His emotional farewell speech at Yankee Stadium on July 4, 1939 inspired the huge crowd with his ability to always appreciate the bright side when he alluded to his troubles and then said, "Yet today, I consider myself the luckiest man on the face of the earth." I am extremely grateful for the fortuitous events and good fortune that have come my way in so many different circumstances throughout my life. When it comes to luck - Lou Gehrig has nothing on me!

1. The Jewelry City

My two brothers and I were born as Democrats and raised as Catholics in an Irish American family where the dinner table discussion usually centered on politics, the Boston Celtics, Red Sox, Bruins or Patriots. We grew up in Attleboro, Massachusetts which is known as the Jewelry City. Enormous quantities of finish and raw stock jewelry were produced at manufacturing plants by generations of workers throughout the area. It seemed as though everybody had at least one friend who had a parent employed by Balfour, Jostens or some other factory.

I couldn't afford a class ring upon graduation from the University of South Florida, but I knew that if I ever wanted one later that our childhood home was only a couple of miles down the street from Balfour where they were made. My generous mom and dad gave me my class ring that Christmas, but it came through with the wrong graduation year. I was still living at home with the factory close by so I walked into Balfour on County Street and told a lady seated behind the counter that I needed the year changed on my ring. Her eyes remained focused on her magazine as she asked me which school. When I told her the University of South Florida she looked up at me with an astonished expression and said, "Oh, you could have mailed it honey. You didn't have to drive all that way!"

Florida is a melting pot of people from all over the country and world. A lot of girls continue to wear their high school class ring during their freshman year in college. I would tell girls at USF that I bet that I could guess where her ring was made. She would take off the ring and look on the inside where it just about always said either Balfour or Jostens so I had 50-50 shot at being right! A girl from Oklahoma or Indiana would look amazed and say, "How did you know that?"

I am the oldest, then Brendan and youngest was our late brother Christopher who we tragically lost just before his 57th birthday. Brendan and Chris were both great athletes and talented basketball players in particular. They both graduated from Bishop Feehan High School with Brendan becoming the school's first basketball player to score 1,000 points which was prior to the advent of the three-point shot. Thus, all of his long buckets only counted for two points making the accomplishment even more impressive. Later in life, Brendan was inducted into the Feehan Athletic Hall of Fame where he would eventually be joined by his son Matthew who was also an outstanding athlete recognized with the same honor as his father. Together they became just the second father and son in the history of the school to be honored in the Hall of Fame.

Brendan would become a trooper after graduating from the Rhode Island State Police Academy, forge an exemplary career in law enforcement and eventually be appointed Colonel and Superintendent of the Rhode Island State Police as well as Secretary of Public Safety by Governor Donald L. Carcieri. We were all very proud to see Brendan take the oath of office at the State House in Providence.

Chris became one of a very select group to play on a high school basketball team that was undefeated in league play and would later go on to purchase the 19th Hole Tavern in Hyannis with his childhood friend David Cronan. The Irish pub is noted for serving a perfect pint of Guinness and the coldest beer on Cape Cod. St. Patrick's Day is a major event in our family as Chris used to host an annual St. Patrick's Day Party which had grown to legendary status over the years featuring corned beef, cabbage, Irish Step Dancers, bagpipers and other beautiful Celtic music.

Our mother, Carol Flynn Doherty, RN, is a Registered Nurse and one of the funniest people in my life. She would care for our family with a steel minded devotion and happy stories to make troubles seem a little better by putting worries behind us.

Our father, Dr. Edward J. Doherty DDS, was a dental surgeon and a great dad. He took us to the Baseball Hall of Fame in Cooperstown and was always there when we needed him. He taught us sports, high morals and patriotism. One of his favorite activities was playing a tape recording over and over again of the radio broadcast of the game when Brendan scored his 1,000th point. He was our dentist until he took ill and passed away at the young age of 57 so he never got to see the Boston Red Sox win the world championship. Many years later in 2004 my brothers and I visited our father's grave which is almost at the top of a majestic hill in the Bourne National Cemetery. It was the day after the Sox finally broke the Curse of the Bambino by winning the World Series so Brendan had the magnificent idea to leave a copy of *The Boston Globe* sports section next to dad's granite grave marker. That sentimental stroke of innate kindness remains firmly planted in the best part of my memory. After saying a prayer we started to make our way down the knoll as we passed another family heading up the hill to visit a grave near our dad. Chris facetiously commented that when those people see the newspaper they might think that dad has the *Globe* delivered here!

Dr. Edward J. Doherty holding Brendan, Carol holding Chris, author, dog Suzie foreground

2. My Mother & My Wife - nobody worked a room better

My mother has always been a powerful and guiding force in my life as one of the strongest willed individuals that I have ever known. Her father, my grandfather John P. "Jack" Flynn, was an outstanding detective with the Taunton Police Department, but she lost her mother Margaret Flynn, nee Brady early in life to a stroke and developed a thick skin with a street smart awareness to compliment her beautiful smile. She worked as a Registered Nurse at Boston Children's Hospital - the same great facility that later employed our daughter, her granddaughter Christine E. Ehlers, RN. My mom also worked at Morton Hospital as well as Boston City Hospital, now called Boston Medical Center, which was the pride of the James Michael Curley administration. She was always in demand for private duty, but was told on more than one occasion to use the back door with the rest of the Irish servants in some well to do homes in the city of Boston. There was never any opposition after mom's determined voice was heard telling them that she was there to render medical assistance and that she would use any door that she pleased including the front door!

My two brothers and I played sports and got banged up from time to time as all kids do so it was comforting to have a mother that was a nurse who was always ready to patch up an injury or diagnose an illness. She would later care for our sick father after he became too ill to continue working and had to give up his dental practice. Mom went back to work full time herself late in life at other hospitals and was still able to summons the energy needed to take care of dad until the day that we lost him.

I was a freshman in college when Brendan was a freshman at Feehan and so on so I only got to see his high school games when I was home for Christmas break for a few weeks on nights when I wasn't working. I got to see Chris play a lot more, but the thing that many people remember most about those games was my mother in the stands with a cow bell that she would ring every time that one of her boys scored. She was always there to support her family and God save the referee who would dare to call a foul on one of the Doherty boys. The sound of that whistle was like a red flag to a bull!

I was lucky enough to be having a pretty good game running with the football on our home field at Attleboro High School one Saturday morning. I think we were playing Durfee High School and my mother and father were standing on the sidelines watching the game. One of my friends told me that there was a guy standing next to my mother who was watching the game while listening to it on the radio. The radio announcer was excitedly calling out my name as I gained yardage on a triple option play. My mother heard my name being broadcast, but couldn't quite hear the guy's radio that well so she grabbed it out of his hand to turn up the volume. The shocked fan turned to my mother and said, "Hey lady, that's my radio!" to which my mother replied, "That's my son!" The guy looked to a nearby Attleboro Police Officer who just shrugged his shoulders.

Mom was always a down to earth realist whose number one priority in life was our family, but she also cared about people that she had never even met like the time she took us to Burger Chef when we were kids. Mom was a terrific cook who seemed to always be in the kitchen so there must have been some urgency for us to end up at a fast food place. After the meal I began to clean up the table to take the trash to the rubbish barrel. Rubbish removal from your own table was catching on as a new tradition in these type of restaurants, but mom insisted that I leave it on the table. She said that the restaurant janitor might have 8 kids to support and if I did his job they might find out that they don't need him and he would get laid off! Who is going to feed those eight kids? They probably didn't even have a custodian, but that is the way mom thinks. Her mundane view of life's challenges was always filtered through a lens of hope for the little guy.

I had never lifted weights to achieve muscle mass until my sophomore year in high school, but for some reason I had a completely natural physique as a very well built young man. I grew up that way and just developed over the years. By the time I reached the 9th grade guys were asking me for my secret. Was I bench pressing an enormous amount of weight, taking some kind of vitamin supplements or something else? Some kids didn't believe it was natural and kept talking about this so one day, sick of hearing this, when I was asked about my biceps by Kenny Blais, a star catcher on our baseball team and a real good kid, I facetiously told him that the secret was my mother's beef stew. Well, it wasn't very long before word spread throughout the school and guys were asking if they could buy some of mom's famous beef stew. Who knows - maybe it was the stew that had me pumped!

Grandpa Flynn had a cottage in Mattapoisett that we stayed in every year for the entire summer so everyone thought it was our place as he was a very generous man. Mom helped me fill out the application for my first summer job that would produce a regular paycheck as opposed to some cash here and there. Mom wrote HARD WORKER in big letters across the top of the application. I got the job scooping ice cream at Gulf Hill in Mattapoisett which is still there today under the name of Oxford Creamery - now owned by Liz & Ken Ackerman, a hardworking, personable couple who continue to uphold the high standard of mouthwatering delicious food and tasty ice cream.. Gulf Hill was owned by a great guy from Fairhaven named Arthur LeClair who was a very young man for owning his own business. I worked diligently for about 11 hours a day and Art always treated me right. Once in a while Art would kid around and remind me of what my mother had written on the top of the application by saying, "Did that say HARD WORKER or HARDLY a WORKER?"

Art, who was also the short order cook, had everything he needed set up around his grill including the cardboard French fry containers already filled with raw fries that were ready to be dumped into the fry-a-later to fill each order. Art asked me to go into the walk in freezer and bring him a tray of pre boxed fries as my very first assignment. I entered the huge freezer and made my way through a jungle of frozen ice cream, hot dogs and hamburgers all sitting on top of the wooden pallets that lined the cement floor. There must have been dozens of small red and white cardboard boxes overfilled with frozen French fries hanging out over the top sitting on a large flat metal tray toward the back of the freezer. I picked up the tray and tried to squeeze by all of the other products toward the exit as my foot tripped on a pallet and the French fries went flying through the air. Frozen

French fries were everywhere including in between the wooden slats of several pallets, down my shirt and one even landed behind my ear. I didn't want to screw up on my first day on the job so I started picking up the fries and shoving them back in the boxes as fast as I could. I hadn't worn a coat because I thought that I would only be in there for a minute so the long tedious task of retrieving frozen French fries in a freezer had me shivering like a wet dog. Art knew that I had been gone for a while so he asked one of my co-workers, my cousin John Cornish, to check on me. John found me scrounging around the freezer floor on my teenage hands and knees with my thick bushy eyebrows carrying a full load of white frost. I could see my breath as I asked him to cover for me and that I would be finished in a minute, but Art sniffed this out and we all had a good laugh.

Almost all of the employees were high school boys so Gulf Hill was a unique place to work with testosterone-fueled stories from a awesome crew including Richard Reilly, David Crowley and my cousin John. One of the few females to ever come behind the counter was Art's beautiful wife Donna. She was drop dead gorgeous so whenever she came in every guy would attempt to steal a glance in her direction and try to scoop ice cream at the same time.

My mother came in every day to order a chocolate frappe. I think it cost 45 cents, but I would cram about five dollars' worth of ice cream into the container for her. One day, before everyone knew her identity, she came up to the counter as one of my co-workers asked if he could help her. Knowing that he wasn't going to produce a five dollar frappe, she immediately pointed to me and said, "No, I want that boy to wait on me." One day mom didn't come in for some reason so wise cracking Art asked me, "Do you think we should call and check on your mother to see if she's OK?"

I got paid $1.65 per hour just like everyone else and was elated to earn a steady paycheck. Art saw how hard that I worked every day so at the end of the summer he calculated my last paycheck at $2.00 per hour. Holy smokes, we eat tonight! He didn't have to do that as I was the only one to get a raise so it was nice to be appreciated for my effort and I was grateful to Art. After getting a job in an Attleboro raw stock jewelry factory for the next summer I recommended that Art hire my brother Brendan, who was most likely the biggest kid to ever work there. Brendan probably served more ice cream than he ate himself, although it may have been a close call.

My mother's assistance in securing a job for me at Gulf Hill was nothing compared to the employment miracles that she would later perform. My dad had worked at the Foxborough race track when, I believe it was called Bay State Raceway, and had been a charter member of the union there while in dental school. He manned one of the well paid pari-mutuels windows at the trotter track and made a lot of friends along the way. The competition was fierce in trying to land a job there and unfortunately, all of dad's connections were gone by the time I needed a summer job in college so the forecast for me working at the track looked pretty dismal. A representative of the racetrack told me that there was an extremely long waiting list for jobs in the pari-mutuels department, thus I didn't stand a chance and should go look elsewhere for some other job. That guy had never met my mother!

Mom gathered her political strength and started making phone calls. Dr. Paul F. Walsh was then the Chairman of the New Bedford School Committee, but more importantly from our perspective, he served as the Chairman of the Massachusetts State Racing Commission. The Racing Commission is a powerful entity that exercises control over all the racetracks in the Commonwealth. Doc Walsh was a dentist just like my dad so my mom played that card to perfection and the next thing I knew I was working at the track in Foxborough.

My dad had paid for part of his dental school tuition by playing High Low Jack and Seven Card Stud. He taught me how to work a Three-Card Monte spread and to calculate odds, but I was never nearly as good with numbers as he was. One time, when he was working at Foxborough, the tote board malfunctioned and caused some kind a devastating problem with the computer inside the track. The race results were delayed as angry gamblers lined up outside of the cashiers' windows demanding payment. Dad saved the day by calculating the odds for the winning combinations with a pencil and paper and eventually everybody went home happy! This pretty much cemented his reputation as a solid guy in the world of gambling with his shining legacy carrying on through the decades to greet me on my first night on the job.

Most of the employees in the pari-mutuels department start off as sellers with some becoming cashiers after years of experience matching wits with cons and thieves playing change games at the window, presenting losing or altered tickets as well as other deceptive endeavors of larceny. One of the most common scams occurs when a railbird places a bet on a perfecta, for example, by buying a ticket for the 7 horse to win and the 4 horse to come in second in the fifth race. The horses have to finish 7-4 for the bettor to collect so if it is not a winner most people discard the ticket by dropping it on the floor, but not some of the mendacious misfits of the race track world. They will hold onto the ticket until the 7-4 combination comes through in the fifth race sometime in the future, maybe two months later. The cashier, who had to move pretty fast to clean up the lines of gamblers, rips the corner off the perfecta ticket after seeing 7-4 above Race 5 and is about to pay out $400.00 when hopefully the wrong date is noticed on the ticket. The employee was required to make up cash shortages out of his own pocket that had been caused by mistakes or thieves so you had to remain vigilant and alert. These positions were all eventually upgraded with the introduction of modern machines that sell and cash, but back in the day it was a whole different ballgame.

John Powers was the Pari-Mutuels Manager and a very nice man. He made me a cashier on my first night on the job probably because I was my father's son so he must have thought that I must be a real genius too! He assigned Gerry Purro, who was an experienced cashier, to teach me the ropes. Gerry was an extremely friendly and well-liked accountant from Franklin. We sat together on one of the many park benches outside of the grandstand and had a coffee as we watched the trotters warm up pulling the drivers around the track in the sulkies. Post time was in one hour so Gerry had a limited opportunity to teach me how to be a cashier. He put me at ease by pointing out to the track and saying, "OK kid, we're going to start from the beginning. That's a horse!"

My mother and father came to the track on my first night expecting to find me selling pari-mutuels tickets. After walking around the enormous facility and not seeing me working as a seller, dad told mom that I must not have gotten on because they never would have made me a cashier on my first night. Dad was a certifiable genius and even he had never been a cashier. Dad reluctantly agreed to take a look at the long stretch of cashiers' windows upon mom's insistence and the shock on his face was evident when they found me cashing winning tickets on the Main Line. It was a busy night, but I found the time to tell my parents that the only reason that I was there was because of mom's political savvy and dad's powerful reputation as a reliable numbers guy.

Quite often I worked on the pari-mutuel windows at an outdoors part of the Foxborough track that was extremely busy on warm summer nights. If my geographic calculations are correct, that section of the facility was located in what is now the north end zone of Gillette Stadium. I used to stand at my post handling action on the same ground that was later used by Rob Gronkowski to spike footballs!

The track provided good income for a while in helping to pay my tuition, but eventually the Handle, which is the amount of money bet on a given night, dropped down low enough on a consistent basis such that I would only show up for work on a Saturday night. The other nights were not even close to being busy enough for a low seniority guy like me to be hired and even on Saturday night I would wait with about 25 other guys for an hour until John Powers would come out and usually signal us to go home without pay by giving us the thumbs down sign. You still had to show up on Saturday night even though there was a slim chance of being hired.

My mom had just put a heaping plate of her delicious piping hot pot roast in front of me at the dinner table on a Saturday night. At least I was going to have a terrific meal before going to the track, but I guess that I must have looked or sounded a little bit down. Mom asked me what was the matter and I told her that I probably wasn't going to make any tuition money tonight as I had to go to the track well knowing that I would most likely be sent home without pay and even have to burn precious gas in my car for nothing. Mom thought for a moment with eyes narrowed and her head slightly tilted as she said, "I'll take care of this."

Within minutes mom was on the phone with the Foxborough track which at the time was called New England Harness Raceway. She told the person on the other end that her name was Gladys Roosevelt and that she was the President of the Golden Age Society of New England. She would like to send seven busloads of elderly gamblers to the track tonight and she just wanted to be sure that the facility was able to accommodate that many people. I got hired by the track immediately after walking in the door along with everybody else available including the other 25 guys who would normally be sent home! They even opened up extra Show windows because that is the usual preference of the elderly. All of the fringe guys were talking about how they must be expecting a heck of a crowd and I was the only one there who knew that we all owed our night's pay to the ingenuity of a loving mother who always refused to take no for an answer. My father would later say, "Only your mother could have thought of that one!"

I had always wanted to work in a courthouse and there was an opening for an assistant clerk-magistrate at the ADC a few years after I graduated from college. James H. Sullivan, appointed by Governor Paul A. Dever, was the great Clerk-Magistrate so he did all of the hiring. He was a friend of my dad's so I had gotten to know him pretty well when he frequented our living room. He was a larger than life figure with an engaging personality that exuded old school Irish wit and charm. I really liked him and always enjoyed our conversations. Just like so many other super pols, Mr. Sullivan was extremely charismatic and always made me feel as though I was the only other person in the room. My dad told him that I was very interested in the job at his court, but unfortunately he said that I shouldn't even bother applying because it was meant for someone else. Dad asked Mr. Sullivan if there was anything we could do or anyone that we could call to make this happen. Mr. Sullivan said that he would like to have me work there, but that his mind was made up. Mr. Sullivan, like so many others, had underestimated my mother.

Mr. Sullivan had a son who was working for the telephone company. Even though he had never practiced law full time, he was a lawyer who had an eye on someday succeeding his father who was gracefully getting along in his years. Jim Sullivan was a very powerful man so there was no doubt in our minds that he was laying the ground work and slowly putting a plan in place to make this happen. Governor Edward J. King was in the corner office at the time so it was common knowledge, at least in our home, that the dynamics and politics of the situation made it necessary that this Sullivan family succession would have to take place during the current gubernatorial administration.

Mom put together an offer that Mr. Sullivan couldn't refuse. She went to work on this project and developed a contact that was extremely close to Governor King. Mom knew that Mr. Sullivan wouldn't want to risk alienating the Governor who would hopefully someday appoint his son to succeed him. The contact came through with a phone call to Mr. Sullivan telling him that the court just couldn't function without me on his staff! I raised my 25-year old right hand to be sworn in as the youngest assistant clerk-magistrate in the Commonwealth on January 28, 1980. Mr. Sullivan retired three years later on Governor King's last day in office and his son Daniel was appointed to succeed him with only minutes to spare before newly elected Governor Michael S. Dukakis walked in the door of the State House. Mom had come through again!

Eighteen year later I was lucky enough to have my name reach the Governor's desk after being interviewed and voted on by the Judicial Nominating Commission as well as passing a background check by detective troopers from the Massachusetts State Police assigned to the Executive Branch. I remain forever grateful to His Excellency, Governor A. Paul Cellucci for appointing me to the lifetime position of Clerk-Magistrate of the WDC with the next paragraph beginning an explanation of that process. Later, I found a religious letter addressed to my mother that was all about me. Apparently, mom had sent a $20.00 dollar bill to some monastery in Alabama requesting employment prayers on my behalf. The letter advised mom that many monks were praying for me to get the job as Clerk-Magistrate! Mom always played every angle!

When Jennifer Lopez became known as J. Lo some friends started referring to my wife Joanne as J. Do and the name stuck, as now she is called J. Do by just about everyone including her mother.

After being promoted to First Assistant Clerk-Magistrate of the ADC the next step up was a lifetime appointment by the Governor of the Commonwealth. Governor William F. Weld occupied the corner office when I began to formulate a plan to try to secure an appointment to the position of Clerk-Magistrate. There were a few openings so J. Do and I decided to shoot for the newly created Falmouth District Court and my focus, quite naturally, was on how to bring about a favorable viewing of my candidacy to Governor Weld.

Governor William F. Weld & author

One of my first calls of many was to a good family friend who was born Margaret Mary O'Shaughnessy in the Borough of Queens, New York and had been elected to the Massachusetts Governor's Council under her married name of Margaret Heckler. She would serve eight terms in the United States Congress after defeating incumbent and former Speaker of the House Joe Martin in the Republican primary. Peggy was appointed by President Ronald Reagan as the Secretary of Health and Human Services and later became the first woman to serve as the United States Ambassador to Ireland. I called Peg for help and she reminded me of some laughs that we had when J. Do and I were honored to have her attend our wedding at Highland Country Club in Attleboro. She happily agreed to contact Governor Weld and called me later to tell me of the conversation. Peg, who was a staunch Catholic dead set against abortion, basically gave the Governor hell for his pro-choice position on human life. At this point I am looking for a job and not an argument or religious lesson so I just listened as she told me about the scolding as well as the nice things that she had relayed about me to the Governor. I have always had a deep admiration for Peg as a devoted public servant and loyal friend so I was extremely grateful for her assistance. She went on to tell me that Governor Weld had asked her if she had contacted Paul. It would not be the last time that I heard that name.

My cousin Kevin D. Callahan was a Bristol County Assistant District Attorney at the ADC. He is a brilliant guy who made his political bones early on with his ear always to the ground and became a legendary advance man for United States Senator Ted Kennedy. It wasn't unusual to see Kevin somewhere in the background as the Senator was addressing a crowd. I told Kevin that I was in the early stages of intelligence gathering and asked him for advice on Governor Weld. I was shocked to hear him tell me that I should forget about Governor Weld and focus on Lieutenant Governor A. Paul Cellucci. Weld had delegated the selection of judges and clerk-magistrates to his Lieutenant Governor! I think it is fair to say that most governors would relish the opportunity to rock someone's world with a lifetime appointment to a highly sought after position, but Bill Weld really didn't care about such matters as he may have had less of an ego than most people in a position of authority. He also knew that the appointment process was in good hands with Paul Cellucci. This all became common knowledge as time went on and the administration developed, but Kevin Callahan was astutely aware of this well before most and he was the first one to tell me about this extremely unusual arrangement.

The application for the position of clerk-magistrate is long, in depth, extensive and very similar to that of a judge. It can't be filled out in one sitting as you have to do research on yourself to be able to go back in your life to produce correctly spelled names, accurate places and precise dates. There are many questions that require an answer that will basically put your best foot forward. Many applications are screened out and never again see the light of day, but I was one of the lucky ones to make the long list and then the short list granting me an interview before the Judicial Nominating Commission. The JNC is comprised of about two dozen lawyers who peppered me with questions to determine my ability. This is a very distinguished panel of highly respected, prominent attorneys including the incomparable Diane M. Bunk who had been appointed by Governor William F. Weld and is now an Assistant District Attorney in Bristol County. Everything is very secretive so I was not told how I did, although I did see Judge Augustus F. Wagner Jr. in the men's room during a break. Gus was very complimentary about my last answer to the Commission and told me, "You really hit that one out of the park!", so it felt good to hear that from the highly regarded former Superior Court Judge who had been appointed by Governor Edward J. King and was then in private practice.

The JNC ultimately voted in my favor and assigned my name to an even shorter list and the shorter list was made even shorter when they voted to send my name along with three others to the Governor's desk for his consideration for the Falmouth District Court. The reality of making it to the Governor's desk in this administration was in actuality making it to the Lieutenant Governor's desk.

The next step was an interview with the Governor's Chief Legal Counsel, Attorney Brackett Badger Denniston III in his office at the State House. Philip A. Rollins, then Cape & Islands District Attorney, thought very highly of him, admiring his intellect and speaking ability so he wanted to convince him to run for public office, but hoped that his name wouldn't hurt. Phil told me that Denniston would be a terrific candidate, but said that he was a man with three last names! Phil, a veritable legend in the criminal justice system, was a political genius who was always very supportive of me. Attorney Denniston is an extremely capable and well-rounded lawyer who was very nice to me and made me feel right at home. We spoke about many different topics that day as I enjoyed the back and forth with a smart and down to earth guy. The interview ended with a hand shake as he wished me well, but stressed to me that I had some competition. It would be months until I heard anything official.

One of the other three finalists for the position was Charles N. Decas, a well-qualified and good guy. Charlie had an extensive background in government including as a State Representative who had served in the legislature with Paul Cellucci and was loved by his constituents as well as his many colleagues in the State House. I was told by a judge who was a former senator that the bond developed between Cellucci and Decas, having served together in the House of Representatives, would be tough for me to overcome. The judge was correct and Charlie was appointed Clerk-Magistrate of the Falmouth District Court by Governor William F. Weld. I got to know Charlie and enjoyed his company at court seminars and social events where I was thankful for some valuable lessons he taught me for the future. He is a nice man who became a great Clerk-Magistrate and did a tremendous job in an entirely new court.

author, Cape & Islands District Attorney Philip A. Rollins

Staff and some management at the ADC felt badly for me and kind of had me lumped into the same category as the other hundreds of applicants who didn't get the job. None of them had been through this process so they really didn't understand that this was no time to be expressing condolences until the Honorable Francis T. Crimmins Jr., appointed by Governor William F. Weld, started explaining the reality of the situation. Judge Crimmins, who was sitting in Attleboro at the time, told them that it was a tremendous accomplishment that I was chosen as a finalist for a lifetime position and was one of only four to make it to the Governor's desk out of hundreds of applicants. It was Judge Crimmins' own idea to do that and I remain grateful to him as I really didn't want people feeling sorry for me. I would have liked to have gotten the appointment, but the truth is that I was just content to be a finalist in my first time out of the box.

J. Do and I had always attended court-related and other events together unless one of us was otherwise engaged. There was a very well attended court gathering that took place not long after the Decas appointment. I think it was a birthday party for Janice P. Johnson, the legendary Victim Witness Advocate from the DA's office, which was held at a golf course clubhouse in Norton. I had a previous commitment so my bride represented me at the function. J. Do was seated at a table with some others who all knew me including a politically astute attorney. Somebody said that it was too bad that I didn't get the job in Falmouth and the lawyer tried to console J. Do by saying it was OK because all of those jobs go to former state reps, senators and big money guys. The general consensus was that I was a nice guy, but it was a lost cause. This attorney didn't realize that my bubbly wife didn't need cheering up as she looked around the table declaring firmly and emphatically that, "Ed Doherty WILL become a clerk-magistrate." I am told by others who were there that you could hear a pin drop as the stunned group quickly realized that my J. Do meant business!

J. Do with daughters Chrissy & Kait

Soon there was an opening in the WDC after the retirement of the great Clerk-Magistrate William H. Barker Jr., a nice man whom I had met a few times who had been appointed by Governor Francis W. Sargent. The application was much easier to fill out this time as I had already researched everything for Falmouth. I received valuable direction and solid advice from Judge Crimmins who shakes more hands every day than the Governor. He was a terrific judge and is a great man who became my lifelong friend. If he is ever in need I will be there in a heartbeat and go through a wall for him as they aren't made thick enough to stop me from helping Frank Crimmins.

I was lucky enough to come out on the positive side of some JNC lists for the WDC and was granted an interview before the same esteemed board of attorneys. The process was much the same as before and my name was eventually sent to the Governor's desk along with five others. This time there were six of us left standing who all wanted the same job.

Attorney Denniston had left his position for greener pastures so I was interviewed by Chief Legal Counsel Paul W. Johnson in his State House office. He is a real gentleman and an extremely intelligent lawyer. I enjoyed speaking with him and recalled thinking during the interview that this brilliant guy was so down to earth that it would be great to have a beer with him. We shook hands at the end and he wished me good luck. It was now a waiting game.

I got a call from a very high ranking government official who asked me who was my toughest competition. When I answered he told me not to worry because that guy had some baggage that would kill his appointment. He said that the Governor should find out about this and seemed to intimate that somebody might drop a dime on the finalist. I immediately said that I wasn't going to do that because if it turned out that I was lucky enough to get the job, I wanted to be able to look that man in the eye and tell him that neither I nor any of my supporters had anything to do with his defeat. My approach was to present myself in a positive way without introducing negativity about anyone.

J. Do wanted to help me. Judges, clerk-magistrates and assistants are prohibited from political involvement, but J. Do had heard me say that I wished that I could volunteer for Paul Cellucci. She decided, on her own, to do what I could not - go to work for the Cellucci Committee. She had a deep appreciation for the humility, intellect and civility of Lieutenant Governor A. Paul Cellucci and, just like many others, wanted to lend any assistance she could in seeing that he would succeed in being elected Governor of Massachusetts. She drove to Boston and worked hard for the Cellucci Committee, rubbing elbows with some interesting people as she developed a keen rapport with his inner circle, all the while working full time in addition to attending Bridgewater State College as well as taking care of a husband, two kids and a dog.

I am lucky to be married to a smart, beautiful and happy wife who always sees the glass as half full. J. Do is well liked, easy going and quick with a laugh. She was working in a bank in downtown Attleboro the first time I saw her. I told a friend that I had just met the most gorgeous girl that I had ever seen in my life. I went into the bank to make a deposit, but instead I made a withdrawal - I took her out!

J. Do participated in many different areas of the Cellucci fund raising operation and even hosted some events herself. Even though I was prohibited from attending political functions and never got to see my bride at these gatherings, many people who were at her times told me that she was an extremely moving speaker in introducing the future Governor. I have, on other occasions, seen her work a room with speed, precision and grace. J. Do moves through a crowd while introducing dignitaries and engaging guests with her warm personality and quick wit. J. Do and I started dating when she was just nineteen years old and the first time that I got to hear her speak to an audience was when she was competing in the Miss Attleboro Pageant. My future bride dazzled the crowd with an extremely powerful, elegant and awe inspiring speech before going on later that night to win the Swimsuit Competition before a packed house.

Lieutenant Governor Cellucci was very impressed with J. Do's ability to bring fresh faces into the campaign and shared some laughs with her about her unique bookkeeping system for donor tracking. She enjoyed spending even limited time with him and gained his acceptance, trust and respect. It became easy to work hard for a remarkable man who may or may not help her husband. She had begun this quest with me as the primary goal, but quickly developed a genuine admiration for Paul Cellucci as she experienced his leadership skills, honesty and integrity up close and personal. The Lieutenant Governor, whose family had owned an automobile dealership in Hudson, even took time out of his busy day and went outside with J. Do to see her new vehicle that was parked at the curb in Boston. The troopers assigned to his State Police detail were guiding him in the opposite direction when he turned the other way and told them, "No, I'm going to see her new car."

One of J. Do's times was scheduled at a Knights of Columbus in southeastern Massachusetts. She had booked the event through the normal channels by speaking with the person in charge of functions there and told him that they were honoring Lieutenant

Governor A. Paul Cellucci. She had the tickets and other material printed immediately after being approved, then went to work on sales to ensure a good crowd. Ticket sales were brisk as voters wanted to honor the statesman who had the well-deserved reputation of being a real gentleman. The sold out event was only a few days away when J. Do received a call from somebody at the Knights of Columbus that the function could not be held in their facility because it was a Catholic organization and the Lieutenant Governor was pro-choice! What!!! They had already given J. Do approval after she had told them who it was for! She immediately scrambled, almost wore out the phone and finally found another venue, but she then had to notify all of these paid guests who had tickets directing them to what was now the wrong location. J. Do didn't have much time to accomplish the impossible, but she did and the successful event went off like a charm. To paraphrase a line from the movie *Dirty Dancing* - Nobody puts J. Do in a corner!

I should mention that even though my name was already on the Governor's desk I had gotten this far along in the process without any help from my bride. I knew that she could not help me with the JNC and that was fine with me. She was warming up in the bullpen to be ready for the ninth inning so we waited for a long time before deciding on a final strategy. My bride then had a private conversation with the future Governor, went into her windup and delivered a fastball right over the edge of the plate on the inside black. It was time to wait some more and that we did.

By now Governor Weld had resigned and vacated the corner office after having been nominated by President Bill Clinton as the United States Ambassador to Mexico. The former Governor wanted to concentrate on the process and hopefully be approved for the new post. Senator Jesse Helms, who was not a fan of Weld, was the socially conservative Chairman of the Senate Foreign Relations Committee. Weld was denied a hearing and ultimately withdrew his nomination, but his resignation as Governor automatically left Lieutenant Governor Cellucci as the Acting Governor of the Commonwealth.

I received a call from Attorney Johnson during a court recess at the ADC. He was very cordial, but had to deliver the disappointing news that I didn't get the job as another candidate had been chosen. I politely thanked him and actually expressed condolences that most of his calls had to be negative. He is a good guy who was just doing his job as it was actually a very nice conversation considering that it was a delivery of shattered dreams.

I was almost lost as to my next move, but it wasn't long until I got another call from Attorney Johnson informing me that there had been an unexpected development and that Acting Governor Cellucci would like to interview me. Attorney Johnson mentioned how impressed he was that I was such a gentleman when previously receiving bad news and told me that he was happy to be able to make this call. Every administration is a little different, but this Chief Legal Counsel would interview every candidate that made it to the Governor's desk and the Acting Governor would only interview the final choice. I was scheduled for an interview with Acting Governor Cellucci, which meant that I had the job!

I drove into the State House and met Attorney Johnson in his office before we both proceeded to Acting Governor Cellucci's office for my interview. I was greeted warmly and enjoyed answering questions in a comfortable atmosphere. The Acting Governor, who I always called Governor, told me that his original plan was to appoint me to another court in southeastern Massachusetts after appointing someone else to Wrentham. He said that it didn't work out so he was happy to offer the position of Clerk-Magistrate of the Wrentham District Court to me. I quickly accepted, shook hands, expressed my appreciation and smiled all the way home.

After working as an assistant clerk-magistrate in the court system for 18 years, the last seven as first assistant, I was well qualified for the position of clerk-magistrate, but so were a lot of others. My bride presented me in the light most favorable to achieving my goal. I fought and legitimately earned my way to the Governor's desk, but there is no doubt in my mind that without my J. Do I would still be working in Attleboro.

After being nominated by the Governor and unanimously confirmed by the Executive Council, I received a call from one of the Governor's staff to schedule my swearing in with His Excellency. I was told that Governor Cellucci was ready to administer the oath of office to me at the State House on Friday which happened to be Opening Day for the Red Sox at Fenway Park. I immediately asked for the following Monday as my brother Chris and I had tickets to the game, a sacred ritual for diehards who look forward all winter to the initial crack of the bat and the first sausage sandwich on the corner of Van Ness and Yawkey. I knew that the Governor was a big baseball fan so I figured he wouldn't mind although some of my friends thought that I must be crazy to put a ballgame over a lifetime appointment, but it wasn't just any ballgame - it was Opening Day! Chris and I got to see Mo Vaughn hit a walk off grand slam in a Sox come from behind 9th inning victory against the Seattle Mariners before we celebrated at J. J. Foley's Cafe! The following Monday immediate family gathered at the State House in Boston to watch me become a Clerk-Magistrate.

Sworn in by His Excellency, A. Paul Cellucci, Governor of the Commonwealth

I was sworn in twice - it is said that the first one is for the dough and the second one, a more ceremonious event, is for your mother. Speaker of the House Thomas M. Finneran was kind enough to grant me permission to hold my swearing in ceremony a few months later in the Chamber of the Massachusetts House of Representatives at the State House. It was a very enjoyable event attended by family, friends, colleagues and even some of my cousins who flew in all the way from Ballyjamesduff in Ireland. My cousin Patricia, from the Lynch side of the family and her husband Aiden O'Reilly, came across the sea accompanied by two of their daughters Ciara and Olive. I was proud to share the day with the O'Reillys as my cousins are a remarkable family brimming with class, kindness and humor. My brother Chris had a hook for a limousine which not only added a level of dignity to the occasion, but also provided needed transportation for our Irish cousins. I was sitting next to Governor Cellucci thinking that my dad would have enjoyed this day had he not been taken from us so early in life. I could see my proud mother sitting with our family in the front row and she would later tell me that dad was with us as she could smell Aramis, his favorite cologne, throughout the House Chamber.

author, Representative Steve Karol, Governor A. Paul Cellucci

author & Bristol County District Attorney Paul F. Walsh Jr.

Stephen J. Karol, the charismatic Lobbyist and former State Representative from Attleboro who had been the distinguished Chairman of the House Transportation Committee and well-spoken Bristol County District Attorney Paul F. Walsh Jr., son of previously mentioned Doc Walsh, took turns saying nice things about me after being introduced to the crowd by Judge Frank Crimmins who I was privileged to have serve as my Master of Ceremonies. Judge Crimmins joked that my cousins came over from Ireland because they thought that a clerk-magistrate was like a Clerk of the Works and could provide jobs for the family!

After taking the oath of office from His Excellency, Governor Cellucci sat down behind me as I looked out at the audience and began to deliver my acceptance speech. I expressed my sincere gratitude to the Governor for having the faith and confidence in me to make this day possible. Governor Cellucci, just like me, was the father of two daughters so he knew what it was like to have young teenage girls in the house. I acknowledged a lot of people and could hear the Governor laughing behind me when I expressed my appreciation to my two daughters for staying off of the telephone just long enough for the Governor to get through!

I concluded my remarks and was escorted out of the House Chamber with the Governor in a ceremonious exit led by Raymond J. Amaru, the House Sergeant at Arms. Ray is a nice man who I would get to know much better later through our mutual friends, Robert A. "Ted" Tomasone, the great Clerk-Magistrate of the Somerville District Court who had been appointed by Governor William F. Weld and the Honorable Michelle L. Kelley the great Clerk-Magistrate eventually appointed by Governor Charlie D. Baker to succeed me. Michelle was later appointed District Court Associate Justice by Governor Baker.

author, His Excellency, A. Paul Cellucci, Governor of the Commonwealth, House Chamber
(Becky Lebowitz photo, The Sun Chronicle)

I continued through the State House with J. Do on my arm and into the Great Hall where we greeted our guests who had formed a receiving line for the reception. It was catered with delicious food as well as beer and wine, but I knew that our friend Jack Riccio would like to have a drink of his favorite liquor. I was initially told that liquor was not allowed so a special legislative dispensation was granted to allow for the serving of Crown Royal for one day only. Jack ordered a Crown Royal and the bartender said, "Oh, you must be Jack Riccio!"

As we were leaving Boston and heading south the sight of the Golden Dome covering the historic State House reminded me of how very lucky I had been on a wonderful day for our entire family. I thanked God for His Blessings and set my sights on the Wrentham District Court.

This chapter is dedicated to two resourceful, driven and talented women - my mother and my wife. I went from the loving care of one into the loving care of the other. They are each beautiful, sweet, gentle and not to be messed with! Their photos should appear in the dictionary beside the word Persevere. They don't take no for an answer and sense promise and hope where others see despair.

Some folks are born next door to a future President of the United States, share work space with a future Governor or happen to know a United States Congressman through some strong social connection, but not these two dynamic ladies. My mother and wife didn't just happen to know somebody who could help me - they worked hard to make one connection after another specifically for me.

I wanted to share their incredible accomplishments with the public even if it means exposing that my long path to whatever success I may have achieved was paved and bolstered by the love of my family. I am grateful for their devotion and extremely proud of their grit so I really don't care if somebody thinks less of me as long as they realize the truth about these ladies that I love who just happen to be the two most fascinating, accomplished and determined women that I have ever known.

3. Courthouses

The Honorable Samuel E. Zoll was appointed to a judgeship by Governor Francis W. Sargent and was later appointed Chief Justice of the Massachusetts District Courts. After being sworn in by Governor A. Paul Cellucci I was asked to meet with Chief Justice Zoll at his office in Salem for a traditional welcoming sit down. The Chief was very gracious and cordial as always while we discussed a myriad of professional as well as personal topics. He told me that he usually sends newly appointed clerk-magistrates to a court for a month of training, but since I had already served as an assistant in Attleboro for eighteen years he asked me to work in the Dedham District Court for only one week.

The Dedham District Court is one of the best run courts in the Commonwealth thanks in large part to a man I had already met - Salvatore Paterna, the great Clerk-Magistrate who had been appointed by Governor Michael S. Dukakis. The court is located in a busy area near Superior Court and within walking distance of many government buildings and stores. The spring weather brought people out to the sidewalks during lunch exchanging greetings from across the street. It was an enjoyable week with a multitude of very helpful people including Chief Court Officer Patti Bellotti whose innate kindness is supplemented by her exuberant personality and outgoing nature. I spent a good deal of my time there with the very popular, capable and personable First Assistant Clerk-Magistrate Philip J. McCue. Even though I had almost two decades of experience in the same position as Phil, it was nice to see how some things were done a little differently in another court. Phil, who is a lawyer and a nice guy, is now the Deputy Court Administrator for the District Courts. He went out of his way to show me the essential basics in Dedham including the best restaurants!

Boston Red Sox first baseman Mo Vaughn was arrested for drunk driving by Trooper Richard M. Ball who would retire many years later after attaining the high rank of Lieutenant Colonel with the Massachusetts State Police. The 1995 American League MVP was represented by one of the best lawyers in the system, Attorney Kevin J. Reddington of Brockton. After arraignment, the best result achievable by any defense attorney is a Not Guilty verdict. Kevin is a down to earth great guy whose confidence in his own legal ability is displayed on his car's license plate - NG. Vaughn was acquitted after an interesting and highly publicized jury trial in the Dedham District Court. The First Justice of the court is the Honorable Michael J. Pomarole, an accomplished jurist with a terrific sense of humor who had established a reputation for integrity and fairness long before his appointment to the bench by Governor Jane M. Swift.

The First Justice at the time, however, was the enormously respected Judge Maurice H. Richardson who was appointed by Governor Francis W. Sargent. Judge Richardson was a nice man with an expertise in mental health issues and many other subjects. His nickname of course, was Mo, hence the license plate on his car that read MO. His parking space on the side of the building was clearly labeled with a sign indicating that it was reserved for the judge. When the press spotted the automobile with MO on the plate parked in the judge's spot during the trial, rumors began to circulate that Mo Vaughn was being shown preferential treatment with the incorrect assumption that they even let the Red Sox star leave his car in the judge's parking space!

I know another attorney with an interesting license plate on his car. My first introduction to Attorney Paul L. Carlucci was in the ADC, but because his office is in Franklin I had the pleasure of hearing his cases much more often in Wrentham. Paul is a formidable lawyer with a quick smile and a good word for everyone.

Paul and his lovely wife Robyn have four children, including Haley who is a very talented actress. J. Do and I travelled to New York City to see Haley play the lead in West Side Story on Broadway. The beautiful and gifted actress was the star of the play with her rendition of Maria. We had a good time and then enjoyed delicious hot pastrami sandwiches at the famous Carnegie Deli on 7th Avenue in midtown Manhattan.

A very favorable and highly sought after criminal disposition, from the defendant's perspective, is a Continued Without a Finding or CWOF. This is usually reserved for someone who is facing a relatively minor charge where the Commonwealth has enough evidence for a conviction, but the defendant has had no previous indiscretions. The case is eventually dismissed after a period of time with the fulfillment of any requirements as ordered by the court, thus the defendant's record without any convictions is preserved by this disposition.

I happened to notice a car in the courthouse parking lot with an interesting license plate that just had to be owned by a defense attorney and found out that the vehicle belonged to Paul Carlucci. His license plate reads CWOF!

Author's Note: I wrote the following which was published after editing in *The Boston Globe* for Tales From the City in the January 25, 2015 issue of the *Globe Magazine* -

> Years ago I worked in the Clerk-Magistrate's Office of the Attleboro District Court where we used an envelope sealer that had a roller turn through a small water reservoir to moisten the glue on envelopes for the office mail. The sealer quickly became known as the "licker" because it licked the envelopes for us. The licker might be found on anyone's desk depending on who was the last to use it. On one busy morning, with a long line of people at the counter within earshot, one of our staff who needed to seal an envelope, loudly asked the rest of the office, "Who's got the licker?"
>
> A disgruntled criminal defendant waiting in line could be heard exclaiming, "No wonder it takes so long in this line. They're all in there drinking!"

Americans report for jury duty throughout our nation to fulfill their civic responsibility and immediately become an integral part of the delivery of justice even if not chosen for a panel. Jurors fill out a very brief juror questionnaire that is collected by the court officers and was then given to me in the courtroom. Reading through these questions and answers would sometimes bring a smile to my face. One of the questions asks the jurors to list their highest level of education. One man apparently misunderstood when he saw the word "highest" because he wrote down that his highest level of education was "5 feet, 8 inches!"

I can't remember which court, but there was a juror who wrote on the questionnaire that he had an extensive background in law enforcement. Everyone thought that he was probably a police officer or federal agent until it was learned that he had been arrested 17 times. He did have an extensive background!

Rosemary T. Carr, who is now retired, was the First Assistant Clerk-Magistrate in the Central Division of the Boston Municipal Court. Rosie is a very nice person and a true professional who could write her own book about all of the things she has seen during her long and storied career in the court system. Rosie has a big heart and quietly helped a lot of people in her time working in Suffolk County including a very young assistant district attorney who was trying his first criminal case while she served as the session clerk. She felt badly for the inexperienced ADA who was getting eaten up by a seasoned defense attorney at every turn. Rosie kept quietly mouthing "object" to the rookie who was nervously considering his options. Finally, after Rosie had mouthed "object" again, he stood up and said, "Objection Your Honor!" causing the judge to ask, "What are you objecting to counsel?" The sheepish ADA then blurted out, "I don't know, I'm just doing what she said!"

The Honorable William F. Sullivan is an Associate Justice of the Massachusetts Superior Court. He is an outstanding judge who greets the jury with interesting stories about John Adams and the Massachusetts Constitution. He is a very smart, terrific guy who had a private law practice in Quincy when I first had the pleasure of meeting him. He was serious when he had to be, but always had a keen sense of humor and a down to earth style.

J. Do and I were making plans to see my alma mater, the University of South Florida, play football against the University of Notre Dame at the famous stadium in South Bend. Bill played collegiate soccer for the Irish so I called him to ask for advice. He was extremely accommodating and congenial in giving me a virtual telephone tour of the iconic campus and surrounding community. Bill even mailed me some information to assist us in familiarizing ourselves with the Notre Dame grounds for a more enjoyable experience, but he would jokingly say later that he regretted being so helpful after USF ended up beating Notre Dame in a weather delayed classic confrontation.

Prior to his appointment as a judge by Governor Deval L. Patrick, Bill was on the short list of distinguished and experienced court appointed attorneys who were qualified to handle serious felonies. The police had brought in a defendant in a homicide case so I called Bill at his office to tell him that he was needed for a bail hearing. Bill, whose excellent sense of humor is always spot on, kiddingly said, "Bail hearing? The Commonwealth is asking for bail?" I knew that he wasn't serious, but replied, "Well Bill, your client is charged with murder." He immediately came back with, "Yea, but it's his first offense Eddie. He'll promise not to do it again and maybe we can work out a CWOF!"

J. Do and I experienced an incredible sense of awe as we walked into Notre Dame Stadium for the first time. Stepping foot on that hallowed ground began the adventure of a lifetime as we surveyed the beautiful green field and thought about the legends who had performed there. Unfortunately, fellow USF grad Tim Mahoney couldn't make it to the game, but he got us unbelievable seats in the front row behind the Notre Dame bench where we were joined by USF Alumni Jim Mittenzwei, Ken & Ralph Terrio and their lovely wives Joanne, Cindy and Tallie. Notre Dame Alumni have a reputation for generosity and warm hospitality that is well deserved. We will never forget being invited to tailgate parties by complete strangers who were extremely kind and gracious with the game ending in a stunning USF upset victory to cap off an incredibly memorable day.

We had a perfect view of renowned Notre Dame Coach Brian Kelly making decisions and rallying his players during the game. Kelly would eventually become the winningest football coach in Notre Dame history before moving on to coach LSU. The celebrated coach, raised in Chelsea close to Boston's Logan International Airport, has spent a lifetime helping others. He and his wife Paqui, a two time breast cancer survivor, were honored by being recognized with the Breast Cancer Research Foundation's Humanitarian Award. I was informed by the terrific story written by Jill Radsken, "Awash in pink for a good cause," *The Boston Globe*, May 21, 2014. Coach Kelly has a spirited sense of humor and never forgot where he came from, "Who made it out of Chelsea?" said a grinning Brian Kelly, who worked as a legislative assistant at the State House before getting out of dodge. "I called it UCLA - University of Chelsea Logan Airport."

Notre Dame, Touchdown Jesus with Joanne & Jim Mittenzwei.

After Clerk-Magistrate James H. Sullivan appointed me to the position of Assistant Clerk-Magistrate he assigned me to Sally A. Bruno to begin the long process of learning my new job. She would later marry David Linton, the ace *Sun Chronicle* crime beat reporter who covered the courthouse. J. Do and I are fortunate that the four of us have remained lifelong friends. Sally has an engaging smile, quick wit and a welcoming personality with a rolodex full of friends from every walk of life. She was one of the most knowledgeable and dedicated court employees that I would ever encounter so I learned from the very best. She was a highly sought after political operative who would later go to work in the State House for Senator William R. Keating before he was elected Norfolk County District Attorney and eventually to the United States Congress from the Ninth Congressional District of Massachusetts. I already knew Sally's Uncle Willie and Aunt Ann who stayed with their children across the street from my grandfather's cottage where we spent summers on Prospect Road in Mattapoisett. Her Uncle Willie is a terrific guy who would make pizza for all of us young kids and watched out for everybody in the neighborhood.

Sally would eventually be put in charge of the entire Civil Department, but at this time handled everything in Small Claims so on Thursdays, which is civil day in most courts, the surface of her desk disappeared under piles of yellow small claims cases. Clerk-Magistrates and assistants would eventually be given the authority to hear small claims cases, but back when I started they were only heard by judges. Sally and I would go into Courtroom One to break down the list before a huge crowd of litigants. Sally would sit in the Clerk's chair and I would stand beside her to address the audience. Sally would write down defaults and other entries as I called the list and announced results until we significantly reduced the number of cases and set aside those remaining to be heard by the judge.

There were always many confused and inexperienced litigants in the courtroom when we broke down the list so I would begin with an opening statement to the crowd in an effort to try to keep things simple. As soon as Sally was seated I would welcome the audience and announce that they should answer by saying either plaintiff or defendant when they heard their name called. I would quickly explain that if they were suing someone and bringing them to court that they were a plaintiff and if somebody was suing them they were a defendant. Sally would then sometimes kiddingly say under her breath so that only I could hear, "If you don't know what you're here for, you're probably an attorney!"

The Honorable John J. Dolan, appointed judge by Governor Edward J. King, was a brilliant lawyer who became First Justice of the ADC not long after I was appointed Assistant Clerk-Magistrate by Clerk-Magistrate James H. Sullivan, the man for whom the courthouse would eventually be named. Judge Dolan was an innovative yet conservative jurist and a true legal genius. I served as his session clerk for many years so sitting in a courtroom with Judge Dolan on the bench was like attending law school by osmosis, and of course I am not implying that my level of acquired knowledge was even close to that of a member of the bar, but it did provide me with a valuable education on many legal issues.

I'll never forget the day that I watched Judge Dolan take an unusually long time to rule on an objection in a civil case. He listened to both attorneys and kept asking questions in an effort to narrow down the issue. Judge Dolan would ask one attorney what he had to say about some particular component of the basis for the objection and then turn to give the other lawyer an opportunity to make his argument only on that one piece of the puzzle. This went on for about 20 minutes, which is about 19 minutes and 55 seconds longer than most objections take, and when Judge Dolan issued his ruling it was only after he had become satisfied that every element of the salient portion of the topic had been explored. Other attorneys seated in the courtroom felt as though they were being treated to the viewing of a legal masterpiece as one commented to me after the trial that Judge Dolan was a real "law man" and the tape recording of the proceedings should be used to instruct third-year law school students.

Back in the day, criminal defendants in Attleboro who wanted their case heard by a jury had to travel to the Fall River District Court. Defendants who wanted the case to stay in Attleboro had to sign a jury waiver stating that they didn't want the case to be heard by a jury. Judges had to verbally explain this to every defendant so by the time I had called dozens of cases by late in the afternoon, a defendant sitting in the courtroom had heard these rights explained to others so many times that some thought of themselves as law school graduates!

Notwithstanding that repetitive and brief legal education, some guys still just didn't get it. I called the case of a Rehoboth resident who was charged with assault & battery in Norton. Judge Dolan asked him if he wanted to have a jury trial in Fall River or waive that right to have his case heard in Attleboro. You knew just by looking at this guy that he wasn't a graduate of MIT as his deer in the headlights expression was accompanied by complete silence. Judge Dolan tried to simplify things sometimes when necessary and this case cried out for simplification so the judge said, "Sir, do you want your case heard here in Attleboro or in Fall River?" The defendant was serious when he then stated, "I want it heard in Rehoboth!"

We come in contact with multiple people, including many confused individuals, in the District Court system so it is no surprise that some are unsure of the responsibilities of courthouse staff. I had grown a mustache that I kept in my early years at the ADC so I was sometimes referred to as the guy with the mustache, which on some days was probably the nicest thing that I was called! Judge Dolan had just sentenced a 20-year old burglar who was standing in the prisoner's dock, to a split sentence that called for a year to be suspended for two years with probation and six months committed to the House of Correction. Judge Dolan, just like most judges, would announce the sentence to the session clerk in a normal speaking volume that usually couldn't be heard by the defendant or most people in the court. I wrote on the criminal docket, then turned to face the defendant and announced his sentence in a loud voice that all could hear.

The defendant would be transported to the House of Correction after being processed in the Probation Department for the suspended portion of his sentence. Immediately upon being brought into Probation the defendant started complaining to Probation Officer

Terrell J. Kiley, who would eventually be promoted to the position of Chief Probation Officer, that six months was a long time to be going to jail and that it just wasn't fair. Terry is a tremendous guy who has heard just about everything over a long storied career in the court system so he doesn't get rattled and knows how to handle everything that comes his way. He told the defendant that the judge says you're going for six months so you're going for six months. The excited defendant looked at Terry and said, "The judge? The judge thought that I was a good guy. The judge didn't say a word. It was that son of a bitch with the mustache that doesn't like me!"

I was the session clerk in Court Room One in the ADC where I called the last case before the luncheon recess. The defendant walked up to the microphone wearing a sling holding his right arm. He explained that his injury had prevented him from working so he hadn't been able to pay his fines. It seemed like a reasonable excuse so Judge Dolan gave him more time to pay, I gave him a date and we recessed for lunch. As I was reaching for my car keys I happened to glance out the front window of the court just in time to see the same guy take his arm out of the sling and stick his right arm out with his thumb up to hitch hike a ride! He could have at least waited until he was down the street!

Judge Dolan was also very helpful to me during the Judicial Nominating Commission and screening process that led to my appointment as Clerk-Magistrate of the WDC by Governor Cellucci for which I shall remain forever grateful. A few years after I retired we lost Judge Dolan, creating a hole in the hearts of his adoring friends and family. The funeral for the venerable justice was private, but he had provided his lovely wife Sue with

The Courts & You - ADC speakers for high school student's program, seated L-R First Assistant Clerk-Magistrate Antonio J. Casale, author; standing L-R Attorneys David C. Manoogian & Peter F. Murphy, Probation Officer & future CPO Terrell J. Kiley, Chief Probation Officer John Carroll, Assistant District Attorney & now First Assistant Clerk-Magistrate James P. Perkoski, First Justice John J. Dolan & Clerk-Magistrate James H. Sullivan.
(Tom Maguire photo, courtesy of The Sun Chronicle*)*

a short list of people who he wanted at the service. J. Do and I felt privileged to be invited and were honored to attend.

    This typist heard a lot of Civil Motor Vehicle Infraction and Criminal Show Cause Hearings during my time in the court system. Hearings are held in various rooms in different courthouses including courtrooms, but I usually held them in my office. There were some very serious cases that called for the issuance of a criminal complaint upon a showing of probable cause. For most cases, however, I tried to be guided by the old adage that there is a difference between a bad guy and a good guy who had made a bad mistake. I would give people a break if warranted with the most persuasive reasons for leniency being that the alleged victim had been made whole, it was a nonviolent crime, the defendant had corrected the problem like registering an unregistered vehicle and the defendant had little or no record. A citation for speeding, for instance, results in the defendant having to pay $25.00 for a hearing, taking a day out of work, trying to find a parking spot, waiting for the case to be called in the courthouse while seated next to a guy who maybe hasn't had a shower in a while and probably some other inconveniences so if I decided to give someone a break and find her or him Not Responsible it wasn't like they didn't receive some level of punishment. Most people don't want to go through that again which causes them to lighten up their foot on the gas pedal in the future or correct some other form of errant behavior.

    People often want to bring family members and friends into hearings even if not percipient witnesses. I usually allowed this, but I always wanted everyone to be identified. A 65-year old woman took a seat in the defendant's chair and her husband sat closer to the door so I asked her the name of the handsome fellow seated behind her. I figured that she would just tell me his name, but I felt bad for the husband when she turned around wearing a quizzical look while inquiring, "Handsome?"

    The Grammy-winning R & B musical group Tavares became an international sensation producing numerous hits including "Heaven Must Be Missing an Angel" and "It Only Takes a Minute" which reached #1 on the Hot Soul Singles Chart. Their widely-acclaimed cover of the Bee Gees "More Than A Woman" can be heard on the *Saturday Night Fever* soundtrack. The group was comprised of five brothers who eventually established roots in the New Bedford area. One of the brothers, Ralph Tavares, lived in South Dartmouth and also worked as a court officer for about thirty years. Ralph worked the Aaron Hernandez murder trial and many other high profile cases, but I got to know him when he would periodically work in the ADC to fill in for someone on vacation or out for a day. We were always delighted to have Ralph in court because of his positive attitude, kindness, humility, professionalism and conscientious work ethic. Sometimes arrestees would be acting up and making noise in the lockup so we would ask Ralph if he would go to the cellblock and calm the prisoners down by singing a song to them!

A small claims plaintiff was looking for the custodian at the ADC to report a spill on the floor outside of the Probation Department. She went up to a man and asked if he was the janitor to which he indignantly replied, "No, I'm a criminal!"

A rental dispute resulted in a hearing before me with the landlord seeking a criminal complaint against the tenant. The tenant, a 25-year old girl, became loud and emotional while telling her story as the landlord had banned her boyfriend from the apartment. She started yelling, "I can't take it anymore. Tell him to let my boyfriend back in. I haven't had sex in 3 months! I want sex!" She then leaned in toward me, lowered her voice and told me, "I need sex bad!" "Sorry," I said, "I'm just here for the probable cause."

I was hearing a case involving a husband and wife who had all kinds of issues with each other. There was no violence, but just about every other kind of problem imaginable. At one point the wife said that the husband won't take out the rubbish and that tomorrow is rubbish day and she knows that he won't do it again. The husband was incensed that his wife was in effect predicting the future. He wanted to point out that she didn't have Extra Sensory Perception. He had intended to make reference to her acting like she has ESP, but instead he inadvertently said to me, "What, does she have ESPN!"

Ronald A. Valcourt was an Assistant Clerk-Magistrate in the Fall River District Court at the same that I was working in Attleboro. We came up through the system together and shared some laughs over the years. Ron is a terrific guy who would eventually be promoted to be the great Clerk-Magistrate of the same court by Governor A. Paul Cellucci. You will never hear anyone say a bad word about Val and I still have the very kind note that he sent to me on an appointment issue.

A middle aged woman was the defendant in a speeding hearing before Ron. She was driving too fast, but Ron decided to give her a break and found her Not Responsible which is the equivalent of a Not Guilty finding in a criminal matter. He ruled in her favor and

L-R Clerk-Magistrates Ron Valcourt & Brian Kearney, J. Do, Clerk-Magistrates & Assistants - Joseph M. Hogan Scholarship Award Recipient Kaitlin Doherty, author, Matt Kearney, Clerk-Magistrate Joe Hogan

went on to the next case. Soon thereafter a loud commotion could be heard in the courthouse hallway. The court officer came into the hearing room to tell Ron that the woman who just left the hearing was extremely upset. Ron told the court officer that he had just found her Not Responsible so she should be very happy.

The woman was beyond agitated as she loudly complained about Ron to the other litigants waiting in the corridor. She was offended and telling anyone who would listen, "How dare that man tell me that I am Not Responsible! I am a very responsible person!"

Until retirement, the great Clerk-Magistrate of the Brockton District Court was Kevin P. Creedon, appointed by Governor Edward J. King. Kevin, who served in the court system for well over four decades, comes from a long line of devoted public servants, one of the most storied and distinguished political families in the history of the Commonwealth. Members of this iconic clan from the City of Champions serve in numerous government positions and three of Kevin's brothers are accomplished attorneys. Kevin's brother Michael is a very personable former state senator who was eventually appointed to a judgeship by Governor William F. Weld and later became First Justice of the Falmouth District Court. I had the distinct pleasure of serving as Judge Creedon's session clerk in Attleboro for about a year which contributed to my real education enormously. Their likeable brother Jake is an outstanding lawyer in private practice who I always look forward to seeing and amiable brother Rob also served in the state senate before being elected as the Superior Court Clerk of Courts for Plymouth County.

Kevin was a Probation Officer before his appointment as an Assistant Clerk-Magistrate in the Taunton District Court where he served at the same time that I was working in Attleboro. He was also a part time talented bartender at Raynham Park while I was working on the windows. One Friday night Kevin had to stop serving an intoxicated patron, but the man was not happy and had some unkind words for Kevin before going on his way. Kevin happened to be on call that night with the Raynham Police who had arrested the same guy who had been shut off at the track. Kevin went to the police station and got a double take from the defendant as he sat down. He released the man, who had a sober ride waiting, and instructed him to go to court to be arraigned on the drunk driving charge the next morning which was a Saturday. This was back when the courts were open on Saturday mornings so Kevin was the session clerk who called the defendant's name in the courtroom and read the charges. The man had now interacted in one way or another with Kevin three times in less than twelve hours! The defendant then had to go to the Clerk-Magistrate's Office during the court recess so when he saw that it was Kevin working the counter he sighed and said, "Man you're like a bad dream. I just can't get away from you!"

Kevin was doing CMVI hearings one day in Brockton after having been appointed Clerk-Magistrate. A 60-year old woman had been cited for failing to stop at a stop sign so the officer read the citation and then turned to file the report away as Kevin addressed the lady by saying, "Yes ma'am, what would you like to say?" The woman winked at Kevin as she lifted up the left lapel on her blue blazer to reveal a hidden political button that read, CREEDON FOR SENATE!

Two heavily intoxicated young women in their mid-twenties had been arrested by the Brockton Police for being disorderly. Kevin released the two friends from the lockup, listened to them thank him and then describe their next problem. One of them was pregnant, they both had babysitters watching their children and were long overdue for their return home. It was 2AM, they had no money left and didn't even have a car to get back home to Plymouth.

The kind-hearted Clerk-Magistrate immediately had a conversation with the shift commander and came up with a plan to assist the two damsels in distress. The women were transported in a Brockton Police cruiser to the town line where they were met by the Whitman Police and continued on a police chain through the towns of Hanson, Pembroke and Kingston until finally being delivered home safely by the Plymouth Police.

The women were very grateful and never forgot how nice Kevin had been in going way above and beyond his job description in helping them. Months later Kevin answered a knock on his door at the Brockton District Court only to find the woman who had been pregnant smiling and holding a baby. She said that she appreciated what he had done for her and wanted him to meet her infant.

She was so thankful that she wanted the Clerk-Magistrate to know that she had named the baby Kevin!

CM & ACM clambake, front L-R, Ann McCormick, Kevin Creedon, Joe Faretra, back, Vinny Capolupo, author, Angelo Ligotti, Bob Arena, Joe Ligotti, Arthur Wilner, Ted Tomasone & Charlie Decas

Attorney John P. "Jack" Mulvee was legal counsel for the Jury Commissioner's Office and is one of the nicest guys you could ever meet. He would come into courts to prosecute delinquent jurors who had failed to appear for jury duty and just about always worked things out by giving the defendant another chance, thus avoiding the issuance of a complaint. He has a terrific sense of humor and is very highly thought of in courts across the Commonwealth.

Jack had an annual outing on his boat that was always a good time featuring distinguished guests like Kevin Creedon, quick witted Court Administrator Dana L. Leavitt and Anthony S. Owens, the great Clerk-Magistrate of the Dorchester Division of the Boston Municipal Court whose hands are so big that my right disappears whenever we shake hands! Tony, a real good guy who was appointed by Governor Mitt Romney, grew up in the Columbia Point projects and at 6' 5" was one of the shortest basketball players on a Don Bosco team whose front court height rivaled that of the Boston Celtics!

Captain Mulvee was doing an admirable job of steering us through some choppy seas as Kevin G. Murphy, the great Clerk-Magistrate of the Chelsea District Court appointed by Governor William F. Weld, told some funny stories. He asked Jack to dock the boat at the Chelsea Yacht Club under the Tobin Bridge where we all enjoyed some libation compliments of Kevin's hospitality and generosity. He was blessed with outstanding Assistant Clerk-Magistrates like Bruce Glazer and Harry Landry as well First Assistant Robert E. O'Leary followed by First Assistant Edward F. O'Neil III. Brian V. Sullivan was another terrific ACM who kept me laughing every time we met. We were all pulling for Sully and ecstatic when Governor Charlie D. Baker appointed him to be the great Clerk-Magistrate of the Lynn District Court. The very likeable Ed O'Neil was a court officer at Middlesex Probate & Family Court prior to his appointment in Chelsea. Ed saw firsthand the financial toll, heartbreak and emotional turmoil of couples getting divorced all day long so when Sully asked him if he had learned anything important in all his time in Probate Court his response was, "Oh yea, stay married no matter what!"

Judge Antone S. Aguiar Jr. was a State Representative from the southeastern part of the Commonwealth who was appointed to the bench by Governor Edward J. King, eventually serving as the First Justice of the Fall River District Court. Judge Aguiar played baseball at Yale and was an all-around really good guy. He had a fabulous sense of humor, an easy laugh and would literally help anyone who found themselves in need. We spent a lot of time working together in the ADC so sometimes we would eat lunch at Morin's Restaurant, where you never get a bad meal. Some people might tell you that I am a fast eater, but Judge Aguiar would finish his entire lunch before I could even eat half of mine! He was always in a good mood, but did things in a hurry as he seemed to always want to expedite everything and move on.

One day Judge Aguiar was presiding over a jury trial in Courtroom Two at the ADC with Nancy E. Clarke serving as the session clerk. Halfway through the trial Nancy, who would rise through the ranks to become First Assistant Clerk-Magistrate, noticed that Juror #5 was asleep in his chair. The jurors in this courtroom are seated on the judge's right, but the judge's attention was focused mostly on the witness testifying from the stand to his left. Nancy quickly realized that Judge Aguiar probably wouldn't notice the sleeping juror as he took notes and then continued to look left to observe the witness answering questions. Nancy thought for a few seconds as to what her responsibility was in this unusual situation and decided to inform the judge without disrupting the proceedings. She leaned in and whispered, "Judge, juror #5 is asleep." Judge Aguiar, who always saw the glass as half full and never wanted to hurt anyone, looked over at the slumbering juror and then said to Nancy, "That's OK, he's heard enough."

Sometimes jurors are now permitted to ask questions of witnesses, but back in the day that would never happen and you never knew how jurors might react during a trial. I was the session clerk on a jury trial back when jurors only listened in the courtroom and then deliberated in the jury room - they didn't ask the witness any questions. The defendant was being tried for assault and battery by means of a dangerous weapon as a result of an altercation at a local establishment. The defense attorney had questioned one of the witnesses for about fifteen minutes and then suddenly paused as if possibly contemplating his next question. Sometimes an attorney will ask the judge if he or she can have a moment which is usually granted, but this lawyer just stood there silently. Judge Aguiar wasn't sure if the attorney had finished so he asked, "Are there any more questions for this witness?" Juror #3 stood up and said, "Yes, I have a few questions."

Whenever Judge Aguiar gave someone a break on a criminal case he would always address the defendant after sentencing in a very stern voice and say, "Don't come back!" It was his way of telling, usually a young man, that he was lucky this time and that he should stay on the straight and narrow by keeping out of trouble so that he won't end up in court again. One night I released a young man on a larceny charge from the Attleboro Police lockup who apparently didn't take Judge Aguiar's admonition to stay out of trouble seriously. Judge Aguiar had given this kid a break three weeks before and now he was under arrest again so I told him that he had to go to court the next morning to be arraigned. The kid looked at me with legitimate fear in his eyes as he said, "I can't go to court - the judge said not to come back!" I told him that we were making a special exception this time just for him!

Growing up in Attleboro made me more familiar with our clientele than Judge Aguiar who lived in Swansea so sometimes I would provide little tidbits of information for him to consider. Judge Aguiar was taking an admission from a teenage defendant so I mentioned that the young man was a very talented high school track star. The police had to chase the young sprinter for some distance until finally apprehending him, but the kid didn't have a record and there was no violence so Judge Aguiar continued the case without a finding. The last thing that the judge said to him was, "Save your running for the track and not from the police!"

One of our regulars in Attleboro was a habitual thief who had been convicted and sentenced to, I think, a year in the House of Correction. His sentence had been stayed for two weeks to get some affairs in order so he appeared in Courtroom One to begin serving his time on the scheduled day. I called his name just before our luncheon break at about

12:55PM. The posture of the case at that point was simply to order the mittimus to issue and for the court officer to bring him to the lockup. I asked him if he was ready to go, but he said that he had one final request. He asked Judge Aguiar if it would be OK to leave and come back after lunch so that he could go to his favorite restaurant for one final meal before being incarcerated. Judge Aguiar would quite often look to me for input so I pointed out that the defendant had already surrendered himself voluntarily on a nonviolent crime thus the judge allowed the request. We broke for lunch and I started walking to Tex Barry's Coney Island Diner in downtown Attleboro. This place is famous for their delicious chili dogs made by Arthur Bombardier, the affable owner who started working there when he was only fifteen years old. Arthur handed me my usual order of three well done chili dogs as I sat down to enjoy the old fashioned feast. Just as I was taking a bite out of my first dog I looked to my right and saw, seated a couple of tables away, the defendant that wanted to have his last meal as a free man in his favorite restaurant. The guy surrendered himself at 2PM to start his sentence with a belly full of chili dogs and a smile on his face! I told Arthur that he should make an ad out of this story because that really was a loyal customer who appreciated the mouthwatering cuisine more than any other and chose Tex Barry's under extreme circumstances!

Judge Aguiar was always proud of his association with his alma mater Joseph Case High School in his home town of Swansea. We were shooting the breeze one morning in his chambers while waiting to enter the courtroom for a jury trial. He was telling me the details of the Case football team's victory that past weekend and mentioned that he was in charge of the stakes. I said that was terrific that they had steaks as I suddenly envisioned thick sirloins sizzling on the grill! I told Judge Aquiar that at Attleboro High School games we only had burgers and hot dogs. "Do you cook the steaks at half time?" I asked. No, he told me - he was in charge of the Marker Stakes that are used to measure for a First Down! Oh, never mind!

Judge Aguiar was hearing a small claims trial back when they were only heard by judges. I swore in the parties who were representing themselves just like in most small claims cases. Judge Aguiar listened to the plaintiff present his case, took some notes and was now ready to give the defendant an opportunity to be heard. The judge wanted to know the defendant's position on some of the issues that had been raised by the other litigant so he asked the defendant, "Sir, what is your position?" to which he replied, "Your Honor, I'm a polisher in a jewelry factory."

A woman who had been arrested for larceny was awaiting arraignment in the WDC holding cell. Apparently her husband was fed up with her criminal behavior so he came to the counter of the Clerk-Magistrate's Office and was dead serious when he announced to our staff, "My wife is in lockup and I want an annulment!" Sorry, we don't do those here!

I needed to know who represented a 40-year old defendant so I asked him, "Sir, who is your attorney?" The poor guy looked confused as he said, "You mean my lawyer?"

Chief Justice John M. Greaney, appointed Hampden County Housing Court Judge by Governor Francis W. Sargent; Superior, Appeals, Chief Justice of Appeals & Associate Justice of the Supreme Judicial Court by Governor Michael S. Dukakis. Chief Justice Greaney is an accomplished man with five gubernatorial appointments to his credit which, as far as I know, is a record for one person.

WDC 2002 Capital Improvements Ribbon Cutting, L-R Representative Michael J. Coppola, Senator Jo Ann Sprague, Register of Deeds William P. O'Donnell, Representative James E. Vallee, Chief Justice for Administration & Management Barbara A. Dortch-Okara, appointed Judge by Governor Michael S. Dukakis; DCAM Deputy Commissioner Neil Johnson, author, Representative Scott P. Brown, Governor's Chief Legal Counsel Steven D. Pierce, Representative Elizabeth A. Poirier, Representative John H. Rogers, Representative David P. Linsky & SJC Associate Justice Robert J. Cordy, appointed by Governor A. Paul Cellucci. (Vin Igo photo). Representative Brown would later win election to the United States Senate and Chief Legal Counsel Pierce would later be appointed Chief Justice of the Housing Court after his appointment as Judge by Governor Jane M. Swift.

WDC 2002 Capital Improvements Ceremony, second row L - R, Somerville District Court Clerk-Magistrate "Ted" Tomasone, Representative James E. Vallee (partially blocked), Representative David P. Linsky, Representative Elizabeth A. Poirier, (unidentified), Register of Deeds William P. O'Donnell, front row L - R, House Ways & Means Chairman John H. Rogers, Massachusetts State Senate Policy Analyst Amy B. Panek, Senator Jo Ann Sprague & Regional Administrative Justice Rosemary B. Minehan, appointed by Governor William F. Weld, a fair minded Judge and nice person who took care of the needs of our region. (Vin Igo photo).

42

You may see acclaimed Falmouth Attorney Drew Segadelli zipping around Buzzards Bay in his 38 foot long cigarette boat. It's easy to tell that the white navy blue striped Scarab is owned by a criminal defense lawyer as soon as you see the name on the boat - *CRIME PAYS!*

Attorney Glen Hannington is a fearless advocate who owns a thriving law practice with offices in Canton and Boston, but I first met him when he was an Assistant Clerk-Magistrate at the Boston Municipal Court and I had the same job in Attleboro. He is a kind, generous man with a terrific sense of humor and a big heart. Glen's late mother also had a fantastic sense of humor and even had a nickname for me. My premature full head of white hair inspired her to call me "The Q-Tip"!

One time we decided to have lunch at the Blue Fin Lounge in Bass Pro Shops in Foxborough. Glen noticed on the menu that there is an upcharge provision to order a double amount of meat for a sandwich. The waitress was taking our order as Glen was speaking with me and contemplating the larger portion. He finally told her, while looking very serious, "We better get the double meat - just in case!" It was just funny the way the words came out of his mouth so we laughed about it later as we tried to think what the poor waitress must have thought that Glen meant when he stated, "…just in case!" She may have thought we were going on a long journey where food was unavailable!

Attorney Tracy L. Wilson is a terrific lawyer with offices in Canton and Quincy who is married to the distinguished Norfolk County Sheriff Patrick W. McDermott. Tracy is also famous for raising money for good causes and pours her heart out every year running in the Boston Marathon. Glen and I had just finished lunch at a Chinese restaurant in Newton and were headed back to court in his car as we found ourselves riding partially along the same route as the runners use in the Boston Marathon. After driving up Commonwealth Avenue to the top of Heartbreak Hill Glen pulled

*Attorney Glen Hannington &
First Assistant Clerk-Magistrate Bill Farrell*

over to the side of the road and facetiously declared, "That wasn't so bad. I don't know what everybody's complaining about!" Glen put Tracy on speakerphone and we all got a good laugh out of our Heartbreak Hill accomplishment!

Glen is very involved with the Cape Cod Baseball League and is not only a sponsor of the Wareham Gatemen, but was elected President of the team. The premier summer league in America is comprised of the best college talent from across our nation with an impressive percentage of players in the Major Leagues having competed on the Cape. Glen asked me to throw out the ceremonial first pitch for one of the games at Spillane Field so I walked out to the mound in Wareham accompanied by my brother Chris and the lady in charge of pre-game events. She was very nice and of course never knows if she is handing the ball to a former athlete so she kept things simple and told me that I could move up closer to the catcher if I didn't feel comfortable throwing the ball all the way in from the pitcher's mound. Before I could start for the mound my smiling brother Chris kiddingly said, "Eddie, if you don't tow the rubber I'm leaving!" I got lucky and threw a strike from the mound which drew praise from the leadoff batter waiting in the on deck circle who tried to make me feel like Pedro Martinez!

We were reading the luncheon menu at a restaurant near Gillette Stadium where the specialty of the house was an enormous 64 ounce prime rib so Glen and I decided that we would both give it a try. We had just taken our first bites of the delicious beef when two huge guys with long beards came in and sat down at the next table. These guys weighed at least 400 pounds apiece with the appearance of anxious and hungry lumberjacks. They both asked the waitress for the prime rib, but she told them that they were all out. She turned and pointed to us as she said, "Those guys got the last 2 ribs!" which caused the lumberjacks to stare in our direction with angry eyeballs that seemed ready to pop out! It would have been nice if the waitress had not pointed us out like we had committed a terrible sin against society, but the big guys ordered some steaks and we got out of there safely with full bellies.

Attorney Glen Hannington

Glen and I were playing in his golf tournament while riding in the same cart on a beautiful day at the Milton-Hoosic Club in Canton. I was fortunate enough to hit a nice drive off the tee right down the middle of the fairway on the 349-yard fourth hole. I took out my 8 iron for the second shot on this majestic par 4, but Glen suggested that I use a 9 so good fortune was with me as the 9 iron lifted my ball and dropped it right on the green. We couldn't see if it stayed on the green as we were hitting from down in a valley that was much lower than the hole, but it looked to be a pretty good shot. I got to the hole first and called to Glen that the ball wasn't on the green and that I couldn't even find it on the edge anywhere. He told me to look in the hole and to my surprise the ball had found its way to pay dirt! I had scored my first and probably last eagle which was quite a thrill for a guy with my limited golf game. Glen surprised me at a sports banquet later that year when he presented me with a nice trophy commemorating the occasion.

Even folks with a solid memory probably wish that they had a better one. I wish that my memory was more precise, but it was far from perfect even long before I qualified for Medicare. Different people seem to experience a level of memory loss in some areas, but not in others. Sometimes I can recall the minutiae of many stories vividly and in intricate detail, but I can't remember who I told them to which has become an inside joke with my family and friends. If I start to relate a story that I have previously told they will hold up their hand with two fingers raised which is their good natured way of telling me that it is a repeat recitation. Glen had just made a long beautiful putt for birdie so we were heading for the golf cart to proceed to the next hole when I started to tell him a story. He smiled and held up his hand with two fingers raised as he said, "I hope the day never comes when I have to hold up three fingers."

Glen is a devout New England Patriots' fan so he has been a regular at Gillette Stadium with his lovely wife Louise and two daughters for many years. Glen was on his way to get something to eat before the game with his daughter Tevis driving. They were on their way to Five Guys when Glen received a call from a criminal defendant who had just retained him on the phone. Glen has a very successful law practice anyway, but the sudden surge in income caused him to tell his daughter, "Forget Five Guys, we're going to Davio's!"

Glen's daughter Nicole is a very gracious and outstanding attorney who is licensed to practice in Nevada and California. She knows a somewhat complex formula for figuring out the speed of a pitched softball. The major league distance between home plate and the pitching mound, 60 feet 6 inches, is somehow compared with the same area on a softball field and entered into a mathematical calculation that produces the ball's velocity as it travels on the way to the catcher's mitt. When Nicole was in law school she was explaining these numbers one day to her father. Glen was duly impressed with his daughter's mathematical acumen, but was thinking of the standard legal fee for a plaintiff's attorney when he told her that when she becomes a lawyer the only math that is important to know is ⅓!

Glen used to take his mother fishing and pulled a trick on her a couple of times that caused me to have an even greater sense of admiration and respect for him. They were fishing in his boat on Cape Cod with both of their lines in the water, but only Glen was catching anything. The next time that he snagged one he nonchalantly set the hook without alerting his mother and then let out enough line so that the fish's movement couldn't immediately be felt through the rod. He then asked his mother to please hold his fishing pole while he took a phone call. She took the rod from his hand and within seconds excitedly cried out that she had a fish! She reeled in her catch and proudly smiled all the way home. Glen successfully pulled that off again one time in Florida resulting in another joyous day for his mother who would eventually go to her grave without ever knowing the real story. The world is a much better place because of sons like Glen Hannington.

Clerk-Magistrate Daniel J. Sullivan asked me to use his office to conduct a show cause hearing when I was an assistant clerk-magistrate in the ADC as there were several witnesses, so the larger space would be able to accommodate everyone. I sat at Dan's desk, listened to the evidence, found probable cause and ordered a criminal complaint to issue against the defendant.

A few weeks later Dan came into my office while reading a note with a quizzical look on his face. It was from the victim in the aforementioned case who had written an extremely nice note praising Dan for conducting a fair hearing and for his intellect, patience, legal acumen and sound judgement. He told me that he didn't remember the case, but that the lady had given him high praise and was obviously very satisfied with the decision. I told him that he didn't recognize her name because he didn't conduct the hearing, I did. It was the case that I heard in his office, but she gave credit to the wrong guy because Dan's name plate was still sitting on his desk when I did the hearing so she thought that my name was Sullivan. We both had a good laugh at the mix up!

The much admired and highly respected Plymouth County First Assistant District Attorney Paul C. Dawley would later be appointed to a judgeship by Governor Jane M. Swift and served with tremendous distinction as the First Justice of the Brockton District Court and as the Regional Administrative Justice. He would eventually be appointed Chief Justice of the District Courts for the entire Commonwealth by the Honorable Paula M. Carey, Chief Justice of the Trial Court who had been appointed and reappointed to her position by the Supreme Judicial Court after having been appointed a judge by Governor A. Paul Cellucci. Chief Justice Dawley eventually retired from the Trial Court and accepted the position of General Counsel for the University of Massachusetts Foundation.

Chief Justice Dawley is truly one of the very best in the business, a highly skilled attorney, brilliant judge and great all around guy. He was my boss for a significant portion of my career and was always much more than fair with me so I shall always be indebted to him for his patience, integrity and kindness.

ADA Dawley was prosecuting a criminal case before Judge Richard J. Chin who had been appointed to the Boston Municipal Court by Governor Michael S. Dukakis and to the Superior Court by Governor William F. Weld. The defendant was represented by Attorney Robert L. Jubinville, a passionate lawyer and former Massachusetts State Police Detective who would go on to win election for a seat on the Governor's Council and later be appointed the great Clerk-Magistrate of the Framingham District Court by Governor Charlie D. Baker. The defendant had been charged with some serious crimes by the Massachusetts State Police and the complexity of the case had required the investigating trooper to produce some supplemental police reports in addition to his initial documents. ADA Dawley wanted to be sure that all of the police reports had been submitted, that they had everything and that there weren't any outstanding supplemental files. He asked the trooper on the witness stand if they had everything or if any of his police reports were outstanding to which the trooper responded, "Well, I do my best, but I think that all of my reports are outstanding!"

I used to put together and MC different functions at the WDC including our annual Law Day Ceremony and Courthouse Speaker Series. President Dwight D. Eisenhower had signed the Law Day proclamation in 1958 to emphasize the importance of the rule of law in the United States resulting in celebrations in many courthouses ever since. Attorney Peter Padula was gracious enough to serve as our Law Day Chairman and I was honored that so many distinguished elected and appointed officials, professional athletes and accomplished members of the community took time out of their busy schedules to participate in our events. Many people in our audience told me how excited they were to be able to meet United States Congressmen William R. Keating & Joseph P. Kennedy III; United States Attorney Carmen M. Ortiz; former Patriots' quarterback Steve Grogan; USN Lieutenant Commander and Medal of Honor recipient Thomas G. Kelley who, it was announced in 2023, would have a guided missile destroyer named for him; the Honorable Paul C. Dawley, Chief Justice of the Massachusetts District Courts; United States Marshall John Gibbons; former Boston Red Sox Manager Joe Morgan; Register of Deeds William P. O'Donnell; Massachusetts Attorney General Martha M. Coakley; Colonel Richard D. McKeon, Superintendent, Massachusetts State Police; United States Senator Scott P. Brown; Channel 4 WBZ-TV CBS Boston News Anchor Lisa Hughes; the Honorable Paula M. Carey, Chief Justice of the Massachusetts Trial Court; US Gold Medal Olympic Hockey Champion Jim Craig; Boston Police Officer Jennifer J. Penton, one of the stars of the TV series "Boston's Finest" who is now a Trooper with the Massachusetts State Police; and many others.

author, Law Day Chairman Attorney Peter E. Padula

Some of our very best speakers were from South Boston including former Boston Mayor & United States Ambassador Raymond L. Flynn, Boston Police Commissioner William B. Evans and Boston City Councilor Michael F. Flaherty Jr. We were also privileged to honor Admiral William H. McRaven who was Commander of the Joint Special Operations Task Force when a team of Navy SEALs killed Osama bin Laden in Pakistan.

author, J. Do, US Senator Scott Brown   *Middlesex County District Attorney & future Attorney General Martha M. Coakley, author*

 Platoon Sergeant Lawrence F. Kirby had been part of the massive Marine invasion force on Iwo Jima and bore witness to the American Flag being raised on Mount Suribachi in what became one of the most iconic photos in American history. The huge Iwo Jima Memorial in Arlington National Cemetery in Washington, DC is one of the most beautiful and patriotic monuments in our nation. It depicts six men raising the flagpole with Old Glory flying as an inspiration to the brave troops that were fighting below. You would expect to see twelve hands from the six heroes gripping the pole, but the sculptor added one more saying that the thirteenth is the hand of God. Larry's awe inspiring speech describing the brutal details of the fierce battle left our audience both teary eyed and appreciative at the same time. Larry Kirby remains as one of the greatest and most moving speakers that I have ever had the privilege to hear.

 We were also honored to have Boston Police Officer Steve Horgan raise his arms in the air in the courtroom to recreate his famous pose from the Red Sox bullpen during the second game of the 2013 ALCS. Legendary *Boston Globe* Photojournalist Stan Grossfeld took the iconic Fenway Park photo of Detroit right fielder Torii Hunter flipping over the bullpen wall in pursuit of David Ortiz's two out grand slam. This is the classic image that made Steve famous as the "Bullpen Cop" with his arms raised in victory and his left hand closed as he stood behind Hunter. Steve told me that he had been eating sunflower seeds in the bullpen when Ortiz connected on the first pitch changeup delivered by Tiger's closer Joaquin Benoit. Grossfeld's camera lens captured the officer's left hand in a fist because Horgan had immediately closed it to hold onto his sunflower seed snack as he shot his arms up in the air!

WDC Law Day, family with BPD Officer Steve Horgan

Toward the end of my career I was still working on trying to secure an appearance from Tom Brady, John Hannah, Ty Law and some other football greats. Three time Super Bowl Champion Joe Andruzzi was a dominant professional football player and continued his legacy of excellence off the field in retirement by teaming with his wife Jen to start the Joe Andruzzi Foundation. The Andruzzis and their staff continue to work extremely hard to raise money to help families that have a member afflicted with cancer. I can honestly tell you that I have never met a nicer couple who have done so much for so many. Joe, whose brothers were New York City Firefighters on September 11, graciously agreed to make a presentation and speak at our Courthouse Speaker Series which was a tremendous success. He regaled the audience with interesting and humorous stories of his family and his time in the National Football League. The standing ovation at the end was well deserved as everyone enjoyed Joe's powerful and heartfelt message of kindness and hope.

I wanted to see if he could come back for our Law Day Ceremony so I spoke with him again just before he left the courthouse. I told him the date and asked if he could possibly make it to Law Day. Joe smiled and facetiously said, "Law Day! That's nice. You're going to have a day for Ty Law?"

J. Do and I were elated to attend the Andruzzi's magnificent cancer fighting fundraising event at Gillette Stadium where a full house gathered to help combat the ancillary manifestations of this terrible disease. We enjoyed speaking with many nice people including broadcaster and former Patriots quarterback Scott Zolak who did a tremendous job as the MC of the event. J. Do told Scott that he looked like Glen Campbell so before you know it they were both singing a few lines from *Rhinestone Cowboy*!

Former NE Patriot & three-time Super Bowl Champion Joe Andruzzi

A lot of interesting people have walked into Courtroom One for our Law Day Ceremonies over the years, but the funniest guest we ever had was professional comedian Paul D'Angelo. Paul was named "Boston's Best Comedian" twice by *Boston Magazine* and has played to sold out shows everywhere. Prior to making people laugh full time he served as an Assistant District Attorney in Essex County and also as a criminal defense attorney. Paul had our audience absolutely cracking up after every joke and short story including the talk his father had with him as a young man. His dad told him that he should be a lawyer when he grows up so a beaming Paul inquired as to the reason. "Is it because I am so intelligent, well-spoken and charming?" he asked. "No", his father proclaimed, "it's because you're the little sneak who's been stealing the change off the top of my bureau!"

J. Do and I have always enjoyed the hilarious standup routines of comics like Steve Sweeney, Mike Petit and others. The best comedy venue that we have ever been to is Giggles Comedy Club in Saugus which is owned by Mike Clarke who runs a top shelf operation and serves as his brother Lenny's Manager. Lenny Clarke is a veritable legend, appearing in hit movies including *Fever Pitch*, *Here Comes the Boom* and *There's Something About Mary* as well as headlining as a much sought after standup comedian for many years. Even though there is no better comic than Lenny and all of our Law Day guests are volunteers, I asked Mike if there was any chance of having his famous brother make an appearance in Wrentham. Mike is one of the nicest and most accommodating people that I ever dealt while putting together courthouse events. Mike was kind enough to commit to me for an appearance by the dynamic comedian about a year in advance, but only if Lenny was not under contract to do a movie. Unfortunately, for us, Lenny Clarke later signed on to do a movie, which I think was *Ted 2*, conflicting with our Law Day date. Mike is a squared away honest man so I think the chances were very good that if I had not retired Lenny Clarke would have had folks laughing in Wrentham someday.

Paul D'Angelo is also one of the many terrific comics drawing laughs at Giggles and another of our favorite comedians there has always been Dave Russo with his dead on impersonations. I told a friend that Russo does Robert De Niro better than De Niro. Tony V cracks up the audience because of his off the wall, yet down to earth style of humor. *The Boston Globe* Correspondent Nick A. Zaino III wrote an interesting story on October 9, 2020 about Tony V and Jimmy Dunn, two friends who are both outstanding standup comics. Zaino quotes Tony V speaking about himself and Dunn together, "We enjoy a nice meal. Most of our conversation at breakfast is where we're going to have lunch."

George A. Mendonsa was the Navy sailor photographed in New York's Times Square kissing a woman wearing a nurse's uniform to celebrate the end of World War II. The iconic photo served as a model for numerous statues and became a symbol of post war happy days. George became somewhat of a celebrity making appearances at county fairs and other venues while posing for photos as he duplicated his famous kiss with women who would line up for a smooch with the famous veteran. Some places even had George working a kissing booth!

George agreed to make an appearance at our Law Day Ceremony after I had a nice conversation with him and his good natured wife Rita. I had his name printed on the invitation as well as the program next to Boston Police Commissioner William B. Evans who was going to introduce him to our audience. Walpole Police Detective Prosecutor William A. Madden II had agreed to pick George up in his cruiser and bring him to the courthouse, but unfortunately George called me to say that he had taken ill and would not be able to come. America lost a powerful symbol of victory over tyranny when George passed away a few years later at the age of 95.

I had called George about a month before Law Day to finalize the arrangements, but Rita answered the phone and told me that George was out making an appearance at some well attended event in Rhode Island. Rita had always kiddingly chided George about kissing other women so I asked her if he was going to be performing his famous pose that day and giving out kisses. Rita quickly answered, "He better not be!"

It was my honor to present the American Ambassador of Philanthropy Award to Donald E. Rodman at our Law Day Ceremony at the Wrentham District Court. Don was a generous man, raising a tremendous amount of money to help children in need with the Rodman Ride for Kids. He also worked very hard to insure success at the Rodman Celebration for Kids at the Seaport Hotel in Boston. J. Do and I were privileged to meet Mark Wahlberg there who went out of his way to spend time with the huge crowd and even became one of the auction items himself by agreeing to play golf with the highest bidder. Mark then offered to play an additional round of golf to raise even more money for the cause! Don Rodman, Mark Wahlberg and other celebrities put smiles on the faces of many disadvantaged kids because of their innate kindness that night.

Philanthropist & great humanitarian Don Rodman (Barry Okun photo)

Detective Prosecutor Bill Madden presented a motor vehicle citation to me during a hearing as evidence that the man had run a red light. Bill is an honorable man, an impressive guy, and a US Marine Corps veteran, so he would be my first choice as a partner in a foxhole. Unfortunately, I couldn't understand the defendant very well, but he kept saying something about jello so I didn't know if he was hungry or maybe had spilled jello on himself in the car or what the problem was with the jello. Detective Madden saved the day by telling me that the poor guy was having trouble with pronunciation and was trying to tell me that the light was yellow! I found him Not Responsible and told him to be careful.

J. Do & Mark Wahlberg

A middle aged woman was cited for speeding by a Walpole Police Officer. Detective Madden, representing the Commonwealth at the hearing, testified that the motorist had exceeded the posted speed limit as evidenced by the introduction of the police citation. The lady testified that she could not have been speeding because she had been listening to Barry Manilow on the radio and it is absolutely impossible to drive fast while listening to that mellow music. She went on and on about how that music is so soothing and has such a calming effect that no one could ever speed under those circumstances. I remember her saying that Barry Manilow is very relaxing and always makes her drive slowly. Detective Madden then kept a serious demeanor as he asked her, "What about "Copacabana"?"

Justice is blind and I always thought that it should also be free, but as previously mentioned a defendant has to pay a $25.00 fee to have a CMVI Hearing, the vast majority of which are for speeding. I had just finished hearings with Bill Madden one morning when he told me that he had noticed a quarter on the floor next to where the defendant sits, but after a few more hearings it was gone. Somebody got a hearing for $24.75!

The Walpole Police had filed a criminal complaint application charging a married couple with shoplifting. Detective Madden presented the Commonwealth's evidence alleging that they had stolen a Fitbit from a local retail establishment. At the time I would at least like to think that Fitbits were a relatively new product because I thought that the detective was talking about some kind of a snack. After hearing thousands of shoplifting cases over the years it is not unusual for me to hear testimony describing the theft of a candy bar or some other easily concealed food item. The detective, who knows well that I would never be confused with being a high tech savvy guy, was kind enough to educate me about Fitbits and that they were a lot more expensive than a candy bar! Fortunately, the police had recovered the stolen goods so that the merchant had not suffered any loss. The 40-year old defendants had a clean record so after a stern admonition from me I denied the issuance of criminal process as I told them to go in peace and sin no more.

Sometimes Detective Madden would take his young children with him to the WDC if he had a light day without hearings or courtroom work. He would be signing criminal complaints while standing at the end of the counter in the Clerk-Magistrate's Office with his beautiful daughter Alexis and attentive son William close by. Alexis had done a terrific job of leading our Law Day audience in the Pledge of Allegiance when she was in the second grade! The kids would be listening and taking everything in as defendants, lawyers, witnesses and others came to the counter with a litany of problems or requests. Six-year old William seemed particularly interested in the long parade of human drama unfolding before him. A defendant came to the counter who said he was turning himself in on a warrant and was told by a member of our staff to start in probation. The young boy listened intently as the next two defendants had the same problem and were also told to go to probation. By now William was an expert on criminal law and courthouse procedure so when a fourth guy came to the counter on an outstanding warrant he knew the drill. Before our staff could tell the man what to do the precocious youngster looked up at the guy and said, "Go to Probation."

author, Bill Madden

Hearings with Medway Police Prosecutor Gerald Tracy were an enjoyable and unforgettable experience. Jerry did an impression of John Wayne that was so spot on you felt like you were watching clips from a movie. He would slip into character and bring the next defendant into the hearing while talking and walking like the Duke! People would get a hearing and a floor show at the same time!

Jerry always got the job done and brought a lot of joy and happiness to those around him in making that court a fun place to be every day. The first time I met Jerry was at the WDC counter where he told me, in his best John Wayne riff, that he had captured the Ned Pepper Gang and had them tied up outside next to his horse!

One time I was a few steps behind Jerry as we made our way through a crowded foyer to the courtroom. Jerry was making his realistic trademark sound that resembles a bicycle horn as people quickly moved away thinking a vehicle was coming through!

Jerry told me that the Chief of Police thought he might be crazy so he had him examined by a psychiatrist. Jerry said he passed with flying colors and kept the examination results in his wallet which he would proudly display for proof of his sanity.

My mother wanted to watch me doing hearings so she came in one day to see justice in action. Jerry, who has the dynamic personality of a game show host, welcomed her with open arms and started regaling her with some of his famous stories. He showed her the tiny handcuffs that he always kept hanging off his gun belt and told her that they were used for the little leprechauns that lived in Medway because they would sometimes act up, get out of hand and have to be arrested. Jerry always told these stories with a straight face so my mom turned to me and said, "I'll have whatever he's drinking!"

I did a lot of hearings with Detective Lieutenant William R. McGrath prior to his well-deserved appointment as Chief of the Wrentham Police Department. He has always been an honorable man who has the courage to call them like he sees them and understands the ever changing components of the real world. Bill even extended himself to help me with a family employment matter for which I shall always remain grateful. The citizens of Wrentham are lucky to have Bill because he stands behind his officers and is a class act with the intellect to make adjustments to benefit everyone.

We were doing hearings one day when Bill got a text message from a Wrentham Police Officer who had just stopped a motor vehicle for speeding. The driver was on his way to the court for a hearing before me on another moving violation so the officer wanted Bill to know that the guy might be a little late!

On another case, Detective Lieutenant McGrath presented evidence through a police report that a defendant had been shoplifting, but the police had recovered the stolen merchandise so the store had not suffered any income loss. The defendant produced a certificate showing that he had completed a four-hour online class teaching him not to shoplift. Apparently classes are now available for the education and rehabilitation of thieves!

A remorseful defendant without any record admitted to speeding after Detective Lieutenant McGrath handed me the citation. He was a nice guy and said all the right things so I gave him a break and found him Not Responsible. This guy must have been pretty conscious of upcoming holidays because it was early September and as he was leaving he said, "Thanks, have a nice Thanksgiving!"

My cousin, the Honorable Joseph R. Welch was appointed District Court Circuit Justice in 1990 by Governor Michael S. Dukakis. He sat in several courts, but spent a good deal of his time on the bench in Quincy District Court where he served as the very first Jury Court Judge. He had an extremely distinguished career even before being appointed to his judgeship, receiving numerous awards and honors as a very popular and highly skilled attorney. I always looked forward to him coming to Wrentham as he was nice man with a tremendous sense of humor.

He was my father's first cousin so he knew my mother very well when they were younger. Joe and my mom hadn't seen each other for quite a while so I set up a lunch date at Fitzy's Pub on a day when he was sitting in Wrentham. All three of us had fun as I enjoyed just listening to them reminisce and speak of old times.

Judge Welch sat in many courts so he had interesting stories from near and far. My mom and I listened attentively as he spoke about a jury court case when he sat at the Edgartown District Court on the island of Martha's Vineyard. He was presiding over a drunk driving case where the defendant had taken the breath test and failed. He blew a .23 which is high enough to usually persuade the defendant to plead guilty, but this man wanted a trial. Judge Welch issued rulings as the trial proceeded until the evidence was closed and the case went to the jury for deliberation. The jurors came back and found the defendant Not Guilty! The verdict was announced and Judge Welch thanked everyone for their service. He then addressed the jury privately and told them that although they certainly had a right to acquit the defendant, he was just wondering how they reached their verdict as .23 is usually considered to be overwhelming evidence in favor of the Commonwealth. He asked if they could please tell him why they had not found the defendant guilty. The jury foreman stood up and said, "Your Honor, you have to understand - the defendant is the only rubbish man on Martha's Vineyard and if he doesn't have a valid driver's license none of us will get our trash picked up!"

Attorney Thomas J. Iovieno is a class guy with an interesting law practice in Canton. Sometimes his name will be in the newspaper representing a client who is well known to the general public through some level of celebrity or acclamation. Tom is one of the lawyers who would frequent the WDC so I would see him quite often. I enjoyed listening to his arguments because he is a highly skilled advocate who knew when to push hard for his client and when to back off. Part of a defense attorney's job is to recognize the strength of the Commonwealth's case as a component of strategic preparation. A strong case calls for a different approach than a weak one and nobody makes that assessment better than Tom.

One day I was hearing a Walpole Police case where Attorney Iovieno represented a defendant who was from South Boston. I administered the oath to the defendant and

Detective Prosecutor Bill Madden before reviewing the case file. The defendant was charged with larceny and was already on probation in the Quincy District Court. Attorney Iovieno's strategy in this case was to have his client admit culpability and request my discretion in stopping the issuance of a criminal complaint. The facts of the case were not in dispute and the defendant had already made restitution, making it easy to find probable cause so I now listened to counsel tell me why his client deserved a break. The well-spoken attorney told me that his client was also his cousin. The cousin had a substance abuse problem which had landed him on probation in Quincy. His Quincy Court Probation Officer had filed a surrender notice which had just been heard recently. The defendant had gone to great lengths to get his life back in order and was now in compliance with all court orders. The judge in Quincy gave him a break on the surrender after recognizing that he was back on the right track. Attorney Iovieno made some salient and powerful points on behalf of his cousin including the fact that his client was still going to be supervised by a Quincy Probation Officer who would be keeping an eye on him. He persuaded me, without objection from the prosecution, to deny the issuance of a criminal complaint and give the defendant a break.

The justice who acted on the surrender in Quincy was none other than Judge Joe Welch so I told Attorney Iovieno that I was giving a break to his cousin who had already been given a break by my cousin!

The Honorable Daniel B. Winslow, First Justice of the WDC, appointed by Governor William F. Weld, the Honorable Daniel W. O'Malley, Associate Justice and later First Justice of the Stoughton District Court, appointed by Governor A. Paul Cellucci and again by Governor Charlie D. Baker, Chief Probation Officer Alessandro Pizzi and their lovely wives were invited to our home where my bride cooked up a veritable feast for an enjoyable get together in celebration of our relatively new management team. Prior to his appointment to the bench, Judge O'Malley had been an exceptional and in demand attorney with a very successful law practice. He had also been a highly skilled heavyweight boxer who retired from the ring with an unblemished and undefeated professional fighting record of 4-0. He trained often at Grundy's Gym in Central Falls where he sparred with stablemate, New England Heavyweight Champion and Attleboro's own John "Dino" Dennis who was ranked 4th in the world. Grundy's is the same facility where my brother Brendan later donned boxing gloves, training that would serve him well during the arduous and demanding Rhode Island State Police Academy. Court officers are trained to keep order and provide protection for court staff as well as the judge, but one of them told me that maybe Judge O'Malley could protect them!

Judge O'Malley, a terrific guy, told me that he had represented George Kimball, the outstanding author and boxing writer for the *Boston Herald* and *Boston Phoenix*. By all accounts he was a smart, strong willed man with the precious gift of self-deprecating humor. According to the obituary written by *Globe* Correspondent J.M. Lawrence, Kimball had lost an eye in a fight which was replaced with a glass orb. He had run for county sheriff in Kansas with campaign ads proclaiming, "Vote for me: I'll keep an eye out for you."

A lot of the *Herald* crew used to drink nearby at J.J. Foley's, an old historic Irish neighborhood pub. Dan told me that Kimball was sitting at the bar one night next to another *Herald* reporter. They were having drinks while engaged in lively conversation when the reporter got up and said, "I'm going to the men's room George, keep an eye on my drink will you." Kimball said, "Sure", then took out his glass eye and put it in his colleague's drink!

The police prosecutor presented credible evidence that a defendant was speeding and was so reckless that I thought that he qualified for operating to endanger. I would look at a defendant's record only after finding that the Commonwealth had sustained its burden of proof. This defendant seemed like a nice guy, but his driving record was so bad he belonged on a bicycle! I couldn't in good conscience give him any kind of a break so I found him Responsible and imposed the full amount of the fine. I asked him if he accepted my decision or if he would like to appeal my finding to a judge. Just like many people in this circumstance he was a little indecisive and hesitant as he tried to make a decision. This guy must have been watching a lot of TV game shows like *Who Wants to Be a Millionaire* because he wanted to use a lifeline. I allowed him to go outside to make a call after asking him again if he would like to appeal when he said, "I want to phone a friend?"

A well-heeled attorney had always done very well in school consistently finishing in the top of his class, but unfortunately his book smarts far exceeded his street smarts and common sense. He pulled up in his Mercedes-Benz outside of the Boston Municipal Court to file a civil case for the first time. He lowered his window and asked a 25-year old man standing on the sidewalk if there were any places to park around there? The man smiled and said, "Yes Sir, I'm the valet so I'll be happy to take your car and park it at our lot around the corner." Terrific thought the lawyer as he handed over the keys and thanked the young man for his courtesy. After concluding his business in the Clerk-Magistrate's Office the attorney asked a court officer how to get in touch with the valet? The surprised court officer told him, "Valet! What valet? We don't have a valet!"

A young man was at the counter at the ADC telling me that he was constantly being mistaken for another man with the same name. The man at the counter had a very short criminal record, or resume as we called it, with only minor offenses, but the other guy had a long sheet full of violent convictions. They both had the first name of Angel and the same last name with dates of birth that were pretty close. Simply by being polite the Angel at the counter was distinguishing himself from 80% of my other customers and seemed like a nice guy.

He told me that he was the good Angel and was frequently being stopped by police and had been arrested once for something that had been done by the bad Angel. The other guy had an outstanding warrant so the Angel at the counter was afraid that he might be arrested again. I checked out his story, police reports, and photos so that I could help him. I gave him a written statement on court stationary listing his date of birth and proclaiming that he was not the individual named in the warrant with the other guy's docket number. I was concerned, although a longshot, that the other Angel would somehow get ahold of this statement, but a quick cost benefit analysis led me to err on the side of helping the Angel at the counter. I signed the paper and gave it to him causing a big smile of obvious relief. He thanked me and reminded me again that he was the good Angel. I wished him well after telling him that I didn't know if I could call him a good Angel, but at least he wasn't the bad Angel!

The judge asked the 45-year old defendant if he wanted to waive his right to a jury trial. "Yes, Your Honor," the defendant stated as he held up his hand and *waved* at the judge!

I have administered the oath to witnesses prior to testifying probably thousands of times during Small Claims and Clerk-Magistrate Hearings as well as while serving as a session clerk with a judge. I would ask the witness, with right hand raised, "Do you solemnly swear to tell the truth, the whole truth and nothing but the truth so help you God?" The answer I am looking for is "Yes", but I have heard many others including yup, sure, right, you got it, you know it, I always do, all the way, you better believe it, bingo, I think so, you betcha, who me?, all true, I didn't do nothin, my wife sent me, yessah, is lying a felony?, I'll try - and the man who said nothing but gave me the thumbs up sign! Obviously, some of these answers necessitated further inquiry and there were even some nervous folks who thought they were supposed to recite the entire Oath over again!

I asked a defendant to raise his right hand to be sworn, but he raised his left. People are nervous so this happens sometimes and I always politely remind them to raise the right hand. This guy, however, raised his left intentionally because he said, "I'm left handed."

The defendant was charged with a new B & E while on probation so he was being surrendered by his probation officer in Courtroom One in WDC. Evidence had already been admitted that one of the items stolen and not recovered from the housebreak was a New England Patriots' jacket with the owner's first name embroidered on the sleeve. The defendant, whose name was different from the homeowner's, decided to wear the stolen jacket to the surrender hearing. That foolish choice of attire pretty much confirmed that this guy was not one of our brightest criminals! He was dumbfounded on the stand when the ADA asked him why the stitching on the sleeve was not his name and in fact the name of the homeowner! You can't make this stuff up!

Upon a finding of sufficient facts, I would usually continue first offense underage drinking cases without a finding to keep them at the show cause level, thereby preserving the young defendant's clean record. The complaint application would eventually be denied after a period of time provided that the defendant had stayed out of trouble which was usually the case.

Sometimes the police would respond to a house party, where the parents were away, and I would ultimately have a hearing with about twenty kids and maybe about fifteen parents who had come with their children all mixed in together. I would start the hearing by matching each complaint application to every kid by having them identify themselves and saying their names one at a time. I looked at one female who was silent and asked her for her name to which she proudly replied, "Oh, I'm a parent! I'm over 21." I made her day!

Attorney Joseph D. Saurino is an extremely talented lawyer and one of the nicest people I have ever known. Joe is a low-key guy who punches way above his weight in every category of life. He is a tireless worker and such a capable all-around guy that no one should ever mistake his kindness for weakness.

Joe is the quintessential definition of a great American success story as he and his two sisters were raised in Pennsylvania by loving parents of modest means. The family used to joke that their favorite Sunday dinner was Potatoes & Point which consisted of a huge platter of potatoes surrounding a tiny piece of meat in the middle. The family would each take a serving of potatoes and then point at the meat! Joe gained inspiration from his mother who was seriously ill and made a promise that if she recovered she would build a shrine to St. Anne which was finally completed with help from her devoted husband. Upon graduation from high school, Joe was the recipient of a full scholarship to Boston University where he played quarterback on the Terriers football team and roomed with future NFL star Reggie Rucker.

After becoming an attorney Joe was leaving his office when he suffered a ruptured brain aneurysm that required more than one operation. The prognosis wasn't good, but he fought his way out of a coma and credits the fine care that he received at Brigham and Women's Hospital and Spaulding Rehab for his miraculous recovery. While rehabbing at Spaulding Joe learned that Governor Mitt Romney was appointing one of his dear friends to the bench. On the day that Judge MaryLou Muirhead was sworn into office as Associate Justice for the Boston Housing Court, Joe's lovely wife Mary Ann brought him a shirt, tie and suit so that he could attend the ceremony. Mary Ann helped him down the center aisle at Spaulding as other patients, who had come to know and love Joe, were yelling and cheering him on with words of encouragement. Joe told me it felt like he was in the middle of an escape plot as he headed for the door! I don't want to take any credit for Joe's healthy rehab program, but he told me that one of the things that kept him going was the thought of getting out of there and having lunch with me at Luciano's in Wrentham, in fact he set that as one of his goals!

Joe became an "ordained minister" through an online ministry so that he could administer the vows at the marriage ceremony of his nephew and bride. He has since performed a number of marriages for family and friends so sometimes he even facetiously refers to himself as Fake Reverend Joe! Anyone kidding about Joe being fake, however, has to be cognizant of a few interesting facts. The place in Pennsylvania where Joe's mom built the shrine was the town of Nazareth, Joe's father's name was Joseph and his mother was Mary. The town in Pennsylvania where Mary gave birth to Joe, her only son, was Bethlehem!

There were a lot of small claims cases to be heard in Wrentham so I called an elderly woman's file first. The 85-year old lady was suing American Airlines, alleging a terrible flight and all kinds of inconveniences. During her lengthy litany of complaints about the flight she stated that the ticket cost $150.00 which the airline was willing to refund. I noticed in the plaintiff's written claim she was asking for $2,000.00 which was the maximum limit at the time. I politely interrupted her long story and asked her how she had arrived at the figure $2,000.00 when she had only paid $150.00 for the ticket? I guess she was thinking of deep pockets when she smiled and said, "It's American Airlines, I'm going for the gold Sonny!" She was a pleasant lady, but after hearing all of the evidence I found for the plaintiff for $150.00.

I always looked forward to serving as a session clerk for Judge Paul E. Ryan whenever he was sitting at the ADC. The South Boston native had been appointed by Governor Edward J. King and was the spitting image of Captain Binghamton from the hit TV series *McHale's Navy*. Judge Ryan was absolutely one of the nicest guys in the system and would routinely revoke fines from indigent defendants who stood before him and then always told the defendant, "Give the money to your kids." I thought that was terrific as the defendant would have been serving time instead of the imposition of a fine if the crime had been serious. There was a probation officer, however, who used to argue against this and almost have a stroke when Judge Ryan would thank the PO for his input and then tell me to revoke the balance due. This unhappy PO's underwear must have been too tight anyway as he usually had trouble achieving a smile. One time the judge told me to wipe out $1,400.00 and I thought that the PO was going to have a nervous breakdown, but nobody was going to persuade Judge Ryan from doing what he thought was right.

Judge Ryan's nephew Michael was the Communications Coordinator for the Office of the Jury Commissioner and a remarkable all-around guy who shares my passion for the Boston Red Sox. He has a Master's Degree in Journalism, is the author of 9 interesting books and gave a well-attended author talk at the Attleboro Public Library which was very enjoyable. The family tradition of excellence continues with Judge Ryan's daughter Pamela serving as a Court Officer in the Hingham District Court and her sister Diane is a Probation Officer in the Boston Municipal Court.

Judge Ryan once winked at me and related that his wife Flo had told him to take out the rubbish right away so he facetiously told her that she couldn't talk to him that way because he was a judge. "Fine, Your Honor," she said, "Put on your robe and take out the rubbish!"

As previously mentioned, my cousin Kevin Callahan served as a Bristol County ADA in Attleboro. Kevin is a terrific lawyer with an engaging personality and an optimistic view of everything in his path. Kevin tried a lot of jury cases so I had a front row seat to some very interesting arguments and the jurors were always entertained listening to his colorful presentations. One time Kevin ended his opening remarks to the jury by stating, "So let's put the meat on the grill and see if it sizzles!"

Kevin always has a nice professional cadence to his speech with a pleasant and pleasing tone. His logical and powerful assertions to the jury were as persuasive as any I have ever heard. Kevin was prosecuting a State Police drunk driving case with the arresting trooper present and ready to testify. His opening statement to the jury was vintage Callahan as he told them how they would hear testimony so vivid that they will imagine they are at the scene with the trooper. Kevin's spot on descriptions made people feel like they were part of the action. "Ladies and gentlemen," he said, "We're going for a ride in this trooper's State Police cruiser so fasten your seat belts!" Kevin was so convincing that one of the jurors started fumbling around in his chair trying to find his seatbelt!

The ADC session was in recess as I made my way through the crowded hall around two defendants who were standing together. The male was wearing a perfectly tailored expensive suit and his girlfriend was sporting an attractive colorful dress. As I walked by, one of our regulars looked at the fashionable couple and said to them, "You guys should be voted the best dressed criminals!"

Robert A. "Ted" Tomasone was the Clerk-Magistrate of the Somerville District Court until retiring a few years ago. He was the President of the Association of Clerk-Magistrates and Assistants for many consecutive terms and was gracious enough to appoint me to the Executive Board where I was honored to serve alongside many of my distinguished colleagues including future Clerk-Magistrate & later Judge Michelle L. Kelley who at the time was one of Ted's assistants in Somerville. Teddy will long be remembered for constantly helping those in need as well as getting an extra 6.25% permanently added to our pay raise statute which continues to benefit members of our association today and every time that the legislature and governor vote on an increase.

Teddy was the host and MC of a biannual dinner that became legendary in the North End of Boston. They used to be held at Joe Tecce's and eventually were moved to the function room upstairs at Filippo Ristorante. The spectacular and plentiful cuisine was consumed by a long

President Ted Tomasone, Somerville District Court Clerk-Magistrate (Eric Adler photo, courtesy of The Sun Chronicle)

list of distinguished guests including great Clerk-Magistrates like Governor Edward J. King appointee Ronald C. Arruda of the Bristol County Juvenile Court, Kenneth F. Candito appointed to the Dudley District Court by Governor William F. Weld, Carlton M. Viveiros of the Southeast Housing Court & Joseph A. Ligotti of the Hingham District Court, both having been appointed by Governor Michael S. Dukakis. The place was packed with Assistant Clerk-Magistrates like Joe's son Angelo J. Ligotti of the Bristol County Juvenile Court, judges, police, attorneys, politicians, professional athletes, restaurateur Paul Cucinatti of Orzo Trattoria in North Andover, and anyone else that Teddy invited. There were usually probably a few hundred people there, but it seemed as though everyone wanted an invitation as it was the toughest ticket in town. In fact, it was so tough that there were no tickets at all as Teddy would call me with the date.

On any given night you might meet hall of famers, world champions and Governors A. Paul Cellucci & Deval L. Patrick; Auditor & pro boxer Joe DeNucci, Senate Presidents Thomas F. Birmingham, William M. Bulger, Therese Murray & Robert E. Travaglini; Heisman Trophy Winner Joe Bellino; renowned Patriots' player & broadcaster Gino Cappelletti; Bruins greats Chris "Knuckles" Nilan, Derek Sanderson & Rick Middleton; Mayor Thomas M. Menino; NECN Sports Anchor Chris Collins; Attorney General Francis X. Bellotti; Celtics legends Thomas "Satch" Sanders & Sam Jones; Celtics owner Wyc Grousbeck; Red Sox owners John W. Henry & Larry Lucchino; Sox Managers John Farrell & Bobby Valentine; radio broadcaster Jerry Trupiano, storied Sox stars Tim Wakefield, Luis Tiant, Jim Rice, Dr. Jim Lonborg, Johnny Pesky & Rico Petrocelli who is an extremely entertaining, dynamic and interesting speaker.

Boston Red Sox Cy Young Award Winner Dr. Jim Lonborg at Ted Tomasone time (Bill Grassia photo)

Quite often I would end up being seated at the same table with one of my childhood heroes - the legendary Red Sox pitcher Bill Monbouquette whose right arm delivered a no hitter for the home town team when I was in grade school. Everybody knew when Monbo was on the hill and he even had a song written about him that was played on the radio. After my shock and awe died down to a reasonable level, Bill and I had some wonderful conversations over the years as he was a splendid ambassador of baseball with firsthand knowledge of many historic events that I had only read about. It was a sad time when he passed away bringing an old time era to a close.

Boston Red Sox two-time All Star Rico Petrocelli, held shortstop record 40 home runs, at Ted Tomasone time (Bill Grassia photo)

Ted would always introduce the dignitaries with great fanfare as he is a natural born MC and never forgot to recognize his erstwhile boss from Suffolk County Civil Superior Court - the great Clerk-Magistrate Michael J. Donovan. Mike is a terrific guy, was an honorable elected official until retirement, and is a well-liked man of his word who seems to know everyone. I always felt as though he and Ted were cut from the same cloth, most especially in terms of Loyalty as they both spelled the word with a capital L. Ted would almost become somewhat emotional while introducing Mike to the audience as it was quite evident that he was eternally grateful to the man who had appointed him Assistant Clerk-Magistrate.

Sometimes I would sit with a very interesting man in his eighties who could tell colorful stories of historic boxing matches. He started boxing himself at the age of 12 and won his maiden professional fight with a first round knockout when he was only 16 by using an older friend's ID to circumvent the age requirement. This charismatic son of Italian immigrants grew up in the North End and eventually sold out the Boston Garden, located only a few blocks from his childhood home on Fleet Street. It was easy to see that he was tough as nails when younger, but he was always extremely nice to me as he is one of those celebrities who really care about people and gave of his time freely. He took out Johnny Saxton in the Boston Garden with a devastating punch in the 14th round resulting in a technical knockout to claim the undisputed Welterweight Championship of the World. This great World Champion who I admired so much was born Leonardo Liotta, but you know him as Tony DeMarco! When young Liotta wasn't old enough for his first professional fight he borrowed Tony DeMarco's birth certificate and the rest is history.

Attorney Philip J. Privitera invited J. Do and I to the grand unveiling of the Tony DeMarco statue at the corner of Hanover & Cross Streets. The beautiful bronze sculpture was a gift from the Privitera Family Charitable Foundation and depicts the legendary boxer throwing his powerful left hook while standing guard at the entrance to the North

End. We all had a terrific time later at Filippo's where people came from near and far to honor the International Boxing Hall of Famer who had defeated eight World Champions in his illustrious career, but if there were a Hall of Fame for nice, classy guys, Tony DeMarco would get in on the first ballot!

Acclaimed Red Sox relief pitcher Bob Stanley, a real gentleman, was one of Teddy's many guests at Joe Tecce's. Steamer is an interesting guy who pitched a lot of tough high leverage innings in some tight spots for the team. He was a minor league coach at the time who seemed to enjoy his job and was welcomed by everyone near our table. It was common knowledge that he had never turned down a request to speak with kids for the Jimmy Fund and was always extremely generous with his time in helping those in need.

It was an honor to converse with the gutsy athlete who set the American League season record by pitching 168⅓ innings of relief in 1982 as he would keep throwing until his right arm almost fell off. Game 6 of the 1986 World Series was a tough loss for Sox fans as Stanley delivered a 3-2 pitch to Mookie Wilson that should have been a routine out, but the ground ball bounced through the legs of Bill Buckner allowing the winning run to score from second. Just prior to that Stanley was charged with a wild pitch that brought in the tying run, but I will go to my grave believing that the pitch should have been ruled as a passed ball. The New York Mets would go on to win that World Series and keep the Curse of the Bambino alive until the Sox finally found redemption and won it all in 2004.

One time, which I think took place in the locker room at Fenway Park, Bob was somewhat unhappy with some things that had been written about him in one of the local newspapers. We all misspeak at one time or another so apparently he wanted to say that he was going to cancel his subscription, but instead stated that, "I'm going to cancel my prescription."

L-R Radio Broadcaster Jerry Trupiano, Boston Red Sox legend Johnny Pesky, author, Detective Prosecutor Bill Madden at Ted Tomasone time (Bill Grassia photo)

The East Boston Division of the Boston Municipal Court has long been a renowned stop on the judicial circuit with such impressive courthouse talent as the great Clerk-Magistrate Joseph R. Faretra who was appointed by Governor Francis W. Sargent. First Justice John E. McDonald Jr., an outstanding judge, was appointed by Governor Deval L. Patrick after having served as an Assistant Clerk-Magistrate in the Central Division of the Boston Municipal Court. Those seeking justice have always been extremely well served by First Assistant Clerk-Magistrate Vincent F. Capolupo, another terrific guy, as well as the very charming and extremely capable retired First Assistants Sandra Caggiano and Deborah A. Nicholls.

East Boston is the hometown of New England Patriots Super Bowl Champion Jermaine Wiggins who was kind enough to relate some interesting stories to us at Teddy Tomasone's famous events. Santarpio's Pizza has been serving delicious food to hungry patrons in East Boston for over 100 years with owner Joia Santarpio carrying on the family tradition. I used to go to the fabled restaurant with a group of guys from the courts to enjoy pizza and other delicacies from their kitchen.

I had the distinct pleasure of meeting Mike Eruzione at one of Teddy's times. He was of course the captain of the famous 1980 Gold Medal Olympic Hockey Team who were forever etched in our hearts from the famous call by Al Michaels, "Do you believe in miracles? Yes!" and will always be remembered as the tough group of talented young college kids who beat the Russians. Eruzione cemented his place in international lore with his steadfast leadership and for scoring the winning goal against the Soviet Union. His father and mother grew up next door to each other across the street from Santarpio's and his dad worked at the famous eatery for almost half a century where he left many fond memories as an engaging and kind person.

Santarpio's is not only famous for their fabulous cuisine, but also for a well-stocked bar that exudes old world charm with seats full of cheerful patrons. Armando Caldarelli is a chef and legendary bartender who has worked there for over 50 years! The personable barkeep is a fantastic guy who they jokingly call Lefty because he can't do anything right!

Attorney Kevin J Reddington is a member of the prestigious American College of Trial Lawyers, an invitation only relatively small group of distinguished attorneys. The ability to effectively communicate is extremely important for any trial lawyer and he is among the very best. His powerful and persuasive speaking ability was evident when he was addressing the jury in a very serious criminal case. The witness had testified against his client during an emotional tear filled session on the witness stand. Attorney Reddington's defense centered on discrediting this witness and convincing the jury not to be swayed by the histrionic crying. The jury deliberated and came back with a Not Guilty verdict which was probably facilitated to some degree by Kevin's closing argument which included, "An ocean of tears cannot float a boat of lies."

It was a hot summer day in Attleboro with the large courtroom windows without screens wide open. A defendant charged with shoplifting jumped out of the prisoner's dock, ran across Courtroom One and jumped out the window. As he was making his escape an overzealous police officer fired his revolver at the alleged thief who turned around before jumping while producing a facial expression of unbridled fear! The bullets didn't hit anybody, but one slug lodged in a wooden railing near the middle of the courtroom. The officer was quickly reassigned to desk duty.

I used to give tours of the courthouse to the Boy Scouts, young school kids, and other groups, so the highlight of my trek through the halls of justice always culminated in the kids trying to stick their pinky fingers into the bullet hole along the side of the wooden bar where attorneys sit.

Elisabeth Sylva was a Field Coordinator for the Administrative Office of the District Courts when we first met and has since been appointed to the position of Assistant Clerk-Magistrate of the Hingham District Court. I am overjoyed for Lissy as she is an extremely likeable, hard working person who was an enormous help to our staff in Wrentham especially during personnel shortages. I always enjoyed speaking with her and wasn't surprised to see her smiling face helping out in the Brookline District Court when I did hearings there. I was filling in for the great Clerk-Magistrate of that court, Edward F. Savage Jr., who was appointed by Governor Deval L. Patrick. Ted is a squared away guy and good friend whose word is his bond so I was glad to be of assistance.

I had just finished a conversation with Lissy and went up to the counter to assist a tired looking middle aged man. He told me that he was there for an IOU so I thought that maybe it was a civil case where he owed somebody money until he told me that he had been arrested the night before after failing a field sobriety test. IOU was close, but he was in for OUI!

Criminal defendants report to the Probation Department for booking prior to arraignment. The defendant's personal and financial information is listed on an intake form and brought to the associate probation officer in the courtroom. The judge, or sometimes the session clerk on behalf of the judge, will ask the defendant if he or she will be hiring his or her own counsel or if they are requesting a court appointed attorney. If the defendant requests that an attorney be appointed the APO will inform the judge if the defendant is indigent and qualifies based on the financial data listed on the intake form.

A defendant in Wrentham had already overheard himself described as being indigent when he was at the Probation counter. Associate Probation Officer Diana L. MacDonald, one of the happiest and best people I have ever worked with, was in the courtroom with the defendant's intake sheet when the judge asked if he qualified for court appointed attorney. Before she could answer the defendant addressed the court himself. He meant to say that he was indigent, but instead told the judge, "Your Honor, I'm indignant."

Court officers are an integral component of the operation of every courthouse as security has become more important than ever. Michael Cotter is one of the best I ever worked with so I always appreciated his advanced skill and proficient demeanor in the courtroom and elsewhere.

Wrentham Acting Assistant Chief Court Officer Brian Scully was always very helpful to me so I was grateful for his assistance. He is a squared away professional who kept decorum in the courtroom and always took pride in doing his job right. One of our staff had brought her young daughter in so Brian greeted the little girl in the Clerk-Magistrate's Office. The girl was a student at Igo School in Foxborough, which was named after the late great Vin Igo who was a bail commissioner, photographer, legendary newspaper correspondent, School Committee Chairman and a real good guy. I used to kid around with Vin that he was one of the very few people who had a building named in his honor while he was still alive! Brian was being very nice to the child while making small talk. "Where do you go to school?" Brian asked, to which she replied, "Igo School." Brian thought that the poor kid had a speech problem and was trying to say, "I go to school," so he said, "Right, but what's the name of the school?" The little girl looked up at him and said, "Igo School." Brian then politely said, "Ok" as he walked away shaking his head.

A neighborhood altercation resulted in the defendant driving by the victim's home while yelling obscenities out the car window. The victim testified on the witness stand during a lengthy hearing about threats and vandalism. Court Officer Scully had to concentrate on keeping his composure while hearing the victim's testimony. The victim wanted to say that the defendant drove by and yelled obscenities out the car window, but instead stated that the defendant loudly yelled terrible atrocities!

Judge John F. St. Cyr was appointed by Governor Francis W. Sargent, serving as the First Justice of the WDC until retiring the year before I started there. I enjoyed being his session clerk many times in Attleboro as he was an extremely courteous, interesting, humorous and accomplished jurist. Officer Scully was in the courtroom when a woman was arraigned for writing a bad check to Mars Bargainland. She admitted to the charge and wanted to make restitution which is sometimes facilitated by the complainant being present so Judge St. Cyr wanted to see if there was a representative of the store in the courtroom. The judge drew a court full of smiles and chuckles when he addressed the crowd by asking, "Is there anybody here from Mars?"

The COVID pandemic adversely affected daily life everywhere including the court system where the backlog of jury trials were headed for unacceptable delays. After a determination was made that all Norfolk County Courthouses were unable to provide adequate ventilation and were too small to allow for proper social distancing, the Trial Court entered into a lease agreement with Lombardo's in Randolph. I had already retired when this plan was put in place, but had gotten to know President & CEO Vincent J. Lombardo, a real gentleman, at Teddy Tomasone's fabulous functions. The legendary venue, well known for weddings, proms and other spectacular events, was retrofitted to be able to accommodate jury trials in the service of justice. Ballrooms became courtrooms, a jury assembly room, and a jury deliberation room. The bridal suite was converted to the judge's chambers and Vincent's Nightclub was modified as a lockup with holding cells for defendants in custody. Court officers brought prisoners into the courtroom by escorting them through the kitchen with everything working out as well as could be expected thanks to the hard work and dedication of everyone involved. Attorney Joseph P. Cataldo of Franklin tried the very first case in this unique jury court and won an acquittal for his client. Lombardo's quickly became famous for having the only courtrooms in America with lighting provided by a huge beautiful chandelier!

Assistant District Attorney Kevin J. Burke was assigned as a prosecutor for the WDC at the time. As soon as ADA Burke heard that he might be prosecuting cases at the transformed Lombardo's facility he quipped, "Looks like I'll be giving my closing argument to the jury from the same floor I danced on at my senior prom!"

A defendant in an assault and battery case was trying to convince me that he hadn't started the fight, thus his punches were delivered in self-defense. He said that he would never have thrown the first punch because he had a heart condition and was in declining health. He testified that he had just visited his cardiologist last week for his annual checkup. The next thing that he wanted to say was that he had been given an EKG test at the physician's office, but instead he told me that, "I even got a KGB test." How did the Russians get involved?

I spoke with a man at the Attleboro Court counter who said that he had been punched in the face and wanted to file a private criminal complaint. I gave him a complaint application and suggested that he was the victim of Assault & Battery, but when I looked at the application more closely later he had written in the offenses section - Salt & Battery!

Another guy at the counter was reaching for his wallet as he told me he was here to pay for his Witness Protection! "You're not in the Witness Protection Program are you?" I inquired. He was paying his Victim/Witness Fee!

Brenda Fiske Todd is a very nice person who worked in the Civil Department before becoming the Judge's Secretary at the ADC. She was at lunch one day when the telephone man came to repair a problem in the court. He inspected the situation and determined that there was a connection malfunction with the phone wires that rested under Brenda's desk in the Clerk-Magistrate's Office. He got down on the floor, rolled over onto his back and slid underneath the desk to begin his work. This was in the middle of the office where Brenda's desk was one of three pushed together so he wasn't visible as staff walked by and I was probably the only one that knew he was under there. Brenda came back from lunch and sat down in her chair. She was leaning over, I think to place her pocketbook on the floor, when she spotted the guy under the desk. Poor Brenda was so surprised that she let out a startled scream and yelled, "There's a man under my desk!" All ended well when the guy pleaded that he was only there for the phone!

Prohibiting cell phones from being brought into a courthouse by the general public is a good idea for more than one reason. Cameras have been used to intimidate witnesses, ringtones are distracting in a courtroom and loud phone conversations anywhere in the courthouse can be disruptive. I have always felt badly, however, for people who don't have a vehicle available where they can leave their cell phone. Some people are dropped off at the court or arrive by public transportation and therefore have no vehicle nearby. Small convenience stores located close to a court will sometimes charge a $1.00 fee to hold the phone for the day, but not every court is located near a store. It would be nice if we could pay for an extra court officer to take possession of cell phones at the entrance. This would make life easier on victims, witnesses, defendants, litigants and others as well as providing even more security because as far as I am concerned we can never have too many court officers.

I was seated at my WDC desk reading a police report to review a warrant request on a nice day with an open window directly behind me. I heard some rustling in the hedges just outside of my window and turned around expecting to see some kind of animal in the bushes, but instead saw a 30-year old man crawling through the mulch around the shrubs. My obvious concern was for the dozens of staff and others in the court because I didn't know if he was mentally ill, planting a bomb or engaged in some other nefarious activity so I immediately called a court officer. The officer quickly responded and discovered that the man was trying to hide his cell phone because he had no legitimate place to store it.

Another day, Walpole Police Detective Prosecutor Bill Madden was signing criminal complaints at the counter when he happened to look out through the window to the far left. He could see a guy moving in the bushes outside the window next to First Assistant Clerk-Magistrate Cynthia J. Kerr's desk. Not knowing what the guy was up to, the detective ran outside to confront him only to learn that it was another defendant trying to hide his cell phone because he didn't have a car.

The Hogan family, as far as I know, absolutely must hold the world record for gubernatorial appointments with a total of four at this writing. The Hogans are a remarkable family of historic achievement with a devoted commitment to public service, all the while exemplifying the very highest ideals of American justice.

The Honorable William T. Hogan Jr., was the great Associate Justice of the Dedham District Court appointed by Governor Edward J. King and was very kind to me when I had to testify in a criminal jury trial as the Keeper of the Records. It was getting close to the luncheon recess when he asked the ADA and defense counsel if they could agree to the evidence that I held so that I wouldn't have to come back after lunch. Unfortunately, that common courtesy is not so common, but Judge Hogan really cared about people so you never forget small acts of kindness like that.

Judge Hogan was the first, but far from the last, member of this legendary Boston family to receive a judicial appointment from a Governor of the Commonwealth. He was a popular, honorable man who left a legacy of friendship and loyalty in setting an example for his accomplished children - three of whom would also be appointed by an incumbent of the corner office.

Daniel J. Hogan is the great Clerk-Magistrate of the Central Division of the Boston Municipal Court. Appointed by Governor A. Paul Cellucci, he also does an outstanding job as the President of the Association of Clerk-Magistrates and Assistant Clerks. His brother Michael is the great Clerk-Magistrate of the Lynn District Court having been appointed by Governor Charlie D. Baker.

Their sister, Judge Mary Hogan Sullivan was the great First Justice of the Dedham District Court so she sometimes sat in the same courtroom chair previously occupied by her father. She had been appointed by Governor Jane M. Swift and also led the Veterans Treatment Court which serves as a national model for specialty courts in helping veterans get through some tough times. Judge Hogan Sullivan bought a copy of my first book and asked me to inscribe it to one of the veterans who was about to graduate from her program. You don't find empathy like that every day so the Commonwealth began to miss her wisdom and caring the day after she retired.

The Trial Court holds conferences all over the state to update court personnel on new laws and procedural changes. There were more of these than ever during the last few years of my career as a result of amended domestic violence statutes and many other important issues with a high level of complexity. I enjoyed these sessions because there was much to learn from the best instructors in the business and it was always nice to be able to socialize with my colleagues.

Most of these were organized by District Courts Chief Justice Paul C. Dawley and his outstanding staff. We all benefited tremendously from the preparation and instruction of Chief Justice Dawley; Brenda Tanous, Executive Assistant to the Chief Justice; Deputy Court Administrators Ellen S. Shapiro, Joseph R. Jackson & John M. Connors; Assistant Deputy Court Administrator Deborah L. Propp; Legal Counsel Michael Shea; General Counsel, now Judge Joseph M. Ditkoff; Deputy General Counsel Sarah W. Ellis; Elizabeth R. Cerda, Special Projects Coordinator; Brien M. Cooper, Clerk of the Appellate Division; Catherine E. DuBois, Administrative Coordinator; Janice L. Bowers, Performance Analyst; Regional Coordinator Jill K. Ziter; Sarah M. Adamson, Confidential Assistant to the Chief Justice & the aforementioned Philip J. McCue, Deputy Court Administrator.

In addition to those mentioned elsewhere, at any given seminar or social event I might have run into great clerk-magistrates like the following, some of whom have retired; unless otherwise specified, they are with a Boston Municipal or District Court:

Keesler H. Montgomery, Roxbury - appointed by Governor John A. Volpe;

Omer R. Chartrand, Barnstable; John "Jack" Devine, Dedham; Duncan E. McLeod, Fitchburg; John L. McGrath, Lawrence; Charles H. "Charlie" Perenick, Concord; Donald M. Stapleton, Stoughton & Richard P. "Dick" Miliano, Somerville - appointed by Governor Francis W. Sargent;

Stephen I. Ross, Orleans; Raymond J. Salmon Sr., Clinton; Philip B. O'Toole, Leominster & Paul J. Burke, Northeast Housing - appointed by Governor Michael S. Dukakis;

Joseph M. Hogan, Natick; Raymond S. Peck, Taunton; Robert F. Arena, Salem; John J. Connors, Brookline & Joseph E. Croken, Malden - appointed by Governor Edward J. King;

Roxana E. Viera, Nantucket; William A. Lisano, Lowell & Laurie N. Dornig, Orange - appointed by Governor William F. Weld;

Michael J. Finucane, Waltham; Leonard F. Tomaiolo, Clinton & Thomas C. Carrigan, Milford - appointed by Governor A. Paul Cellucci;

Thomas J. Begley, Framingham; Daniel F. Langelier, Winchendon; Daryl G. Manchester, Wareham & Kenneth P. Halloran, Falmouth - appointed by Governor Jane M. Swift;

Liza H. Williamson, Edgartown; Edward B. Teague III, Falmouth & Doris A. Stanziani, Haverhill - appointed by Governor Mitt Romney;

Marybeth Brady, Malden; John S. Gay, Springfield; Charles J. "Chuck" Ardito III, Barnstable; Robin E. Vaughan, Stoughton; John D. Fitzsimmons, Plymouth & John F. Kennedy, Uxbridge - appointed by Governor Deval L. Patrick;

Brian M. D'Andrea, Worcester; Eric T. Donovan, Brighton & Brockton; Brian J. Costa, Salem; Pamela Gauvin-Fernandes, Wrentham; Kirsten L. Hughes, Stoughton & South Boston - appointed by Governor Charlie D. Baker;

Judge Frederick V. Gilgun, Woburn - appointed Clerk-Magistrate by Governor Endicott H. Peabody & Judge by Governor Edward J. King;

Judge David E. Stevens, Brockton - appointed Clerk-Magistrate by Governor Francis W. Sargent & Judge by Governor Edward J. King;

Judge Paul F. X. Moriarty, Hingham - appointed Clerk-Magistrate & Judge by Governor Edward J. King;

Judge Robert B. Calagione, East Brookfield - appointed Clerk-Magistrate by Governor A. Paul Cellucci & Judge by Governor Jane M. Swift.

His Excellency, Governor Charlie D. Baker, left his imprint on the Massachusetts judicial system with a vast number of appointments of clerk-magistrates, judges, and all seven justices of the Supreme Judicial Court! Governor Baker is an honorable man of great integrity, compassion, intellect, and kindness so his positive impact will continue to be felt through his magnificent appointments long after his last term in the corner office.

Governor Charlie D. Baker

Although I didn't work in the Juvenile Court, I had enough contact to appreciate the hard work and dedication of the great Suffolk County Juvenile Court Clerk-Magistrate Donna M. Ciampoli, a nice person appointed by Governor Jane M. Swift as well as the great Norfolk County Juvenile Court Clerk-Magistrate Robert L. Ryan and the great Plymouth County Juvenile Court Clerk-Magistrate George P. Roper, both terrific guys who were appointed by Governor Deval L. Patrick.

Not enough credit is given to the District & Boston Municipal Court Assistant Clerk-Magistrates in our system who work tirelessly to keep the courts running smoothly every day. First Assistant Clerk-Magistrate Raymond J. Salmon Jr. of Leominster is one of the best in the business - smart, cheerful and someone who can always be counted on.

The following, some of whom have retired, are all a credit to the system:

First Assistant Clerk-Magistrates Maria T. Abascal, Lawrence; John T. Colton, David C. Belger & Jody M. Menard - Parece, Taunton; Robert Bloom, Quincy; Terrence B. Downes, Lowell; William G. Farrell, Somerville; William A. McEvoy Jr., Newton; Sharon Hague, Fall River; Diane M. Joy & Arthur Wilner, Brockton; Brendan T. Keenan, Worcester; William P. Casey, Lynn; Sean P. Coleman & Felicita G. Bermingham, Natick; A. Daniel "Archie" Keohan, Stoughton; Andrew P. Quigley, Hingham; Paul F. Troy, West Roxbury; Beverly J. Mahan, South Boston; Richard C. "Dick" Morrissey, Springfield; Timothy F. Murphy & Patricia F. McDermott, Brighton; David Nobrega, Wareham; Darryl S. Whitney, Marlborough as well as -

Assistant Clerk-Magistrates Patrick J. Clifford, Karen P. Dever & John Roache, South Boston; Thomas Brophy, Antonio Gibbs, Janet M. Mattoli, William O'Brien & Noreen E. Prime, Brockton; Jean M. Alexander & Christopher Ghiloni, Quincy; John J. Clough, Dorchester; Thomas F. Quinn & Daniel Day, Lynn; Stephen P. LeDuc, Marlborough; Olga Grabau, Cambridge; Barbara Gould, Natick; Mark Fabiano, Wrentham; Douglas A. Cox, Paul W. Shannon & Joseph A. Kirnon, Roxbury; Ann M. McCormick, Wareham; Damon J. Borrelli, Stoughton; Robert C. Tringale, Somerville; Darlene Acevedo-Cotto, Attleboro; Michael D. Prosser, Worcester; Ronald R. Petralia, Framingham; Irene F. McGowan, Thomas J. Hobin Jr. & John L. Kowalski, Dedham; Gregory V. St. Cyr, Nancy K. Wasserman & Cynthia Vincent Thomas, Fall River; Thomas Hibbert Jr., Patrick T. Walsh & Thomas W. Alfonse, New Bedford & many others, some of whom are mentioned elsewhere on these pages, have set a high standard of excellence throughout the court system.

The Central Division of the Boston Municipal Court has long been the home base for some talented and distinguished Assistant Clerk-Magistrates that I have always held in high regard including Andrew J. Burke, Robert J. Kelley, Kevin F. Callahan, Mark Concannon, Michael Sher, Brendan Creedon, William J. Lavery and the ever-upbeat Denise M. Donovan who is now serving justice in Wrentham.

Lavery is a great guy who never has anything bad to say about anyone and always finds the humorous side of every situation. He was working the counter at the BMC when a man walked up and told him the name of the case. Bill could see that it was a police hearing so he asked him if he was a witness or the defendant to which the man replied, "I'm the guy that did it!"

Michael J. McEneaney was the Bail Administrator with jurisdiction over the entire Commonwealth for many years. Mike was a man of unrivaled integrity, setting a tone of cooperation in a sometimes confusing field of overlapping criminal jurisdictions. He was able to resolve minor issues quietly before they became major problems so his dynamic professionalism was always appreciated.

Upon Mike's retirement, he was succeeded by the ever-capable Catherine M. Coughlin, appointed Bail Administrator in 2014. Cathy had big shoes to fill, but the work ethic she displayed as the First Assistant Clerk-Magistrate of the Newton District Court prepared her well for this new opportunity. Cathy and I shared some laughs at a conference in Chatham. She is smart, convivial, intelligent and well-versed in the applicable law so the Commonwealth remains in good hands.

I inherited a very talented staff and was able to hire more myself after my appointment as Clerk-Magistrate of the WDC. I had appointed Attorney Michelle L. Kelley, now Judge Kelley, to the position of Assistant Clerk-Magistrate for a vacancy that had never been filled. I had been fortunate enough to get a bill approved by the House, Senate and Governor, but unfortunately without the necessary funding for the job. The statute remained intact with no money for a few years until the appropriations system changed that allowed me to make the appointment. Michelle was eminently qualified with the most well rounded and impressive resume that I had ever seen. She was already an Assistant Clerk-Magistrate in the Somerville District Court where she had been appointed by Clerk-Magistrate Ted Tomasone. She had established herself with a reputation as an honest, diligent, innovative, street smart, hardworking attorney.

Michelle hit the ground running in Wrentham being already well versed in the law and court procedure, but every office is just a little bit different so naturally she had to learn local customs, meet new people and develop a feel for a courthouse that was new to her. On her very first day on the job in Wrentham, just as Michelle was getting acclimated to her new environment, a disturbed middle aged woman drove her car up on the courthouse lawn in between the building and a long row of parked employee's vehicles. The poor lady somehow miraculously avoided hitting other cars, trees or the courthouse wall as she quickly drove right by and very close to the window next to Michelle's desk at about 50 MPH. Michelle couldn't believe her eyes as she smiled and turned to ask our staff, "Do we have a drive-thru window in this court?"

The counter in the Clerk-Magistrate's Office of the WDC is covered with clear glass. After my appointment I started cutting out photos from the newspaper of local police officers, attorneys, staff and others of interest for placement under the glass. I would also insert positive news clippings about various events so that people would have something to see and maybe read to occupy their time while waiting for our staff to assist them on a busy day. It became a veritable Hall of Fame as one of the court officers was happy that the photo that he gave me of his daughter, a proficient hockey player, found a spot under the glass. A defendant was standing at the counter engaged in a news clipping when Michelle approached him and asked, "May I help you, sir?" The guy said, "Yeah, just a minute though, I'm right in the middle of this story!"

Michelle and her husband Tom, a terrific guy, were hosting a Halloween party for friends, family and staff at their house. There was a huge turnout of invited guests including Michelle's sister Kim, her parents Pat and Tom Gremo as well as her uncle Paul Riggieri who are all from the Worcester area. WDC First Assistant Clerk-Magistrate Lesley Hazeldine's brother Jimmy is a Norfolk Police Officer who happened to be on duty that night so he stopped into the party for a few minutes to say hello during his shift. Of course, Jimmy was wearing his police uniform so as he walked in, Michelle's father and uncle who had never met him, looked a little concerned that there might be a problem so Jimmy told them it was just a Halloween costume to put them at ease. After a while Jimmy had to return to patrol so Michelle's uncle happened to be watching as the officer walked out and got into his Norfolk police cruiser. When Uncle Paul saw the police car he said, "Wow, they really go all out for Halloween around here!"

Michelle and Tom's son Matt led the audience in the Pledge of Allegiance at our Law Day Ceremony when he was in the 4th grade and their daughter Madison testified on her mother's behalf at the confirmation hearing before the Governor's Council when she was in high school! Madison's awe-inspiring speech could not have been better as the packed State House chamber listened to the young girl relate heartfelt stories about her mother delivered in a passionate, impressive, beautiful and powerful cadence.

Author's Note: The subject of the story below, Assistant Clerk-Magistrate Michelle L. Kelley, succeeded me upon being appointed Acting Clerk-Magistrate by the Honorable Paul C. Dawley, Chief Justice of the District Courts and was later appointed to the lifetime position of Clerk-Magistrate of the Wrentham District Court by His Excellency, Charlie D. Baker, Governor of the Commonwealth. She would later be appointed Associate Justice of the District Court by Governor Baker. She continues to receive high accolades for her leadership in that position today. I wrote the following, when Michelle was my assistant, which was published in "Tales from the City" in *The Boston Globe* for the June 28, 2015 issue of the *Globe Magazine*:

> Clerk-Magistrates and Assistants are on call with police departments after court hours to set bail on arrests throughout the Commonwealth. Most defendants are admitted to personal recognizance with a $40 release fee. Assistant Clerk-Magistrate Michelle Kelley, Esq. received a call late one night from the Millis Police Department informing her of a stray cat on Main Street. After realizing

that the police had confused her with the Animal Control Officer, Kelley told the dispatcher, "I think you've got the wrong number unless that cat has $40."

Cynthia J. Kerr extended a warm greeting to me on my first day at the WDC. She had been employed in the Clerk-Magistrate's Office since the age of 18 and had worked her way up the ladder to the position of Office Manager at the time of my appointment. Cindy is a very smart and extremely caring person with the innate courage to exhibit leadership and strength when needed. Eventually, I appointed Cindy as an Assistant Clerk-Magistrate where she did a terrific job of resolving many difficult cases in a fair, intelligent and dignified manner. After I retired she was appointed to the position of First Assistant Clerk-Magistrate by my successor, Clerk-Magistrate Kelley.

I personally trained Cindy on most of her new duties by engaging her in lengthy

Swearing in of Judge Michelle L. Kelley

conversations about various responsibilities including the issuance of search warrants as well as having her sit in on my show cause hearings. After a while she was ready to hear small claims cases which can run the gamut from being relatively simple hearings to somewhat complex trials. Most small claims litigants are pro se so they come to court without an attorney and represent themselves. Some are more familiar with the process than others, but one of the most misunderstood components for non-lawyers is simply how they should address the court. Salutations such as, "Good morning Mrs. Clerk, Madame Clerk, Ms. Clerk-Magistrate, Your Honor, Mr. Clerk", and others are heard regularly in courtrooms throughout the Commonwealth. Cindy was at the civil counter just before entering the courtroom to conduct her very first small claims hearings. There was a litigant at the counter who must have known that Cindy was an Assistant Clerk-Magistrate so I guess the word "magistrate" was foremost in his mind when he addressed her by saying, "Good morning, Your Majesty." We all had a good chuckle when Cindy laughed and politely declined my offer to get her a gold crown!

Lesley J. Hazeldine was another outstanding clerical employee who I promoted to Assistant Clerk-Magistrate and was promoted again to First Assistant Clerk-Magistrate by Clerk-Magistrate Kelley after Cindy Kerr's retirement. She did a terrific job of producing all of the graphics, design components and emails for our Law Day Ceremonies as well as our Courthouse Speaker Series. Lesley took care of my emails and handled some extremely sensitive issues for me in a very professional manner.

I also spent a lot of time training Lesley for her new position and had her sit in on my hearings for a while. Her very first hearing on her own was a CMVI case with the Millis Police. The exuberant defendant walked into the hearing and immediately told Lesley that she had a nice smile. He wasn't a bad guy and his infraction wasn't egregious so she gave him a break and found him Not Responsible. I was proud of her because she did a terrific job of serving justice with the hearings on her first day. Lesley opened a piece of candy after the hearings that had a wrapper printed with expressions like a fortune cookie. It was a nice coincidence that the wrapper read, "Your smile is your best accessory!"

Lesley used some of the money that she had earned from bail release fees to purchase a relatively expensive game for her nephews for a Christmas present. Lesley told them, "Just so you know boys, four guys had to get arrested for you to have this!"

I was honored to promote Paula J. Padula to the position of Office Manager. She is a nice person who had my back every day with her leadership ability, keen listening skills and warm personality making her a perfect fit for the job. Paula put out many fires before they ever got to me and saved me from a lot of headaches along the way.

Sometimes terminology can vary from court to court. A criminal summons in the ADC is called a "future" at the WDC because it has a future date. During my first month on the job in Wrentham, Paula was looking for a case and thought that I might have it on my desk so she asked me if I had a future. I told her, "Well, I certainly hope so Paula!"

Paula, who was voted the Cutest Girl in her Franklin High School class, makes a delicious apple crisp and was always strong enough to be able to poke fun at herself. Paula set up all of our hearings so she was speaking with a police officer at the counter who was new on the job and trying to learn the system. This poor guy was telling Paula about all of his problems and difficulties that went back years and years. Paula politely listened to this long litany of mental anguish and perplexing personal episodes that seemed to have no end. After the officer had finally walked away Paula told our staff, "That poor guy's in worse shape than I am!"

Most of our staff were female so when somebody would call in sick or go home ill Paula was right on top of it and knew that I didn't want to hear intricate details about some of their problems so she would tell me, "She has female problems." Enough said!

One day Paula answered the phone and tried to assist a woman of Asian descent where there may have been somewhat of a language barrier. Paula thought that she heard the woman say that her last name was Fu, but being unsure she asked her to spell it. The caller then loudly, slowly and emphatically stated that the spelling of her last name was F U which caused Paula to hold the phone away from her mouth and say, "This woman is not very nice at all."

There were an inordinate number of motor vehicle accidents on Route 140 in front of the courthouse. When we heard a crash somebody in the office would say, "Sounds like somebody's going to be asking Paula for a hearing!"

Paula was so thoughtful that she came into my office holding an envelope full of decorative bows because she knew that I had just wrapped a wedding anniversary gift for my bride. I didn't know she was bringing me a bow so when I saw her with an envelope in her hand I reached in my pocket for my money as I thought she was collecting donations for something. Paula stated that I was well trained and laughed as she said, "You see a woman with an envelope and go right for the wallet!"

Paula was a terrific Office Manager, but just like me, not a person who would be described as high tech savvy. Paula issued a very brief memo to our staff that simply stated, "Be sure to check your email." Jackie Landry, who was later promoted to Operations Supervisor by Clerk-Magistrate Kelley, said that she read part of the memo, became exhausted and had to put it down! She said that she will read the rest of it tomorrow!

Cheerful Bookkeeper Kristen L. Orlando has a huge heart and genuinely cares about everyone. Part of her responsibility is the return of bail upon disposition of a criminal case. A defendant at the counter had been his own surety so Kristen asked him for a photo ID so she could give him a check. He said it was in the car, didn't feel like retrieving it and started to hand his cell phone to Kristen while asking, "Can you call my lawyer and ask him what I look like?" As soon as Kristen answered in the negative he asked her, "How about if I lift up my shirt. I have my name tattooed on my back?" Kristen told him "No" and that we needed his photo ID. The guy walked away out to the car while shaking his head as if we had an unreasonable policy. Even Kristen can't keep everybody happy!

Judge James M. Sullivan was appointed by Governor Jane M. Swift and is now the highly thought of First Justice of the Plymouth District Court. He previously sat as an Associate Justice in many courts including Wrentham and was new to our court so many of our staff had not yet met the affable judge when he walked into Courtroom One through the public entrance wearing a suit while holding a coffee. Court was not in session as Kristen was calling the small claims list to separate defaults from hearings and assumed that Judge Sullivan was one of the litigants so she called out to him, "Sir, you're not allowed to have that coffee in the courtroom. What's your name?" He said, "Jim" prompting Kristen to ask, "Jim what?" After the humble jurist told her, "Jim Sullivan" she said, "Well, you're not on my list. What are you doing here?" Before he could answer, the court officer told Kristen that he was the new judge! Kristen later went into the judge's lobby to apologize, but Judge Sullivan just laughed and thanked her for doing a thorough job.

A distraught older woman was at the counter crying. She had been arrested for drunk driving and felt like her world was coming to an end. Kristen immediately started to console the poor lady by telling her that she will be able to get through this and that everything will be okay. Nobody possesses a higher level of empathy than Kristen Orlando as she has the listening skills of a psychologist and a heart that beats to help others. I only began watching this demonstration of kindness as Kristen said goodbye to the lady and gave her a big hug. After seeing the emotional hug I thought that she was probably one of Kristen's relatives or friends so I inquired after the lady had gone. When I asked Kristen who she was the sympathetic Bookkeeper replied, "I have no idea. I just thought she needed a hug and to let her know everything would be okay."

Kristen answered the phone and assisted a woman who was calling in sick for jury duty. She told Kristen that she couldn't fulfill her civic obligation because she had to go to the hospital as a result of contracting some rare disease that required her to receive her 56th blood transfusion. She then told Kristen that she has had so many blood transfusions that she doesn't even know if she's still Irish!

*Ashley MacDougall, Jackie Landry, Paula Padula,
Carol Indelicato, Cindy Kerr & Kristen Orlando*

Kathleen M. McKeon, appointed by Governor William F. Weld, is the great Clerk-Magistrate of the Woburn District Court. She is pleasant, good natured and one of the hardest working state employees in the Commonwealth. One of the first staff that I hired was her 19-year old niece Jodi B. Lazarus, a very nice person with a terrific sense of humor who I would come to think probably had the highest IQ in the building. She worked her way up through the system and was eventually appointed to the position of Office Manager by Clerk-Magistrate Kelley.

A guy had been arrested by the Wrentham Police for mowing his front lawn while he was completely naked. He appeared for arraignment fully clothed, but after seeing other men wearing a suit and tie in the courtroom, he surprisingly felt badly that he was not properly dressed. He told Jodi, who was working the counter when he was leaving, "The next time I come here I'm going to wear a suit!" Jodi told me later, "He said he was going to wear a suit. Let's hope it's not his birthday suit!"

A defendant gave Jodi his motor vehicle citation to request a hearing. There were a lot of other people at the counter who needed help so Jodi may have been speaking fast as she told the man that he would get a notice from the court in 4-6 weeks. The guy was surprised as he said, "That's a long time - 46 weeks!"

Sometimes clerk-magistrates and assistants sign criminal complaints that are stacked up on the counter after having been processed by staff. I may have been signing a complaint that was ordered to issue by one of my assistants at a hearing or vice versa. I had just signed a complaint for larceny against a defendant who was alleged to have stolen the property of Juicy Couture. I have seen a lot of unusual first names, but I had to chuckle when thinking that somebody had named a baby Juicy until being told by Jodi that Juicy Couture is a store in the Wrentham Outlets carrying women's clothes and other items!

Jodi Lazarus

Jodi always had enough confidence to poke fun at herself with self-deprecating humor as one time she told me, "If looks could kill, I would be doing life in prison!"

A woman called the WDC to say that her husband couldn't make it to his court date today because he was too drunk and wanted to know if there would be any adverse consequences. Operations Supervisor Jacqueline A. Landry, a real All Star with a heart of gold, told her that a warrant would issue for his arrest. The wife didn't understand what a warrant was so she asked if it could be explained in a simpler way with different words so Jackie told her, "Police, handcuffs!"

A confused defendant was at the WDC counter so Jackie tried to assist the man. He was answering a criminal summons for an arraignment, but when Jackie inquired as to why he was in court the man replied, "I'm here for an arrangement." Jackie told me later that she wanted to tell him that there was a flower shop down the street!

It's always helpful to our staff if the defendant knows his or her case docket number. A guy called Jackie and wanted to say he had a docket number, but instead told her that he had a "doctorate." He didn't mean a Ph.D.!

Our staff spend a good deal of time typing a legal document called a mittimus which authorizes the court officers to hold the defendant in custody and be turned over to the

Deputy Sheriff for transport to the House of Correction. The most common reasons for a mitt are that the defendant has been unable to post bail or for a commitment of incarceration for a period of time. Jackie happened to notice one of our regulars at the counter for whom she had been constantly typing bail mitts. Someone must have posted bail for him as he was no longer in custody so after he left Jackie said, "I'm glad he's out of jail. I'm sick of typing his mitts!"

One of the best things that I have ever done was to hire Ashley K. MacDougall who is bright, hardworking, conscientious and pleasant so she was always a joy to be around. She anticipated my needs and never had to be reminded of anything so it came as no surprise that she was later promoted to Sessions Clerk by Clerk-Magistrate Kelley.

A 50-year old woman was at the counter who apparently believed that she hadn't aged over the years and didn't want our staff to confuse her with being a juvenile. Instead of simply saying that she was on probation she started the conversation with Ashley by stating, "I'm on adult probation."

Carol A. Indelicato was a Case Coordinator II before retiring and is a very nice lady who, amongst other duties, processed Civil Commitments for our office. She always did an outstanding job of dealing with the relatives of some troubled people under very difficult and sometimes emotional circumstances. Carol was assisting an elderly couple who had petitioned to have their adult son committed as an inpatient under Section 35. After completing the necessary paperwork for the petition Carol called the psychologist so that the son could be examined. The busy doctor can't always respond immediately so the parents were becoming somewhat impatient as it was taking longer than they had originally envisioned. Apparently they were thinking about the delicious homemade food at Nicky's Restaurant when the elderly mother said to Carol, "I hope the doctor gets here soon. We don't want to miss the senior citizen's special today at Nicky's!"

One time a member of our staff who was famous for being long winded started to tell a story to a bunch of us in the vault prompting quick witted Carol to say, "Wait a minute, let me go get a chair!"

Anne-Marie Gooley is a very kind person of many talents. She is a Case Specialist in the Civil Department, but I think her true calling is party planning. Her organizational and inter personal skills are amazing so courthouse functions really improved dramatically after I hired Anne-Marie! Sometimes she would even use empty criminal case files as risers under the tablecloths when setting up a table for our courthouse parties. She is one of those innovative entrepreneurs that use dynamic creative ability to make something positive out of nothing. I was glad to see Anne-Marie and her parents after I retired when I was having breakfast with Bill "On the Grill" Prodouz at Leo's Restaurant in Buzzards Bay after a morning of surfcasting. She was wearing a big smile that day just like the first time we met!

Anne-Marie and I were having a conversation in the office just outside the walk in vault when a defendant came to the counter. He wasn't sure which courtroom to go to so he inquired as to where his case would be heard. I asked him to check for his name on the printed docket in front of him and then asked if his name was on the list to which he replied, "Oh yea, I'm on the list all right, my wife's shit list!"

Michelle Kelley was instrumental in my bringing Marissa Palladini into the office for an internship.

L-R future Judge Michelle Kelley, Lesley Hazeldine, Anne-Marie Gooley

Marissa is a very nice girl who did terrific work for us. She was probably already familiar with some criminal terminology as her father and stepmother are both local police officers. Our staff always did an awesome job of hanging decorations in the office for the holiday season including a tiny Christmas tree standing on the counter. Marissa seemed genuinely appreciative of being included with her name on a small stocking on the little tree.

After I retired Marissa did another internship at the United States Supreme Court in Washington and was later hired to work at the court by Michelle, eventually leaving for a paralegal position with a civil litigation law firm in Boston. She will be graduating from law school in May, 2023 so the court system will benefit from her superior intellect, well-reasoned logic and innate kindness. Marissa's Washington internship was also done during Christmas season so she was given an ornament to place on their tree, but it was so tall she had to get into an electronic lifting machine to get up high enough for the placement. The size of the Supreme Court's massive tree dwarfed our mini counter tree, but the Feds always get a bigger budget than the state!

Katie Stoico is a hardworking, likeable young lady who I hired and promoted. Eventually, she decided to leave the court for another position so I hope that she is as happy today as she made our office while there.

I was always quick to publicize any compliments about our staff so that they would know that they were appreciated. Sergeant First Class Michael Seery was a US Army Recruiter who would come in to do background checks on applicants. He was at our court counter often enough to see how busy our staff were and was grateful for their assistance. He told me that they were extremely helpful, knowledgeable, professional and that we have a real model court. When I relayed this to our staff in a meeting and told them the sergeant had said that their hard work made this a model court, Katie, who could have been a standup comic, asked, "Do you think he said that we were a model court because we're all beautiful models?"

An attorney was waiting for the arrival of a psychologist to examine his client so he came to the criminal counter and asked, "Is the doctor here yet?" Katie smiled and said, "You need to go upstairs to see Carol. She deals with doctors, we deal with dockets!"

Some defendants want to tell their entire life story to our busy staff so Katie came up with a simple yet ingenious and sensitive response to politely stop the long speeches. A guy was on the phone telling Katie why he should be given a break and not be sent to jail when she cut in and told him, "Unfortunately Sir, I'm not the person you have to convince."

Katie was processing a criminal complaint for a threat on one of her first days on the job. The defendant had stated that he was going to put a bullet in the victim's head so she asked me if she should type "to kill" or "do harm"? Before I could answer she said it was going to be a head shot so let's go with "kill"!

I cleaned the snow off some of our staff's cars as I was leaving court for the day. The next morning Katie asked me if I had cleaned her car and thanked me. I told her that I should have told her that it was me so she wouldn't be worried that it was some stalker to which she replied, "That's all right, a stalker is OK as long as he cleans off my car. No 209A there!"

Anna McGorty did an outstanding job as a victim witness advocate for the Norfolk County District Attorney's Office which is located in the basement of the WDC. Anna retired before I did and everyone was sad to see her go. She is sweet, kind and funny putting forth her very best effort to help any number of victims of crime while wearing a beautiful smile on her face every day.

One time Anna wrote a criminal docket number on a coffee filter so I asked her if she was out of paper and she smiled as she said, "Cutbacks in the DA's Office!"

Anna was at our counter speaking with Kristen Orlando so as I walked by I overheard part of their conversation as Anna asked Kristen, "Is she the one who killed her husband?" Thinking that I may have possibly missed a homicide case in lockup I asked, "You're not talking about one of our cases are you?" Anna laughed and said, "Oh no, we're talking about the TV show *Desperate Housewives!*"

Kristen Keating worked in the Norfolk County District Attorney's Office as a victim witness advocate. The hardworking, outgoing professional helped a lot of victims every day and used her refined communication skills to make their world just a little safer. One time she ordered a sub from a local sandwich shop and asked that it be delivered to the courthouse. The delivery man didn't know that the DA's Office was downstairs so he came to the Clerk-Magistrate's counter and announced, "I've got an order for Kristen!" Kristen Orlando was only kidding and drew a big laugh when she asked, "Is it already paid for?"

The Wrentham Probation Department has an outstanding, professional staff that was second to none. Pam Callahan, Mary Masters, Paulie Aiello, Donna LaCasse as well as Probation Officers Andrew S. Gassman, Stephen R. Spiewakowski, Gary Borders, Colleen Hannon, Joseph Bianculli and others were always more than helpful to me.

Kathleen Littlefield is the Probation Office Manager. She is a tremendous asset to the court system as her dedication to task is always accompanied by a positive attitude and a cheerful demeanor. A criminal defendant had his destruction of property case disposed of and came to our counter to have his bail returned. He didn't have any ID so Kristen asked him if anyone in the court could positively identify him to which he replied, "Yes, Kathleen Littlefield was my CCD teacher!" He may have needed a few more religious lessons from Kathleen!

WDC Probation Officer Gail Weinberg-Kraus is a very nice person who works hard at her job and truly cares about people. She is extremely compassionate with a sympathetic, understanding nature about her that is genuine and sincere. One of her new probationers was somewhat burned out from drugs and having difficulty understanding what she was trying to explain. He told Gail that his brain didn't work as fast as it used to, that he was having trouble processing the info and asked if she can speak a little slower. Gail was honestly not trying to be a wise guy when she then stated very slowly and dramatically, "My name is Gail," to which the probationer replied, "Hey, I said I was a little slow, but I'm not a f***in idiot!"

Some very talented and dedicated Chief Probation Officers have worked at the WDC including Sandra L. Adams who holds that post today. CPO Alessandro Pizzi and I attended monthly management meetings and got to be fast friends. Al came to America from his native Italy when he was only seven years old aboard the fabled *Andrea Doria* which would sink off of the coast of Nantucket three years after his safe passage. Young Al, who only spoke Italian at the time, was reunited with his mother in New York City and eventually with his father who was working in Venezuela to support his family, thus at one time all three members of the family were living on different continents. Al learned and mastered America's Past Time becoming a highly-skilled baseball player and coach in his adopted town of Franklin. The hardworking young man who had emigrated from a farming community in the Abruzzi Province of Italy earned a bachelor's and master's degree from Assumption College and another master's from Northeastern University before becoming a Probation Officer. I remember when I was honored to speak before a huge crowd at Al's retirement party and how some people were crying tears of joy because they loved him so much. I told the audience that although Al is a humble man, he had never let his humble beginnings limit or define his future. If you google American Success Story a photo of Al Pizzi should pop up because he is an honorable man who came from nothing and rose to the top of his profession where he left an indelible mark with positive accomplishments that will never be forgotten.

Three young men had been arrested together for larceny less and were now being booked standing next to each other at the probation counter at the WDC. CPO Pizzi was on the inside of the counter asking them questions to complete the intake form used to assist the judge in determining indigence eligibility. Al asked the first guy how much money he made per week. The defendant hemmed and hawed about not working regularly and finally told Al that for the last pay period he had earned $37.00 for the whole week. Al wanted to know if that was his take home pay or before taxes and deductions so the jovial CPO asked, "Gross?" The defendant next to him thought that Al was belittling his friend and declared, "You think that's gross man, I only made $25.00!"

Jurors chosen for trial are selected from a much larger group called the Jury Pool. Al was walking in the hallway of the court one morning when he was approached by a man reporting for jury duty who wasn't sure where to go. Al directed the gentleman to head downstairs to the Jury Pool Room causing the surprised man to exclaim, "You have a room here with a pool for the jurors?"

CPO Pizzi happened to be in the courtroom on a busy day in the First Session. Two young scruffy defendants who looked like they hadn't seen soap and water since the Clinton administration were standing in the prisoner's dock as they were arraigned for B & E in the night with intent to commit a felony. The ADA read off a list of stolen items that the defendants were alleged to have taken from a local physician's home including a Phi Beta Kappa jersey. The judge, noticing that one of the defendants was wearing a Phi Beta Kappa shirt, looked at him and inquired, "I take it that you're a member of the Phi Beta Kappa Academic Honor Society?" The confused defendant responded, "Huh?"

Carol A. Silvia was appointed Acting CPO after Al Pizzi retired. Carol is a true professional whose intelligence, kindness and listening ability equipped her to resolve small difficulties before they grew into big problems. We became very close as she even connected me to Charley Soares, the legendary writer and famous angler, who took me fishing in his home waters of Sakonnet. That was like having Larry Bird ask a kid to shoot some hoops in the driveway!

Eventually Carol was appointed Chief Probation Officer in the Fall River District Court so Terrell J. Kiley took over while maintaining his position as CPO of the ADC. Of course, I already knew Terry from my time in Attleboro so it was no surprise that he continued to do an outstanding job.

Lillian Amaru was a Probation Officer in Wrentham and did a terrific job as the Assistant Chief Probation Officer and then as the Chief Probation Officer toward the end of my career. I always enjoyed our management meetings where we had a good time and shared a lot of laughs about our families while getting the business of the court done in the process. I could always count on Lil as she is an honorable person of the highest integrity so her word was always her bond.

Lil described the details of a stop she had made at Dunkin' Donuts with her husband Mike. Lil stayed in the car while Mike went in to get the order. He asked the young girl behind the counter for a bagel with cream cheese on the side. He wasn't sure why the young lady had made such a quizzical facial expression, but she gave him his order and he went back to the vehicle. Only when Mike opened the bag in the car did he realize why she had looked so confused. Lil and Mike had a good laugh when he took out the bagel and discovered that the cream cheese that he had asked for on the side had been smeared on the bagel all along the side!

Lil retired a few years after me so they had a drive by retirement party for her due to the restrictions of the coronavirus. She stood outside on the courthouse steps greeting a long line of vehicles slowly driving by as well-wishers yelled out car windows with horns sounding. J. Do and I rode by with our granddaughters four-year old Addie and two-year old Lucy waving from their car seats in the back. A half dozen police cruisers had blue lights flashing and sirens blaring in appreciation for the true professional whose remarkable devotion and innate kindness made the court a better place every time she walked into the building.

I don't remember the name of the band, but a couple in their twenties were having a good time at a concert at Gillette Stadium where they were enjoying the music along with thousands of others when the band started to play the woman's favorite song. The young lady really liked this particular selection so much that she was inspired to remove her clothing and engage in sexual relations with her boyfriend right at their seats. They were charged by the police and ordered to appear in the WDC.

The woman had a respectable job and no criminal record so the talk of the day at the courthouse was how this one song was responsible for causing her out of character behavior. I was in the courtroom as she was arraigned when an attorney from Worcester leaned in toward me and whispered, "Eddie, can you get me the name of that song so I can play it for my wife!"

Attorney Daniel Del Vecchio Jr. was a devoted trial lawyer and a very nice man. He put on incredible Bar Association clambakes at his lakefront home and could not have possibly worked any harder for his clients. After the jury got the case to begin deliberations he would always call his lovely wife Anne and say, "Annie, it's in the box!" She would then pray for a NG because Dan told me he would take any help he could get! I always thought it was fantastic to see a couple who had been married for so long performing as a team in a high stakes enterprise of human drama.

Attorney Dan Del Vecchio

Dan told me a story about another defense attorney who specialized in drunk driving cases. Long before cell phones, the lawyer and his wife went out for the night leaving their nine-year old daughter at home. A man who had been arrested for drunk driving called the house from a police station and asked for her father so the girl told him that he wasn't home, but she could tell from the conversation that the guy had been drinking heavily. It wasn't unusual for the little girl to hear her father speaking with clients on the phone so she had always listened and paid close attention to his legal advice. It was almost as if this youngster had started to attend law school before the age of 10 so when the impatient drunk driver called back a third time from the booking room the nine-year old told him, "Listen, I don't know when my father is coming home, but don't say a word to the police and don't take the Breathalyzer!"

One of the best Christmas parties of the year was hosted by a group of very generous lawyers at the old Joe Tecce's in the North End. Attorneys Willie J. Davis, Roger Witkin, Paul O'Rourke, Michael P. Doolin, Robert Zanello, Frances Robinson and Robert L. Jubinville sponsored the festive occasion with delicious food and an open bar where a good time was enjoyed by all. Attorney Doolin was later appointed Superior Court Judge by Governor Charlie D. Baker. Attorney Witkin always greeted us warmly with his engaging personality and keen sense of humor. Roger gave out pencils that touted his criminal law practice with one of the best slogans I have ever seen - Reasonable Doubt at a Reasonable Price.

A defendant sent a cashier's check to the court for his fine payment. He had written the reason for the check on the bottom left as - "me being an idiot."

The Welfare Department in Attleboro, which I think eventually had another name, used to prosecute alleged deadbeat dads with the initiation of criminal proceedings for non-support. I probably conducted show cause hearings on hundreds of these cases over the years. The typical case involved an unwed mother who was receiving public assistance testifying on behalf of the Commonwealth to identify the defendant as the father of her child. This was long before the advent of precise medical technology so sometimes I would be asked to observe facial similarities between the child and defendant. It wasn't very scientific and far from the stronger level of proof available now since the development of DNA evidence, but we all did the best we could.

The Welfare representative, defendant and the mother holding her child would be seated at the hearing. After administering the oath to the parties, I would always start the hearing by asking the mother if the defendant was the father of her child. I would ask that same question to every mother who would then always answer in the affirmative. The hearing would proceed with testimony from the mother, welfare representative and defendant. Sometimes I would deny the issuance of criminal process based on the defendant's admission to paternity and the acceptance of an 18-year support debt. Other times I would hear the testimony, weigh the evidence and ultimately either allow or deny the issuance of a criminal complaint.

The easiest decision that I ever had to make brought one of these non-support hearings to an immediate conclusion. I asked the mother, who was seated before me holding a young baby, if this was the father of her child. She said that he looked kind of familiar, but that she really didn't know who the father was because she was sleeping with so many different guys that it was all a blur! The thought had crossed my mind that she may have been trying to help the defendant by having the taxpayers support the child, but after hearing that testimony I couldn't issue a complaint in good conscience. Denied.

A lot of theft occurred at the Emerald Square Mall in North Attleborough and the Wrentham Outlets so shoplifting became a very common crime in both courts where I worked. Clothing and other items would probably be less expensive if the merchants didn't have to factor in the price of larceny. The Wrentham Police charged a man in his late 20s who just couldn't make up his mind as to which was his favorite store. He was charged with shoplifting on the same day from Tommy Hilfiger, Perry Ellis, Calvin Klein, J. Crew, Bass Shoes, Armani, Burberry, Cole Haan and Banana Republic. He must have been shoplifting for that hard to find gift!

Homelessness has long been a problem in many communities across our nation resonating with me while helping a gentleman on a frigid winter day at the ADC counter. The homeless defendant was turning himself in on a default warrant for a minor crime because he wanted to be held in jail to escape the cold. He spoke of incarceration like it was a trip to Bermuda or as he called it - "three hots & a cot!"

A guy from Norton had 22 restraining orders issued against him from 11 different plaintiffs! Maybe he was just misunderstood!

Edward F. Siudut served with distinction for many years as the Chief Probation Officer of Norfolk County Superior Court. He was a rugged 6 foot 7 inch solid guy who perpetually seemed to be in a good mood so I always enjoyed his company at court conferences and other functions. Big Ed, who played professional basketball in Italy, was selected by the San Francisco Warriors in the second round of the 1969 NBA Draft after a stellar collegiate career at the College of the Holy Cross. Lew Alcindor and Jo Jo White were taken in the first round before him.

John J. "Boots" Connelly was the popular Chief Probation Officer of the Norfolk County Probate & Family Court and was also a talented athlete who had starred in football and baseball for Boston College. Al Pizzi, Big Ed and I were in the neighborhood so we decided to stop into Boots Connelly's office to say hello. It happened to be on a Wednesday so as soon as we were told that the CPO was not in, ever comical Big Ed remarked, "Boots takes Wednesdays off, he thinks he's a dentist!"

Attorneys Jo Anne and Marybeth Hopkins have an extensive law practice and are frequently representing someone in the Attleboro and Wrentham District Courts so I had the privilege of getting to know these sisters many years ago and continued to hear their clients' cases throughout my career. They are both outstanding lawyers who I would recommend to anyone with their keen sense of humor and incomparable kindness always making them a pleasure to be around.

Some members of the Norfolk County Bar Association volunteer their time every year at the Boston Food Bank at an event to assist in the effort to provide sustenance and other needs for those less fortunate. J. Do and I joined a couple of dozen attorneys one day to help with this noble program. There are many different phases of this magnificent operation that came to fruition that day because of these volunteers from across the county. We worked side by side filling boxes with food and other items such as soap and shampoo that we selected off a conveyor belt that travelled by in front of us. The boxes had to be filled very close to a certain weight and then put on a table behind us to be weighed for accuracy and continue on for shipment. Marybeth, a recipient of the Bar Association's Pro Bono Award, would pick up the boxes that we had prepared and weigh them on a scale.

This assembly line was working very well as we felt some sense of satisfaction in being able to contribute, even in some small way, to the benefit and wellbeing of others. J. Do and I did the best that we could to fill each box to the allotted weight requirement, but Marybeth was right there to insure a better level of precision. One time I inadvertently failed to put enough items in one of the boxes which was quickly discovered on Marybeth's scale. She brought the box over to me and politely told me that I was 3 pounds underweight. I thanked Marybeth and told her that it was the first time in my entire life that I had ever been accused of being underweight!

The Honorable Francis T. Crimmins Jr. of Stoughton sat in the ADC quite frequently while using his superior intellect as well as his engaging sense of humor to make court sessions extremely memorable and much more enjoyable. As mentioned previously, I was honored to have him as my MC for my swearing in ceremony in the House Chamber at the Massachusetts State House. Judge Crimmins is a real pro as he did an outstanding job while standing close by as I raised my right hand to take the oath of office for Clerk-Magistrate from His Excellency, A. Paul Cellucci, Governor of the Commonwealth.

I was also honored to serve as his session clerk in Attleboro, but as a result of a staff shortage I would sometimes have to set him set up for a jury trial in the morning and then leave to conduct show cause hearings, issue search warrants and fulfill other duties in our busy court. I would turn on the tape recorder, swear in the first witness and place the exhibits in front of Judge Crimmins before leaving. I would usually check in with him just before lunch, but many times in a hectic office I wouldn't be able to make it back to the jury court until the end of the day. Court Officer Timothy B. Ahern started calling me the "Closer" because I would enter at the end, but the nickname given to me by Judge

Crimmins celebrated my late entrance with a comparison to the end of a train. He started calling me the "Caboose" and he still does today because I walked into the courtroom last.

Our oldest daughter Kaitlin married Jon in a beautiful ceremony that began outdoors at the Sea Crest Beach Hotel in North Falmouth. She asked me to perform the ceremony so I called the Governor's office to begin the paper work process for the One Day Marriage Designation. I told the lady who answered the phone that I wanted to marry my daughter and the shocked woman replied that I can't do that in this state! I quickly realized the ambiguity that I had presented and told her that I just wanted to perform the ceremony. Judge Crimmins came through as always and loaned me his judicial robe that he had worn while serving justice in courtrooms throughout the Commonwealth. Frank is a lot taller than me so I had to be careful to not trip on the robe as I walked into the ceremony with J. Do on my arm!

Judge Crimmins' robe (S. Campbell photo)

Massachusetts State Judges take turns when the court is closed participating 24/7 in the Judicial Response System to receive phone calls for emergency situations that cannot wait until the opening of the courthouse. They hear a wide variety of requests and on any given night may issue a restraining order on behalf of an abused woman or order that a limb be taken from a patient in a hospital. There are several different types of courts under the umbrella of the Trial Court so judges would tend to become proficient in their own field and experts in those kind of cases heard in their own division. A Juvenile Judge, for instance, probably knows juvenile law and procedure better than a Land Court Judge and vice versa. They are all, however, on call with Judicial Response to address emergencies involving every category of law.

Judge Crimmins, appointed to the District Court Department, was on call when he received a request that would have been brought in the Probate and Family Court Department during normal working hours. A man had perished in a deadly motor vehicle accident and his fiancée was holding out hope that she could still become impregnated by the deceased. Judge Crimmins was very sympathetic to the lady and acting with an abundance of caution decided to call his good friend the Honorable James V. Menno, who was an Associate Justice in the Plymouth County Probate and Family Court after having been appointed by Governor William F. Weld, to discuss this unusual case. The lady was represented by Attorney Edward J. McCormick III who filed a Motion to Harvest Sperm. Judge Crimmins allowed the motion and brought positive closure to an emotional case stemming from a terrible tragedy. An interesting ancillary component of this atypical proceeding was that both judges as well as the petitioner's attorney are all graduates of the same school - Xaverian Brothers High School in Westwood!

Judge Crimmins was eventually appointed to the position of First Justice of the Stoughton District Court. Unfortunately, one of the most common cases that judges hear every day are requests from abused women for restraining orders under Massachusetts General Laws Chapter 209A, but on this day Judge Crimmins was hearing a 209A request from two women against the same man. Abuse complaints from more than one woman against the same man are more common than you may think, but it is unusual to have two women in the courtroom at the same time seeking a protective order against the same defendant. This particular case, however, was extremely unusual because not only were the two women in the same courtroom at the same time against the same defendant, but they were also both currently married to him! One of the wives lived in Randolph and the other in Canton and of course the defendant lived with each wife separately in both towns. One marriage had gone on for six years and the other for four with each woman thinking that she was the only wife and not being aware of the other marriage! Judge Crimmins listened to this emotional plea for justice from these two ladies who were both victims of the very same con artist. The judge was very sympathetic in spending an inordinate amount of time trying to be helpful to them as he granted their requests and issued the protective orders.

Judge Crimmins and I spoke later about the traumatic level of hurt and anguish for these poor women and the incredible logistics necessary for the defendant to pull this off for so long. I wondered aloud how the defendant managed Christmas, Thanksgiving and other holidays and then Judge Crimmins pondered, "Eddie - how did he do Valentine's Day?"

Judge Crimmins was on the bench in the Stoughton District Court when a middle aged woman said that her lawyer was requesting a second call. Judge Crimmins allowed her request while asking for the name of her attorney. She said his name was George Himmelesq. Never having heard that name the judge asked where he was from to which the lady replied that his office was in Braintree. Judge Crimmins quickly realized that she had put two words together to make one and that she was represented by George Himmel, Esq.!

Judge Crimmins decided to leave the bench for a challenging and prestigious position in local government. The court system's loss was their gain as he excelled in more than one leadership post, made lots of friends and continued to take his job more seriously than himself.

He would eventually go on to found Ab Initio Elder Law Solutions, LLC in his hometown of Stoughton where his firm serves the public in private practice through representation in many areas, but with a concentration on elder law. One day he was interviewing an applicant to fill an opening for a para-legal position in his office. During the interview the lady asked if it was possible to have an arrangement where she could be allowed to work flex time. The self-deprecating former judge told me later that he had never heard of flex time and thought that maybe she was requesting time to work out and exercise at the office!

The Stoughton Chamber of Commerce hosted a Roast of Judge Crimmins so I agreed to be one of the Roast Masters in front of a sellout crowd who paid to witness their friend on the receiving end of some good natured barbs. I mentioned the economic impact on the local community when the judge goes on a diet. I told the crowd - I'm not saying that Judge Crimmins eats a lot of sweets, but when he gave up ice cream for Lent they had to lay off three high school kids from Crescent Ridge Dairy!

Judge Crimmins' late father was also named Francis, but everyone called him Mike. He stood 6 foot, 7 inches tall and was described years ago by some as the tallest man in Norfolk County. He proudly served our country in one of the bloodiest conflicts of World War II while helping to defend his battalion's section of the American lines that ran 80 miles along the dense Ardennes Forest through the snow covered hills of Luxembourg and Belgium. This bucolic setting had become a war zone as the Nazis unleashed their final major offensive to the west. Judge Crimmins' dad was lucky to survive after being blown out of a tank that had been hit by an exploding Nazi shell. He met General George S. Patton Jr. on the battlefield where he was immediately asked why he wasn't wearing Army issued boots. The senior Crimmins responded by telling the famous General that the Army couldn't find any that were big enough to fit him. A phone call was made by General Patton and a new pair of correctly sized boots were delivered soon thereafter.

After six frigid weeks of intense winter combat, 19,000 brave American soldiers had lost their lives in a crucial Allied defense of freedom by stopping Hitler's last full scale effort to continue with his imposition of tyranny and design on world domination. We owe our nation's security and the preservation of democracy to the valor of Francis T. Crimmins Sr. and all those who fought there including the rest of Patton's courageous Third Army as well as our fearless allies. The Nazi assault had failed with the defeat so devastating that Germany's surrender would come just three months after the last shot was fired in this historic turning point of the war which came to be known as the Battle of the Bulge.

It should come as no surprise that Judge Crimmins is a scholar and a devout patriot having grown up in a house under the tutelage of his loving mother and the inspiration of his heroic dad who had been through hell to come back to father an extremely talented family in Stoughton. It is obvious that Judge Crimmins inherited his love of country from his dad as the United States Constitution and Declaration of Independence are documents that he absolutely reveres. His friends and colleagues are very familiar with a unique expression that the Harvard grad proclaims as a sincere compliment. The highest form of praise that Judge Crimmins can bestow upon someone is when he says that, "You are a great American!"

When a defendant admits sufficient facts on a criminal charge the judge has to conduct a colloquy to be satisfied that the admission is free, voluntary and understood. The judge asks a series of questions designed to ensure that the defendant is sober and intelligent enough for the proceedings to continue. Sometimes a defendant's answer may be ambiguous enough to cause the judge to inquiry further. Judge Crimmins was unsure of a defendant's sobriety so he asked him, "Sir, how long has it been since you had your last drink?" We knew it was trouble when the guy immediately looked at his watch!

Another question asked by judges during the colloquy has been the source of some interesting answers over the years. The judge will ask the defendant, "How far did you go in school?" High school, college and sometimes a graduate degree is the usual reply, but I have heard responses such as, "All the way", "To the end", "Until I got thrown out" and the 65-year old man who said, "Oh Christ, I don't know - it was a long time ago!"

I usually attended Somerville District Court Clerk-Magistrate Teddy Tomasone's times in Boston twice a year with Judge Crimmins and Walpole Police Detective Bill Madden. Attorney Glen Hannington would usually get there before us so we would join him at his table. Different guests, including Attorney Martin F. Kane II, would be seated with us so it was always fun and interesting. Marty is an outstanding attorney who specializes in divorce work and is one of the best guys in the business. One time the congenial advocate was seated to the left of Frank, Bill, Glen and I for this festive occasion that had become a time honored tradition in the North End where Teddy had grown up. The event ended with Teddy saying good night before putting the microphone down as always so everyone started shaking hands as we all said good bye. The multitude of hands to shake on the way out was like a long receiving line with the Governor at the end, but first we bid farewell to those at our table. Frank, ever the jokester, extended his hand to Marty, the Divorce King, and facetiously said, "See ya Marty, and hey - don't take any calls from my wife!"

I always enjoyed conversations with ADA David T. Turcotte as he was an interesting, humorous prosecutor who was always well prepared. The first time we met was just after a bail hearing in the ADC and later he happened to be in the Clerk-Magistrate's Office where he overheard me speaking with our staff about processing a complaint for a defendant in lockup who was charged with possession of THC. The full name of the substance had to be typed into the old fashioned trifold criminal complaint, not just the three letters. This was long before Google or spell check and nobody in our office knew how to spell it including me. Dave was kind enough to help us and immediately, without hesitation, spelled out tetrahydrocannabinol! We were all happy for him when he was appointed to a judgeship by Governor William F. Weld.

Attorney Richard J. Silva Jr. is a brilliant lawyer, an honest man and a real good guy. He represented a defendant before Judge Turcotte, on a busy day in the criminal session of the Fall River District Court. Judge Turcotte was conducting a colloquy when he asked a 45-year old man, not Rick's client, how far he had gone in school. The man replied, "Well, it was about a mile each way Your Honor."

Legendary Boston Attorney Marty Kane once said, "Love is grand, but divorce is 50 grand!"

A large stack of Massachusetts State Police cases sat in a pile on the side of my desk as I was about to start hearings in the WDC. Trooper Kevin Collins is a squared away State

Police Prosecutor who takes pride in his job, his appearance and his professional demeanor. It was always a pleasure working with him because he understood that some people deserve a break and others don't. I was always grateful for his competence, intelligence and adept approach to problem solving. He could be tough when necessary, but wasn't afraid to smile.

We were about half way through the list when Trooper Collins called the next case and directed the defendant to have a seat in front of my desk where I was seated. The 80-year old man sat down as his twelve-year old grandson took the seat next to him. I swore them in and listened to Trooper Collins testify that the gentleman was charged with operating without a license, uninspected, unregistered and some other motor vehicle offenses. I asked the man what he would like to say and he started explaining a long story in a thick Irish brogue that was sometimes hard to understand. His young grandson was doing the best he could to help his grandfather as the older man suddenly began to get frustrated with his inability to articulate his presentation. I told him not to worry as he was doing just fine and asked if he had any documents that he could show to Trooper Collins. He immediately blurted out that he had a shitload of paperwork in the truck! The grandson quickly whispered to him that there was no swearing in court, but the poor Irishman seemed confused as he asked his grandson, "What do you mean. I've got a shitload of it right out there!"

He brought in the proper documents which satisfied the trooper so I denied the request for criminal complaints and sent him on his way after thanking the young man for being such a good grandson.

Trooper Collins presented me with a citation alleging that the 45-year old woman seated in front of me was speeding. I thanked the trooper and asked the defendant what she would like to say. It sounded like the pleasant lady was saying, "I was nice," so I was thinking that maybe she was trying to tell me that she was nice to the trooper who had stopped her. The poor lady had a lisp, however, and was explaining that she had been stopped on the way home from work so she wasn't saying "I was nice", it turned out she was saying, "I work nights." Not Responsible.

William R. Fitzpatrick Jr. was a tall, barrel chested, broad shouldered, good natured trooper who looked like he just came out of central casting for the Massachusetts State Police. He was assigned to the Foxborough Barracks so I did hearings with him both in Attleboro and Wrentham. He was prosecuting the state police cases in Wrentham when he looked at his list and recognized the name of the next defendant he was about to call. He told me that he had this kid on his team in Little League when he was a coach. He brought the defendant in and presented evidence of speeding, driving on somebody's lawn, hitting a mailbox and all kinds of reckless operation that I think went on for miles. The kid seemed like a nice guy who just didn't know how to operate a motor vehicle safely. After the hearing when the defendant had left, Fitzy smiled at me and said, "I just want to remind you that I was his Little League Coach and not his Driver's Ed Instructor!"

A 40-year old woman was charged with a breakdown lane violation so Fitzy presented the citation to me. Her friend was sitting behind her at the hearing as the defendant told her story. She said she was in the breakdown lane because her friend had a bad case of "explosive diarrhea." The friend raised her hand and said, "That's me. I'm the one with the diarrhea!" I asked her how she was feeling now and quickly found the defendant Not Responsible to get them out of my office.

On another occasion Trooper William R. Apgar was prosecuting cases for the State Police. Bill and I had done hearings together in both courts for years. He went by the nickname "Grumpy" and projected a gruff exterior that hid a kind heart and caring persona. He called the case of a 17-year old girl who was charged with speeding. The veteran trooper presented the citation to me which showed the young kid to be travelling at 85MPH in a 65 zone. She had been clocked by an experienced trooper which, in my opinion, is overwhelmingly strong evidence in favor of the Commonwealth. The nervous teenager stated that she was in fact going that fast, but it was because there was an emergency. She said that she was headed for work and it was urgent that she get there quickly because somebody else had called in sick. This polite girl was very nice, but much too young to be a doctor or a nurse so I asked her where she was employed. She stated that she worked at Somerset Creamery! I then asked her rhetorically, "So if you don't make it on time somebody doesn't get a frappe?" I could immediately see that she understood the folly of her actions and argument so I told the doe-eyed young lady, who had no previous record, to be more careful before giving her a break and finding her Not Responsible.

Grumpy directed an 85-year old gentleman facing a hefty fine into the hearing, but before I could even swear him in he asked me, "Do you give senior citizen discounts on speeding?" The trooper presented the citation showing the defendant to be going 97 MPH which he admitted to so I asked him why he was going so fast. He told me that his girlfriend had called and asked him to come to her place and he wanted to get there before she changed her mind! I found him Not Responsible after asking him to be careful in the future if she calls again.

Grumpy used to like to watch the *Jerry Springer Show* and would sometimes relate stories about the unfortunate characters that appeared on the program. He asked me if I watched it, but I told him that I didn't need to see it on TV because I got to witness it live every day in the courthouse!

I was doing hearings at the Natick District Court, probably for some conflict case. There was one memorable case where I quickly ascertained that the defendant was not going to be nominated for the Nice Guy of the Year Award! There was strong evidence from the Commonwealth that the defendant had threatened a woman with a snow shovel. Obviously all women are equal as victims of crime, but this case just seemed to get worse when testimony revealed that the woman was a nun!

I was hearing a criminal harassment case being presented by Foxborough Police Officer Joseph D. McDonald, a gentle giant who was loved by all. The defendant seated before me had a tattoo on his forearm that clearly read, "Hit me or I'll hit you." Facing that type of charge, it might be a good idea to wear a long sleeve shirt!

I was doing Walpole Police hearings with Detective Bill Madden when Joe's name came up. A very experienced defendant smiled and told us, "Hey, Joe McDonald really lost some weight. He looks great, huh!" You're probably a frequent flyer if you notice the prosecutor's weight loss!

I always found people who have come from large families to be some of the nicest folks around and Sergeant Kevin D. Roake of the Norfolk Police Department is no exception. The South Boston native, who comes from a family of seven children, could certainly handle himself, but always seemed to be smiling and in a good mood with the glass half full. Kevin was the prosecutor sometimes for the hearings for his department and called the case of a man who was charged with speeding. The defendant was carrying some written material which he had been reading in the hall while waiting for his case to be called. I asked him to have a seat and swore him in as the front cover of his instructional manual was clearly visible on his lap. He could have turned it over so that I couldn't see the title, but instead propped it up as if he wanted me to see that he was reading *How to Beat a Speeding Ticket*. I have never read that manual, but Chapter One should be titled - You Get More With Honey!

A 30-year old woman who was cited for speeding testified that, "I wasn't speeding, I never speed. I always drive slowly because I hate people who speed, as a matter of fact I get sick to my stomach when I see somebody driving too fast!" She was wearing a NASCAR tee shirt!

A 17-year old girl came before me for a speeding hearing on a busy day. The girl was doing a nice job of representing herself and telling me that she was a good kid as her mother, seated behind her nodded in agreement every time the defendant said something positive about herself. It was a terrific, heartfelt presentation, but when I noticed that she was wearing a sweatshirt that read - Franklin Drama Club I just had to ask, "How do I know that this is not an act?" The good kid was found Not Responsible.

A 30-year old woman came in for a motor vehicle hearing while holding the hand of her three-year old son. As soon as I offered the lady a seat the kid looked at me and started screaming and crying uncontrollably. "You've wearing a tie," she said, "so he thinks you're the doctor!"

A good relationship between District and Superior Courts is important for bail reviews, indictments on bind over cases and other issues for the swift delivery of justice. I was truly blessed to spend my career in two counties where both were well known for their great staff in Superior Court. Bristol County Clerk of Courts Marc J. Santos, First Assistant Clerk Philip F. Leddy, Assistant Clerk Marcel W. Gautreau and the rest of the outstanding team were always very helpful to me. Norfolk County Clerk of Courts Walter F. Timilty, First Assistant Clerk Mary K. Hickey and the entire office were always ready to be of assistance including the Assistant Clerks in the photo below.

Author accepting Amicus Curiae Award from Norfolk County Bar Association in Superior Court. L-R Asst. Clerks Brian G. Roche, Janice C. Uguccioni, Nancy J Delaney, CPO Milton L. Britton Jr., Asst. Clerk M. Diane Gibbons, Asst. Clerk & now Judge Joseph P. Hurley III, Asst. Clerk James M. McDermott, Court Officer Timothy J. Rose, Staff Sergeant James Dunn from Dedham American Legion Post 18, author, Attorney Richard J. Sweeney, Register of Probate & now Sheriff Patrick W. McDermott, Judge Kenneth J. Fishman, Clerk of Courts Walter F. Timilty, Trial Court Chief Justice Paula M. Carey, Father Thomas Bouton, Clerk-Magistrate Salvatore Paterna, Register of Deeds William P. O'Donnell.

Although I never worked in Plymouth County, I have been summoned to the City of Champions for jury duty. It was always a pleasure to see Clerk of Courts Robert S. Creedon Jr., First Assistant Clerks David M. Biggs & Patrick W. Creedon as well as Assistant Clerks Brendan P. Sullivan and Adam J. Baler who is now the great Clerk-Magistrate of the Plymouth District Court, appointed by Governor Charlie D Baker.

The security officers who worked the courthouse door were commonly referred to as Blue Shirts as that was the color of their uniform. One of the Blue Shirts was a nice young guy who liked to go to Dave & Buster's, a restaurant where customers can accumulate reward tickets that can be exchanged for various gift items.

An attorney was making her way through the metal detector while carrying a high end pocket book from Dooney & Bourke that had D & B displayed on the outside of the leather.

The Blue Shirt, upon seeing D & B and thinking it was from Dave & Buster's said to her, "That's a nice bag. I'd like to get one of those for my wife. How many tickets did it cost?"

A defendant was in the prisoner's dock where he just caught a sentence of 6 months committed. His two children, aged 4 and 6, came over to give him a hug and say goodbye. He told the kids, "Daddy is going away for a long sleepover!"

Attorney Thomas R. Leedham Jr. was a class guy and a very capable lawyer. He represented a man who was on trial for stealing a horse's harness that had not been recovered by the police. The man had vehemently protested his innocence and told anyone within earshot that he wasn't a thief. Tom did a magnificent job for his client and earned him a verdict of Not Guilty. Immediately after hearing the verdict the defendant leaned over to Tom and asked, "Not Guilty? Does that mean I get to keep the harness now?"

Attorney James H. Fagan is a good friend and a tenacious criminal defense lawyer with an office in Taunton. He served as a State Representative for many years, eventually becoming Chairman of Post Audit & Oversight and was later appointed Chairman of the Ethics Committee. The good-natured advocate is a man of his word and his word is his bond so a handshake from Jim holds more weight than any written contract. Our families had known each other even

Representative Jim Fagan

before Jim was working as a kid behind the counter with his dad at Hanson's Drug Store on Broadway where he served frappes to my uncle, Dr. Thomas F. Doherty and his friend the immortal Ted Williams.

Jim and his mother both had Sister Jane Regina, many years apart of course, at St. Mary's Grammar School. When Jim was in Kindergarten the good Sister told him, "James Fagan, you're incorrigible!" The happy four-year old didn't know what that meant, but seemed to like it. By the time Jim was in 8th grade one of the nuns told him, "Mr. Fagan you're wasting time, you're not doing anything." He responded with, "Don't worry Sister, when I grow up I want to be a lawyer, it's good practice!"

Jim's Christmas parties at his office on Dean Street were the stuff of legend. It was a veritable who's who of interesting people in a jovial atmosphere where J. Do and I always had fun. It was so well attended that we had to travel down back streets to find a place to park, but it seemed that no matter how far away we were as soon as we got out of the car roaring laughter could be heard coming from the party!

One of Jim's clients was driving along a road in North Dighton. He had been drinking and may have had one beer too many as his vehicle collided with the passenger side of a fire truck that was on its way to a call. The impact caused the car to roll over on its side with the driver still behind the wheel secured by his seat belt as the firefighters rushed in to render aid and assistance. The driver looked up and upon seeing the firefighters said, "You guys do a great job, how did you get here so fast?"

The police would never bring an intoxicated criminal defendant in custody to the courthouse today, but back in the day one fell through the cracks. The drunken defendant, arrested for public drinking, was standing in the prisoner's dock while holding onto the wooden railing as he swayed back and forth to maintain balance. The judge addressed the defendant and tried to ascertain if he knew what was going on by asking, "Sir, do you know why you're here?" "No, Your Honor," came the inebriated reply. "You're here for drinking," the judge stated. "Great!" declared the defendant, "Let's get on with it. Who's got a bottle?"

One of my favorite police prosecutors was Detective John D. Maloney from the Franklin Police Department. John was appointed Assistant Clerk-Magistrate by Clerk-Magistrate Kelley after my retirement. It is a very busy department and John always did an outstanding job of pursuing justice with the balance needed for every different case. He called the case of a 17-year old boy and brought him before me on a speeding hearing. The defendant came in with his mother and was represented by Attorney John J. Hickey Jr. who is a terrific lawyer and a fun guy on the golf course. I asked the defendant to raise his right hand before administering the oath to him. The oath is actually a question to which most people quickly respond by saying "Yes", but this kid just sat there silently. I think the poor kid was extremely nervous and not wanting to suggest an answer, I told him that he had to say yes or no. He then said, "yes or no" which caused Attorney Hickey to instruct him to reply in the affirmative. Attorney Hickey did a nice job of convincing me that he was a good kid so I found him Not Responsible.

A woman was testifying during a hearing while her five-year old son was seated behind her. She said that the defendant, who was alleged to have stolen her TV, had called her a shithead and a whore, but she spelled the profanity for the sake of the young boy which I thought was nice. She went on continuing to spell the names she had been called which included just about every profane word in the dictionary, but then she suddenly blurted out, "Then he called me a f***in' asshole!" She didn't spell that one!

Millis Police Detective Sergeant Domenic J. Tiberi is a good man who always had a positive outlook during hearings so I enjoyed listening to him prosecute criminal and CMVI cases. He called the name of a woman who was charged with speeding. The lady sat down and told me, "I was so nervous waiting for this hearing that I lost four pounds!"

A Habeas Corpus, commonly referred to as a Habe, is a legal document that I would sign routinely to order that an incarcerated inmate or defendant being held on bail by another court, be transported to Attleboro or Wrentham. There is a singing group, which I believe is comprised of all attorneys, who take their name from Habeas Corpus - they are called Habeas Chorus!

The Honorable Warren A. Powers was appointed First Justice of the WDC while I was Clerk-Magistrate, but we already knew each other very well as I served as his session clerk many times while working at the ADC. Judge Powers was a much beloved Assistant District Attorney in Norfolk County before being appointed to the bench by Governor William F. Weld so we spent several years together working in two neighboring courthouses.

He likes to cook and is considered an expert on various spices and different kinds of marinades. He had heard that I was trying to lose some weight so he brought in a buffalo steak for me at the Attleboro Court. Apparently, this steak has very little fat content so he told me that I could now enjoy eating a delicious piece of meat while everyone else who was on a diet was consuming a sorry bowl of lettuce!

Judge Powers is a deeply religious man who tries to do the right thing every day. I still have the small metal rosary that he gave me to keep in my pocket for my hearing before the Judicial Nominating Commission and the baseball cap with an embroidered eagle that he presented to me after travelling a considerable distance to locate a symbol of my luckiest day in golf. We are both serious Red Sox fans so I still cherish the souvenir that Judge Powers brought back for me from Red Sox Spring Training in Florida.

He knew that I attended Opening Day at Fenway Park every year and that I would always meet some guys on the corner of Van Ness and Yawkey to eat a pre-game sausage sandwich with peppers and onions. This particular Opening Day happened to fall on Good Friday so Judge Powers was worried about my probable menu selection and insisted that I eat a tuna sandwich as he pointed to the sky proclaiming that I didn't want to get the Big Guy mad at me! He even pulled out some cash to try to pay for my tuna so when I got to the ballpark I kept thinking about how much Judge Powers genuinely cared about me and I couldn't let him down.

Carole A. Coyle was a Criminal Clerk who would eventually be appointed to the position of Assistant Clerk-Magistrate of the ADC. Carole, who is now retired, is a very popular and likeable person who had been a conscientious, hardworking and pleasant member of the staff since she was eighteen years old. She took a phone call from a rehabilitation facility that was located in Fall River informing her that a female defendant would not be able to attend the court session as she was detoxing from a heroin addiction. Judge Powers was on the bench when Carole came into Courtroom One to relay the information to me. Judge Powers was in the middle of speaking with two attorneys sidebar as Carole whispered to me so as to not be disruptive. The name of the facility was Star and Judge Powers only overheard part of the conversation as Carole told me that the defendant wouldn't be here because she was in Star. He flashed a quick grin as he asked Carole, "Star Market?"

At one time several of my staff at the WDC were all on the same weight loss plan which involved a point system to keep track of food intake. There always seemed to be desserts and other food items sitting on top of a table in the middle of the walk in vault, out of view of the general public, which is primarily used to hold criminal cases and office supplies. Different points were assigned to various snacks so it was common to see a number written on yellow sticky notes attached to a bag of pretzels or other provisions. Judge Powers walked into the vault and quickly noticed an open bag of potato chips with a sticky note listing the potential damage - five points. Judge Powers, who likes to eat as much as I do, looked at me and laughed as he said, "Five points, you don't want to be the low scorer!"

Judge Powers did an outstanding job of rendering justice in his many years in the court system and is now enjoying a well-deserved retirement with his lovely wife Holly.

Carole Coyle went to assist a man standing at the counter in the ADC who was visiting from France. He wanted directions to somewhere in the city so Carole kindly joined him outside of the office and led him to the end of the hallway where it would be easier to point out the correct street through the double glass doors. There was a bit of a language barrier, but he seemed to understand her so far. Carole wanted to know where he had left his car to facilitate her directions so she asked him where he had parked. Apparently he didn't have a car so he just pointed down with both hands and explained in his French accent, "I am with my feet."

A jury court was established on the second floor of the ADC in the early 1990's. Prior to that victims, defendants, attorneys, police and witnesses had to drive to Fall River to have a case heard by a jury so it was much more convenient for everyone to have justice served in Attleboro. A criminal defendant has a right to a jury trial and even though most cases are resolved without one the defendant's right to be judged by a jury of his or her peers is a sacred tenet of our system that was fought for by our Founding Fathers. Courthouse staff including Brenda L. Quinn, the gregarious Probation Department Office Manager, Janice P. Johnson, the ebullient DA's Victim Witness Advocate Supervisor, and Carole Coyle coordinated and supervised the tremendous clerical work and administrative functions, including the recall of outstanding warrants from Fall River, which went into the preparation and creation of the jury court in Attleboro. Their dedication and prominent role in this process helped to resolve unique issues with the transition from the previous court and ensured the success of the new court from the beginning.

The Honorable John B. Leonard, who was appointed by Governor Edward J. King, was assigned to sit in the new jury court and I was his session clerk. The judge was a former Assistant District Attorney in Bristol County and also served as an attorney for the Federal Communications Commission in Washington, D.C. which was probably at the root of one of his many famous expressions that he would use to recognize simplicity, "This isn't an FCC case counsel!" Whatever Judge Leonard lacked in physical stature was made up for with his booming voice and decisive actions. He sometimes wore a gruff exterior demeanor that hid a big heart with his terrific sense of humor rating second to none on and off the bench. I had to try hard not to laugh from his comments while writing down criminal sentences as fast as I could to keep up with his brisk tempo. In its infancy, the court would have forty cases scheduled for trial on many days when the reality is that the jury only has time to hear one. Cases were being resolved at a record pace as the backlog was slowly but surely being diminished. Guys were going to jail in such a hurry that court officers kept extra handcuffs close by. I wrote so fast that I didn't even have time to look at faces as I read the sentence to a defendant and quickly reached for the next file. My hands were moving faster than a shoplifter on Christmas Eve while I actually kept an extra pen handy as I really thought that I might run out of ink at any given moment.

Court Officers Howie Werman and Tim Ahern, both enthusiastic pros with a great sense of humor, were brought in to handle the security responsibilities for the new court.

The assigned prosecutor was Assistant District Attorney Kevan J. Cunningham who would later be appointed to a judgeship by Governor William F. Weld. Kevan with an A, as we called him, was one of the top ADA's in Bristol County and would eventually be appointed as the First Justice of the Taunton District Court and then as the Regional Administrative Justice where he continued to serve with extraordinary distinction until his recent retirement. He became my boss in that position and I couldn't have asked for a better one. Judge Cunningham is smart, funny, fair, considerate, experienced and caring. Although he is a legal genius, he remains grounded with a genuine hand shake and a quick smile. Judge Cunningham would be as comfortable having a conversation in the White House as he would be in a homeless shelter as he was one of the most admired and well respected members of the judiciary. He was without a doubt one of the greatest judges in the system and one of the best all-around guys that I have ever known. It was a lot of fun working with him in the jury court and it was my honor to serve under him after we had both been promoted.

Some defendants have trouble keeping up with the payment schedule for their fines. The Probation Department used to collect the fines that were ordered by a judge and would give a defendant an extension when warranted if an honest effort were being made to make payments. I have never seen a judge be unreasonable in the enforcement of money collection, but it should come as no surprise that many defendants ignore their responsibility to pay a fine, costs or what is much worse - restitution because that money goes toward making a victim whole. Many don't even bother to show up in court to ask for an extension which results in the issuance of a warrant. A defendant stood before Judge Leonard after being arrested on a warrant for failing to make restitution payments for over a year. His nonchalant wise guy attitude presented a portrait of disrespect as he answered Judge Leonard's only question. The judge read him the riot act for ignoring his obligation and then asked how he was going to pay the money. The defendant spoke in an arrogant tone and said, "The check's in the mail." Judge Leonard pointed to the prisoner's dock and said, "It's in the mail! OK, go have a seat in the Post Office!"

I was speaking with a couple of attorneys in the hallway outside of Courtroom Two when Judge Leonard came walking up behind me. We all had a good laugh when the judge leaned in toward me and said, "These guys are both lawyers Eddie, watch your wallet!"

I announced a criminal case, but the defendant was not present which usually calls for the immediate issuance of a default warrant. The defendant's attorney was present, however, and asked the judge to hold off on the warrant as his client may be a little late because he is probably trying to find the courthouse. Judge Leonard unfurled the defendant's three foot long criminal record and said, "Counsel I think your client knows where the court is located!"

A handcuffed defendant stood before Judge Leonard after having been arrested on a default warrant for failing to appear. His attitude was less than exemplary as his excuse for ignoring his court date was that he didn't have a ride. Judge Leonard feigned sympathy as he told him that we would get him a free ride for his next appearance causing the defendant to temporarily imagine that he had stumbled into some new perk. His smile quickly disappeared when realizing that the free ride was in the Sheriff's van for transport from the House of Correction!

A defendant, who was going to be needing money, was standing in open court with his mother behind him. The mother opened her purse and took out a fistful of twenty dollar bills to see if she had enough causing Judge Leonard to proclaim, "Hey lady, put that cash away in front of all these lawyers!"

A defendant was standing behind his attorney as the lawyer addressed Judge Leonard in open court when the judge noticed the disrespectful defendant smirking and not taking the mater seriously. Judge Leonard immediately declared, "Counsel, I'll put your client in the can for so long that even a Habe won't get him out!"

If Judge Leonard gave a defendant a break on a reduced sentence, for instance, I would announce the disposition just before he would tell the guy, "That's the only break your getting so when you get out of jail don't come back and ask me for a pension!"

When a defendant would complain that he didn't want to go to jail Judge Leonard would tell him, "If you want to dance you've got to pay the fiddler!"

The state would provide lunch for the impaneled jurors so the court officers would call a local sub shop to place the order early enough to ensure delivery by the 1:00PM recess. The jurors would be entitled to a regular sub sandwich, chips and a drink - nothing fancy, but a good quality lunch before returning to hear more testimony. After lunch everyone would be assembled in the courtroom except the jurors who would enter last after the court officer announced, "All Rise, Jury Entering", as the panel found their way back to their seats. Most of the jurors had just consumed turkey, chicken or some other kind of sub and always had a surprise laugh when Judge Leonard asked them, "How was the lobster?"

Then there was the defendant who wanted to ask Judge Leonard for a public defender, but his request was just a little bit off as he said that he wanted a public offender!

J. Do was called for jury duty on a day when Judge Leonard was on the bench. The beginning part of the jury selection process involves a series of questions from the judge to the potential jurors to weed out any potential conflicts. J. Do raised her hand after being asked if she knew anyone involved with the case because the defendant's lawyer was Attorney Roger M. Ferris, a gifted advocate and great guy who had invited us to his office parties that he hosted right down the street. She was asked to approach the bench and imagined some heavy legal inquiry as she came to the sidebar, but Judge Leonard speaking in a hushed tone asked her, "You're quite a bit younger than your husband aren't you Mrs. Doherty?" It was determined that she was qualified for the jury so I actually had to swear in my own wife!

I was honored to attend the State House swearing in ceremony for Judge Kevan J. Cunningham upon his appointment to the bench. He took the oath of office before a huge audience of family and friends including Kevan's lovely wife Sheila who serves as a Bristol County Assistant District Attorney in Juvenile Court. Sheila comes from an extremely talented and incredibly accomplished family. Her late father overcame great obstacles to rise up and graduate from Harvard Law School with seven of his eight children following his lead to become attorneys. The only one who didn't go to law school became a doctor! Kevan is one of those rare people that you never hear anyone say a bad word about so I'm sure that anyone who knows him was ecstatic that he went from ADA Cunningham to Judge Cunningham.

An impressive array of influential speakers took turns praising Judge Cunningham from the powerful microphone at the Speaker's rostrum in the House Chamber. Kevan had previously served as an Assistant Attorney General so it was nice to hear from his erstwhile boss, former Attorney General James M. Shannon who had previously been elected to the United States Congress and had quickly become one of the select few young Representatives who genuinely had the ear of Speaker Tip O'Neill.

Bristol County District Attorney Paul F. Walsh Jr. stole the show with some heartfelt and funny stories about the new judge. Judge Cunningham had been one of the top ADAs under DA Walsh and the story of his job interview was hilarious. Paul Walsh had won the election, but had not yet been sworn into office as the new District Attorney so he met Kevan in a sub shop in New Bedford to recruit him. They shared a pizza as the soon to be DA interviewed Kevan for a job by elaborating on his vision of prosecution and the future of the office. Paul did most of the talking as Kevan ate pizza and listened to a lengthy and powerful presentation. Paul really wanted Kevan as a top assistant and said that they could do great things together. Paul was hopeful that Kevan would accept the position, envisioning them working in unison to form the nucleus of a great team and do positive things for the people of Bristol County. Kevan had hardly uttered a word as he listened and they finished the pizza. Paul was now satisfied that he had said enough about his philosophy on trying cases, law enforcement, criminal justice and the court system. It was now time to hear from Kevan so he asked the future judge if he had any questions. Kevan looked right into Paul's eyes and said, "Yes, I have a question. Can we order another pizza?"

After Judge Cunningham retired we were invited and honored to attend his portrait unveiling in Courtroom One of the Taunton District Court. J. Do and I joined Judge Cunningham's family, colleagues and many friends for the historic occasion where Father Edward A. Murphy of St. Andrew the Apostle Parish in Taunton led us in prayer. The quick-witted priest from Cork, Ireland had the audience laughing at some of his observations of the man of the hour. We heard humorous and heartfelt remarks from retired Massachusetts Appeals Court Chief Justice Phillip Raposa who served as the MC and whose impressive career, including endeavors in international criminal justice, warrants a book in itself. Judge Raposa had been appointed to the district court and superior court bench by Governor William F. Weld. He was later appointed to the Appeals Court by Governor A. Paul Cellucci and as Chief Justice by Governor Mitt Romney. I was always impressed with his keen intellect, fairness and compassion when I served as his session clerk in Attleboro when he was a District Court Judge. District Courts Chief Justice Paul C. Dawley seemed to represent the thoughts of everyone present in his powerful speech praising the high standards of judicial excellence and admirable quality of compassion for which Judge Cunningham is known. The funniest speaker of the day was Judge Cunningham himself who regaled the audience with amusing anecdotes and interesting stories from his years of service. The beautiful portrait of Judge Cunningham was finally revealed to be a distinguished rendering of the brilliant yet humble jurist who always did the right thing. It had been concealed during the ceremony by an enlarged photo of the guest of honor taken when he was two years old sporting a bow tie and a big smile. The ever self-effacing Judge Cunningham commented that the childhood photo had been taken when he still had a full head of hair!

Attorney Louis S. Xifaras is a terrific lawyer and an unassuming guy. Lou and his lovely wife Maxine invited us to a party at their home in Mansfield so we were mingling with some of the other guests and enjoying the night.

J. Do had answered a lady's question by telling her that we lived only a couple of miles away from the party. An hour later the same lady was within earshot as J. Do spotted the dessert table and announced, "I think I'll get a sweet." The surprised woman asked J. Do, "I thought you lived just down the road. Why do you need a hotel suite?"

Raymond L. Flynn was an All American basketball player at Providence College before being selected in the fourth round of the NBA draft by the Syracuse Nationals, the franchise that would later become the Philadelphia 76ers. The 76ers traded his NBA rights to his hometown Boston Celtics where he was the last man cut on a very talented team.

He has spent his entire life devoted to helping others in such noteworthy endeavors as a neighborhood street worker for Youth Activities, Stonehill College Head Baseball and Basketball Coach, Boston City Councilor, Suffolk County Superior Court Probation Officer, State Representative, Mayor of the City of Boston and his current avocation - volunteer baseball and soccer coach for special needs children which he says is, "the best job I ever had."

After making his mark with a reputation of hard work and honest representation he went on to be reelected Mayor of the City of Boston two more times and had been chosen by his colleagues as the National President of the United States Conference of Mayors. Mayor Flynn resigned during his third term when appointed by President Bill Clinton as the United States Ambassador to the Holy See.

As previously mentioned he was one of our best speakers at our Law Day Ceremonies, told some hilarious stories and was universally loved by all. Mayor Flynn was our Keynote Speaker that day in 2012 and I had asked United States Senator Scott P. Brown to say a few words as our Special Guest. Scott is an exceptional lawyer and a nice guy who would later be appointed United States Ambassador to New Zealand and Samoa by President Donald Trump. His beautiful daughter Ayla, of American Idol fame, did a terrific job of singing our National Anthem. They were all great, but I started getting calls from various news agencies the next day inquiring about my political involvement.

Mayor Flynn, as I have always called him, had endorsed Senator Brown in his reelection campaign and had appeared in ads supporting his candidacy that began, I believe, not long before Law Day. Some anonymous gutless coward started spreading lies and dropped a dime on me telling news outlets that the campaign ad was my idea and that I had brought the two men together. Clerk-magistrates are prohibited from political involvement so if true I would be in violation, but it wasn't true. I had known Senator Brown even before he was a State Representative and my brother Chris knew Mayor Flynn much better than I did. I had gotten to know these two political icons independent of each other, had not introduced them to one another and had nothing to do with the TV ad so it was pure coincidence that I had asked them to be part of the same program. Jealousy is an ugly human emotion.

I first met Roger J. Oliveira when he was serving with distinction as an Assistant Clerk-Magistrate of the Southeast Housing Court. Roger is the son of hardworking immigrants who came to America seeking a better life from across the sea. He is a smart and personable patriot who is well liked by everyone. You frequently hear the expression that someone would give you the shirt off his back - Roger really is that guy. Roger played basketball for Salve Regina University in Newport where he was a star point guard and winner of the prestigious John Havlicek Award for the Commonwealth Coast Conference. He had gotten to know Mayor Flynn through his college roommate, the Mayor's son Edward M. Flynn, who would become a Suffolk County Superior Court Probation Officer before being elected President of the Boston City Council.

I have known Attorney Joseph C. Ferreira since he was Chief of Police in Somerset so J. Do and I were very happy when he was elected to the Governor's Council for District 1 succeeding the much beloved Dr. David F. Constantine, who had voted for me. Back when I was working I had lunch with a bunch of guys including Joe more often than with my wife. Joe is a very accomplished lawyer and good friend who continues to insure that the best judicial candidates are screened properly for our court system.

Roger invited me to have dinner at his parent's place in New Bedford so I asked Joe to come and meet some more of his constituents. We had a terrific time that night where I enjoyed meeting one of Roger's many friends - David E. Wojnar who is Chairman of the Acushnet Board of Selectmen, having served on that body for many years and Senior VP of Government Affairs for Provi which is headquartered in Chicago. The real star of the night, however, was Roger's mother who kept coming out of the kitchen with huge platters of all kinds of delicious food! Mrs. Oliveira, a diminutive woman with a big heart, had prepared a veritable feast that could have fed three times as many mouths! There were all different kinds of incredible appetizers, hearty soups and an assortment of delicious entrees that would have made an army happy! She kept going back to get more food for us so Roger burst out laughing upon seeing my stunned expression. After eating for about forty five minutes I was as full as ever when she asked in Portuguese if I wanted more so Roger interpreted and told the kind hearted smiling chef that I said thank you for the wonderful banquet.

Roger told some funny stories that night including when he was at a campaign event for Mayor Flynn, advertised as New England Sports Stars for Ray Flynn at the Corrib Pub in West Roxbury. Many famous sports legends attended to show support for the great Mayor. Somebody asked the Mayor to list the best college basketball players he had ever seen play. Mayor Flynn started naming some all-time greats and may have been a little generous with his last selection, but he was all about making good people feel good and nobody did that better than the future United States Ambassador. His recitation of legendary college players included John Havlicek of Ohio State, Oscar Robertson from the University of Cincinnati, Dave Cowens of Florida State and of course Roger Oliveira of Salve Regina University! Jim Nance said, "Huh, Roger who?"

Mayor Flynn is a columnist and the author of The ACCIDENTAL POPE, a very enjoyable novel written with Robin Moore. Roger, his father Rogerio and mother Maria are all listed on the page of Acknowledgements. Although a brilliant work of fiction, my brother Chris is included in the book and an off duty Swiss Guard even goes out for a drink at the 19th Hole Irish Pub!

Roger started as a Court Officer, doing a tremendous job as he worked his way up to Assistant Clerk-Magistrate and then Acting Clerk-Magistrate. A couple of years after I retired he received a well-deserved promotion when he was appointed Clerk-Magistrate of the Bristol County Juvenile Court by Governor Charlie D. Baker. It is nice when good things happen for a great man so I was extremely happy for Roger and his family.

Unfortunately, tragedy struck not long after the swearing in ceremony. His dad passed away suddenly only two weeks after watching Roger take the oath of office after having been nominated and confirmed to the only lifetime position in the state of Massachusetts. God was with the Oliveira family as Roger's proud father had lived long enough to see the process come to fruition with the appointment of his oldest son by His Excellency, the Governor of the Commonwealth.

Attorney Gerard F. Malone was the ADA in Charge of the District Courts for the Suffolk County District Attorney's Office before going into private practice. He has represented many famous clients from the world of sports and beyond. Gerry is a brilliant lawyer with a dynamic personality and a nice way about him which only serves to increase his rate of success.

Attorney Gerry Malone
(Eric Adler photo, courtesy of The Sun Chronicle*)*

Some court officers had put together a golf tournament for court staff, police, attorneys, ADAs and others. A catered Bar-B-Q was being prepared for the post tournament buffet which featured delicious ribs and many other mouthwatering dishes. This became a topic of conversation as the day wound down and guys were starting to get hungry out on the golf course. Gerry's foursome was way ahead of mine which meant that he would be getting to the food long before me. We passed each other in our golf carts going in opposite directions on the 14th hole so I yelled to Gerry and kiddingly asked him to save me some ribs to which he replied, "Eddie, I hear that the bone is the best part!"

The defendant broke into Liquor World in Franklin where he stole lottery tickets and cigarettes. A police chase ensued and the defendant was eventually apprehended in a stolen motor vehicle. After posting bail in the WDC he was released from the lockup, but not having any transportation he stole a car from the courthouse parking lot and drove to Boston to do more B & E's!

The remarkable Quinn family of southeastern Massachusetts has made many positive contributions to the impartial delivery of justice with unparalleled accomplishments in upholding the highest standards of honesty and fair play. The Honorable Thomas M. Quinn Jr. was a morally sound judge, a great man and a fun guy to be around. Judge Quinn, appointed by Governor Michael S. Dukakis, presided over the Juvenile Court which is located in the lower level of what is now the James H. Sullivan Courthouse in Attleboro. We worked in the same building, but in different courts so I never had the pleasure of attending the session with Judge Quinn although we would frequently pass each other in the hallway and stop to exchange pleasantries for a few minutes. He was a Holy Cross grad and a big sports fan so he would sometimes kid around about a football coach with the same name as mine who had coached the Crusaders. We would discuss the Red Sox and current events until we both had to get back to work. I really enjoyed speaking with the humble jurist who always wore a smile, treated people right and had an upbeat message as he made his way through the halls of justice.

Judge Quinn was the father of seven children, at least three of whom followed him into a career in law. His son Thomas M. Quinn III is a real gentleman and the District Attorney of Bristol County where he does an outstanding job of prioritizing the prosecution of criminal cases for the ultimate protection of the people there. His brother John represented the Ninth Bristol District as a State Representative and is now the highly principled Assistant Dean of Public Interest Law and External Relations at UMass School of Law. Their brother Matthew, an engaging and good-humored man of unrivalled integrity, is the First Assistant Clerk-Magistrate of the Falmouth District Court.

Judge Quinn's brother Jay was a District Court Judge and one of my favorites for many reasons. Judge James M. Quinn, appointed by Governor Michael S. Dukakis, was a very nice guy who knew the law and never thought that he was better than anyone else. I had already witnessed his superior legal ability and dedication in the courtroom when he was an attorney for Mass Defenders so it was no surprise that he was such an articulate judge. I saw him wrestle sometimes with difficult cases when it came to sentencing after a trial and even on admissions of sufficient facts because he worked hard to serve justice as close to perfect as possible. I was privileged to have a front row seat in watching an honorable man do so many good things for so many.

Judge Quinn also had a terrific sense of humor which is a valuable asset in the court system. We see tragedy all day so it is better for your health if you try to laugh when you can. The police had brought in three alleged car thieves that were ready for a bail hearing at the ADC on the Wednesday afternoon before Thanksgiving. Each defendant had an attorney appointed for the purpose of bail only and they all did their best to present their clients in the light most favorable for release, but the ADA was able to show a record of convictions and defaults on all three so Judge Quinn set a high bail. A defendant who cannot post bail is held in custody until his next court appearance at the jail section of the Bristol County House of Correction which was run, at the time, by Sheriff Edward K. Dabrowski. As soon as I announced Judge Quinn's bail decision one of the defendants started complaining to the judge from the prisoner's dock. He was loudly protesting the amount of the bail by stating that he will never come up with the money so he will miss Thanksgiving Dinner at his mother's house. Judge Quinn politely said, "Good luck gentlemen," as the three were being led away by the court officers. The judge then turned to me and said, "I hear Dabrowski puts on a heck of a turkey dinner!"

I felt badly that Judge Quinn had gotten some water trapped in his ear canal one day. He told me that he thought that he had half of New Bedford Harbor swishing through his head. He would tilt his head to the side of the judge's bench in an effort to alleviate the problem to improve his hearing and sometimes he would stand up to do this during the court session. The court officer, upon seeing the judge stand, would loudly announce, "All Rise. Court is now in recess." Judge Quinn would quickly try to wave off the court officer and sit back down followed by the court officer's cry of, "Court is now in session. Please be seated." I think this happened three times that day and the court officer never got used to it.

The quality that I most admired about Judge Quinn was that he had the utmost respect for everyone including the courthouse staff. The traditional time to break for lunch is 1:00PM in every court, but it is entirely up to the judge, thus anyone working in the courtroom has their lunch time governed accordingly. Well-meaning judges try to do what they think is the right thing by asking the session clerk to call one more case at 1:00PM, then another case and this other matter won't take very long so before you know it it's 1:30. The friend you were supposed to meet, the dog you were going to let out or the phone call you were going to make will all have to wait as you hurriedly shove a sandwich down your throat while reviewing a detective's affidavit who is applying for a search warrant. I had the honor of spending many court sessions with Judge Quinn and he always asked me to announce a recess at 1:00 and I mean always. He knew that people had a life and he had such an abiding respect for the courtroom staff that he would interrupt an attorney in mid-sentence at the magic hour to call for a recess. Personal plans could be made when Judge Quinn was sitting so it was nice to feel respected. We were all in agreement - there was nothing that we wouldn't do for Judge Quinn! I always said that Judge Quinn should have been the #1 speaker in judicial seminars for new justices. I wasn't tied to the courtroom during the second half of my career, but I will never forget the innate kindness and huge heart of the great jurist from the Whaling City.

My first contact with Attorney Stephen A. Lechter was in the ADC not long after I was sworn in. Steve is a brilliant lawyer and a fascinating guy with a nice way about him.

The Honorable John J. Dolan, First Justice of the court had designed a Civil Case Conciliation Program that I was asked to administer under his guidance. Local attorneys were kind enough to volunteer their time to participate as Conciliators with a goal toward reducing our Civil back log by bringing parties together in the hope of reaching a settlement. Even where no agreement could be reached there was often a beneficial narrowing of issues that would serve to reduce trial time. Steve Lechter was one of those Conciliators who did an outstanding job of facilitating the speedy delivery of justice through his ability to negotiate, remove emotion from the process, suggest realistic solutions and cause others to be able to find common ground.

Steve has his own law practice with his office situated in the city of Attleboro a stone's throw from the street where I grew up. His superior legal acumen and positive approach to problem solving resulted in a unanimous decision by the Supreme Judicial Court that was extremely favorable to one of his clients and established new case law in Massachusetts. Steve's client was forced off the road by another motorist causing personal injury and damage to his motor vehicle. The insurance company denied the claim because there had been no contact between the vehicles. Steve successfully argued that his client had no other choice but to swerve off the roadway to avoid the other vehicle. He went on to show that there definitely would have been contact caused by the reckless behavior of the other driver if not for the commendable driving skill of his client. His client may have saved lives by this action and should not be penalized for doing the right thing. The Justices agreed making this a landmark case which still stands as good law today. Steve Lechter not only beat an insurance company and saved the day for his client, but established solid case law that continues to ensure justice for anyone finding themselves in a similar situation in the future. The gravity of this important decision has been hailed by some as a vital victory for the proper standards of public safety in the Commonwealth.

Jeffrey A. Wordell and William P. Healy, two of the nicest guys in the system, were both Probation Officers in the ADC. Jeff had a sophisticated and refined voice that sounded like the maître d at Buckingham Palace which belied his mundane nature and kindness driven personality. I was standing next to them in an otherwise empty courtroom one day as they were discussing another member of the court staff who was alleged to be lazy, habitually late and always getting away with all kinds of things that would have cost others their job. They went on and on about her not being held accountable until finally Bill stated, "This is unbelievable. She should be fired!" Jeff, speaking in his somewhat aristocratic tone, responded immediately by saying, "Oh no, we wouldn't want that." A shocked Bill Healy inquired as to why she shouldn't lose her job. We all laughed when Jeff declared, "Because - we want her to stay around. She makes the rest of us look real good!"

WDC First Justice Daniel B. Winslow

The Honorable Daniel B. Winslow was the First Justice of the WDC before leaving for the State House in Boston to become Chief Legal Counsel for Governor Mitt Romney and would later serve as the State Representative for the Ninth Norfolk District. He became the Executive Vice President and Chief Legal Officer of Rimini Street, a Las Vegas global provider of enterprise software and is now President of the New England Legal Foundation. Judge Winslow, pursuant to his responsibility as the First Justice, scheduled a monthly meeting with the chief probation officer, chief court officer, assistant district attorney in charge, and myself. These meetings were always informative, interesting and fun. He had a terrific sense of humor and would produce some funny anecdotes to make extremely dry reports more palatable. He is a legal genius who was always trying to devise some new method for making the court system better for everyone. Even when we disagreed it was always without being disagreeable. We had an abiding respect for each other so I would like to think that we got some good things done together.

I used to fish the east end of the Cape Cod Canal so often that some of the other surfcasters started calling me East End Eddie which I used for my pen name in magazine and newspaper articles as well as for my first two books. Judge Winslow, upon hearing of my pen name and recognizing that the WDC is located on East Street, told J. Do that, never mind East End Eddie, he knew me back when I was East Street Eddie!

Attorney Thomas E. Giblin dispenses great legal advice from his law office in Medfield and tells terrific stories to his legion of friends in courts and venues all over the Commonwealth. Tom is a good natured guy with an outstanding sense of humor who knows the inside background on many of the most famous political events in

Massachusetts history. He regales his audience with interesting stories and unique expressions.

Tom and I were leaving Boston in his car coming home from a Red Sox game along with Norfolk County First Assistant District Attorney Dennis C. Mahoney, a truly nice person who was very helpful to me with prisoner issues involving the four state prisons in my territorial jurisdiction. Tom started to tell a story about a man who apparently was very reserved and shy. Dennis and I had a good laugh as Tom told us that the guy was, "…as quiet as a church mouse!"

Attorney James P. Perkoski had been appointed as a Special Assistant District Attorney for Bristol County and assigned to the ADC for many years. Jim is a very popular, smart, honest and outstanding representative of the Commonwealth. The designation of Special in his title allowed him to be able to practice civil law in addition to his duties as a prosecutor so he deservedly had the best of both endeavors. Jim is still working in the same court today after having been appointed years later as First Assistant Clerk-Magistrate by Mark E. Sturdy, the great Clerk-Magistrate who was appointed by Governor Deval L. Patrick and had previously served as an ADA and Assistant Clerk-Magistrate.

I always admired Jim's calm demeanor during some incredibly hectic days in Courtroom One when there were sometimes so many defendants, attorneys and others that it was standing room only for most of the day. I saw the fruits of his negotiating skill when defendants admitted their guilt and always respected his legal acumen during some hard fought procedural issues before and during criminal trials.

Some might say that the courthouse custodians may have been less than diligent in their cleaning duties, but I always thought that most of the place looked pretty good. ADA Perkoski would stand in the same general area in the courtroom while questioning the witness on the stand or addressing the judge. One afternoon he spotted a rather large portion of what appeared to be a clipped fingernail on the floor just beyond the witness stand. Apparently, he thought someone was clipping their fingernails and, these remains at least, had survived the custodian's dedicated hunt for filth. Jim saw the fingernail the next day and the day after that. The fingernail had found a permanent place next to the delivery of justice as Jim noticed it sitting there for weeks, months and then years whenever he stood in his usual place in the courtroom. The discarded body part kind of became somewhat of a fictitious security blanket for Jim as he jokingly played a little game in his own mind. Whenever he began his closing arguments he only had to look over and see the familiar fingernail to quickly imagine that everything was still right with the world.

Attorney Edward F. Casey was a very successful and prominent lawyer who had been appointed Associate Justice of the Bristol County Probate & Family Court by Governor Edward J. King. He was a friend of my dad and our families knew each other from school and elsewhere. Judge Casey's swearing in was scheduled for Courtroom One at the ADC. Clerk-Magistrate James H. Sullivan asked me to stand next to the Governor and introduce him to the receiving line of hundreds of guests. It was an honor for a 26-year old guy like myself and most especially because I knew that my father and J. Do would be in that line.

The custodians were ordered to clean the court and make everything perfect for the big day. As soon as Jim Perkoski heard where the ceremony would take place he immediately figured that the fingernail's days were numbered and that his security blanket would soon find a new home inside of a vacuum cleaner bag. The swearing in went off without a hitch and Governor King was very gracious with his time. The next time that ADA Perkoski assumed his position in the courtroom he glanced over past the witness stand to look for his long time token of security. Surely it would be gone by now after such lengthy preparations for the Governor and all the dignitaries. What a surprise - the fingernail was still there! The custodians had missed it, he thought, so all remained right with the world!

Sometime later, Jim reached down to pick up the fingernail himself only to realize that it wasn't a discarded fingernail at all. Apparently, at some point a heavy object had fallen on the flooring material imprinting a small, perfectly crescent shaped dent in the floor.

The Caseys are one of the most preeminent and remarkable families to ever come out of the city of Attleboro. Judge Casey's son Edward is a very well respected, popular attorney and his kind hearted sister Jane, one of the smartest kids in our class, was voted the female designation of "Most Likely to Succeed". Their sister Jennifer is an extremely talented attorney who at one time worked for Touchstone Pictures and Walt Disney Pictures where she negotiated and drafted talent deals for motion pictures as well as various production contracts. Judge Casey's other son John was one of the nicest kids at Attleboro High School and would later become an accomplished, honest and highly skilled attorney. J. Do and I were lucky to be able to benefit from his legal expertise when he represented us in a somewhat complex land closing. John is a down to earth guy who has helped countless people in need with his mundane nature allowing him to always poke fun at himself. He was appointed to a judgeship by Governor Mitt Romney and was soon appointed First Justice of the Norfolk County Probate & Family Court, eventually rising to the prestigious position of Chief Justice of the Massachusetts Probate and Family Court, having been appointed by the Honorable Paula M. Carey, Chief Justice of the Trial Court, which put him in charge of every Probate Court in the Commonwealth!

Before becoming a judge, John was gracious enough to agree to testify before the Governor's Council on my behalf and was driving us to the hearing when he took a wrong turn that became only a minor inconvenience. I was sitting in the front passenger seat as John looked over at me and said, "Ed you're the one who's supposed to be nervous and I end up taking a wrong turn!"

Not long after passing the bar exam John was appointed Assistant City Solicitor for the City of Attleboro. It was a unique job as he was like an assistant district attorney, but only for one police department. Serving in this position made John the court prosecutor for the Attleboro Police where he excelled in establishing a reputation of integrity and fairness. He would be praised as the subject of an extremely positive editorial on the Opinion page of *The Sun Chronicle* as a result of his efforts to utilize consecutive as opposed to concurrent criminal sentences in the interests of true justice.

One day the Attleboro Police arrested a shoplifter and brought him to court in custody for arraignment. The defendant was alleged to have stolen some food items from Fernandes Super Market and sprinted out into the parking lot with the police in hot pursuit. As he ran toward the street he realized that the police were gaining on him and closing the gap so he started shoving stolen Hostess Twinkies in his mouth and gobbling them down as he was running. John prepared for a potential bail hearing by reviewing the police report and the defendant's lengthy criminal record as he considered if he should request that the judge set bail in the case.

The defendant was a frequent flyer who was a well-known thief to everyone in the courtroom except visiting Judge C. George Anastos, a Nantucket judge who would sit in Attleboro from time to time, but not often enough to recognize the local criminals. I read the charges to the defendant and entered an automatic not guilty plea just before the judge inquired if the defendant had a record. Assistant Chief Probation Officer Robert A. O'Connell responded with, "Oh yes, Your Honor" as he feigned exhaustion after lifting the volumes of paper listing the defendant's criminal record and handed it to the judge. Judge Anastos, who had been appointed by Governor John A. Volpe, was clearly troubled by the sight of so many convictions. He flipped through pages and read portions of the record aloud while proclaiming in a loud stern voice, "Larceny, Larceny, Larceny, Larceny." This continued for some time until he looked over at the defendant who was handcuffed in the prisoner's dock and asked, "Do you know what they do to people who steal in Iraq?" Judge Anastos' voice seemed to get louder and more determined with every word as the experienced defendant's eyes widened at full attention. "Do you know what happens to a thief in Turkey? Do you know what would happen if you were caught stealing a loaf of bread in Iran?" the judge said. The usually happy-go-lucky defendant was now frozen in fear and unsure if he should speak. Judge Anastos leaned forward toward the defendant and declared, "If you steal over there they will put your arm on a block of wood and take an ax." The judge paused as I noticed the defendant's eyes somehow getting even wider. The judge continued at thundering decibels, "Then the ax will come down and they will chop your hand right off!"

Assistant City Solicitor Casey quickly addressed the court by saying, "We won't be requesting that Your Honor! The Commonwealth is only asking for $50.00 cash bail."

Another Attleboro High School graduate and former Assistant City Solicitor for the City of Attleboro also became a judge. Attorney Robert S. Ovoian was appointed as a District Court Judge by Governor Charlie D. Baker. He is one of the best liked and greatest all-around guys that I have ever known so I was extremely happy, along with everyone, for his appointment to the bench.

After I had retired I happened to be in the New Bedford District Court which is a bustling yet extremely efficient center of justice thanks in no small part to Peter J. Thomas, the great Clerk-Magistrate appointed by Governor A. Paul Cellucci and James B. "JB" Sheerin who does an outstanding job as the First Assistant Clerk-Magistrate. I took a seat in one of the courtrooms to kill some time and immediately noticed that the jurist sitting in this very busy criminal session was none other than Judge Ovoian. After a while he smiled when he saw me sitting toward the back of the courtroom and found me in the building later during the court recess as we enjoyed catching up on old times. Bob played several sports in high school and was a tenacious basketball player. We graduated together and as far as I know, 1973 still stands as the only class in the history of Attleboro High School to produce both a judge and a clerk-magistrate.

Litigants were always treated fairly by the Honorable Ernest I. Rotenberg, appointed by Governor Francis W. Sargent. Judge Rotenberg served as the First Justice of the Bristol County Probate & Family Court where he surrounded himself with policies of kindness and professionalism. Chief Justice John D. Casey had high praise for Judge Rotenberg explaining that, "He was also one of the creators of the pretrial conference which is a fundamental part of our case management system and has been followed in our court departments." He was a legal genius who even did magic tricks for little kids to calm them in the emotion filled atmosphere of a family break up.

I knew some probate judges and staff because we all worked in the same building in Attleboro. The probate judge, seated on the bench in the courtroom, issued his ruling on a divorce case. He addressed the husband and stated, "Sir, I'm going to give your wife $800.00 per month." The man looked up at the judge and said, "Gee, that's awful nice of you your Honor. I'll try to pitch in a little bit myself sometimes!"

Marriage can sometimes produce some funny quotes like this one from Patrick Murray - "I've had bad luck with both my wives. The first one left me and the second one didn't."

Margaret F. "Peggy" Albertson, appointed by Governor Mitt Romney, was the great Clerk-Magistrate of the South Boston Division of the Boston Municipal Court until being appointed to a judgeship by Governor Charlie D. Baker. She is a smart lawyer, a very nice person and a tremendous credit to the court system. Peggy succeeded John E. Flaherty the longtime great Clerk-Magistrate of that court having been appointed by Governor Maurice J. Tobin in 1945. I first met Mr. Flaherty when I attended Executive Board meetings of the Clerk-Magistrates Association with my boss, the Clerk-Magistrate of the ADC, James H. Sullivan. Mr. Sullivan, a past President of the group, was an automatic member of the E-Board so I was always by his side. Being 25 years old put me about 30 years younger than the next youngest person at the table. I listened to about fifteen Clerk-Magistrates from all over the Commonwealth discuss court related relevant issues of the day. Votes were taken by going around the table with each member saying yes or no until it got to me and, being the only nonmember, I would smile and remain silent as I was the only one without a vote. Years later, however, as mentioned previously, I was honored to accept appointment to this esteemed body myself by the Clerk-Magistrate of the Somerville District Court, President Ted Tomasone.

Mr. Flaherty was a great guy who had been previously employed in some very interesting jobs. Running as a Democrat, the witty Irish American had been elected as a State Representative and served as the Minority Leader of the Massachusetts House of Representatives. The Democrats were not yet in the majority back in those days or Mr. Flaherty would have been elected Speaker of the House.

He had also been appointed to the position of official Greeter for the City of Boston by Mayor Maurice J. Tobin who would later be elected Governor of Massachusetts. A holiday was coming up that was celebrated by Polish Americans so the Mayor wanted to firm up his support in that community by paying homage to General Casimir Pulaski who had fought against the British in the Revolutionary War. He asked Mr. Flaherty to throw a memorial wreath off a Boston bridge in honor of the Polish born war hero whose Calvary tactics were credited with protecting the retreating troops of General George Washington at the Battle of Brandywine Creek. Mr. Flaherty put a nice wreath in the trunk of the car and drove to the nearest bridge that night. This was during World War II so all American bridges were being guarded by our soldiers to thwart any potential sabotage efforts by the Nazis. Mr. Flaherty parked the car near the bridge and proceeded to open the trunk when an American soldier pointed a rifle at him while yelling, "Halt, who are you and why are you here?" Mr. Flaherty told the soldier that he wanted to throw a wreath off of the bridge to which the startled soldier, thinking there was a body in the trunk, replied, "Don't move! You're not throwing Aretha off of my God Damned bridge!"

Mr. Flaherty hosted a tremendous St. Patrick's Day party at the South Boston Court every year on a Sunday when the facility was closed. We would enjoy the party inside and then watch the parade from a reviewing stand in front of the courthouse. One time J. Do was standing there between myself and Boston Mayor Kevin H. White as we watched the enormous parade proceed by in front of us. One of the guys in the parade yelled up to us, "Remember to get your Irish Flu Shot - Guinness!"

Sean P. Murphy is the great Clerk-Magistrate of the West Roxbury Division of the Boston Municipal Court. He was serving as an Assistant Clerk-Magistrate when Governor Deval L. Patrick made the court system a much better organization by elevating him to the lifetime post. Sean's warm smile, sincere handshake, superior intellect and innate sense of fairness have positively affected the lives of countless defendants, victims, witnesses, staff and attorneys since his first day in office. Sean always does the right thing regardless of pressure or what may be the popular way out. If courage, kindness, humor and fairness were listed together in the dictionary there should be an accompanying photo of Sean Murphy.

I was sitting next to Sean at one of these aforementioned conferences that was held at The College of the Holy Cross in Worcester which just happens to be his alma mater. Sean accidently bumped into his coffee cup and spilled the contents on the table in front of our seats. We thanked the nice waitress who came over with a towel and cleaned it up. By sheer coincidence Sean had a Holy Cross class reunion the very next day which was held in the same room and he ended up being seated at the same table. Somehow Sean managed to spill his coffee again and the very same waitress came over one more time for the clean up! Sean apologized as the waitress, upon recognizing him from the previous day, wore an expression of shock and disbelief!

Sean and I were sitting near each other on a couch in the lobby of a Nantucket hotel during a Clerk-Magistrates' Conference. Wives, girlfriends, and others were out shopping so Sean and I were having a conversation while I was waiting for J. Do to return. My better half soon walked in with the rest of the radiant shoppers and told us that she had bought Seven7 Jeans for $50.00. Neither Sean nor I realized that Seven7 was a brand name for the clothing so Sean, quite impressed with my bride's bargain hunting skills rhetorically asked, "You got seven pairs of jeans for 50 bucks? Wow!"

Sean comes from an extremely talented family with siblings making their positive mark in many professions including his sister Liz who retired as a sergeant from the Massachusetts State Police. She completed the Police Academy in the same class as Maureen Kearney who would also retire as a sergeant and was the sister of Natick District Court Clerk-Magistrate Brian J. Kearney.

The wonderful nurses at Tobey Hospital in Wareham were preparing me for my colonoscopy as I had a conversation with Dr. Kevin R. Murphy who I had just met for the first time. I was almost sure that we had never met before, but there was something very familiar about his voice, facial expressions and laugh. I just couldn't put it together as the anesthesia was starting to take effect and the room was beginning to slow down. Just before I went out Dr. Murphy noticed my job listed on the chart and told me that his brother Sean was the Clerk-Magistrate of the West Roxbury Court! It was the last thing said before Dr. Murphy operated on me so when I woke up I wasn't sure if I had heard correctly until we had another conversation. He is a highly skilled physician and an extremely nice man so the incredible talent in that classy family goes far beyond the field of law.

A middle aged woman came in for her hearing for bad checks with the assistance of her service dog. I offered her a seat as her beautiful yellow lab sat down on the floor next to the chair. I asked the lady to please raise her right hand to be sworn and as soon as she raised her hand the dog raised his right paw. I administered the oath with the lady responding in the affirmative and the yellow lab let out a ruff! I know the dog didn't lie!

Each morning the public side of the counter in a District Court Clerk-Magistrate's Office is crowded with people being serviced by a devoted staff of hard working professionals who are processing criminal complaints and other legal documents to be ready for the opening of the court session at 9:00AM. Attorneys, police prosecutors, assistant district attorneys, victims, defendants, plaintiffs, witnesses and others are crammed into a relatively small area at the counter to ascertain information such as where their case will be heard so that they can go to the correct courtroom. Many of these people are understandably unsure of the process and can sometimes be extremely confused. I asked a gentleman if I could help him, but he seemed even more confused than most so sometimes it is best to start with the basics. I usually begin by asking if the case is civil or criminal. The word "civil" didn't seem to get a response so I asked him if it was a criminal case. As soon as he heard "criminal" he said, "Oh no, I didn't hit him that hard!"

Every morning the priority for the Clerk-Magistrate's Office is to process the arrests from the night before for the arraignment session. The data gathering component for this procedure has improved dramatically over the years with the advent of the universal use of fax machines and computers. Back in the day, when I was appointed to the ADC, arrest information was taken over the phone in the morning from the police by our staff. The five police departments in our district would be called with our staff hurriedly writing down information relayed on the phone by each police prosecutor. The defendant's name, address, date of birth and offenses were hand written on a separate piece of paper for each arrest with this information eventually being used to provide the data to type the criminal complaints. These phone calls could sometimes be quite lengthy with the process of speaking on the phone with the police called "taking arrests."

Attorney Theodore J. Koban, a very nice man and an excellent lawyer whose office is directly across the street from the courthouse, called early one morning wanting to speak with Nancy Clarke who at the time was the hardworking and dedicated Office Manager. Kim Eames was a very nice Criminal Clerk who is now a Registered Nurse in the Emergency Room at Sturdy Memorial Hospital. Attorney Koban asked to speak with Nancy and was told by Kim, who had answered the phone, that she was not available. Kim told him, "I'm sorry, Nancy is taking arrests," to which Attorney Koban inquired, "She's taking a rest! It's only 8:30 in the morning. Is she tired already?"

The session clerk in the courtroom asked the defendant to raise his right hand to be sworn. The defendant must have thought that he was being arrested again because he raised both hands!

I was leaving in my car to head home at the end of the day and noticed a pair of women's high heels sitting in an empty space in the WDC parking lot. Who knows what that story was!

Attorney Peter E. Padula of Franklin is an outstanding lawyer and one of the nicest guys that I have ever known. I have always enjoyed his company because of his kindness and low key yet terrific sense of humor. I was also good friends with his Uncle John Padula who was affectionately referred to as the Master. John was a generous and well known philanthropist who had quietly helped many in need. He did Jimmy Durante impressions and was a natural born entertainer. I used to eat at his Franklin home, along with about a dozen other friends, on Wednesday nights where The Master would cook up an incredible feast while regaling us with stories and song. The Master had a golf tournament every year so we all got to say that we played in The Masters! He was a great golfer with an unusual swing as he actually would hit himself in the head with the golf club shaft on the backswing, but the ball would usually go straight down the middle of the fairway. He was a great man whom I was honored to call a friend.

We were playing golf one day when the Master got a phone call from one of his tenants who was complaining that there was a mouse in the living room of his apartment. The guy wanted to know what was going to be done about the rodent. I heard John tell the guy on the phone, "That mouse isn't paying rent so throw him out!"

The Master was trying to collect rent from an uncooperative tenant when an argument ensued. The guy's German shepherd attacked John in the hallway where he lost his eyeglasses and wristwatch in the process of making his escape. The Master let out a hearty laugh when I called him the next day and told him that I just saw a dog walking by the courthouse wearing eyeglasses and a nice wristwatch!

Judge Frank Crimmins, author, John Padula, comedian Scott Record, John's daughter Diane

The Master paid for his nephew Peter's tuition for law school which led to a memorable situation in the Massachusetts Supreme Judicial Court. After Peter graduated from law school and passed the Massachusetts Bar Exam he had to go to be sworn in at the SJC in Boston along with all of the others in the same situation. All of those about to become new attorneys were asked to raise their right hands to be sworn. The Master was proudly standing behind Peter as all of the right hands were raised when the thought crossed his mind that since he had paid the tuition for law school that he should be a lawyer too. The Master raised his right hand along with everyone else and took the oath himself!

Pete is not only a terrific lawyer, but he was a star baseball player and all-around athlete as well so he decided to try out for the boxing team while in college. He told his Uncle John that he was going to take up boxing to which the wise cracking Master replied, "Boxing! What are you boxing - oranges?"

I heard many of Attorney Padula's cases over the years including a felony allegation where Pete represented a man from Ireland who was charged with assault & battery by means of a dangerous weapon, to wit: an Irish Shillelagh. He hit a guy with it three times and it broke on the third blow. Pete said that it was very important to his client that it be known to me that the Shillelagh had been made in America because if it had been made in Ireland it wouldn't have broken no matter how many times he had hit the guy!

Nobody ever did more to help veterans than Veterans Service Officer Dale L. Kurtz, a West Point Grad and a terrific guy. I was fortunate to have hundreds of nice people participate in Court Cards for Combat which I put together in support of our troops overseas for the Christmas season. Court staff, attorneys, police, firefighters and others would write Christmas cards to our men and women in the military and drop them off at the court. Walpole Police Detective Prosecutor Bill Madden's contacts as well as some others including Cape Cod 4 the Troops assisted me in getting the huge shipment delivered and distributed in Afghanistan and other far away outposts to reach Americans in uniform. Local school teachers had kids write thousands of holiday greetings during class to show appreciation for the sacrifices made by those protecting our nation so that we could continue living freely in the greatest country on the face of the earth. Mark R. Jeffries was the great Clerk-Magistrate of Southeast Housing Court who was appointed by Governor Mitt Romney. Mark is a terrific guy who was always very helpful in personally delivering boxes of cards to our court every year. His wife Catherine is a teacher and could always be counted on for an enormous batch of cards from her students as I remain grateful to her and so many others for their dedicated endeavors. A second grader wrote, "Dear Soldier, please be careful of the Taliban because those evil bastards might sneak up behind you!"

The Honorable Emogene Johnson Smith was the First Justice of the WDC during the last years of my time there. She was a fair minded judge who called 'em like she saw 'em with a flair for style as one of the best dressed ladies in the Commonwealth. The black robe hid her colorful, classy outfits so those in the courtroom never got to appreciate her dynamic fashion sense. Ema, appointed by Governor A. Paul Cellucci and sworn in by Governor Jane M. Swift, is a kind person who was thoughtful enough to come to one of my surfcasting seminar book signings at Bass Pro Shops in Foxborough where I was happy to inscribe and sign a book for her.

Ema, who is African American, grew up in the state of Mississippi so she knew firsthand about the injustice and horrors of racial discrimination. She attended segregated public schools until graduating from high school and had a front row seat to some of the defining moments of the civil rights movement.

After graduating from law school and passing the bar exam she was appointed as an Assistant District Attorney for the District Courts in Suffolk County by legendary District Attorney Newman A. Flanagan. District Attorney Flanagan was amongst the many dignitaries who attended Judge Johnson Smith's swearing in as the First Justice where the oath of office was administered by the Honorable Lynda M. Connolly, Chief Justice of the Massachusetts District Courts. Chief Justice Connolly, who had been appointed by

Governor William F. Weld, is a nice person and a terrific judge so we were privileged to have her in Wrentham. I remain grateful to her for appointing me to the Massachusetts District Court Task Force on Security at a perilous time in the court system and the world. I was honored to serve as the MC of this event and pleased to see so many of Ema's friends and colleagues turn out for this momentous occasion.

I spent a lot of time putting together our annual Courthouse Speaker Series, Law Day and other events so I will always remain grateful to Ema for giving me complete latitude with the selection of speakers and creation of the entire program. The First Justice is the head of each district court so it would have been extremely difficult and onerous if I had been required to seek her permission every time for the hundreds of phone calls and emails that were needed for our events. I truly appreciate the trust that Ema had in me.

Her husband Jerry is a retired Boston Firefighter who, Ema told me, has to sign a document every year attesting to the fact that he is still alive and thus continues to qualify for his pension! I gave Ema some striped bass filets which Jerry used to cook a meal that he hadn't eaten in a while. Ema told me he loved his grits with the fish I caught that morning at 5AM before court so it doesn't get any fresher than that!

The monthly management team meetings in the office of the First Justice were always interesting with Ema because we got the business of the court taken care of and had a lot of laughs along the way. One day most of our team were seated in Ema's office sharing some stories as we waited for the Assistant DA to join us so that the meeting could begin. These meetings would sometimes be attended by different people with the assistant chief probation officer, for instance, in place of the chief probation officer and so on. Ema and I had been conversing and laughing with the others when the ADA came in and had a seat. Ema wanted to start the meeting, but it somehow slipped her mind as to where I worked. She looked around the room and said, "OK, I guess the only one we are missing is a representative of the Clerk-Magistrate's Office." I had been sitting right next to her for 20 minutes so I smiled at Ema and said, "I work in the Clerk-Magistrate's Office." Her jaw dropped as she apologized profusely for her minor gaffe. I laughed and told her not to worry about it as I had made much worse mistakes when she turned to the window behind her desk and proclaimed, "I just feel like jumping right out of this window!" I was glad she didn't because she was an outstanding judge and is still a good friend.

I used to go home after work and try to forget some of the horrific testimony that I had heard in court, but cases involving the abuse of children and animals seemed to find a permanent place in my mind. There are many cases much worse than the one I am about to describe, but this stands out for being extremely unusual. A corrections officer working in a watchtower high over MCI Norfolk noticed something outside of the prison off in the distance. He focused his binoculars to see a dog running loose with something that appeared to be taped in his mouth. The animal control officer responded and found the poor canine with a TV remote control shoved almost down his throat that was being held in place by heavy tape wrapped around the dog's closed mouth. The poor mutt was part collie with a snout long enough to contain most of the remote.

The dog owner appeared at the hearing, but didn't contest the facts of the case. The 40-year old defendant began his defense by telling me he loved that dog. He said that the dog kept grabbing the clicker off a table so he taped it inside its mouth to teach it a lesson. Maybe the defendant learned a lesson when I issued a criminal complaint for cruelty to animals with a quick arraignment date.

Some unique circumstances were created as a result of having another state bordering portions of our territorial jurisdiction. The North Attleborough Police were chasing a kid in a stolen car who would not stop. The suspect was 17 years old which, at the time, meant that he was an adult in Massachusetts. The police pursued the stolen vehicle with the young man behind the wheel from North Attleborough into Cumberland, Rhode Island. He was eventually apprehended and placed under arrest, but the criminal adult age threshold in Rhode Island is 18 so as soon as he crossed the state line he became a juvenile. I think it was about 2:00 AM when the North Attleborough Police called me to discuss this unusual circumstance with a view toward my making a bail decision. This situation presented a multitude of questions in gray areas to which there is probably no absolute definitive answer. I told the officer that the defendant would still be charged as an adult in Massachusetts, but the arrest, custody rules, and rendition proceedings would have to be governed by Rhode Island juvenile law. I had no authority to set bail on a defendant in another state, but the defendant had been drinking so the Cumberland Police held him in protective custody thereby obviating the need for any further involvement on my part. The defendant waived rendition in a Rhode Island courtroom the next day and was returned to face adult criminal charges in Massachusetts.

If you work in the court system long enough you will eventually hear every imaginable excuse for everything and some will be true! A defendant at the counter was late for court and had already been defaulted with a warrant ordered for his arrest. As one of our staff was retrieving his case to be brought back into the courtroom he said, "I drove by the courthouse three times. I didn't know it was a court. I thought it was a Masonic Temple!"

Bob Halpin, a great guy in a busy forum, serves in the finest tradition of public service as the Court Administrator of the United States Immigration Court in Boston. Under his signature on notes or letters to me he would always write - A Federal Clerk!

Judge John H. O'Neil was a brilliant legal scholar with a huge heart. He served with distinction as an Assistant Clerk-Magistrate in Bristol County Superior Court before being appointed to the bench by Governor Edward J. King. He was one of the very few judges who had previously worked in a Clerk-Magistrate's Office which I think colored his perception of the entire system in a very positive way. Maybe I'm partial to clerk-magistrates and assistants, but I have always thought that prior experience in one of those positions produced some of the very best judges in the system. Judge O'Neil really cared about the court staff as he knew what they were going through because he had been there himself. There have been other outstanding jurists with experience as clerk-magistrates and assistants including Judge Paul K. Leary, appointed by Governor William F. Weld; Judge Dennis P. Sargent, appointed by Governor Deval L. Patrick; Judge Stephen S. Abany, appointed by Governor Mitt Romney; Judge Richard A. Eustis, Judge Douglas J. Darnbrough, Judge Joseph P. Hurley III, Judge Margaret F. Albertson and Judge Michelle L. Kelley who were all appointed by Governor Charlie D. Baker. The aforementioned Judge Thomas M. Quinn Jr. and Judge John E. McDonald Jr. had that experience as well. Judge O'Neil spoke in a somewhat aristocratic manner which belied his mundane nature and keen sense of humor. He was an honorable man and a really good guy whose his photo should be in the dictionary next to the word "class."

I was about to start my morning as his session clerk on a busy day in Courtroom Two in Attleboro as I waited in the judge's lobby for Judge O'Neil to use the men's room. The water for the toilet in this antiquated facility would continue to run long after flushing so Judge O'Neil tried to make some adjustments to the mechanism in an effort to alleviate the problem, but to no avail. Finally, he came out of the men's room, looked at me and said, "Let's go into court Eddie. I didn't come here to fix the plumbing!"

One day I was serving as the session clerk with Judge O'Neil in Courtroom One for the Small Claims hearings long before the law changed authorizing clerk-magistrates and assistants to hear these cases. I had just called a case and sworn in the parties when Sally Bruno, now Sally Linton, came in to the courtroom to quickly inform me that I was needed elsewhere. I had to interrupt Judge O'Neil to tell him that I was leaving the court because my wife was about to give birth to our first baby. "Go", he said.

Judge O'Neil would sit in courts all over the region, but was not in Attleboro very often. The next time he returned was two years later which just happened to be on the same day that J. Do was going into labor with our second child. We only have two children, but due to the circumstance Judge O'Neil thought that we must have several. I remember him commenting that every time he comes to Attleboro my wife is having a baby and then asking, "Eddie, how many children do you have anyway - about a dozen or so?"

Some of the towns from both of the courts to which I was appointed bordered the state of Rhode Island so my brother Brendan and I often discussed similarities and differences in the two systems as well as attorneys and defendants that were familiar to both of us. One time Brendan was working on an organized crime case that alleged a RICO charge in Rhode Island with the defendant working in my judicial district in Massachusetts. At the time, Brendan was a detective corporal with the Rhode Island State Police Intelligence Unit which was tasked with the investigation of La Cosa Nostra and other related organized criminal activity. Brendan arrested the defendant and transported him to the ADC where I was serving as the First Assistant Clerk-Magistrate. The defendant was arraigned as a fugitive from justice by Judge O'Neil.

Judge O'Neil would pass away many years later, but not before becoming First Justice of the Fall River District Court and later seeing his son John appointed as Clerk-Magistrate of the same court by Governor Deval L. Patrick. John is a terrific guy, outstanding lawyer and great Clerk-Magistrate who carries on the family tradition of judicial excellence with fairness, common sense, humor and compassion.

The defendant waived interstate rendition, essentially agreeing to be transported to the state of Rhode Island in the custody of my brother. The rendition waiver was signed by the defendant, Judge O'Neil, Brendan and myself. It was really a routine process that is sometimes repeated a few times per week, but since it was so unusual to have brothers signing the same legal document involving two different states I knew that our mother would be very proud because she absolutely lived for this kind of thing. I showed her a copy of the rendition waiver bearing the signatures of two of her sons which brought a smile to her face as she beamed with pride in relating this story to anyone who would listen!

Working as a paid LBJ Intern for Congressman James A. Burke in Washington during part of my junior year in college was the experience of a lifetime. I remember walking by the United States Supreme Court with a genuine sense of awe and respect as I thought of the monumental decisions made in that hallowed chamber and how they affect the lives of every American.

Katharine Whittemore wrote a fascinating review in the September 30, 2012 issue of *The Boston Sunday Globe* on *The SUPREME COURT: A C-SPAN BOOK FEATURING THE JUSTICES IN THEIR OWN WORDS*. Edited by Brian Lamb, Susan Swain and Mark Farkas, the book reveals many interesting facets of the storied institution. She explains that, "The Lawyers Lounge, where attorneys do last-minute prep, is stocked with cough drops and aspirin. William Suter, the Clerk of the Supreme Court, was in basic training with Elvis Presley." We also learn that there is a basketball court on the fifth floor of the building, high above the deliberations of justice, which she quotes as being called, "the highest court in the land."

Unfortunately, for multiple reasons, there are many repeat offenders in the court system. Some guys get paroled, then convicted of a new crime and get sent right back to jail for a few years. We used to say that defendants like that are said to be doing life in prison on the installment plan.

I was very proud of my hardworking staff at the WDC especially when we were shorthanded and changing over to a new computer system resulting in unavoidable delays. An impatient middle aged woman wanted to pay her fine and was not happy when told that it would be a few more minutes. The angry defendant was pacing back and forth at the counter while loudly expressing her displeasure with our incompetence. Even though I was appointed and not elected, she pointed a finger at me and said, "And you - I can't believe I voted for you five times."

Franklin Police Lieutenant Jason C. Reilly is a real nice guy who comes from a family of law enforcement which includes his sister Jody who retired as a lieutenant with the Massachusetts State Police. I have never met her, but know their brother John very well. I first met John when he was a dispatcher for the North Attleborough Police and was pleased to watch him rise through the ranks. J. Do and I were honored to attend the swearing in ceremony when John was appointed to the position of Chief. Both of these guys are squared away, professional and a true credit to their family. They are all the children of Lieutenant Philip J. Reilly who I first met while working in Attleboro. Phil graduated from law school at the tail end of his distinguished state police career and I always enjoyed our conversations.

Jason, a detective at the time, had finished presenting evidence in a hearing so now it was the defendant's turn to speak. The defendant held up a photograph that he wanted me to examine. I wanted to be sure that Detective Reilly could also see the photo so I asked him to turn it a little bit so the detective could see it. The defendant must have thought that I was talking about some kind of electronic security device because as he turned the photo he asked, "There, is that OK? Can the detector see it now?"

At another hearing Jason read from a police report to present evidence of shoplifting against a young man and his girlfriend who were alleged to have stolen 12 cans of baby formula. Some people just can't put their best foot forward as the man said that he couldn't remember stealing anything. He didn't deny it, just couldn't remember! His girlfriend stated that there was no way that she would steal 12 cans of baby formula because that just wouldn't be right. She told me that she would never do that and said that she had only stolen six cans! I started feeling bad for the poor hungry infant until being informed that there was no baby. I then remembered that baby formula is commonly used to cut heroin.

Norfolk County Assistant District Attorney James M. McLaughlin is an outstanding lawyer and a really nice guy. He eventually left the DA's Office for greener pastures and, although wishing him well, we were all sorry to see him go. Jim was in the courtroom arguing for bail during a hearing on a busy day. This adversarial procedure requires the prosecution to point out some level of negativity about the defendant so some take what they hear personally. Jim convinced the judge to set bail on the fifty-year old defendant so his eighty five-year old mother came to our counter to post the bail. The court officer brought the defendant to the counter where he stood next to his mother and said, "Ma, that DA was a real asshole!" to which his elderly mother replied, "Shut up, you're the asshole!"

Some people watch so much TV that they become close to the characters on the screen. I asked a woman at the counter in Wrentham if I could help her so she explained that she wanted to have her husband committed for some mental health issues. She told me that her doctor had sent her so I asked her the name of the doctor and she told me, "Doctor Phil."

The great Robert L. Moscow was appointed Clerk-Magistrate of the Cambridge District Court by Governor Michael S. Dukakis. My good natured friend is now enjoying a well-deserved retirement after a long illustrious career in the court system. Bob is absolutely one of the nicest and smartest guys that I have ever known so a huge void was left upon his departure.

Bob is not afraid of self-deprecating humor and his low key approach is laudatory as he gets a lot done without calling attention to himself. His lovely wife Dawn is a psychologist so we would jokingly say that Bob should be her #1 patient. They were both at a party at our house where they met my mother. After I introduced Bob to my mom she said hello, looked at Dawn and said, "So Bob, this pretty girl must be your daughter!"

Bob was an Assistant Clerk-Magistrate in Norfolk Superior Court when he applied for the position in Cambridge. People who were tuned into appointments from the corner office at that time were saying that the Governor was appointing so many women that a male didn't stand a chance. A judge was speaking with Bob about this after hearing that he was interested in the Cambridge job. The judge told Bob that if he wanted the job he had better get a sex change operation to which the quick witted public servant replied, "Oh no, I'm not going through that again!"

I was seated next to Bob at a clambake that is put on every year by the Clerk-Magistrate's Association. It is always a fun time with good food and lots of laughs. Bob had never eaten a lobster so I started showing him how to take it apart for consumption. He paid attention and was a good student, but said that he was having trouble concentrating because the lobster was staring at him! Bob could always find humor anywhere!

I first met Stephen R. Fratalia when he was working as a Juvenile Probation Officer at the WDC. Steve, a good guy, and his lovely wife Anne host an annual party just before Thanksgiving at Napper Tandy's in Norwood. It is always well attended with police officers, attorneys, probation officers, district attorney's staff and others including the best former judge in the history of the Commonwealth - the Honorable Francis T. Crimmins Jr. and his lovely wife Joanne. The air is filled with laughter together with the legendary voice of Dublin-born Dave Hickey and the sweet sounds of his guitar.

I had just been put on a diabetes medication that prevented me from having more than two beers. J. Do and I were seated with Attorney Barry R. Crimmins, the judge's brother, and his ever humorous wife Janet. Barry got up and headed for the bar as he asked me if I wanted another beer. I had already consumed my nightly allotment so I thanked him, but said that I couldn't because my doctor says I can only have two. Barry immediately replied, "Eddie, you need a new doctor!"

An alleged member of a famous motorcycle club owned a pig farm out in the middle of nowhere which allegedly provided cover for some illegal activity and hellacious parties that would continue into the wee hours. The owner of the pig farm was arrested and transported to the ADC for arraignment. He was represented by Attorney Victor Wade who was a terrific criminal lawyer and a very funny guy. The defendant was handcuffed in the prisoner's dock as the assistant district attorney and Attorney Wade discussed the upcoming bail hearing. I usually entered the courtroom with the judge, but for some reason I was already sitting in the session clerk's seat and waiting along with everyone else for the judge to come in for the bail hearing. The defendant was being charged with drug distribution for a substantial amount of narcotics.

Attorney Wade had just told the ADA that his client wasn't a drug dealer and that they had arrested an innocent man. The ADA reached into his briefcase and pulled out a huge clear plastic bag full of all kinds of pills and capsules of seemingly every color in the crayon set. It was a veritable rainbow of narcotics in yellow, red, blue, green and purple that the police had confiscated from the pig farm. "He's not a drug dealer," the ADA said as he held the bag up, "then what's this?" Attorney Wade immediately declared, "Those are vitamins for the pigs!"

I was pushing a grocery store cart out of Stop & Shop full of a dozen 18 pound frozen turkeys for my staff for Christmas when an elderly woman wished me a Merry Christmas. Upon seeing all of the turkeys she said, "You must have a big family!"

You never know who you are going to meet at different events. I was doing a book signing in Taunton at the Holiday Inn when a nice man from Plainville took a look at my book and decided to buy one. As I was inscribing it to him he told me that he remembered me from the court and that I was nice to his son.

A very nice elderly lady from Franklin contacted me with an unusual problem. Her son had some substance abuse issues and was in need of money to be able to post the $3,000.00 bail set in his criminal case. Her son's roommate had scraped together $2,000.00 so she came up with the balance and said it was OK to put the entire $3,000.00 in the roommate's name which made him the surety. Tragically, her son died of a heroin overdose which ended the case and made the bail eligible for return, but the roommate kept the whole thing and wouldn't give her the $1,000.00 dollars.

I referred her to the police and did the best I could for her, but nothing was happening for this poor lady who had not only lost a son, but was now out a substantial sum. It is not my job to conduct investigations and make phone calls to track down criminals, but I made an exception for this sweet woman who had been through enough. I phoned police detectives, chiefs of police, town clerks and many others mostly in cities and towns north of Boston in an effort to locate the roommate. Sometimes I would only be a couple of weeks behind him after he vacated some flop house and moved on. He was finally tracked down, brought to justice and ordered to make restitution. More than two years had passed since she had buried her son, but it was a good day when I was able to tell her that the defendant had made his last payment and the Probation Department had put her final check in the mail.

I had already worked in Courtrooms for a few years with many different judges when Judge Patrick J. Hurley was assigned to Attleboro for the day. He is a tall distinguished looking gentleman who immediately greeted me with a smile and handshake as he projected a mundane aura of just being a regular guy. I was pleased to meet him and honored to serve as his session clerk in Courtroom One. The now retired jurist was a brilliant judge and an incredibly nice man. After disposing of several criminal cases by way of admission and scheduling other cases for hearings we began a criminal bench trial. This was long before the advent of jury trials in Attleboro so the defendant had elected to have his case heard by a judge. I called the case, swore in the witnesses and sat down for the opening statements by the assistant district attorney and defense counsel. Judge Hurley then said something that I had never heard before or since. He leaned forward and whispered, "Eddie, you can take off and go have an iced tea for the rest of the afternoon if you want."

Judge Hurley, who had been appointed Associate Justice of the WDC by Governor Michael S. Dukakis, was later appointed to the Hingham District Court by Governor William F. Weld and eventually named First Justice of that court. He had also served with great distinction as an Assistant Clerk in the Norfolk County Superior Court and as the Clerk of the Supreme Judicial Court. His wife Cynthia was a school teacher so when it came time to name his boat the humble judge facetiously told me that he had combined part of a school teacher's day with a favorite component of his own job. He named the boat *RECESS*.

It was a sad day in the history of the Massachusetts Court System when Judge Hurley retired from the bench. I was honored to be present with a full house for his portrait unveiling at a beautiful and emotional ceremony at the court. He is a great, great man who helped a lot of people in his outstanding career so I hope that he is enjoying retirement because he is surely missed on the bench. Judge Hurley always had the courage to do the right thing and made many lives better along the way. His warm smile, innate wisdom and simple acts of kindness will never be forgotten. Many judges have succeeded him, but no one will ever replace him.

I saw the horrible results of domestic violence almost daily in courthouses and police stations with the terrible sight of blackened eyes peering through bloodied faces on so many battered defenseless women. A coward's fist can do a lot of damage to a helpless and vulnerable victim. Governor Cellucci had once said, "The most dangerous place for a woman in Massachusetts is in her own home." As always, the greatest Governor in the history of the Commonwealth was correct of course, and unfortunately that horrific statement is also true just about everywhere else in the world.

I certainly recognize that there are many different types of domestic violence, but I am only speaking to the one that I saw the most - a man abusing his wife or girlfriend. One of the more troubling aspects of domestic violence is the reality that so many wives and girlfriends make up with their abuser, drop a restraining order and take him back into their lives. There are multiple factors driving a woman back into a bad situation including economics, love for her hungry and distraught children as well as the stigma of family rejection from those who only see her charismatic husband when he is sober. Everything seems to be working against her so thank God for domestic violence prevention groups like New Hope and others that have been there for so many women in need.

Every person that I hired at the WDC was given personal training by me so that they not only would be prepared to assist victims, but also so that they would recognize that my personal involvement served to create a heightened awareness of the gravity of this important issue. I was honored to serve on the Fatality Review Working Group of Governor's Council to Address Sexual Assault & Domestic Violence where I was privileged to be able to participate with multiple dedicated professionals including Executive Director Tammy Mello, Bristol County Assistant District Attorney Courtney J. Cahill, Dr. David Adams from Emerge and the legendary domestic violence victim's champion Toni K. Troop, former Director of Communications and Development for Jane Doe Inc.

I would sometimes share the highs and lows of my day in the courthouse with family and friends, but always remained vigilant in not mentioning the victim's names or any other confidential or identifying information. Sometimes I would express sadness in explaining how a woman had returned to a violent home and been beaten again. My mother could never understand how these poor ladies could make up with the bad guy and let him return to the marital home, notwithstanding my efforts to explain all of the powerful conditions driving them back into a cycle of terror. I told mom that not every woman is as strong as her and she said that I must be right because if somebody ever laid a hand on her he would never get another chance to hit her again. She then explained what she would do with a meat cleaver! I'm not advocating homicide as the answer, but I did wish that more victims had the strength of my mother so that they could at least permanently remain away from a guy in a relationship that should be over. Everybody, whether weak or strong, should try to enlist support along with the services of domestic violence prevention organizations. Nobody should be subjected to abuse.

A young woman in her early twenties from a very nice family was alleged to be the victim in a domestic violence case. She made it very clear, just like so many before her, that she didn't want to press charges against her assailant. She wanted to have the A & B case against her boyfriend dropped, but the ADA requested a bench trial which was scheduled before the Honorable Daniel B. Winslow. She was in the courtroom when her boyfriend was convicted so she made one last attempt to influence Judge Winslow and try to persuade him to be lenient with the defendant. In an effort to prove her love for him she screamed in open court, "Judge, I'll f*** him right now on the bench right in front of you!" She was still yelling as she was placed under arrest for disrupting court proceedings and led away by court officers.

I have had the considerable privilege of meeting, knowing and/or working with many distinguished jurists, some who are mentioned elsewhere as well as some listed below.

Some may have achieved a higher judicial designation, but this only reflects gubernatorial and presidential appointments.

Judge James R. Lawton - appointed by Governor Endicott H. Peabody;

Judge Dennis L. Collari - appointed by Governor Francis W. Sargent;

Judge John P. Concannon, Judge David H. Kopelman, Judge Mark E. Lawton, Judge John A. Markey & Judge Roger F. Sullivan - appointed by Governor Edward J. King;

Judge Mark S. Coven, Judge Allen J. Jarasitis, Judge Roanne Sragow, Judge James W. O'Neill, Judge William W. Teahan Jr. & Judge Robert J. Kane - appointed by Governor Michael S. Dukakis with Judge Kane later appointed to Superior Court by Governor A. Paul Cellucci;

Judge Bernadette L. Sabra, Judge Gregory R. Baler, Judge Deborah A. Dunn, Judge Mary M. McCallum, Judge Stephen S. Ostrach, Judge Don L. Carpenter, Judge Gregory L. Phillips, Judge Edward R. Redd & Judge Leon J. Lombardi - appointed by Governor William F. Weld;

Massachusetts Supreme Judicial Court Chief Justice Margaret H. Marshall - appointed to the SJC by Governor William F. Weld & as Chief Justice by Governor A. Paul Cellucci;

Superior Court Judge Kenneth J. Fishman, Judge Lance J. Garth, Judge John M. Julian, Judge Toby S. Mooney, Judge Francis L. Marini, Judge Michael F. Flaherty Sr., Judge Paul J. McCallum & Judge Kevin J. O'Dea - appointed by Governor Jane M. Swift;

Judge Andrew M. D'Angelo & Judge Daniel J. O'Shea - appointed by Governor Mitt Romney with Judge D'Angelo later appointed to the Appeals Court & Judge O'Shea later appointed to Superior Court by Governor Charlie D. Baker;

Judge Joseph I. Macy, Judge Gilbert J. Nadeau Jr., Judge Thomas S. Barrett, Judge Brian F. Gilligan, Judge Ronald F. Moynahan, Judge Thomas C. Horgan, Judge John P. Connor Jr. & Judge James J. McGovern - appointed by Governor A. Paul Cellucci with Judge McGovern later appointed again by Governor Mitt Romney;

Judge John A. Canavan III, Judge Mary L. Amrhein, Judge Mary Dacey White & Judge Robert G. Harbour - appointed by Governor Mitt Romney;

Judge Cynthia M. Brackett, Judge Paula J. Clifford, Superior Court Judge Renee P. Dupuis, Judge Thomas L. Finigan, Judge Franco J. Gobourne, Judge Michael A. Vitali, Judge Neil A Hourihan, Judge Mary Elizabeth Heffernan, Judge Jeanmarie Carroll, Judge Julieann Hernon, Judge Lawrence Moniz, Judge Susan L. Jacobs, Judge Steven E. Thomas & Judge Margaret R. Guzman - appointed by Governor Deval L. Patrick with Judge Guzman later appointed to the United States District Court for the District of Massachusetts by President Joseph R. Biden Jr.;

Judge James M. Stanton, Judge Robert Harnais, Judge Edward H. Sharkansky, Judge Paul M. Cronan, Appeals Court Judge Joseph M. Ditkoff, Judge Harold P. Naughton Jr. & Judge Brian Walsh - appointed by Governor Charlie D. Baker. Judge Cronan is the brother of my brother Chris' business partner and close friend David Cronan, so class and honor really run deep in that family.

I had some interesting conversations with Judge Angel Kelley who was appointed to the District Court bench and later to Superior Court by Governor Deval L. Patrick. I always enjoyed her company as she is a smart, dignified, outstanding judge who came to her position with an incredible resume of accomplishments attended by a spirited sense of humor that is guided by an innate quality of kindness. I still have the beautiful congratulatory note that she wrote to me many years ago. Judge Kelley was eventually nominated to the United States District Court for the District of Massachusetts by President Joseph R. Biden Jr. It was my great honor to attend her Investiture Ceremony at the United States District Court in Boston with Natick District Court Clerk-Magistrate Brian J. Kearney. A huge crowd of family, friends and colleagues gathered to enjoy the culmination of her success. The federal court was the beneficiary of the state court's loss once Judge Kelley was confirmed by the US Senate so we are all lucky that some of the salient issues facing our nation are now in her very capable hands.

Massachusetts was experiencing a severe financial crisis when I was promoted to First Assistant Clerk-Magistrate at the ADC so I was told that I could either not accept the promotion or take the promotion without additional remuneration with the hope that I might get paid in the future! I chose the latter with the hope for a retro check someday as my young family could use the money. I waited for months and months, but to no avail. Finally, in a last ditch effort to secure my pay raise, I drove to Boston and entered the outer office of Chief Justice for Administration and Management John E. Fenton Jr. who had been appointed to his judgeship by Governor Francis W. Sargent. I didn't have an appointment and even though we had never met, the Chief Justice greeted me like a long lost friend! I was just a little guy in the huge court system, but this great man made me feel like a million dollars! He removed a big cigar from his mouth, offered me a seat and told me that my dilemma had never been brought to his attention. He made a phone call right in front of me as I heard him tell the person on the other end my name and then, "This guy needs to get paid right away and I want him to get a retro check for the full amount back to day one." Wow, I expressed my appreciation and thanked him repeatedly! I had heard of his reputation for assisting people so I wasn't surprised, after that display of kindness and class, to receive a nice check for the full amount soon thereafter. Our system of justice and the entire Commonwealth lost a huge champion of integrity when Chief Justice Fenton passed from this world.

I personally knew most of the attorneys mentioned in this chapter and consider it a tremendous privilege to have worked in the same realm as them. They were honest, hardworking and conscientious advocates who did the best that they could every day for their clients.

It was my pleasure to engage in interactions and hear objections as well as powerful arguments from lawyers including former Bristol County Assistant District Attorney James D. McKenna who had served with distinction as Chairman of the School Committee and been reelected time after time by the voters of North Attleborough because he is a down to earth, intelligent, skilled advocate with a huge heart.

Attorney Thomas P. Gay is a brilliant litigator, honest man and one of the nicest guys in the system. He serves in leadership positions for the Wareham Gatemen of the Cape Cod Baseball League, there is nothing that I would not do for Tom.

I was introduced to Attorney Daniel M. Rich from Norton by his mother Frances who was a Criminal Clerk when I worked in the ADC. Dan is a very sharp lawyer and a real nice guy which is no surprise to anyone who knew his sweet mother.

Attorney Francis M. O'Boy from Taunton, an intellectual dynamo, fierce advocate and great guy, will always be remembered for his unique style of objecting in the courtroom. He never said, "Objection", but instead would humbly ask the judge, "Pray Your Honor's judgment."

Attorney Robert E. Cutler Jr. is the elected Foxborough Town Clerk who discovered and reported what appeared to be fraudulent or forged signatures on statewide ballot initiatives which resulted in a criminal investigation. Bob is a skillful lawyer, an honorable man and a good guy.

I knew the Shanley brothers growing up in Attleboro as they were all nice kids and legendary tennis players, including my classmate Terry, so I was happy when Edward K. Shanley, better known as "Charlie", passed the bar and started practicing with the law firm of Coogan Smith, LLP. He is a class guy just like his brothers and a terrific lawyer.

There are numerous honorable and accomplished attorneys licensed to practice in the Commonwealth and beyond, many mentioned elsewhere on the pages of this book, so at the risk and absolute certainty of omitting the names of many outstanding lawyers who I saw at work or socially, some are listed below;

Jack M. Atwood, Arthur M. Bakst, Mark E. Barnett, Bryan M. Beatty, Lynn M. Beland, Mark J. Beland, Peter V. Bellotti, Kelly Ann Bennett, John G. Birtwell, Dennis P. Bisio, Daniel T. Blake, Robert C. Bliss, Steven C. Boozang, Judith A. Borges, Eugene F. Boyle, Eliot T. Brais, William F. Brennick, John J. Brooks III, R. Andrew Burbine, John W. Burke, James M. Caramanica, J.W. Carney Jr., James M. Cassidy, Louis F. Cerrone, Robert C. Chamberlain, Stephen D. Clapp, Harold Cohen, Michael C. Connolly, J. Jerome Coogan, Richard R. Cornetta Jr., Frank C. Corso, Robert M. Costello, Joseph A. Croce, David L. Crowley Jr., Jean N. Crudale, John F. X. Davoren, George C. Decas, Elaine M. DeMeo, Christine J. Doherty, John L. Drury, Michael J. Duggan, Gerard J. Dupont, David G. Eisenstadt, Stephen J. Fallon, Robert H. Fennessy Jr., Robert E. Ficco, Philip F. Filosa, Elliott Fine, Jordan H. F. Fiore, Elissa A. Flynn - Poppey, Patrick Francomano, Joan M. Fund, Kathleen M. & John T. Gaffney Jr., Dale E. Galasso, Victor J. Garo, Lee Garrison, Vincent M. & Salvatore J. Germani, Francis J. Gillan III, Patrick M. Gioia, Daniel E. Goldrick, Robert L. Goodale, David J. Gormley, Dale E. Grant, Frank J. Gross;

Kevin F. Hampe, John B. Harwood, Van L. Hayhow, John M. Healy, John J. Hoffman, Jarvis Hunt, John F.D. Jacobi III, Stephen L. Jones, Howard M. Kahalas, Paul F. Kenney, Paul V. & Stephen J. Kenney, John P. Kivlan, Ronald G. Koback, Joseph F. Krowski, Kevin P. Landry, Keith G. Langer, Robert N. Launie, John P. Lee, Maureen A. Lee, James M.

Lewis, Elizabeth Y. & Bruce H. Lint, Frank A. Lombardi, Paul F. Lorincz, Bradford N. Louison, Margaret M. Madden, Charles J. Maguire Jr., Elizabeth Maitland, Linda J. Maloney, Robert S. Mangiaratti, John C. Manni, David C. Manoogian, Christopher M. Markey, Robert P. Marks, Charles R. Mason, James P. McCarthy, Wesley A. McClure, Frederick M. McDermott, Michael T. & Timothy J. McGahan, John J. McGlone III, Austin W. McHoul, John W. McIntyre, Carol Mercier - Locke, John H. Michelmore, Clifford A. Monac, Peter S. Mrowka, Charles D. Mulcahy, Paul G. Murphy, Peter F. Murphy, John T. Murray, Stephen E. Navega, Paula A. Nedder, Gerald J. Noonan, Robert F. Nugent Jr., Richard A. Nunes, William F. O'Connell;

Anthony R. Pelusi Jr., my classmate Patricia M. Perry, Thomas D. Petrowski, Bradley W. Phipps, Fiore Porreca, Alfred Puller, Kerri A. Quintal, Bruce G. Rich, John J. & Neil J. Roche, Paul M. Rockett, Brian D. Roman, Gerald W. Roque, Dale E. Rose, Julie A. Rougeau, Robert J. Roughsedge, Jeffrey N. Roy, John P. Rull, Jonathan C. Rutley, Ralph Ryan, Steven P. Sabra, Camille F. Sarrouf, Richard P. Schmidt, Gordon O. Simard, John W. Skurchak Jr., Victor T. Sloan, Henry J. Sousa Jr., Stephanie A. Sousa, George I. Spatcher Jr., Mandy L. Spaulding, Florence M. & Francis J. Spillane, Neal R. Steingold, AnDré D. Summers, C. Samuel Sutter, Edward J. Sweeney III, Michael S. Szymanski, Bruce E. Thompson, James D. Thrasher, A. Stephen Tobin, Cheryl A. Tracy, Philip A. Tracy Jr., John S. Tuohy, William R. Tuttle, Talbot T. Tweedy, Edward W. Valanzola, Sallie K. Vallely, Edward F. Vaughn, William B. Vernon, Anthony M., Janet M. & John P. Vignone, Max Volterra, Andrea J. Wagner, William M. Wainwright, Douglas B. Weilding, Joshua D. Werner, Sara Holmes Wilson, Nancy Maloof Winn, Paul F. & Thomas J. Wynn, Frank A. Yee Jr., and several others.

4. "Gruffy"

Brian J. Kearney served with great distinction as an Assistant Clerk-Magistrate in the Boston Municipal Court before being nominated and appointed the great Clerk-Magistrate of the Natick District Court by Governor Jane M. Swift. Brian's father, Detective William P. Kearney, was a well-respected Boston Police Officer, his sister Maureen retired as a sergeant after a distinguished career with the Massachusetts State Police and his brother Stephen hung up his gun belt after keeping the streets safe during decades of legendary service as a Wareham Police Officer. Prior to his appointments in the court system, Brian had entered the family business as a patrolman in Boston and Cape Cod before being promoted to sergeant. Brian Kearney is one of the most honorable, kind, generous and funniest guys in the system. He would call me every year to personally invite J. Do and I to the Natick District Court Christmas Party. One time I told him that I couldn't make it because I had already committed to something else on that day so he changed the Natick date just for me! Who does that? No one could have a better friend!

Brian had always enjoyed being a canine officer on those police departments and was given the nickname "Gruffy" by the great Governor's Councilor Michael J. Callahan based on a shortened version of McGruff from the old TV ad featuring McGruff the Crime Dog.

L-R Governor's Councilor Michael J. Callahan, Natick District Court Clerk-Magistrate Brian J. Kearney, author at Tampa Homecoming - USF vs Syracuse

Gruffy actually trained dogs for his own police departments as well as for many others in Massachusetts and beyond including a large German shepherd named Bear. He had trained Bear to walk up to the water fountain in the Wareham Police Department, stand up on his hind legs, depress the button with his left front paw and lean in to get a drink of water! A booking sergeant was in the process of taking information from a defendant who was extremely intoxicated. The man was swaying back and forth in his seat as he noticed

Bear walk into the booking room. The dog walked over to the bubbler, stood up and pushed the button with his paw as he leaned in to get a drink. The guy was rubbing his eyes in disbelief as Bear continued to quench his thirst. As soon as Bear had finished and got down on all fours the phone rang. "Booking," the sergeant declared after answering the phone. He paused for a moment to listen, looked at Bear, moved the phone away from his ear and started to hand it to the dog as he said, "Bear - it's for you." The defendant was rumored to have quit drinking immediately.

A woman called the Wareham Police Department to report that her house had been broken into and that the suspect may still be in the area. Patrolman Brian Kearney and his trusty canine Bear had already been tracking a suspect for numerous house breaks so he was dispatched to the area where he and his loyal German shepherd began a backyard search with the dog trying to pick up a scent. The reporting party became impatient as she didn't know that Gruffy had already responded and was diligently looking for the suspect nearby. She dialed the station again and complained that she had already called about her home being broken into and that no police had come to her house! The dispatcher told her that the officer was already there and if she looked out the window she would probably see him in the backyard. She looked through the window and spotted Patrolman Kearney with the dog on a leash walking slowly through her backyard. "Oh, that's just great," she told the dispatcher, "As if my day isn't bad enough - my house gets broken into and they send me a blind cop!"

Gruffy actually taught one of his dogs to retrieve a can of beer for him from the refrigerator. Finn would access the refrigerator by biting down on a rope attached to the handle to pull the door open. The beautiful yellow lab would then pick up a can of beer in his mouth and proudly deliver it to his master. Gruffy was eventually able to teach the dog not to bite down too hard on the beer cans, but not before they went through an entire case of Bud Light full of tooth holes squirting beer all over the basement floor!

Patrolman Kearney responded to a disturbance call in Boston along with his partner. The man causing the ruckus, who identified himself as Jesus Christ, was creating a commotion and wouldn't calm down or cooperate so he had to be arrested. He insisted that he was Jesus Christ as Gruffy gently guided him into the back seat of the cruiser while ensuring that his head passed safely through the entrance. Gruffy is always extremely polite and courteous with everyone, but he was really extending a remarkably high level of respect and consideration to this defendant. When his partner asked him why he was being so nice to the guy Gruffy smiled and responded, "Hey, he said he was Jesus Christ. You never know!"

Sergeant Kearney handcuffed a suspect in Boston and had him seated on a curb few yards away from his parked police cruiser. His canine partner Bear was in the back seat with his head out the partially opened window furiously barking at the defendant. Gruffy got between the defendant and Bear as he pretended that the dog was communicating with him through the continuous loud barking. He looked at Bear, as he barked, and said, "What's that boy?" (more barks) "This guy is armed, dangerous and wanted with a bunch of warrants out for him!" (more barks). The defendant started yelling at Bear and screamed, "That's not true! Don't believe a word he says. That dog is a f***ing liar!"

Gruffy's father, Detective Bill Kearney, had an outstanding career with the Boston Police Department. He and his partner were the first narcotics officers in the city and Detective Kearney was the first Boston Police Officer to arrest Stephen Flemmi, the future career criminal who would later come to be known as "The Rifleman" and eventually be sentenced to life in prison for ten murders.

Detective Kearney's brilliant career was unfortunately interrupted when he developed lung cancer. Chemotherapy doses would cause him, just like all patients, to be tired and lethargic so Gruffy would drive him into the Dana-Farber Cancer Institute for his treatments and then take him home. Gruffy always had his dog Mac in the back seat of the car when he picked up his dad for the trip into the clinic. The beautiful yellow lab would have his tail wagging in the back of the car and would excitedly greet Bill when he got into the front passenger seat as a harmonious rapport developed between the two. He enjoyed the time with his son as they swapped funny stories through the Boston traffic with Mac patiently listening from the back.

Unfortunately, Mac had to be put down to relieve him of his pain and suffering from an incurable ailment. Gruffy hated to lose his trusted and loyal friend, but he knew that it was the right thing to do. The next time that his father got into the car he inquired about Mac. Gruffy told him about how the poor dog had been sick and suffering in pain so that he had to be put down as they drove off for his dad's cancer treatment. His father expressed how sorry he was that the poor dog had to die and then facetiously correlated the dog's situation with his own as if Gruffy might put him out of his misery! They both had a good laugh when he told his son, "You know, I don't have any pain! I just want you to know that I feel great. I'm fine!

A very young Brian Kearney once asked his father, "Are there many murders in Boston dad?" The veteran detective replied, "Oh yea, just like the vitamins - one a day!"

Gruffy was directly responsible for saving lives on two different occasions in the court system. He administered CPR and started life saving procedure to a victim in distress before being assisted by court officers in Framingham where the process resulted in the man regaining his breath. It was only about a week before that Gruffy had saved another life on Nantucket where he had been assigned to temporarily work at the District Court on the island. Gruffy was hearing a small claims case when the plaintiff suddenly dropped to the floor in the middle of his presentation. Gruffy quickly started CPR and took care of the man until the ambulance arrived. The plaintiff called Gruffy later from the hospital to ask if he could continue with his testimony on the phone! Gruffy had to say no, but apparently the plaintiff had already said enough before collapsing in the courtroom as he prevailed in the case. Gruffy not only saved his life, but he ruled in his favor on the small claim!

Section 35 of Chapter 123 of the Massachusetts General Laws outlines the procedure to be used in a substance abuse petition for a civil commitment. Everyone in the system is familiar with Section 35 as it is frequently used to help people address a terrible problem.

Gruffy had to end a telephone conversation with me because he said that he had to take care of a Section 140. I asked him what the heck is a 140 and he said that his court averages 4 Section 35s per day so he calls it a 140!

Gruffy was in church attending the Sunday service with his family when the priest, as always, held up the host and proclaimed, "The body of Christ." That statement, as is customary, was immediately followed by the altar boy ringing the bell. A little kid, about four years old, heard the bell and yelled, "Ice cream man!"

The Natick District Court and Framingham District Court are now housed in the same building in Framingham. First Assistant Clerk-Magistrate George R. Marinofsky, Assistant Clerk-Magistrate Ronald R. Petralia, Chief Court Officer Michael Farrell, Deputy Chief Court Officer Robert Jackson and Officer Brian Waldron are all great guys who work there and contribute mightily to the success and positive reputation of those courts. Troy Boone, another great guy who worked in Wrentham and Framingham, is now the Chief Court Officer in Marlborough District Court. It was my pleasure to meet the Honorable David W. Cunis, First Justice who was appointed by Governor Mitt Romney, when I attended one of their Law Day events and I had already been acquainted with the Honorable Douglas W. Stoddart, appointed by Governor A. Paul Cellucci, whom I had enjoyed speaking with at a judicial seminar. It was nice to see the Honorable Lynn Coffin Brendemuehl, appointed by Governor Deval L. Patrick, attending the funeral services for Brian Kearney's mother. Judge Brendemuehl, a very nice person and terrific judge, would sometimes sit in Framingham and is the First Justice of the Concord District Court, where Ann Tavares - Colicchio, appointed by Governor William F. Weld, serves as the great Clerk-Magistrate.

It was a monumental day in the history of the Framingham District Court when Governor Deval L. Patrick appointed the great John A. DeLuca Clerk-Magistrate. I had gotten to know John when we were both Assistant Clerk-Magistrates so I was very happy for him, his family and the court as it is always nice to see an assistant get promoted. Unfortunately, John passed away in 2020, but will always be remembered as an honest public servant and a loyal colleague. Gruffy came up with a unique idea to remember our friend. A beautifully engraved granite bench now sits in front of the court in memory of John after having been unveiled at a nice ceremony that J. Do and I were honored to attend along with a huge crowd.

John was hearing State Police cases on a busy morning in the Framingham Court. The 20-year old defendant was alleged to be speeding at over 95 MPH on the Massachusetts Turnpike. He was wearing a Yale Baseball jacket so after inquiry, the defendant confirmed that in fact he did play hardball for the Ivy League School. Upon hearing that Trooper Stephen Belanger of the Weston State Police Barracks stated, "I hope you have a good arm and you can throw as fast as you drive!"

John called a civil case in the courtroom one day that described a transaction not usually seen in a lawsuit. The plaintiff had obtained a default judgment in another state and filed a Supplementary Process action on the foreign judgment in the Framingham Court. The gist of the plaintiff's complaint was dissatisfaction with the defendant's services who happened to be a prostitute!

Two females had been arrested and were in the holding cell awaiting arraignment at the Natick District Court. They were both charged with narcotics trafficking as they were alleged to be so-called "drug mules" in the narcotics trade. It was suspected that they may have hidden some of the drugs in a bodily orifice which would require the issuance of a search warrant for examination. A search warrant is needed for a probe of any crevice in the human body as a cavity search is considered extremely intrusive. Probation Officer David DiGiorgio mentioned that it looked like they were probably going to need to have a cavity search done and after overhearing this Head Account Clerk Meme Grant declared, "What!!! Why should the state have to pay for a dentist for something like this?"

Gruffy did the cooking for Natick Police Sergeant Danny O'Callahan's retirement party at the Natick District Court. The place was packed with judges, probation officers, attorneys, police prosecutors, Assistant DA's and other court personnel all enjoying a fabulous spread of delicious food. The only problem was that nobody had a pot big enough to cook the corn on the cob until Natick Police Detective James Ordway saved the day and volunteered his cauldron for the gathering. The pot was large enough to hold an enormous amount of corn to feed the whole crowd. Toward the end of the celebration some of the guests may have misunderstood when Sally Crane of the Clerk-Magistrate's Office yelled across the room to the detective, "Hey Jimmy, thanks for bringing the pot to the party. It was great!"

I had gotten to know Natick District Court Chief Probation Officer Daniel T. Marzilli very well from attending so many of their Christmas parties and cookouts. Dan, now retired, was a great CPO who could solve any problem with his engaging personality and terrific sense of humor. I always enjoyed his company because he was able to see the funny side of seemingly every issue.

Gruffy enjoys cooking and putting a smile on hungry faces so these were not just little get togethers with a few cold snacks. At least two grills were working to full capacity in the courthouse parking lot where you could hear the sizzle of steaks, burgers, dogs, chicken and more! Dan Marzilli donned an apron to man one of the grills where he monitored a full load of fresh asparagus. So much asparagus was piled up on the grill that Dan had to concentrate on carefully moving around the enormous load of vegetables to ensure proper cooking.

Gruffy was tending to various meats close by on the other grill when a retired judge saw all the food and commented that this is great as they seem to have everything you could want at a cookout. Gruffy motioned toward Dan's grill and kiddingly told the judge, out of the CPO's earshot, that they even had crates of asparagus delivered from Marzilli Farms, owned by Dan's family, which of course was not true. The judge was astonished as he walked over to Dan and started asking him all kinds of questions about raising asparagus. He asked the CPO how long it takes for asparagus to grow to maturity; how many are in a pound and if they have to be watered daily! Dan was busy cooking and trying to be polite, but after the judge left, he had a serious look on his face when he told Gruffy, "The judge has lost it, he's gone, really gone!"

George L. Shea Jr. was the Second Assistant Clerk-Magistrate of the Boston Municipal Court and one of the best guys in the system. The now retired Shea has an outstanding sense of humor as evidenced by a call he made to the Natick District Court asking for Gruffy. Marcia Frasier answered the phone and inquired as to what it was regarding to which George replied, "I'm Kearney's probation officer checking up on him." Marcia, a very nice person, but somewhat naïve, told Gruffy that his probation officer is on line two and later asked him, "So, what are you on probation for anyway?"

Thomas Connolly was the Director of Security for the Trial Court. I knew him well and always found him to be an even keeled straight shooter and real good guy. He was very upset about a misunderstanding one day, however, when he called Gruffy about a food bill for the prisoners. A court officer had picked up the lunch order of seven bologna & cheese sandwiches for the prisoners in custody, but the kid at the sub shop had hit the wrong key so, although the price was correct, the receipt that went to Boston read seven steak & cheese subs! Connolly told Gruffy, "I'm brown bagging it and you guys are feeding steak & cheese to the prisoners!"

James Comerford is one of the very talented Assistant Clerk-Magistrates employed at the Quincy District Court. Jim is a great guy and a brilliant author who has written five different books on various subjects including principles of criminal, tort and insurance law. After I had written my first book, I facetiously mentioned to Gruffy that between Jim and myself, we have written a total of six books!

Marcia Frasier answered the phone at the Natick Court to hear the caller say that a woman who was court regular had died. The alleged decedent was a well-known defendant with an outstanding warrant so the court employee got emotional and started crying as she was about to recall the warrant until Gruffy told her, "Don't do that - I just saw her alive downtown!"

A defendant was alleged to have stolen some items from Macy's so Gruffy was in the middle of the shoplifting hearing when he answered the phone. Attorney John H. Rogers, the popular House Majority Leader, was on the line, Gruffy was almost finished with the hearing so instead of telling John that he will call him back he said that he will be right with him and set the receiver down on the table. John could clearly hear the ensuing conversation including Gruffy ordering the defendant to stay out of Macy's. Gruffy could hear John yelling into the phone, "Can I get that Macy's stay away order for my wife?"

As previously mentioned, Natick District Court sessions are now held in the same building that houses the Framingham District Court. The van from the House of Correction transports prisoners that are held in custody for both courts and on this occasion one of the defendants was confined to a wheelchair. A court officer assisted by pushing the wheelchair into the courtroom with the seated defendant being tried for some violent crimes. The evidence wasn't going very well for the defense when the lengthy trial had to be continued to the next day for additional testimony. The court officer wheeled the defendant out of the courtroom and down next to the prisoner's holding cells to await the arrival of the custody van. The court officer didn't bother to put the defendant into a cell because the need for the wheelchair seemed to eliminate the possibility of escape. The court officer's eyes were diverted for a moment when suddenly the defendant jumped out of the wheelchair, burst through the door and bolted across the parking lot. Gruffy said that the defendant seemed to get healthy real fast and looked like he ran a 4.3, 40-yard dash between parked cars until sailing over the perimeter fence like an Olympic athlete. The escapee's freedom was short-lived as he was quickly apprehended by the Framingham Police that night. When Gruffy told me that the man had jumped out of the wheelchair he said, "We work miracles at this court!"

Gruffy married the lovely Attorney Maryanne Lewis who is an inspiring, dynamic and powerful speaker. J. Do and I have known their son Patrick J. Kearney, since he was a very young man so it goes without saying that we were absolutely ecstatic when he won the race for State Representative for the 4th Plymouth District comprised of Marshfield and most of Scituate. I got to the polls an hour early just to compensate for potentially getting lost in an unfamiliar town so that I could hold a Kearney sign on primary day as well as the general election. I shook so many hands that I imagined my tired right arm feeling a little like Jim Lonborg's after Game 7 of the 1967 World Series. A whole army of colorful characters were out in force to help Patrick. One of the guys supporting a sign next to me was Frank "Snacks" Crowley whom I had previously met when he worked security at the Framingham District Court until retiring. I enjoyed campaigning with the loquacious and good-natured gentleman who had been given the nickname "Snacks" by Gruffy. Patrick's younger brother Matthew did an excellent job of running his campaign so it was nice to see the love of two brothers united in an all-out effort to achieve a common goal. Patrick is and will continue to be a great State Representative for the constituents of his district as well as for the entire Commonwealth.

Patrick is a very well-rounded individual whose many talents include singing, fishing, playing lacrosse and hockey. Even prior to graduating from the Massachusetts Maritime Academy he had worked on commercial fishing vessels and charters. Patrick holds a Captain's License from the US Coast Guard and is such a gifted surfcaster that I profiled him as the youngest fisherman in Legends of the Canal which is one of the chapters in my first book, *SEVEN MILES AFTER SUNDOWN*.

Gruffy and Patrick were at the Garden enjoying the Bruins game as Boston defeated the New York Rangers for their 10th straight victory. A guy recognized Patrick and said, "Hey, you're the kid from the fishing book that I got for Christmas! I've read it 5 times and can't wait for spring!" While flattered that somebody read my book 5 times, this poor guy really needs to be introduced to the joy of the public library!

State Representative Patrick Kearney, 4th Plymouth District, (Gruffy Kearney photo)

    I had heard great things from Gruffy about John Doble long before meeting the now retired Bourne police detective who had been assigned to the Cape Cod Drug Task Force. JD, who played high school football with Gruffy, is a talented photographer who was very kind and generous to let me use his beautiful photos in my first book as well as PowerPoint presentations for my seminars. He is a terrific guy and legendary surfcaster who I see quite often when we are both wetting a line on the Canal. JD went from catching criminals to catching fish!

    Gruffy had told his young son Patrick that it was better to be addicted to fishing than drugs so Patrick took that to heart immediately. He may have caught more heavy stripers than any other student in history while attending Massachusetts Maritime Academy, located right on the west end of the fabled Cape Cod Canal and always enjoyed the sport like John Doble. John once described the attachment to surfcasting through the sensation of a fish hitting your line hard when he said, "The tug is the drug!" One time Gruffy told me, "Patrick is addicted to fishing and John Doble is his supplier!"

    Practical jokes and funny stories seem to run in the entire Kearney family. Laughter is contagious and this crew are full blown carriers. Patrick takes his job seriously, but not himself. When the kids were young Gruffy took eight year old Patrick and six year old Matt out to dinner one night in Cambridge. Upon being seated in the restaurant Gruffy told his boys to stay put and he would be right back as he left the table and headed for the men's room. When he was returning to the table he noticed a small crowd of people speaking with his sons. He was greeted by the manager, assistant manager and some waitresses who were all very welcoming, engaging and happy to see him. Complimentary extra appetizers and entrees were sent to the Kearney table as the manager told them how honored he was to have them there and to just ask if they needed anything at all. Gruffy sat down as he thanked them for their warm and genuine hospitality.

As soon as the manager and his staff left the table Gruffy asked his boys what the heck was going on. The mischievous young lads then let on that they had told the waitress that their father was the *Phantom Gourmet*!

Both of Maryanne and Gruffy's sons, Patrick and Matthew, graduated from Boston College High School. I told Gruffy how much I liked the motto of BC High - "A man for others." It has such an honorable ring to it with a noteworthy and admirable goal. Gruffy liked it too, but he facetiously said that the motto for his school was, "Let's do it to them before they do it to us!"

I have always admired those who have the courage to use self-deprecating humor to poke fun at themselves. President Abraham Lincoln was probably the most famous to tenaciously get laughs at his own expense, but Gruffy is cut from the same tough cloth. Gruffy, a hardworking kid with part time jobs, excelled in athletics including as a multi-talented high school quarterback. He was very proud of his son Patrick when he made the National Honor Society at Boston College High School and congratulated him on this magnificent achievement. Gruffy went on to tell Patrick what an honor it is and how they had such a nice ceremony and dimmed the lights when he attended Bourne High School. There was enough ambiguity and lack of specificity in his voice to lead Patrick to believe that his father might have received the same honor as he was about to accept. Patrick has always held his father in the absolute highest regard and although never doubting his intelligence, was kind of surprised at what he was possibly learning about his dad's high school years. Patrick looked at his father and inquired, "Dad, you were on the National Honor Society?" to which Gruffy replied, "No, I was the guy who got the room ready for the other kids. I was the janitor!"

Attorney Maryanne Lewis is a former State Representative who served in the leadership of the Massachusetts House of Representatives as a Division Leader. I would imagine that Patrick Kearney is the only State Rep in history to be raised by parents holding the positions Clerk-Magistrate and State Representative.

The family had gathered at the rehearsal dinner for the wedding of Maryanne's sister Kate and Larry May where the State Rep was asked to give a toast to the soon to be newlyweds. The quick-witted solon raised her glass and proclaimed that, "When the wedding vows are official, the groom's name will automatically be changed. As soon as he becomes a married man he will no longer be known as Larry May, his new name is Larry Will!"

Gruffy was a well-qualified former Police Sergeant and Assistant Clerk-Magistrate working at the Boston Municipal Court when he was appointed by Governor Jane M. Swift to become the Clerk-Magistrate of the Natick District Court. Notwithstanding his solid credentials and deeply held commitment to public service there were news stories circulating regarding his powerful family political connections. Gruffy's mother, Marguerite, was scanning through the newspaper when she stopped reading and called out to him in the next room. "Brian, just how bad are you anyway?" she asked to which he then inquired as to what she was talking about. "Well,", she told him, "the Herald has a story about Osama bin Laden on page 6, but they've got you on page 1!"

Mrs. Kearney's sharp wit and good-natured ribbing was on full display when she kidded with Gruffy as they were watching *Jeopardy* on TV one night. Gruffy correctly answered one of the questions to which his mother replied, "You must have seen this before! What is this a repeat?"

I was one of a bunch of Gruffy's friends who took his mother to the dog track in Florida where we all had an enjoyable time and a lot of laughs. Mrs. Kearney paid close attention as I taught her how to play a quinella and to calculate the odds on the tote board at the Palm Beach Kennel Club in West Palm. She was my best student!

Mrs. Kearney's last years were spent living in Massachusetts with her daughter Maureen where she was the beneficiary of round the clock loving care. Mrs. Kearney and her husband had raised a half dozen children, three of whom became police officers like their father. Gruffy and the other Kearney siblings - Stephen, Michael, Ann and Bill helped out tremendously, but being in the next room meant that Maureen was the one who provided the bulk of nurturing and continuous support. Even though Mrs. Kearney was afflicted with the usual difficulties associated with advanced age, she never lost her keen sense of humor. One day Maureen drove her mom for a doctor's appointment and waited with her for the physician to come in. The doctor entered the room and asked Mrs. Kearney if she had any pains. She looked at the doctor and said, "Well, I've got six kids!"

Gruffy's sister Maureen was a retired sergeant from the Massachusetts State Police. One night, while still on the job, she told the troopers on her shift at the Bourne Barracks that she was going to buy them dinner from the Way Ho in Buzzards Bay. Sergeant Kearney called the restaurant to place the take-out order, but there was a misunderstanding in the conversation which resulted in Benny, who was taking the order, becoming shocked and instantly worried. She told him that she needed enough food to feed four hungry troopers, but Benny thought that she had said that she needed to feed four hundred troopers! "Four hundred troopers! Oh no!"

We were having a good time in a fishing tournament aboard the Magpie out of Scituate Harbor. Jim Lewis, Gruffy's brother-in-law, was the skipper of this vessel with a crew of John McNamara, myself and others. We were a carefree group of anglers who laughed and joked on our way out to the fishing grounds. We trolled for hours catching mostly bluefish and by day's end had broken the previous record of 54 fish caught to win the tournament. Jim, a nice guy who always sees the glass as half full, put us on fish all day so it was quite an honor to be a member of the winning team with a final tally of 98 fish to our credit!

Bluefish are hard fighting sport fish that will always put up an exhilarating battle right to the finish. They have razor sharp teeth lining powerful jaws so they require your full attention. Toward the end of the afternoon my rod suddenly bent over again as Johnny Mac yelled, "Fish on!" while Jim eased the throttle back to slow the boat for my next bluefish engagement. I lifted the rod out of the flush holder and started to crank in some line on what looked like about a 14 pound bluefish that was pulling hard and jumping out of the water while doing aerial acrobatics like a circus performer. I was already pretty tired from reeling in heavy fish all day and this one was no picnic. The war suddenly got more intense when another bluefish of about the same size hit the other hook on the same lure. Now I had two on the same line! One bluefish can be a tough fight, but two clashing together adds new meaning to the definition of exhaustion.

Jim knew that my hands would be full for a while and that I would therefore be defenseless against his never-ending mischievous pranks and practical jokes. Both of my hands were completely engaged in the conflict so I could do absolutely nothing when Jim snuck up behind me and quickly pulled my shorts down around my ankles! As I continued to reel in the fish, I could feel the cool ocean breeze on more than just my face!

Dozens of friends and family could be found staying at Jim's huge summer home in Scituate on any given night. Friendly people were constantly in and out lending a festive party atmosphere to the seaside villa. Gruffy loves eating ice cream sandwiches so he devised a scheme to prevent them from being gobbled up by everyone else in the house. He put the box of ice cream sandwiches in a brown paper bag and wrote BAIT in large black letters on the outside before placing the disguised goodies in the freezer. Jim had intended to go to the bait shop before heading out to sea, but instead grabbed the bag marked BAIT out of the freezer and drove to his boat. He set his bearings for just west of Stellwagen Bank and looked forward to a nice relaxing day of cod fishing. He turned the engine off after arriving at his favorite spot and reached for the bag of bait. As soon as Jim opened the bag to bait the first hook, he was surprised to discover a puddle of melted ice cream! Cod don't bite for ice cream sandwiches!

Gruffy invited me to fish in a tournament out of Scituate Harbor in Kevin Mullaney's boat. Kevin is a terrific guy who is nicknamed "Monger" as in fishmonger. He always sees the glass as half full and is a good guy with whom to wet a line. I had brought along some of J. Do's famous candy bar brownies which are absolutely delicious. Gruffy and I tend to see the world through the same lens so it is not surprising that we both have a good appetite. We gobbled down about a half dozen brownies as "Monger" put the boat in gear and headed for Provincetown. We trolled for bluefish and landed some nice ones on a bluebird day out on the ocean. I had to go below deck for a moment where the brownies were so I asked Gruffy if he wanted another one while I was down there. He immediately said, "Yes, please!" as I made my way down. I grabbed the box of brownies and stopped for a moment to tie my shoe. The 15-second delay caused Gruffy to yell down to me, "Hey Eddie, don't forget those brownies!"

When I was first in the market to buy a Canal Bike to hold surfcasting gear, I was searching newspaper ads everywhere in an effort to find exactly what I wanted. I had looked high and low and finally found a bike that had everything I needed to become a nice Canal Bike except for the color. It was perfect except for the multi colored paint job that included red, black and green with yellow and orange shooting stars plus a group of purple florescent astrological symbols that made it look like a relic from Woodstock! I told Gruffy that I had finally found the ideal bike, but that the color was just too much for me.

I wanted to ride to my fishing spot and not become part of a psychedelic parade! Gruffy thought about it for a second and told me that I should definitely buy that bike. I was surprised that he apparently found this color scheme to be acceptable so when I asked him why I should buy it he said, "Because, it's so ugly nobody will steal it!"

Three of us were heading down A1A in the Florida Keys in route to Key West to meet up with some great guys and hopefully some saltwater fish. Gruffy's brother-in-law John DiCarlo, an outstanding plumber, was waiting for us with retired Wareham Police Officer Neal McCabe, Sherborn Police Detective Sergeant Michael B. McLaughlin, who is now retired after serving as the Acting Chief and Framingham Police Detective Matthew Gutwill, who was assigned to DEA where his dangerous work was being recognized internationally. Gruffy was driving the rental convertible with the top down on a beautiful day as we passed Islamorada and continued south into Paradise. I was in the front passenger seat with Doug Mann telling us jokes and funny stories from the back. Doug owns a flooring business, but he could make a nice living as a standup comic so we were really enjoying the show! We were all wearing big goofy looking dark colored oversized hats that flopped over our ears to protect us from the tropical sun. We looked like Jed Clampett on steroids as you could almost hear the theme song from *Deliverance* playing in the background! A nicely colored new car passed us that had an attractive and different shade of blue that I had never seen before so as the vehicle went by, I mentioned to Gruffy that it was a pretty color. He turned his head toward me and pretended to be serious as he stated, "Don't ever say the word "pretty" while you're wearing that hat."

We rented a charter and were having a good time catching different kinds of fish about 30 miles south of Key West when we suddenly spotted a huge nuclear powered submarine surface from the depths of the Atlantic. We were only about 60 miles from Cuba so Gruffy looked at me and said, "Hey Eddie, make sure that's one of ours!"

Gruffy tries on former New England Patriot & 3x Super Bowl Champion Joe Andruzzi's Super Bowl ring (Judge Michelle L. Kelley photo)

5. Law Enforcement

By the time I was born my maternal grandfather Jack Flynn had retired from the Taunton Police Department where he had served as a highly regarded detective for many years. He had to drop out of school early, I think in the third grade, to help put food on the table for his family to survive. Whatever he missed in formal education was made up for with a Ph. D. in street smarts. Grandpa Flynn was a big man who had a Depression Era mentality that had molded his jovial demeanor with an abundant supply of caution. I spent a lot of time with him as a kid and remain grateful for everything he taught me. It seemed like he knew everybody in the Silver City as people would yell greetings to him from passing cars as we walked down the sidewalk which always made me feel as though I was in the company of a celebrity. His police badge that he gave me before he passed is still proudly displayed on my bureau.

My grandmother had died young so Grandpa lived alone later in life and wanted to protect his home from break-ins when he was out, although he wasn't concerned about a confrontation with an intruder when he was at home because a burglar meeting him would have been destined for the worst day of his life. He had devised the best security system for his house that relied upon common sense for providing protection that never failed. He didn't need a sophisticated electronic burglar alarm as his simple method required no installation or wiring and worked like a charm. Nobody ever broke into that house and if they were ever thinking about it the notice on the door was what probably changed their mind. Grandpa's foolproof system was a note taped on his front door that read, JIM - GONE TO GET MY GUN. BE RIGHT HOME, JACK.

Grandfather, Taunton Police Detective Jack Flynn (middle) with recovered stolen silver

Just like most police officers, Grandpa Flynn spent a lot of time in the courthouse. One day he had brought a prisoner into the Taunton District Court and decided to observe another case that had just been called. A 40-year old man stood before the judge on an assault & battery charge. When the judge inquired as to why he hit the victim the defendant stated that he had been called an Irish son of a bitch. The judge then said that while that is not a nice thing to say, it is certainly not a good reason to punch someone. The defendant thought for a moment and responded, "Judge - how would you like it if somebody called you an Irish son of a bitch?" The judge leaned forward and proclaimed, "Well, I'm not Irish." The defendant thought for a moment and then asked, "Judge - what if somebody called you whatever kind of a son of a bitch you are?"

My mother used to see Grandpa, her father, come home after working details at Roseland Ballroom where he had to break up fights and make arrests to keep the peace. He would walk in the house sometimes with his shirt covered in blood and always reassured my mom not to worry because the blood was not his. Just like most police officers, seeing the dark side of life every day left him skeptical, suspicious and always on full alert. Trust was a hard earned and rarely experienced human emotion for survivors of the Great Depression like Grandpa Flynn.

I remember when a new face came on the scene to protect consumers from faulty products including dangerous cars having mechanical failures resulting in deadly accidents. Ralph Nader was almost universally praised as an honorable man and champion for the little guy. Nader would go on to save numerous lives and win many awards for his contributions to humanity including the Gandhi Peace Award and many others. He was not popular with some automobile manufacturers though as it looked like he was going to cost them money and ultimately, he did. When I spoke with Grandpa about Nader he immediately stated that, "General Motors will hire him for a million dollars a year to make sure there are four tires on every car!" In other words, Nader will take a legal bribe and stop the negative publicity about the car companies. Grandpa's innate skepticism governed his thinking by quickly producing the theory that everyone was out to make a buck so Nader must be too! It turned out that Nader was the real deal and will be recorded in history as an honest American hero, but I learned a lot from Grandpa's thought process and I'd like to think that I have led a more cautious life infused with his lessons.

Grandpa Flynn owned one of the first cars equipped with headlights that turned off automatically 30 seconds after the key was removed from the vehicle so most of America had not yet seen this magnificent invention. I was a young kid riding in the front seat of his car when Grandpa parked on the side of the curb in downtown Taunton. We got out of the car and started to walk away when one of his slew of friends stopped to say hello and upon noticing the headlights said, "Hey Jack, you left your lights on." Without missing a beat, Grandpa said thanks, turned toward the headlights and pursed his lips as he blew toward the lights as if blowing out candles on a birthday cake. The timing was perfect, the lights went out and the guy's jaw dropped as his face froze in a state of shock!

Sometimes I felt like we were taking a tour of southeast Massachusetts as Grandpa had friends everywhere. He was very close to Vinny Walsh who may have lived in Bridgewater. We would pull into Mr. Walsh's driveway where Grandpa would be greeted like a visiting dignitary. The whole family loved Grandpa so I was also treated like Royalty. Grandpa and Mr. Walsh went way back and had been friends forever so I always enjoyed our visits there as stories were swapped in a room full of laughter.

The story goes that one day not long after World War II Mr. Walsh just happened to mention to Grandpa that he would really like to buy a Volkswagen for a graduation present for his daughter. He had tried everywhere to no avail as our country had been at war with Nazi Germany where the automobile was manufactured. Mr. Walsh had a lot of valuable connections, but he told Grandpa that no one could get their hands on this car. Grandpa looked at Mr. Walsh and softly said, "Vinny, what color do you want?" At first Mr. Walsh thought that Grandpa was kidding, but he was elated when a brand-new Volkswagen was delivered to his driveway the next week!

Mr. Walsh was the head of the ticket office at the Boston Garden and was so grateful that he told Grandpa that he could have tickets to any games for the rest of his life. Grandpa had no interest in sports as he viewed ballgames through the lens of his own hard-fought upbringing where time was considered wasted unless the activity produced immediate income and turned the Yankee dollar! He thanked Mr. Walsh, but was really just happy that he could deliver on the car and put a smile on his daughter's face.

The Boston Celtics were hoisting World Championship banners to the rafters on a regular basis that had been produced by future Hall of Fame players that would become household names on legendary teams that would establish a basketball dynasty. I was never any good at basketball, but my dad was a big fan and taught me the game at an early age. Grandpa called basketball Bally Bally, but would sit patiently next to us as we talked about the Celts beating somebody. This was long before I had ever met Mr. Walsh and his family at their home and we knew nothing about Grandpa's connection to him as we continued speaking about the team. My dad mentioned that someday he would take me to a game at the Garden, but it might not be for a long time because even though they weren't always sold out it was sometimes hard to get good tickets. Grandpa piped in and asked us where we wanted to sit? What!!!

Grandpa came through as Mr. Walsh got seats for dad and I near half court that I remember being just about 10 rows back from the parquet floor! We had these seats so often that one time a guy thought that dad worked there. Legendary Boston Celtics coach Arnold "Red" Auerbach won many World Championships and eventually left the bench to sit in the audience when he became General Manager. He could have had any seat in the house, but he chose to sit not far from us at the same distance from the floor because it afforded the best view of the entire game. My memory from over a half century ago was close to correct as Attorney Jan Volk, who had done a remarkable job as another of the longtime Celts General Managers, told me many years later that Red sat in Row 8! Not that we needed validation, but Red's choice of seating only served to confirm the value of our reserved spots. I always kept an eye out for Red toward the end of the game because dad had told me that he only lit his cigar when the Celtics were assured of victory. Dad was right and Red was never wrong - cigar smoke always meant a win was coming!

Later in life, I had the distinct pleasure of meeting Bill Russell, Tommy Heinsohn, John Havlicek, Thomas "Satch" Sanders, Bob Cousy, Sam Jones and Larry Bird.

I was there with dad for Championship games against the Los Angeles Lakers and many other historic contests where a floor full of basketball greats seemed almost common. We watched the great Bill Russell position himself perfectly to snare 40 rebounds from the Lakers in Game 7 as the Celtics tasted victory again in the 1962 NBA Finals. We heard Joe

Dillon, an MDC Water Division worker, break the respectful silence by yelling from a high balcony, "We love ya Cooz" on March 17, 1963, Bob Cousy Day in celebration of the guard who made behind the back passes look easy and was more accurate than anyone else in the league. Thousands of Celtics enthusiasts walked by a car inside the Garden that was a gift to the "Houdini of the Hardwood" from the Celtics that day. The vehicle was covered in so much dust that fans wrote messages on it with their fingers. After my eight year old right index digit dragged through the grime to spell, GO COOZ, I told dad that I would never wash that finger again!

Eleven-time NBA World Champion, five-time NBA MVP Boston Celtic Bill Russell, RFK Golf Tournament, Hyannisport Club

Christopher J. Dolan is one of the most squared away, best natured and nicest guys that I ever met in the system. He started as a dispatcher with the North Attleborough Police Department where he eventually became a police officer before moving on to the same job with the MDC. Chris graduated from the Massachusetts State Police Academy and was promoted to detective in the CPAC Units of the Bristol and Plymouth County District Attorney's Offices. He participated in the investigations of future convicted murderers Gary Lee Sampson, Aaron Hernandez and other homicides while establishing a reputation of honesty and determination. The now retired detective sergeant and his lovely wife Lisa would celebrate St. Patrick's Day at the 19th Hole Tavern where we shared a few toasts together and always had some laughs.

My great-grandfather John T. Brady came here from Ireland carrying his fishing gear and very little else. I inherited his beautiful trout creel that would hang over his shoulder while he wet a line so I have always proudly displayed it in our home. We were in the middle of moving into our new house so the creel was the first thing I hung on the wall in our family room next to the fireplace. Chris called after court hours requesting a search warrant so I gave him our new address, but told him that he would have to maneuver between disorganized furniture and unpacked boxes as this was our first night in the new home. Chris made his way through the obstacle course while walking by bare walls and presented me with the affidavit which I read and approved. Just before leaving he noticed that the only thing on the wall was the fishing creel and smiled as he said that he wasn't surprised at my priorities!

It was always easy taking a call from Chris because he understood that just because he was awake at 2AM, most people including me were in bed. Some guys call at off hours and want to make small talk about the Celtics because they must think that the rest of the world is awake with them! My wife would be asleep next to me so I would try to answer the phone quickly to stop the ring. Chris knew exactly what I needed to know so he would tell me, for instance, the defendant's name, town, that he had release money and a sober ride home without my having to ask. My wife would be trying to continue sleeping as I spoke as little as possible so Chris' routine was perfect and helped extend the warranty on a long marriage even longer! Chris had little codes for typical arrests so instead of telling me that the defendant was arrested for drunk driving, operating to endanger and operating without a license he would say, "We have a guy here for Plan A."

I always enjoyed doing hearings with Wrentham Police Lieutenant Richard Gillespie, a smart police officer with a keen sense of humor. Dick had finished reading the police report alleging larceny against the 45-year old defendant from Boston seated before me. He had been caught in the act so I guess he figured that his only defense was to state that he had a clean record. As soon as we heard him declare that he had led a crime free life, Dick looked at the defendant's record and said, "What about that homicide conviction in Dorchester?" "Oh, that was a long time ago," the defendant proclaimed, to which Dick replied, "Yea, but the guy's still dead!"

Just like all teenagers, I was guilty of using poor judgment now and then as sometimes common sense isn't so common in kids. I was a sophomore at Attleboro High School sitting in the front seat of a friend's car as we made a left on Wall Street and travelled down County Street away from the center of Attleboro at about 9PM. I know one of our friends was in the back seat and there may have been one other guy back there with him. As we passed a guy who may have been just a little older walking on the far sidewalk he decided, out of nowhere, to give us the middle finger while wearing a facial expression of intense anger. I said to pull over, got out of the car and walked across the road toward Mr. Miserable as I loudly asked, "What's your problem?" I may have mixed in a few other choice words as well as he walked toward me and asked, "What are you going to do about it?"

We met right in the middle of the street on top of the yellow lines where we began to trade punches. None of our blows were landing dead on or doing much damage until my right arm got hurt pretty badly blocking a left hook. I kept my right up because I didn't want him to know that I was now fighting almost one handed. Meanwhile traffic was backed up as people were driving over the sidewalk to get around the County Street fisticuffs with some of them yelling out the car window at us. I was too busy to see the drivers, but one woman who sounded like an elderly lady with a high-pitched voice shouted, "You two assholes should go home right now!"

Some high school fights last about 10 seconds, but we kept going. I threw a left as my opponent jerked his head back just enough so that I only caught the tip of his nose. The punch didn't cause much real harm, but it smashed his nose good enough to cause a blood flow that looked to be sufficient for a transfusion. Suddenly he decided that wrestling was the better option as he charged into me while grabbing the back of my upper thighs, burying his bloody nose in my stomach and body slamming me into the macadam. We both landed on my back as I injured an ankle during the landing. I got him in a partial headlock with my left arm, but his neck was so big that I couldn't get my wrist under his chin to shut off his air supply.

County Street, also known as Route 123, is a very busy street that goes right through the center of the city. We were fighting just below a rise in the road so a car speeding toward the center would travel over the hill and be upon us in no time! Vehicles were backed up past Brennan Junior High School during most of the fight which had provided an added degree of safety as cars had to slow down before driving up on the sidewalk, but now that the traffic congestion had cleared a driver operating a fast moving vehicle wouldn't be able to see us until almost on top of us after cresting the hill.

We were both getting tired rolling around on the blacktop when a speeding car came flying over the hill with screeching brakes causing it to stop only a few feet from our faces which were lit up by the high beam headlights. I guess we both had a come to Jesus moment at the same time with the realization that we were lucky to be alive as we simultaneously released the grip on each other and got up. Mr. Miserable staggered toward the sidewalk and I limped back to the car in the other direction. My friends were cheering and yelling as I made sure that the blood on my shirt didn't belong to me.

Somebody must have called the police because we had only driven about a mile when we saw blue lights behind us and pulled over on Cliff Street. Attleboro Police Captain Walter Heagney Jr., who went by the name Larry and whose son Kyle is now Chief of the same department, and another officer shined their flashlights in the car as the captain stated that they had a report of us attacking a guy on County Street. I immediately replied that it wasn't my friends, only me. I obeyed his order to get out and was searched for weapons as he asked me questions. I would get to know him later through my job in the court and on this night he was very direct, professional and in control as always. I was polite and kept referring to him as officer because I was too young to recognize his rank. I told him that I shouldn't have gotten out of the car, but that the guy had been rude by giving us the finger. I guess that I must have made a pretty good case for myself, probably because I was honest and polite, as Captain Heagney smiled, softened his tone and suddenly started treating me like I was the victim. He made sure that I was OK, said that he was going to find my assailant and took off with blue lights flashing and the siren blaring.

I learned a lot about life that night as I was wrong to get out of that car on County Street. I did something stupid that could have resulted in a criminal charge or even death, but I was lucky. The incident also reinforced my knowledge that civility and politeness can sometimes carry the day. Another decade would go by before I found myself working in the court system, but this night taught me that justice isn't always blind. The long road to justice has been paved with the blood, sweat and courage of honorable men and women who held fast to their beliefs while sometimes having to stand up against seemingly insurmountable obstacles. Sometimes good fortune causes justice to swing your way so like the renowned ragtime jazz pianist Eubie Blake once said, "Be grateful for luck."

I had just finished hearings at the WDC when I got a call from Attleboro Police Chief Roland D. Sabourin Jr. who I knew well from my time at the Attleboro Court. As a matter of fact, Rollie, when he was a lieutenant, was the very first police officer to call me on my first day on the job for a couple of alleged car thieves.

We exchanged pleasantries and he then told me that Captain Walter Heagney was dying in the hospital as it looked like there wasn't much time left for the long-time public servant who had become a venerable law enforcement institution in the city. Rollie said that he was short a few years, but a bill had passed the House and Senate to create a full pension to provide for the captain's wife. The end of the Legislative session was near so the Heagney bill, along with many others, was sitting on Governor Cellucci's desk awaiting his signature. Rollie expressed urgency as speed was of the utmost importance because it had to be signed by the Governor before the captain passed or they would have to start all over again in the next Legislative session. Rollie said that it had already been verbally approved by Governor Cellucci and that he was definitely going to sign it anyway, but success was dependent on timing. Rollie asked for my help and I quickly agreed to make a call.

As I was dialing the governor's office in the Massachusetts State House my mind harkened back to the kindness of Captain Heagney when he spotted a few 8-year old kids at Hayward Field on a slight rise high enough for us to catch a glimpse over the fence of the Attleboro High School football game. My parents would have given me admission money if I had asked, but I remember Captain Heagney, who may have been a patrolman at the time, motioning for us with his hand as he opened the gate to let us into the game for free. His Irish American face was a welcome sight as he told us to, "Have a good time boys." I also thought back to how lucky I had been when I was frisked by the captain on Cliff Street after doing something stupid on County Street.

I got through to the governor's office at a very busy time and had a conversation with one of his top aides. Governor Cellucci signed the bill the next day and the pension enhancement became law. The Governor was going to sign it anyway, but I was happy if my call helped with the timing and assisted in even some small way because Captain Heagney passed away soon thereafter.

I had first met Captain Heagney's son Kyle when he was a patrolman in the same department as his father. He is a squared away, honest, smart and very capable police officer with an unfiltered laugh so I was glad when he was named the Chief of Police in Attleboro. David Linton, the talented crime beat writer for *The Sun Chronicle*, quoted Chief Kyle P. Heagney in a 2020 front page story about the protests resulting from the death of George Floyd who was killed by police in Minneapolis. There were some good ideas born out of this tragedy that were being demanded by protesters including various levels of police reform, but there were also some terrible proposals being put forth like the complete elimination of police departments! Linton's interview with Chief Heagney produced a quote that left no doubt about his feelings when he said, "Getting rid of police departments? I think it's going to be as effective as a screen door on a submarine."

My brother Brendan was promoted many times through the ranks of the Rhode Island State Police before eventually being appointed to the position of Superintendent with the rank of Colonel and spent a good deal of time as a detective in the Intelligence Unit. After retiring Brendan coauthored a powerful and interesting book with Joe Broadmeadow entitled *"it's just the way it was"* which chronicled the battle against the Mob in New England. Brendan included stories about various topics, but the main focus of the book is his fascinating up close and personal interactions with the New England Mafia.

J. Do always had high praise for Arthur J. Brillon who was one of her classmates at Bishop Feehan High School. I got to know him later as a conscientious and hardworking police officer for the City of Attleboro. Artie always seemed to be in a good mood with an honest smile and a cheerful greeting. My contact with him was always positive and professional as he really is one of the good guys. Artie helped solve many significant crimes during his many years as a detective and retired at the rank of lieutenant. I was privileged to speak at his retirement party where a sold-out crowd gathered to celebrate and toast a popular public servant.

The release announcement for Brendan's book caused Artie to remember the famous scene in The Godfather movie where a dead fish is wrapped in a newspaper to symbolize that a mob hit had been carried out resulting in a murder. The line that we all remember from the sequence is, "…He sleeps with the fishes."

I had already written my first book about fishing so Artie texted me, "Brendan's book is about people 'sleeping with the fishes' and yours is about catching them!"

Steven D. Ricciardi was the (SAC) Special Agent in Charge of the Boston Field Office of the United States Secret Service. I was honored to have Steve speak at our Courthouse Speaker Series where he captivated our audience with interesting stories of his protection details and criminal investigations. One time his eight-year-old son was upset because Steve had missed a series of his hockey games while protecting the First Lady, so the young boy wrote a letter to Hillary Clinton asking for his father back! Steve was away so often on so many protection details all over the world that his two oldest sons convinced the youngest boy that their father was in prison. Steve's wife heard about it at a Little League game where the other wives felt badly that her husband was doing time, not so! It was my pleasure to speak at

Steve Ricciardi, Special Agent in Charge, Boston Field Office, United States Secret Service

Steve's retirement party at Ned Devine's in Faneuil Hall where a huge crowd gathered to thank a good guy for his many years of service to our country and to wish him well.

I was hearing Foxborough Police cases on a busy day where the hallway was so packed with defendants and attorneys that it was difficult to move through the crowd. The defendant seated before me was a forty-year old woman who was angry as she sat down and didn't get any more pleasant during the hearing. She was convinced that people were conspiring against her by making up stories and various lies. She said she knew that she wouldn't get a fair hearing which was exacerbated by her realization that there were so many guys named Doherty involved with her case. The incident had been investigated by Officer Kevin Doherty of the Foxborough Police, a squared away, nice guy who is now a sergeant on the Burlington Police Department. His police report was being read into evidence by Foxborough Officer Paul Doherty, a good guy who served as the department prosecutor. It was obvious the woman was getting uncomfortable as Prosecutor Doherty stated his name and identified the author of the report as Officer Doherty. She immediately glanced at the name plate on my desk revealing the presence of another Doherty! I told her that we weren't related, but she looked at me with horrified skepticism! After finding probable cause I issued a criminal complaint and told her she would be getting a summons in the mail. She headed for the door while shaking her head, declaring it a kangaroo court full of brothers and cousins. She opened the door to the crowded hallway where Attorney Michael P. Doherty just happened to be right outside my office speaking with a client! It's a good thing she didn't know his name!

Lieutenant George G. Bussiere, who retired as a captain, was the prosecutor for the Attleboro Police during a good part of my time at the city court. He was a nice guy, an Army veteran and old-fashioned dedicated police officer who could sniff out a lie like a dog on a bone. Buzzy called me by my last name and spoke in a staccato cadence that sounded like a human police report so I always envisioned him in the place of Sergeant Joe Friday on the TV show *Dragnet* stating, "Just the facts, ma'am."

As I would start calling arraignments in Courtroom One Buzzy and the other police prosecutors would be seated at their table off to my left. I called the case of a man who was ready to admit to sufficient facts, different from but tantamount to pleading guilty. The nervous defendant was about 40 years of age with no criminal record except for two OUI arrests. It is not unusual for people to be uncomfortable in court, but this guy looked like he was ready to have a stroke with perspiration running down his neck. He was sweating like Jethro Bodine before a math test!

The defendant had agreed to attend a second offense drunk driving program which would be enforced by a 30-day House of Correction suspended sentence with probation. He would only do time for noncompliance, but when I read the sentence to him, he thought he was going to be locked up immediately for a month! As soon as I announced 30 days HoC and before I could say suspended, he defecated in his pants. The loud sound of roaring flatulence and putrid smell of feces rapidly permeated the courtroom. The defendant's backside was only a few feet from the prosecutors' table producing vomit-ready facial expressions on the police. I vividly recall one prosecutor waving his hand in front of his nose as he turned away in search of fresh air. I felt badly for the defendant so I quickly told him he wasn't going to jail. Buzzy made it a point to come up to me during the recess and say, "Well Doherty, you really scared the shit out of that guy!"

I had already been working for several years at the ADC when a woman in her mid-thirties was assaulted by three cowards near the railroad bridge on Pleasant Street in Attleboro. Two of the lowlifes held her down while the third reprobate brutally raped her. This despicable crime went unsolved for 26 years until retired Detective Lieutenant Art Brillon, now a Special Investigator with the Bristol County DA's Special Victim's Unit, and Attleboro Police Detective Lieutenant, now Deputy Chief Timothy D. Cook Jr. used DNA evidence to identify the assailant. A warrant was issued and eventually served on the defendant after long hours of research, dogged determination and hard work that finally paid off. Hopefully, justice will bring at least some sense of relief and closure to the poor victim.

Clerk-magistrates and assistant clerk-magistrates may be on call for various duties with the police departments in their district whenever the courthouse is closed on weekends, holidays and at night. Some of those responsibilities include setting bail on arrests and releasing criminal defendants as well as the issuance of arrest warrants and search warrants. The ADC had a rotating schedule such that one person would be on call for a week and then get one or maybe two weeks off at night, but each court devises their own plan.

The defendant pays a fee to procure his or her release from the police lockup. The amount of the release fee has changed a few times over the years and it remained at $40.00 per defendant at the time of my retirement. Most defendants are released on personal recognizance so $40.00 is all that they will need. If the clerk-magistrate or assistant sets bail then the defendant, his or her family or someone else will have to come up with the bail amount and release fee in order to procure his or her freedom. If the bail is set at $500.00, for instance, the defendant will need $540.00 to be released. The $500.00 bail will be returned to the surety once the criminal case has been resolved, but the $40.00 is kept by the clerk-magistrate or assistant.

Multiple arrests in busy police departments can sometimes result in lucrative nights for clerk-magistrates and assistants causing the unfortunate human emotion of jealousy in some others. It is not always as easy as it seems, however, as there are positives and negatives just like in any job. No one would look forward to getting out of a warm bed at 3AM after having worked a full day in the court, to start the car in a snowstorm with the wind chill at 20 below zero and drive to the police station over partially plowed roads to speak with one ungrateful drunk. Multiple concert arrests on warm summer nights made up for those dangerous cold rides in the snow, but even a pocket full of cash comes with exhaustion and inconvenience.

It certainly helped tremendously to have an understanding and helpful family with a job that often required riding around to different police stations at all hours of the night. I was a peripatetic night owl traversing the streets of my judicial district in all kinds of weather. There were no cell phones when I first started taking bail and eventually it was considered a huge improvement when we acquired a modern invention called a pager or beeper as they were called. J. Do used to handle my phone calls when I was between lockups and sometimes even when I was home asleep.

J. Do helped me enormously by taking our two young daughters out of the house from about 11AM to 1PM on Saturdays and Sundays so that I could get a little sleep and be able to continue functioning. This would be appreciated by anyone who has done the job and I could not have even come close to continuing without my bride's kindness.

There are probably hundreds of court officers working in the Commonwealth and Jeffrey J. Pugsley is quite simply one of the very best. Pugs is an extremely amiable, yet low-key guy who would give you the shirt off his back. Everyone loves him for his professionalism, keen sense of humor and dedication to task. Although he is an average size guy, I always felt well protected with Pugs on the job because I really think that he could handle any situation. Upon my request, he gave me the family photo below that shows his grandfather Sergeant Arthur S. Pugsley, on the left, retiring from the Boston Police Department and carrying his uniform on his last day on the job. The seven police officers on the right are all of his sons saluting their father. They are lined up according to age with the youngest on the lowest step and Jeff's father Jack the second from the bottom. The seven boys had one other sibling - the youngest in the family was a girl.

Sergeant Arthur S. Pugsley leaving BPD, saluted by seven sons. (photo by Charles Dixon, courtesy of The Boston Globe Library Collection at the Northeastern University Archives and Special Collections)

I had just finished releasing several prisoners from the Attleboro Police Department lockup shortly after midnight and was heading for the door when the shift commander told me that they had just brought in an arrest that was being processed in the booking room. My job in those days entailed being on call 24/7 and operating on an average of three hours sleep so I would try to do what I could to make life a little easier on myself whenever possible. Rather than sit and wait for the defendant to be booked which would essentially delay my trip home to bed by about a half hour, I decided to walk down to the booking room to review the case as he was being fingerprinted. He was under arrest for writing and passing several bad checks valued at thousands of dollars and had a criminal record of convictions for fraud and larceny. The sergeant asked me to consider bail on the paper hanger, as bad check artists are called. In reviewing the defendant's record, I noticed that he also had numerous other outstanding bad check charges pending so I set his bail at $1,000.00 cash. As soon as I announced that I had set his bail at $1,000.00 cash the paper hanger looked at me and asked, "Will you take a check?"

The amount of the release fee has changed over the years, but at one time it was $20.00 for quite a while. One of the usual defendants at the Attleboro Police lockup found himself in trouble for minor offenses on a regular basis. He was a nice guy, but just like so many others, alcohol abuse was the root of all of his problems. He kept a folded 20 dollar bill in a different section of his wallet away from the rest of his cash so that it would always be there when he got arrested. He would spend all of his money on beer and whiskey, but never reach for the tucked away 20 dollar bill. He lived by that rule, thus always had enough cash to insure his release from a cell. I was filling out his recognizance form one time when he looked at me and said, "I never drink my last 20!"

The officer accidently left out a letter while typing his police report for the arrest. He meant to describe approaching the driver's window, but instead had inadvertently typed, "I approached the driver's widow."

It was a busy Friday night at the Attleboro Police lockup where I needed to speak with the shift commander who was in the booking room with three more arrests. I had already set bail on one of our regular B & E guys so I was walking by his cell on my way to booking. He had been apprehended as a result of motion detectors and activated floodlights which at the time was some real cutting-edge technology. He complained to me that the world is changing too fast and that it just isn't fair for a poor thief like him!

When the release fee was $40.00 per prisoner I used to jokingly tell my friends that I would get to keep $5.00 and J. Do got $35.00!

Sergeant Lawrence M. Brennick Jr. is a hilarious guy who would call the house frequently, mostly about prisoners, because he was a shift commander at the Attleboro Police Department. J. Do had also gotten to know Larry and his lovely wife Christa pretty well at various police functions and courthouse parties. Larry was one of the funniest guys in the system and kept us laughing as he found humor in just about everything. His stories were fascinating, including the one of him operating a tank when he was in the service in Germany. Larry somehow miscalculated and drove the tank right into some unfortunate guy's house. The tank commander opened the hatch and looked out to see the inside of a living room as he started screaming, "Brennick - get us out of here!" Larry tried to comply, but hit the wrong button causing the gun turret to start to turn with the high caliber cannon sweeping through the home and taking out the second floor.

Lieutenant Lawrence Velino would also call our home quite frequently as he was a shift commander with the same department. One time J. Do answered the phone to hear Larry Velino, without identifying himself, ask for me. She thought it was Larry Brennick and asked, "Is this Larry?" Velino, of course replied, "Yes" and J. Do dove into a whole conversation asking about his wife, how he was doing and eventually handed the phone to me. Lieutenant Velino immediately said, "Gee Eddie, your wife is really nice and so friendly." I don't think that I ever got around to telling him what really happened.

Attorney John M. Moses served as an Assistant District Attorney, but for most of my time in Attleboro he was a truly great criminal defense lawyer with the Massachusetts Defenders Committee which included some of the hardest working and most highly skilled advocates in the system including Attorney John L. Holgerson, Attorney W. Alan Zwirblis, Attorney Alvin Youman, Attorney Kathleen V. Curley, who would later marry John Moses and Attorney James M. Quinn, who went by Jay and, as previously mentioned, would eventually be appointed to a District Court judgeship. Mass Defenders provided free legal service for indigent defendants who were charged with some of the most heinous and consequential crimes in the state. This list of offenses were not only serious felonies, but they were all what we called Bind Overs as they were bound over to a grand jury if a judge found Probable Cause after a hearing in District Court. These cases were so serious that the District Court lacked jurisdiction so the final outcome would be heard in Superior Court. The list of these crimes would be amended from time to time as the legislature and governor would sometimes grant the District Court jurisdiction even though the potential penalty exceeded five years in state prison. For instance, assault and battery by means of a dangerous weapon is a 10-year felony that was a Bind Over case when I first started in Attleboro, but the law was eventually changed so that the case could be heard at the District Court level. These hearings would not always be necessary as sometimes the defendant was directly indicted.

Unfortunately, some defendants really didn't appreciate the high degree of expert legal service that they were getting from Mass Defenders representation and the most amazing part was that it was all free of charge! I was still standing in Courtroom One in Attleboro during a court recess while John Moses was speaking to his client who was handcuffed on the custody side of the railing in the prisoner's dock. This particular defendant grew up in the system so I knew him well and was very familiar with his long history of inflicting serious physical and emotional pain upon innocent victims. If true justice were really served, he would have caught a bullet behind his left ear long ago, but John, being the legal genius that he was, had found deficiencies in the Commonwealth's case and had worked out a terrific deal for his client so that he would only have to serve six months committed.

I almost couldn't believe it when the ungrateful felon went berserk and started screaming obscenities at John for doing a lousy job!

David T. Proia was a good guy who I had known since high school. Dave was sworn in as an Attleboro Police Officer and promoted until eventually reaching the high rank of captain. We had many telephone conversations and discussions at the police station over the course of our careers together. Dave had a nice way about him with an easy laugh and a tremendous sense of humor. I was releasing prisoners on a Sunday morning as Dave would escort them to me from the cell block. He told me about a guy in cell 5 who had asked for a drink of water. The good captain had all of the defendant's booking data on his desk, but just made friendly conversation as he handed the prisoner a cup of water. Dave asked the guy what he had done to get locked up to which the response was, "Nothing! I was just minding my own business and watching TV when the police smashed open my door and placed me under arrest! Unbelievable. This has got to stop!"

Dave smiled at me and facetiously said that it was an epidemic! It's happened again! Police are kicking down doors and grabbing law abiding citizens! Dave then told me that the arrest was the result of a drug raid in which I had issued a search warrant for the defendant's apartment. The defendant had told Dave that he had done nothing wrong, but failed to mention the suitcase full of heroin that the detectives had found hidden under his bed when they executed the search warrant.

Detectives used to come to the courthouse or to my house from time to time to ask me for an arrest warrant or search warrant. Dave always worked very diligently to prepare the affidavit so that he would be able to demonstrate the necessary level of Probable Cause for the warrant. One time he told me that after he had completed an affidavit, he would always review it for potential defects before presenting it to me and that he measured success with a unique and interesting test. Dave said that as he was reading his own affidavit, he would be searching for any weaknesses that might be uncovered by Attorney John Moses. He told me that as he read through each sentence, he was saying to himself, "What would Moses say?"

John Moses had become the gold standard by which perfection was measured which served as a tremendous compliment to a dedicated and brilliant lawyer. I was gratified that I was able to tell John about that high praise of his legal skill before he passed away.

A man stole a corporate ATM card, purchased goods at a few different locations and was arrested after an investigation by NAPD Detective Daniel B. Arrighi and Officer Kory Kiser. One of the defendant's mistakes leading to his arrest was the use of his own store rewards card to accumulate discount points!

I had nominated Detective Arrighi for the Rotary Club's Distinguished Service Award and was glad that the committee voted to honor him as the Outstanding Public Employee from many candidates in two different towns. He was an honest, diligent and hardworking police officer who kept the streets safe by taking a proactive stand against drunk drivers. It was not unusual to hear stories of intoxicated drivers taking circuitous routes around

North Attleborough to avoid arrest and Dan Arrighi is probably more responsible for that reputation than anyone. As a North Attleborough resident for many years I was grateful for the superb level of safety afforded my family and sometimes wondered how many lives had been saved by the aggressive approach of Dan Arrighi.

He is also well known for his remarkable ability to obtain confessions in some serious criminal cases. The only one hearing more confessions than Dan Arrighi was the parish priest! Dan's professionalism and hard work was recognized upon his retirement from the NAPD when he was hired as a Sexual Assault Kit Initiative Investigator by the Bristol County District Attorney's Office where he continues to work on violent cold cases today.

Patrick W. McMurray has held many impactful state, federal, and private sector positions in his long, distinguished career. As a Special Agent with the United States Secret Service he ran a Financial Fraud Task Force from the Boston Field Office and was part of the Presidential Protection Division which took him around the world. President Bill Clinton introduced Pat to Pope John Paul II causing him to tell me that, "Shaking the hand of a Saint will never be forgotten." Pat was holding two sets of Rosary Beads in his right palm as he and the Pope shook hands and a few months later, put one of them in his father's casket.

He served in many other prominent capacities including as the Special Agent in Charge/Country Attaché in Canada when Governor A. Paul Cellucci was appointed United States Ambassador to Canada by President George W. Bush. Pat got to know the Ambassador, his wife Jan, and their family during many government, ceremonial and social events at the American Embassy in Ottawa and elsewhere. Pat speaks in great reverence and awe of the humble Ambassador from Hudson who brought law enforcement partners closer together and was well respected by everyone. Although a humble man himself, Pat's resume is replete with significant and very impressive accomplishments having protected presidents and other world leaders. Pat doesn't like to speak about himself so I had to coax personal information from him and even though he has rubbed elbows with some of the most famous people on the planet, Pat told me that "…the highlight of my career was being affiliated with Paul Cellucci."

The presidential debate between Vice President Albert A. Gore and then Governor George W. Bush was held in October of 2000 at UMass Boston. Pat, in DC assigned to Major Events, was put in charge of security for the debate and ancillary proceedings. Secret Service Assistant Director David O'Connor's sister in law Denise Schultz had a friend in Winthrop with an outgoing, industrious, handicapped son named Owen. Owen was a very politically astute 20-year old whose dream was to meet Governor Bush so David called Pat to ask if this could be arranged. Pat set a plan in motion and Denise brought Owen to a hotel at Logan Airport where Governor Bush would be receiving an endorsement from the State Police Association of Massachusetts. While Owen was sitting in his wheelchair waiting for Governor Bush he became very excited when he spied another of his heroes in the same venue - Governor A. Paul Cellucci! This was long before Pat had ever met Governor Cellucci so he introduced himself to a trooper in the Governor's security detail who then relayed the request to His Excellency who reacted favorably without hesitation. Governor Cellucci spent over a half hour with Owen as they went back and forth over current events and national affairs. Not many elected officials would spend that much time with one kid, but Paul Cellucci had a heart of gold and really cared about helping people. Owen had a photo taken with Governor Cellucci and another one later with the future President of the United States, so Pat had laid the groundwork for a day that the young man will never forget.

Upon taking his post in Canada, Ambassador Cellucci made many friends, quickly becoming an integral part of Canadian life representing the United States. He was scheduled to play a round of golf one day at the Royal Ottawa Golf Club in Quebec with Pat, Dawson Hovey, Assistant Commissioner of the Royal Canadian Mounted Police and Ken Anderson, Assistant CIA Station Chief. Pat got to the course early and was taking some practice chips when a limo pulled up with Canadian Prime Minister Jean Chretien who always referred to Pat as the American Body Guard. The Prime Minister asked, "American Body Guard, what are you doing here?" When Pat told him he was waiting for the Ambassador the Prime Minister didn't realize that a foursome had already been formed and happily declared that he would golf with them. Displaying some diplomatic thinking himself, Pat formed a threesome of Ambassador Cellucci, Prime Minister Chretien and Assistant Commissioner Hovey which was followed on the golf course by the twosome of Pat and Assistant Station Chief Anderson. Pat teed off from a hole on the back 9 and sliced a long shot into the next fairway right at the distinguished threesome which elicited an incredibly loud yell from a voice easily recognized as the Prime Minister! The speeding ball zipped by the startled leader of our northern neighbors finding the grass and not his head, thus averting a potential international incident!

After 9/11 Ambassador Cellucci personally asked Pat and CIA Station Chief Tom Higgins to handle the security increase needed for the American Embassy. American air space was suddenly restricted and closed because of the terrorist attack on that horrible day resulting in many flights having to land at Gander International Airport in Canada. Pat accompanied Ambassador Cellucci and Prime Minister Chretien later to thank those people for their generosity, kindness and hospitality.

Pat accompanied Ambassador Cellucci and Prime Minister Chretien on the flight to New York to view the horrific devastation at Ground Zero. After reaching out to the Secret Service on the ground, Pat went to the cockpit to speak through the pilot in requesting to fly over the sacred spot where so many innocent Americans had died. They landed, took a boat across the Hudson River and walked to the hallowed site where President Bush had previously stood atop the rubble while making an impassioned speech with a promise for justice. The Ambassador and Prime Minister paid their solemn respects in a dignified and serious undertaking at a very sad place in our nation. When they returned to Canada, however, Ambassador Cellucci's keen sense of humor kicked into high gear when he saw a photo of Pat with Prime Minister Chretien in an Ottawa newspaper that had been taken on their trip to New York. The Ambassador kidded with Pat that, "You got more press than me!"

Pat has many fond memories of his time in Canada including the time when acclaimed Irish Tenor John McDermott joined him and some of his law enforcement colleagues kidding around with Ambassador Cellucci in the kitchen of the diplomatic residence. They were all inside the huge walk in cooler when McDermott suddenly burst out in song!

Pat and his wife Sue have kept in touch with the Cellucci family after the Ambassador's passing, getting together for dinner on occasion. Pat was serving as the Commonwealth's Undersecretary of Homeland Security and Homeland Security Advisor when we swapped emails about some forgotten subject, but the one part that I will never forget and was honored to receive, was Pat writing that Jan Cellucci had said to say hello to me. It certainly meant a lot to me because she is the kind widow of the great statesman who had appointed me for life.

Pat, his wife Sue, and some others joined the Celluccis at their home in Hudson two days before the prodigious Ambassador passed. Pat, prominently mentioned in the book *Unquiet Diplomacy* by Ambassador Cellucci, told me that it, "was an amazing honor to say goodbye to a great man."

McMurrays at Ambassador's residence. L-R Pat, daughter Kaleigh, Jan Cellucci, daughter Jacki, son Brooks in front, wife Sue, Ambassador Cellucci

Leo J. Acerra, a good guy who grew up in Roslindale, became a police officer in Millis. He was the prosecutor for his department so I always enjoyed doing hearings with him as Leo was firm when necessary, but always down to earth, pleasant and cooperative with a terrific sense of humor. He sat in the front passenger seat of a cruiser on his first day on the job in Millis as his training officer Sergeant Hugh Mick drove him around to show him the town. A radio call requested their location so the sergeant responded by saying they were at the traffic light. Leo, who had just left the big city, tried to be helpful by telling

Sergeant Mick that he forgot to say which light. The sergeant smiled and said, "This is Millis - there's only one traffic light in the whole town!"

Captain Charles F. "Ted" Dolan was the Chief of Detectives for the Pawtucket Police Department Special Squad, a select unit comprised over the years of elite detectives like Eugene Champagne, Sergeant Joseph I. Monteiro, Captain Patrick J. McConaghy and others. Detective Captain John S. Seebeck, a conscientious, outstanding police officer, was also sometimes assigned to Ted's unit. Joe Monteiro is a nice guy who probably knows baseball statistics better than any of us so it was always a pleasure to see him in uniform working a Pawtucket Red Sox game. Pawtucket was the AAA affiliate of the Boston Red Sox where future stars could be seen playing on their way up to the major leagues. McCoy Stadium was located right over the state line from Attleboro where I grew up so it was a frequent destination for us. I would be sitting with Greg Murphy, originally from Pawtucket before moving to Attleboro, watching the game as Joe would lean over while rattling off stats on the pitcher warming up in the bullpen. I used to kid Joe that he had the best job in the world because he was getting paid while watching his favorite sport! Ted, Joe, Murph and I went to games together elsewhere including Fenway Park and even drove to New York to see the Mets play Milwaukee at the old Shea Stadium in Queens where we had terrific seats thanks to Murph's friend Dave Nelson who was the First Base Coach for the Brewers.

The last game that Jacoby Ellsbury played at McCoy prior to his initial call up to the majors was also the same night that Ted Dolan was honored by throwing out the first pitch in Pawtucket. We all showed up to see Ted prepare to take the mound in his Red Sox uniform. When I told him that he looked great he said that he was all warmed up and ready just in case a call comes in from Boston needing a relief pitcher for the eighth inning! A member of the Paw Sox staff was assigned to escort Ted to the mound for his big pitch. Murph, who had been coached by Ted in American Legion Baseball, tracked down the escort in private beforehand and asked him to hand a note to the Guest of Honor once he was on the pitcher's mound. We all watched in anticipation as he was handed the note and read it. Murph had written, "The only thing you know about pitching is that you couldn't hit it!" Ted smiled and delivered a strike for the beginning of an enjoyable event.

Ted spent a good deal of his retirement time, until his passing, at Red Sox spring training in Fort Myers. His lovely wife Rosemary would drop him off at the ballpark and pick him up after the game near a certain mailbox on the sidewalk outside of the stadium. Ted would wait for his ride at the designated pick-up site so Rosemary called the Red Sox spring training facility "adult day care!"

There was an Irish pub in Pawtucket called the Irish Club although there was no sign so many people drove right by it without even knowing there was a bar inside. My brother Brendan introduced me to the bartender, a nice man named Patrick J. McCabe who lost all his cash in a card game on the ship from Ireland when he immigrated here as a young man. Without money the South Armagh native wasn't going to be allowed to disembark so he got word to his cousin in Brooklyn that he needed help. When the vessel docked in

New York Harbor a couple of NYPD Officers announced that they had a warrant for the arrest of McCabe as they came on board and took him off the ship. The ruse worked like a charm and Pat was happy to find himself safely on American soil.

Pat had spent many years quenching the thirst of his customers and was universally loved by all. When somebody at the pub bought you a drink Pat would put the beer in front of you and say in his Irish brogue, "You've got a friend", as he pointed out the paying patron to you. I have had drinks in pubs from Maine to Florida, from the Carolinas to California and all the way to Ireland, but nobody else has ever delivered a beer to me with that nice warm expression used by Pat. David Cronan, Pat McCabe and my brother Chris are without a doubt the best bartenders to have ever served me a cold pint of Guinness.

Pat had been a farmer in the old country and wanted to grow a batch of his own tomatoes in Pawtucket. He bought some 24-inch high tomato plants that had the green stalk with off shooting vines already immersed in the container's soil. He planted them outside in a patch of soil behind the Irish Club and watered the agricultural phenomenon daily hoping for a fine crop, but the big red tomatoes pictured on the label just weren't showing up so he took a good-natured ribbing from guys asking when they could order a BLT! Ted Dolan and Pat McConaghy bought some full size beautiful red tomatoes from the supermarket and headed over to the pub one night after closing. They used paper clips to attach the tomatoes to the vines and secured them well enough so that they were still hanging there the next day when Pat showed up at the bar. Pat spotted the supposed fruit of his labor, which still had the Stop & Shop stickers attached, and proudly declared, "Faith and begorrah, my prayers have been answered!"

I released a defendant from the Mansfield Police lockup and instructed him to report to the ADC for arraignment in the morning. He said that he couldn't afford to hire a lawyer so I told him to request a court-appointed attorney. The next day he asked the judge for a court-*anointed* attorney!

Attleboro Police Sergeant Kevin W. Noble was one of the most conscientious, knowledgeable and professional members of law enforcement that I met during my career. He is a veteran of the Persian Gulf War and was awarded a Master's Degree in Criminal Justice while protecting people as he patrolled the streets of the city. Kevin is a man of many talents as he is also an accomplished brew master producing a tasty beverage dubbed A.P.D. Attleboro Pale Ale. I still have a bottle with the Attleboro Police badge proudly displayed on the label.

The Attleboro Police had some terrific functions for retirement parties and other events alongside the huge outdoor fire pit at the Attleboro Elks. A long metal shish kabob rod would be used to secure impaled chunks of meat that each person would hold over the open flame. My bride couldn't make it to one party so I was doing the cooking for myself which in itself is a bad sign! During a momentary lapse in judgment, I grabbed the hot metal rod without hand protection, inflicting terrible burns and unimaginable agonizing pain. Kevin responded to my screams, quickly retrieved a first aid kit from his cruiser, applied Silver Sulfadiazine after cleaning my wound and covered it with a sterile bandage. The cream worked miraculously by taking away the pain instantly so I will always be grateful to Kevin for his quick thinking and decisive action. After retirement, Kevin earned a Ph. D. in Public Safety specializing in Criminal Justice so he is now Doctor Noble and although he is not a medical doctor, Kevin sure performed like one the night he saved me at the Elks!

David A. Patterson is one of the most interesting guys that I have ever known. He is a detective sergeant with the Massachusetts State Police Gang Unit where he excels at undercover work in some of the most challenging assignments facing law enforcement involving potential danger at every turn. Dave literally puts his life on the line on a regular basis to make the streets of our communities safe for the rest of us. We were having lunch one day when Dave surprised me with some extremely sophisticated surveillance equipment that could be used to fool even the most paranoid suspect.

Dave was kind enough to speak at our very first Courthouse Speaker Series where he was very well received by the enthralled audience who listened to him speak about brutal encounters with armed criminals and close calls with homicidal reprobates. He has made more undercover narcotics buys than any other police officer in New England. One of the funniest stories he told was about a narcotics investigation that he had worked on with Sergeant Mike McLaughlin in Sherborn. There was a two-pound bag of marijuana being held as evidence from another case at the Sherborn Police Department and they wanted to use it as bait in a drug transaction for their current investigation. The Chief of Police wouldn't allow it however, probably because of concerns about the chain of custody as I believe the case was still open. Dave and Mike aren't easily deterred so they came up with a plan that was simple yet effective culminating in a successful conclusion to their investigation. They didn't have real marijuana so they created some fake pot. The two experienced police officers decided to improvise by using a lawn mower to cut Dave's front yard and proceeded to fill a large plastic bag with the grass clippings from the lawn!

Dave's wife Sheryl was also a Massachusetts State Trooper assigned as a Narcotics Division Investigator in the Worcester County District Attorney's Office. They met during a relatively large narcotics sweep that led to several arrests and put a severe dent in the drug trade in that section of the state. Dave had told me that Sheryl had cancer so I would check in with him from time to time and ask how she was, but of course he was never able to say that everything was great. When Sheryl passed she also left their five-year old daughter Emily who has to be one of the cutest and bravest little girls that I have ever met.

Sheryl's funeral was held at Our Lady of Mount Carmel Church in Worcester. Every pew was full as people came from near and far to pay their respects to the beautiful trooper, mother and wife who was taken much too young by the dreaded disease. The standing room only overflow crowd, which included Lieutenant Governor Timothy P. Murray, listened attentively as Colonel Marian J. McGovern delivered a heartfelt and humorous eulogy. The Colonel said that she and Sheryl were both Worcester girls so there was a lot in common with many nice stories to share. The funeral mass was obviously a sad and solemn ceremony, but the priest was able to introduce a moment of levity with a funny story. He told the congregation that when a young couple come to him to begin to make the arrangements for marriage, he always asks them how they had first met. The whole church burst out in laughter when he said that to this day, Sheryl and Dave are the only couple that he has ever joined in matrimony who said that they had met during a controlled drug buy!

Edward F. Davis III, is a natural born leader who served as the Boston Police Commissioner during the horrendous events surrounding the Boston Marathon bombing. I called to ask him to speak at our Law Day Ceremony, but he said that he was not available that day because he had been asked by former Police Commissioner William J. Bratton to meet with him in the western part of the state. I always found Commissioner Davis, who now heads his own security consulting firm, to be confident, intelligent, courageous and refreshingly honest.

I had been appointed to the Bristol County Homeland Security Task Force which is still being run by the legendary Colonel David W. Gavigan Jr. This group provided a tremendous opportunity for intelligence sharing with outstanding members like K9 expert Captain Alan H. Driscoll, SE Mass Sector Director Douglas P. Forbes Jr. from Massachusetts Emergency Management Agency (MEMA), George L. Pereira from TSA, Framingham State University Police Chief Bradford J. Medeiros, retired Deputy US Marshall & Private Investigator Roger C. Bryant, Attorney John P. Hebb who is a retired detective from the Sherborn Police, FBI Intelligence Analyst Julie Flinn Ferringer, Thomas A. Smith from Comcast and Deputy Sheriff Ronald A. Bettencourt as well as many other talented people. Colonel Gavigan is great guy and an absolute wealth of knowledge with contacts all over the world. Dave asked me to speak at a seminar he had put together at Wheaton College in Norton entitled Responding to Sexual Assaults so that I could engage the audience in some of the court functions for these horrific crimes. I had a previous commitment which I was able to move because Dave Gavigan means the world to me. I had already been working in Wrentham for years at this time so it was nice to revisit my previous judicial district and be able to see some old friends from the Norton Police Department like top notch Detective James C. Franco, who would later be promoted to lieutenant, and others.

Officer Peter J. Morse retired from the Attleboro Police Department, but is still employed as a terrific actor. He played one of the FBI Agents who arrested John Connolly toward the end of the movie in *Black Mass* and was kind enough to be introduced at one of our Law Day Ceremonies. The movie was based on the book of the same name written by the much-acclaimed author Dick Lehr. Peter's mother, Patty Reynolds, is a Session Clerk at the ADC.

Sometimes you will hear police officers say that they are made to look like geniuses by dumb criminals. A guy broke into a home, stole a TV and didn't get caught, but he broke into the same home two days later and was apprehended by the police. The reason for the second B & E was that the first time he had forgotten to steal the remote control for the TV!

A 47-year old intoxicated man walked into the Norton Police Department and stated that he was there to bail out his girlfriend. He was told that his girlfriend was not in custody as she had not been arrested. He then left the station and went to his car where he was arrested and charged with 3rd offense drunk driving.

I was releasing prisoners on a busy night at the Attleboro Police Station. I always had the highest regard for Patrolman James F. Dufort who was an excellent officer and a real good guy. I played high school ball with his brother John so I knew that he came from a hardworking honest family. Jim was standing in front of me speaking with Detective Sergeant Art Brillon so I could hear their conversation as I filled out another recog form. They were talking about one of their brother officers, Detective Alex L. Aponte, a good guy who would eventually retire as a sergeant. Alex was about to get married for the fourth time so Artie asked Jim if he was going to go to Alex's bachelor party. Jim said, "No, I can't make it, but I'll go to the next one!"

A mother and her son were drinking heavily at a Patriots' game so the mother decided to drive her son's car home because he was too drunk. They were pulled over by a Walpole Police Officer who administered a field sobriety test to the woman and as this was going on the son decided to urinate on the side of the road. The family outing ended with them both being arrested - the mother for OUI and the son for open and gross lewdness.

A guy got caught passing bad currency. The giveaway was the portrait of Abraham Lincoln on the twenty dollar bills instead of Andrew Jackson!

J. Do and I were always appreciative for the invitation to the wonderful Christmas Party put on by the Norfolk County Prosecutors Association at the Cathay Pacific in Quincy. It was nice to be able to socialize with so many distinguished members of this esteemed group including Norfolk County Register of Probate Patrick McDermott who would later be elected Sheriff, his lovely wife Attorney Tracy Wilson and many others. The food is absolutely fabulous, delicious, and plentiful with a terrific service rating. The piping hot appetizers and entrees are served family style with each oversized platter sufficient for a very large family!

They also provided top notch entertainment including the extremely funny Chris Tabb, one of the best comedians in the business. Chris does a tremendous job of adlibbing with members of the audience as he keeps everyone laughing with an assortment of rapid-fire jokes, humorous observations and hilarious stories. At one point Chris, who is African

American, stated, "... I'm from Mattapan and if you don't know, Mattapan is an old Indian word that means 'many Black people!'"

James B. Roche retired from the Brighton Division of the Boston Municipal Court where the great Clerk-Magistrate had rendered justice for well over two decades after having been appointed by Governor William F. Weld, having previously served in the Governor's Cabinet as the Secretary of Public Safety. He had been appointed Deputy Director of Operations for the United States Marshal Service in Washington by President George H. W. Bush and as the United States Marshal for the District of Massachusetts by President Ronald W. Reagan. He was also appointed by President Reagan to the Advisory Board of the National Institute of Justice with his impressive resume replete with listings of significant positions of authority governing the safety and security of our nation at the highest levels. A single appointment by the President of the United States or the Governor of the Commonwealth would be considered by anyone to be an incredible honor and tremendous achievement, but Jim Roche has a total of five presidential and gubernatorial appointments to his credit which may be the combined world record!

Jim made an extremely interesting appearance on CNN while serving as Deputy Director of the US Marshall Service. He was interviewed in Washington on *Larry King Live* along with the former wife of a cult leader and an attorney. The well-spoken Deputy Director answered Larry King's questions and explained that the cult leader had threatened to kidnap a judge in Arkansas and of his subsequent arrest in Tampa on a fugitive warrant.

Edwin Meese III, Attorney General of the United States, had appointed a Blue Ribbon Commission to study the idea of integrating the radio and other communication systems for all federal law enforcement so that they would be on the same frequency. Jim, US Marshal for the Bay State at the time, didn't think this was a good idea and spoke with the FBI SAC, DEA, and other federal partners who all agreed that this possible development could actually hamper and confuse transmission of emergency communication. The Chairman and members of the AG's Commission planned visits around the country to speak with federal agencies and take the temperature of various stakeholders. The US Marshal Service in the Federal Courthouse at Post Office Square in Boston was their first stop.

Jim had served as an usher in his friend's wedding in Missouri where the groom had given him a beautiful decorative box of high-end cigars. Jim doesn't smoke, but decided that the classy wooden box of cigars looked good on a shelf behind his desk. The Chairman and other Commission members arrived from Washington and sat down in Jim's office to discuss the proposed communications merger. Jim was hoping to convince this group of the potentially dreadful results of this notion when he noticed a cigar in the Chairman's jacket. He offered the gentleman one of his cigars which was accepted with a smile after observing the top quality of the product. The Chairman was so elated and filled with anticipation over this gift that he asked if anyone would mind if he smoked the cigar during their meeting and everyone told him to go ahead. Unbeknownst to Jim, one of the deputy marshals had put a joke store explosive charge in the cigar, never imagining that it would be smoked by someone else. The enthusiastic Chairman lit the cigar, took a drag and boom! Exploded shredded tobacco was everywhere as a repentant Jim explained that he was just as surprised as everyone else as he didn't intend for this to happen. The radio proposal was eventually shot down so Jim was happy even though the path to success was bumpier than planned!

It was always nice to see Jim at Clerk-Magistrate Association meetings, seminars, boat rides, clambakes and other functions. He is one of the nicest, best natured guys in the system who did a great job at every stop along the way. Jim was serious when needed, but always kept his terrific sense of humor intact while entertaining with his outstanding gift of storytelling. He even has a funny tee shirt that reads, "Irish Pubs - the official sunscreen of Ireland!"

We were having drinks on a boat skippered by Robert Karam, one of the smartest and nicest guys I have ever known. Bob has the cell phone numbers of some of the most influential people in our country, yet maintains the humility of a down to earth guy. Some other clerk-magistrates and John Polcari Jr. were aboard as we headed to Martha's Vineyard for lunch. John, a real gentleman with a nice sense of humor, spent his life working in restaurants so he feels compelled to walk around the boat taking drink orders even though we tell him to relax. I mentioned that my doctor had told me that two glasses of red wine are supposed to be good for your health so Jimmy Roche immediately said that he had heard the same so he figured that a dozen glasses of wine must be really good for you!

Not long after graduating from the Massachusetts State Police Academy Jim was having a couple of beers at a bar in downtown Boston. The young trooper was still so fresh out of the academy that his hair had not yet grown back from the shaved off trainee haircut. He had an off-duty revolver in his pocket as he left the pub and headed for his car, parked on Tremont Street. He was walking down LaGrange Street when a guy came up to him out of an alley brandishing a knife and told him to hand over his cash or he was going to start cutting! Jim said, "Wait a minute, let me get my wallet" as he reached into his pocket. Jim then pulled out his pistol, put it up to the guy's neck and said, "As soon as you start cutting, I start shooting!"

The armed robber dropped the knife as Jim pondered his next move. He had been taught in the academy to avoid controversy especially after drinking so he really didn't want to arrest the guy and bring him to a barracks or courthouse. He ordered the man to walk deeper into the alley and then told him to take off all his clothes. The naked assailant was shivering on the chilly October night as Jim gave him back his wallet and left with all of his clothing. Jim drove off and dropped the garments in a nearby dumpster. There was no arraignment needed for this case of instant justice!

A thirty three-year old man met a woman through a dating app and decided to stop at Bristol County Savings Bank in Attleboro Falls during their first date. The woman, who had no idea what was about to happen, waited in the car while her date went inside and stuck up the bank! He was arrested and eventually sentenced to a total of five years for armed robbery and related charges. Veteran reporter David Linton wrote a terrific story depicting the details of the unusual incident for *The Sun Chronicle*. The newspaper headline was descriptive and telling, "Worst First Date Ever?"

A man parked his pickup truck outside of a convenience store and left his German shepherd in the vehicle while he went in to get a pack of cigarettes. The truck was parked at the curb facing down a steep hill with the road eventually ending at an intersection with traffic going left and right. The dog jumped in the driver's seat and somehow bumped the stick into neutral causing the truck to start to roll down the hill. Tom, who was stopped in traffic at the bottom of the hill, thought he was seeing things as he looked up to his left and saw the speeding truck rolling downhill heading for the intersection with the dog behind the steering wheel looking through the windshield! The truck crashed into the rear of a car stopped at the traffic light in front of Tom, but miraculously there were no injuries. A trooper was also in the line of traffic several cars back so he could see the crash, but not the dog in the truck. The trooper got out of his vehicle to render aid and investigate the accident. Tom was sitting in his car with the window down and tried to tell the trooper about the dog as he hurried by, but the trooper told him he would be with him later after he gets the truck driver's license and registration. Tom told the trooper that he didn't know if the vehicle was registered, but he was sure that the operator didn't have a license!

A woman got a traffic citation in the mail after letting her daughter use her car. The camera at the toll booth had photographed the license plate of her vehicle as her daughter drove through without paying. The daughter didn't realize that she had done anything wrong because she chose the lane with the lit-up sign that read NO CASH because she didn't have any!

It seems as though some people are just allergic to police. I have had defendants at a hearing tell me that they have a right to be rude to a police officer in our country. Even though that is a true statement, it is also true that a police officer has a tremendous amount of discretion. Aside from the fact that civility should govern our speech anyway, it also just doesn't make sense to give a police officer a hard time, but then again, rude nitwits are sometimes referred to as continued job security. It is not illegal to be rude, but disrespectful behavior just might call an officer's attention to something that is against the law.

An Attleboro Police Officer was sitting in his parked cruiser next to a curb in the center of the city with the windows down on a hot summer night. The driver of a speeding car raced by and upon recognizing the officer yelled some profanities out the window along with the officer's name. The officer activated his blue lights and siren as he gave chase to the misguided insolent operator. After pulling him over and running his information the officer discovered that the driver had a revoked registration and was operating on a suspended license. A guy with a suspended license shouldn't even be making eye contact with a police officer, but truth is sometimes stranger than fiction. He was arrested, of course, but by the time I released him several hours later, he knew enough to finally keep his mouth shut!

When we were kids our family was coming home to Attleboro from a summer vacation in Hyannis. My dad was driving with my mom in the front as my two brothers and I talked in the back seat of our station wagon. We were on major roads, but dad was exceeding the speed limit and going about 80-85 MPH. Suddenly there were blue lights on our tail as dad pulled over to the side. He handed his license and registration to a Massachusetts State Trooper who was loud and unhappy. He yelled at dad that he had clocked him at 85 MPH! Dad politely told him that he didn't realize that he was going that fast, but that if the trooper said so then he must have been. The trooper suddenly became sweeter than key lime pie and told dad to slow down and let us go.

I was amazed at the way our dad handled that situation as he stressed the importance of civility to us on the ride home, but I was even more amazed when we were stopped two more times by a total of three different troopers before we got to Attleboro with the same result. Although I wouldn't recommend this routine to anyone, dad was the best, three stops - no tickets!

Sergeant Leslie A. Sheldon was a shift commander with the Norton Police Department. He was a good guy and an honorable police officer who always tried to make bad situations better. He would get frustrated sometimes if he didn't know the answer to one of my questions about a prisoner, but I always told him not to worry and get back to me. He had a terrific sense of humor so we had a lot of laughs over the years. Les had false teeth that apparently didn't fit properly because he was always taking them out and leaving them around the police station. One time I heard him yelling down the hall to other officers, "Has anybody seen my teeth?" Sometimes he would call me on the phone to tell me about some arrests, but I couldn't always understand very well because it would sound like slurred speech when his teeth were out. The communication would always improve after I politely asked him to put his teeth back in!

The police were able to arrest two bank robbers soon after the holdup because they had decided to use a getaway car that was easy to track down. The robbers fled after calling a cab!

It was a busy night at the North Attleborough Police Department as I released about a dozen defendants and set high bail on a domestic A & B case. The defendant had a record of violence and was alleged to have beaten his girlfriend so I set his bail at $5,000.00 and headed for the door. The defendant's girlfriend approached me as I was walking by the booking room and asked if we could talk. The area surrounding both of her eyes was completely blackened in the perfect circles that I had seen so many times before. It was about 8:00 PM as she spoke slowly through swollen bloody lips asking me when I would be back out making my rounds again because she planned on driving to quite a few places in southeastern Massachusetts to borrow money and try to raise the $5,000.00 for her boyfriend's bail!

This wasn't my first encounter with this type of circumstance, but it still shocked me every time. The poor girl was still recovering from a vicious beating and she was about to embark on an arduous journey to benefit her assailant. The thought was prevalent in my mind that I could actually help make life easier on her and save her weakened body from a long onerous nighttime trip if I simply reduced his bail to personal recognizance and charged him $40.00 instead of $5,040.00. I kept his bail at $5,000.00 and she wasn't able to raise the money that night anyway, but I struggled with those kind of decisions many times because my focus was always on helping the victim while being fair.

Our young daughters were still opening presents from Santa Claus on Christmas morning when I had to head out for the Attleboro Police Station for some left over Christmas Eve arrests including a last minute holiday shoplifter, an OUI, and guy charged with disturbance of the peace because he just couldn't shut up even after being advised by the responding officer. The officer, who I knew to be kind and reasonable, almost bent over backwards to avoid arresting the loudmouth on Christmas Eve, but some unfortunates practically beg to be taken into custody.

I released all three defendants and was left with a guy on a default warrant for a domestic A & B. His wife, who was the victim, and his three young kids were waiting to speak with me in the hallway entrance to the station. It wasn't hard to guess what they wanted and sure enough she asked me to release her husband as she told me that he was a great guy and a terrific father. All three kids, the oldest looked to be about 7, were crying and begging me to release their father. One kid was holding onto my leg while she screamed about loving her daddy.

I didn't have the authority to release someone on a default warrant, but I have been known to bend the rules once in a while in the interest of justice. However, not only had this defendant proven himself to be irresponsible by failing to appear in court resulting in the issuance of a default warrant, but the original crime was for beating up his wife. I felt very badly for this poor family, especially on Christmas Day, but I had to say no and leave him in the lockup.

Sometimes domestic violence cases develop differently than you might expect. A Mansfield woman had received a protective order from the ADC against her husband under Chapter 209A. The defendant had a clean record and there was no allegation of actual physical violence, but she did state that he had threatened her. The 209A included an order that the defendant stay away from her and the marital home. There is now tremendous coordination between District Courts, where most restraining orders originate, and Probate Courts that divide assets and finalize divorces, but this case occurred long before defendants were routinely ordered to make payments to plaintiffs in 209A cases. The defendant in this case apparently recognized that his wife would be needing money during these proceedings. He left an envelope containing $300.00 in cash with a note to his wife saying he loved her at her front door, rang the doorbell and ran. The plaintiff opened the envelope, pocketed the cash and called the police to report a violation of the no contact order. Police officers have tremendous discretion in many cases, but not for violation of a restraining order. Arrest is mandatory so the police did the right thing and took the defendant into custody. There is no justification or excuse for a husband threatening his wife, but I think most people would feel some level of sympathy for this man.

Domestic violence prevention laws have changed dramatically since I started working in the system in 1980. Statutes were eventually amended so that there is now absolutely no discretion regarding post arrest release from a police lockup for violation of a 209A. The defendant is essentially detained in what is tantamount to being held without bail. It is not technically held without bail because no bail decision is permitted to be considered, but the defendant is not going to be released from the police station.

Back when I had the authority to release someone for a 209A violation I would rarely exercise that discretion and never when there was an allegation of violence. There was one arrest, however, that I will never forget. A North Attleborough woman had a 209A against her boyfriend that included the usual stay away order. She started feeling amorous a few weeks after the order was issued and invited the boyfriend back into the apartment for some wine, appetizers and a nice candlelight dinner. Apparently, the boyfriend ended up consuming so much wine that he was unable to perform sexually later in the bedroom. She immediately called the police, said he was useless and had him arrested for violation of the no contact provision in the order. Police officers must have guidelines as clear as possible in a dangerous, ambiguous and ever-changing world. They did the right thing in making the arrest, but now it was up to me to make a decision on his release. Today he would be ineligible for bail, but I read him the riot act and explained that, at least with respect to arrest, it doesn't matter that she invited him in to violate her own order. After being satisfied that he understood the gravity of the situation, I released him and ordered him to appear for arraignment in the ADC the next day. He assured me that there would be no more trouble and that he would never go back to her apartment. His eyes then dropped down at the floor with a sense of sadness enveloping his face as he said, "None of this would have happened if I didn't drink too much. The real crime is that I couldn't get an erection and that's probably a felony!"

A clerk-magistrate or assistant will issue a warrant at the request of the police only after a finding of probable cause. The police have already had to demonstrate probable cause for the warrant to issue, thus there is no need for that determination once the arrest has been made.

The police also need probable cause to effectuate a warrantless arrest although they don't need to demonstrate it at the time of the arrest. The ruling on the Jenkins case by the Massachusetts Supreme Judicial Court caused a new procedure to be implemented in the Commonwealth in the early 90's. A Jenkins Hearing is now required within 24 hours for any defendant arrested without a warrant who is still in custody. Courts accomplish this requirement in different ways so the ADC Clerk-Magistrate decided, which was his right, that he and his assistants, of which I was one, would take turns calling all of the police departments in the jurisdiction of the Taunton District Court and they, in turn, would call our police departments on Saturdays, Sundays, and holidays. I ended up making many time-consuming phone calls where I would have to sometimes speak with three different people in the same station to be finally told that I didn't have to do any Jenkins Hearings because they didn't have any prisoners. When I became a clerk-magistrate in Wrentham I made sure that the other Jenkins option would be used where the police in my jurisdiction would call us if needed.

The Jenkins Hearing procedure basically involves speaking with a police officer on the phone, usually the shift commander, and asking questions to determine if there is probable cause for the warrantless arrest. The police have to demonstrate that the different elements of each crime have taken place. For the crime of assault & battery, for instance, the police have to demonstrate that there was an assault, which is an offer of force or violence and a battery, which is an unwanted touching. This is not rocket science as probable cause is usually established pretty easily so a clerk-magistrate or assistant has to guard against the hearing becoming routine and almost perfunctory. It is an important safeguard in our system, however, because even though there is almost always probable cause, there have been some frightening exceptions.

I was making my ADC Jenkins calls on a weekend morning prior to my 1998 appointment to Wrentham. The Taunton Police Lieutenant, commander of the day shift, told me that he had a fresh arrest on an A & B case. Fresh is slang for warrantless so a Jenkins Hearing was necessary as the 24 hour time limit was approaching. He read the salient portions of the police report to me on the phone and explained that the 60-year old defendant who had no criminal record, had raised his fist to his wife of 40 years then ran out of the house as he yelled that he hated her. The lieutenant answered in the negative when I asked him about the battery and if there had been any touching. I'm pretty sure that this was Lieutenant Michael J. Silvia who was a squared away police officer with whom I had dealt with many times and who had previously impressed me with his high level of integrity and absolute professionalism so I knew that he would do the right thing. Silvia, who would eventually retire as a detective captain, kept looking in the police report for something to substantiate the more serious charge, but the shock in his voice was evident when he came up empty.

The bail determination on this defendant was not my decision as my only responsibility was the Jenkins Hearing. The lieutenant told me that the defendant was being held without bail so I assumed that decision was reached based on the serious charge of assault & battery on the woman. The Clerk-Magistrate was told that the guy had hit his wife! There is no provision in the Jenkins Hearing procedure allowing or not allowing for what I did next. I found probable cause for the lesser included charge of assault based on the fist raising and instructed the lieutenant to immediately call the Clerk-Magistrate and inform him that I had found probable cause for a much less serious offense so that he might reconsider his bail decision. It is a very serious crime for a man to threaten his wife, but pales in comparison to the act of hitting her.

On another occasion a young woman approached a uniformed police officer and pointed out her ex-boyfriend who she said had just approached her in violation of her 209A stay away order. The young man was arrested and booked at the police station where it was expected that he would remain for the weekend as alleged 209A violators were, by that time, not eligible for release. Nancy Clarke, the First Assistant Clerk-Magistrate of the ADC, was on call with the police so she conducted the Jenkins Hearing on the phone. During her conversation with the officer, she learned that the 209A had expired and had not been renewed. Police departments have a copy of all restraining orders issued for their jurisdiction so apparently the arresting officer had made the arrest without calling the station to check on the validity of the order. Nancy then did the right thing and immediately ordered the defendant released, something she thought that she would never have to do.

The importance of a Jenkins Hearing cannot be overstated. There is usually at least a minimum of probable cause for almost every warrantless arrest made in the Commonwealth, but when part of the system breaks down Jenkins provides a valuable failsafe for the proper delivery of justice.

One of the functions of a clerk-magistrate or assistant is the issuance of search warrants upon a demonstration of probable cause in a sworn affidavit. I have been asked to issue search warrants involving the crimes of murder, narcotics violations, stolen property and others. The vast majority of search warrants that I have issued have usually been for the police to enter a home which is the most sacred turf in American society pursuant to the values set forth in our Constitution. I took my responsibility seriously because, even though almost all police officers mean well, I was sometimes the only thing between an overzealous, yet hardworking detective, and the sanctity and privacy of a home. I have reviewed countless search warrant affidavits from many honest and honorable police officers during close to four decades in the court system. The laws that govern our behavior allow us to live freely in the greatest country on the face of the earth.

Opinions vary, even from scholar to seminar, with respect to the definition of the clerk-magistrate or assistant's impartiality when considering a search warrant affidavit. Some will proclaim that I was supposed to simply deny the search warrant request if there was an underlying lack of probable cause and not to engage in conversation or offer an explanation to the affiant. I never did that, not even once. The typical search warrant request comes from an involved investigation where the police have spent numerous hours sometimes over weeks and months putting together a criminal case. Sometimes probable cause would have been established if an overlooked detail, related to me verbally, had been included so I might suggest that the evidence become part of the affidavit. The detective had enough evidence, but just needed to demonstrate probable cause on paper.

Later in my career police detectives started requesting search warrants to allow for the attachment of a GPS device to a vehicle so that they could easily track movements or follow it. GPS is the product of advanced technology that serves as another efficient tool to help police solve crimes. Police utilize this procedure after demonstrating probable cause and obtaining a search warrant, but I am of the opinion that a warrant should not be needed if the vehicle is parked on a public way such as a street in front of the suspect's home. Quite often police, armed with a search warrant, have to enter private property to attach a GPS device to a car parked in a driveway and I am happy that that is the state of the law. I can't see any expectation of privacy, however, for the outside of a vehicle parked on the road. The police are not entering private property and they are not searching inside the vehicle so I think that a search warrant should not be required for that case.

Hypothetically and farfetched yet telling, if the budget and policy-making would allow for the hiring of enough police officers to have one standing on every street corner in America with a communications radio there would be no need for GPS or a search warrant because the police could continue to observe the vehicle in motion as a result of this incredible infusion of funding. Justice shouldn't turn on money so a search warrant shouldn't be needed when it can be rendered obsolete by cash. In stark contrast, all of the money in the world providing for millions of police officers could not reveal an ongoing crime inside of a home where the police would still need a search warrant.

Having said that, however, regardless of my opinion, I always complied with the actual case law.

I issued a search warrant for an alleged drug dealer that had an unusual twist in the affidavit. The next door neighbors were using a baby monitor for the safety of their infant, but the electronic device was picking up narcotics transaction conversations through the target's cordless telephone in the next apartment. The detective provided details and did a nice job in a showing of probable cause.

Trooper David M. Manning of the Massachusetts State Police responded to a motor vehicle accident on 495 North in Franklin. He could see headlights shining out of the woods from a car that went off the road into the forest. A witness told the squared away trooper that she had asked the operator if she was OK, but couldn't get an answer because she was "shitfaced." When Trooper Manning went into the woods and asked the operator for her license and registration, she replied by asking the trooper what she was being pulled over for!

An 18-year old armed felon had just been arrested for bank robbery and was being guided into the back seat of a Brockton Police cruiser. He was vehemently declaring his innocence and complaining that the police had the wrong man. This was long before the advent of the covid pandemic so the only people with masks on in a bank were stick up guys. He kept saying he was innocent and would never do such a thing. One of the officers told him that the bank teller had positively identified him to which he replied, "How could she do that? I was wearing a mask!"

Maybe my view of reality is somewhat jaded after having been up close and personal with so many alleged and convicted criminals during my career, but when I first saw people wearing masks to combat the covid pandemic my initial thought was that some stick up guys would see this as an excellent opportunity to blend in and pull off an armed robbery!

The arresting officer secured the defendant in his cruiser after placing him under arrest for drunk driving. As a courtesy, the officer asked the defendant if he wanted him to get anything out of the car before he had it towed to which he replied, "Yea, get me my bottle of whiskey under the front seat will ya!"

Ashley MacDougall's father was a police officer in Medway which is one of the towns in the territorial jurisdiction of the WDC. Joseph R. MacDougall, who is now retired, was an outstanding police officer and a real down to earth good guy. Big Joe was coming home from his part time seasonal job as a Santa Claus when a woman waived him down to say that there was a guy passed out from drugs in a car nearby and that she wasn't able to wake him. Big Joe, who was still dressed in his Santa outfit, went over to the young man and shook his shoulder to bring him out of the stupor. Joe didn't need to use Narcan because as soon as the startled guy saw Santa Claus, he came right out of it and woke up immediately!

Ashley was a very popular name the year she was born so as she got a little older, she found herself surrounded by kids with the same name. Her dad would call out for his daughter at the playground and a bunch of little Ashleys would come running so he gave her a nickname to distinguish her from all the other kids. Big Joe started calling his daughter Chief and still does to this day. Ashley told me it's funny when she is speaking with her father on the phone while he is out with friends as they think he is talking to the Chief of Police and it's even better when they hear Big Joe end the conversation by saying, "I love you Chief!"

Thomas J. Noonan was a former Massachusetts State Trooper, an honorable man and a terrific guy. Later, he was already working at the Worcester District Court when he was appointed to be the great Clerk-Magistrate of that court by Governor Michael S. Dukakis. Tommy served his community and the entire Commonwealth with great distinction for well over half a century and was one of the finest gentlemen that I have ever known.

The Japanese attack on Pearl Harbor left our shocked nation with a universal sense of outrage because the bombings had occurred at a US Naval Base where over 2,400 American lives were lost on our own soil. This tragic assault on democracy and other events of World War II served to inspire a powerful wave of patriotism throughout the United States. Young men enlisted in our armed forces at a record pace in an effort to stop the advance of tyranny that threatened the shores of our homeland. No one felt a deeper sense of pride in the greatest country on the face of the earth than a very young Tom Noonan. Even though he was underage, a burning desire to fulfill an innate patriotic obligation caused Tom to drop out of school and enlist in the United States Navy when he was only 14 years old! He had actually completed basic training and was ready to defend our country when his true age was discovered and he was asked to go home. The following paragraph from Tommy's obituary best describes his Irish wit and beautiful sense of humor.

"By the time he was able to re-enlist it was the end of the war and he would later tell his large and extended family that he didn't need to because 'once the Germans and Japanese heard rumors of his potential return they threw down their artillery and surrendered!' God save the Irish!"

Attorney Richard J. Sweeney is a smart and very experienced lawyer with a law office in Quincy. It was always a pleasure hearing his clients' cases as he is a terrific guy who provides an outstanding, vigorous defense and understands the real world. Prior to passing the Massachusetts Bar Exam he served as a Boston Police Sergeant patrolling the city streets and commanding a Drug Control Unit covering Area E-5.

One day at the beginning of his shift he was sitting on his motorcycle pulled over to the side of the curb on Adams Street at Lower Mills in Dorchester. Rick was filling out motor vehicle citations with common data such as the date and anything else that would apply to every operator in anticipation of violations that day. He had just completed preparing a few partial citations when he observed his first customer of the day run a stop sign right in front of him. Rick activated his siren and blue lights prompting the operator to pull over to the side of the road. He approached the vehicle and was just about to ask for the driver's license and registration when he noticed that the operator was a nun! All of the passengers in the front and back were also nuns! He had pulled over a car load of nuns! Rick told the driver to be careful and to have a nice day as he started to walk back to his police bike realizing that his pre-written citations would not be used on this case!

The North Attleborough Police conducted a raid on an old farm house where there was an illegal gambling operation taking place inside of what I think was a barn. Dozens of men were brought in to the police station under arrest and waited in a long line to be processed. The defendants in line slowly made their way by the desk where I was seated filling out the recognizance forms. They were brought to me individually after being booked as I was releasing every one of them in what was an easy decision for me as these were nonviolent crimes. Detective Sergeant Brian F. Coyle, who also served as the court prosecutor, had a terrific sense of humor and always made people laugh even in tense situations. He was near the front of the line helping with the mass production when he looked toward the back at the last defendant and loudly stated, "There he is. That one was the lookout!" Dozens of angry guys immediately turned around to see who had been asleep on the job!

The Massachusetts State Police have a special Truck Team unit that enforce safety regulations on commercial vehicles. Troopers inspect the outside and inside of a vehicle to ensure compliance with fire extinguishers and many other safety features. They will even slide under a vehicle and inspect parts of the truck that were unfamiliar to me at a hearing. It is not uncommon for some of these violations to result in significant fines. I have conducted hearings where the defendant had been assessed extremely large fines by troopers including one for over $20,000.00! I'm not even close to being an expert on motor vehicle safety components, but this enforcement helps to keep the roads safe for everyone. One of the most common offenses that we would see from this team was for operating an overweight vehicle or speaking in the vernacular - he was overweight. Detective Sergeant Coyle was prosecuting a North Attleborough case and discovered that the defendant also had an open state police case pending so he asked Nancy Clarke what the guy was charged with. Nancy responded that the defendant was overweight which brought a smile to Brian's face as he said, "Oh, Christ, are we charging people with that now?"

Brian was easily one of the hardest working guys in the system as he served as the police station custodian in addition to his duties as detective sergeant and court prosecutor. He would wear jeans and a sweatshirt while cleaning the station before changing into a suit and tie for the courthouse. I had set high bail on 3 alleged car thieves from Boston on a Friday night that preceded a Monday holiday so it looked like the defendants would be locked up all weekend. Brian was swabbing the floor with a mop outside of the cell block on Saturday morning when all three of these guys started yelling at him and disparaging his intellect. They were saying cruel things about him being a janitor, but Brian kept his cool and told them, "You'll find out!" "What do you mean?" one yelled, "We'll find out what?" Brian was greeted with the same level of rudeness and humiliating language on Sunday morning and again on Monday. He said the same thing every day in response to their insults, "You'll find out!" On Tuesday morning Brian walked in wearing a three-piece suit and tie while telling the trio of nitwits, "Time to find out!" The defendants wore facial expressions of shock as they were put into the van and taken to court. I called their cases together for arraignment in Courtroom One. The three handcuffed dopes stood up in the prisoner's dock and listened to me read the charges, but as soon as I finished Detective Sergeant Coyle stood up to address the judge saying, "Your Honor, the Commonwealth is requesting bail." I heard one defendant, while looking toward the detective sergeant, say to the others, "Holy shit, that's the same guy!" I will never forget their horrified expressions as it dawned on them that the man who they had treated so disrespectfully was the prosecutor in charge of the bail argument!

Three men in their 30s were arrested for skinny dipping in a North Attleborough pond. They were all visiting the United States from Poland and had their release fees so Brian Coyle called and said, "Eddie, we've got the Polish swim team down here ready to go!" The wet trio were polite and no trouble, but they didn't quite understand that the problem was that they had been naked and not that they had been in the water. When I released the last one he said to me in a heavy Polish accent, "Tell me, is there anywhere that we can swim in America?"

North Attleborough Police Officers responded to a breaking and entering in progress. They apprehended two males inside of a residence after walking right up to a third suspect standing in front of the house on the sidewalk. The man on the sidewalk had been assigned to be the lookout, but he didn't notice the police coming because he was legally blind!

The officer escorted the next prisoner out of the cell block and directed him over to the desk where I was seated at the NAPD. I asked the young angry looking defendant to have a seat to which he responded by getting in my face and yelling, "Who the f*** are you!" I asked the officer to return him to his cell and heard him say that he thought that he was getting out and who was that guy anyway? The officer closed the cell door and said, "Oh, that guy? He's the guy who decides if you get out!"

I used to drive an old Ford LTD that had been purchased for me by a friend. The vehicle had previously been used as an unmarked New Hampshire State Police Detective's car so it was big, heavy and solid. I am the kind of guy who ranks safety as the most significant feature in a car so this one suited me just fine. When I saw headlights coming at me on my way home from a police station at 3:00 AM my first thought was that I was hoping it was a police cruiser because if it wasn't there was a high likelihood that it was a drunk driver. I knew that I was driving what was probably one of the safest cars on the road for accident protection.

I don't know much about cars, but I quickly learned that rear main seal problems result in constant oil consumption. I eventually had to get rid of my anti-drunk driving car as it became too expensive to maintain. I was driving it to the North Attleborough Police Department one time when I started to smell gasoline. Officer Paul Lalancette was not only a conscientious police officer and is a really good guy, but also a terrific auto mechanic. After I released some prisoners, Paul went out to the parking lot to look at my car and discovered a leak in the gas tank. He said it wasn't too bad so I could drive it a short distance, but knowing that I still had not yet given up the terrible cigarette habit Paul said, "It's OK to drive home, but this might be a good time to quit smoking!"

The police detectives from one of the towns in my district were getting nowhere as they interrogated a B & E suspect at the police station. Even though they didn't have enough solid evidence they really liked this guy for the crime, but just couldn't get a confession. Finally, one of the exasperated detectives declared that the suspect was going to have to take a lie detector test. He placed the suspect's hand on the top of the copy machine and asked him if he had broken into the house in question. The suspect stated, "No" as the detective pushed the button for copy. The machine lit up and produced a photo of the defendant's hand as the detective announced, "It says you're lying!" The suspect confessed and led the police to a cache of stolen goods.

A defendant was arrested for drunk driving by the Plainville Police. His booking photo shows him wearing a tee shirt that reads TOWN DRUNK. He probably didn't want the jury to see that!

J. Do and I had already been retired for about three years when we were honored to be able to attend the retirement party for Officer Scot Taggart from the Foxborough Police Department. Scot is a good guy who performed many different tasks for the department including a stint as a police prosecutor for the WDC. Scot understood the real world and recognized that there is a vast difference between a bad guy and a good guy who had made a bad mistake.

Scot also worked details at Gillette Stadium for concerts, Patriots' games and other events. Ashley MacDougall came up with the idea for the tee shirts that were produced for his retirement party to celebrate the first concert that he ever worked which was also the very same band as the last one that he worked with several years in between - the Grateful Dead. On another night Scot was working behind the band when the Rolling Stones played to a sellout crowd and continued playing after the concert to record a video. The Foxborough Police were receiving complaints of loud music coming from the stadium at 3:00 AM so Scot and some other officers were the ones who had to ask Mick Jagger and company to leave the stage. Jagger and Keith Richards were very nice in thanking Scot for stopping them as they were all very tired.

Scot is an extremely decent and caring individual so anybody who ever got arrested by him probably had to work pretty hard to make that happen! It was a wonderful party and a terrific send off for an easygoing and conscientious police officer.

I spotted Attorney Joe Cataldo across the room at Scot's party, a nice man and one of the best criminal lawyers that I have ever witnessed in action. His father Paul, another great attorney and practical joker, was one of the first lawyers that I had the privilege to meet when I started in Attleboro. Joe came over to the table to say hello to J. Do and I so we talked for a while before dinner was served. I told Joe that I was enjoying retirement with our grandchildren and that I was lucky that I could fish almost every day. During our conversation Joe noticed that I was wearing a wristwatch and facetiously expressed surprise that I needed a watch during retirement. I told Joe that the watch was to keep track of the tidal changes in the Cape Cod Canal!

I was in the process of releasing a defendant from the Foxborough Police lockup who had been arrested during a Patriots' game. As soon as the officer gave him back his property he said, "Hey, where's my other shoe?" The officer then informed him that he was only wearing one shoe when he was arrested!

The next young man was escorted out of the cell and brought to me by an officer who had been told that the defendant had the necessary release fee and was ready to go. I only took cash, but had at one time or another been offered everything from a check, credit card, IOU, handshake, promise, wristwatch and even an old car! The officer instructed the defendant to sit down next to me, but it turned out that the guy didn't have enough money for bail and then asked me if I would take a Dunkin' Donuts gift card!

My morning at the court started with reading a drunk driving police report for probable cause. The officer asked the driver if he would do a field sobriety test to which he replied, "No, that's OK, just arrest me!"

There used to be a Chinese restaurant named the Yummy House which was located on the corner of Park and Union Streets in Attleboro. The restaurant was situated almost directly across the street from the Attleboro Police Station at a busy intersection which was often bustling with foot and vehicular traffic especially on warm summer nights. It wasn't unusual for me to drive by this active area a few times per night on my way to releasing prisoners from the lock up. The food was good with a line of customers sometimes going out the door to the sidewalk. The most memorable part of those drives, however, was the enticing smell of delicious cooking that permeated the air in the nearby surrounding downtown community. On a hot summer night, with my car windows down, I would pick up the scent of the Yummy House as I travelled under the railroad arch down the street with the smell filling my vehicle as I drove by and pulled into the Attleboro Police parking lot.

Sometimes the wind direction carried this appetizing aroma right into the prisoner cell block. I would release prisoners who would thank me and say that they had to go get some Chinese food immediately. I released one guy on a Sunday morning who gave me the fee and quickly dropped down to tie his shoe as if the place was on fire. The shift commander was Lieutenant Joseph E. Fitton, a real good guy who would later retire as a captain. Joe asked him why he was in such a hurry. The defendant looked up at both of us and said, "Are you shittin me? I been locked up here smelling that food for two days. I got get outta here and order an egg roll!"

I had just released a well-known thief from the Attleboro Police lockup a few days before Christmas. He had a lengthy record for larceny, but never any violence or court defaults. Not to minimize his deviant behavior, but compared to the violent criminals that I frequently arraigned, this guy was an easy decision for release on personal recognizance. The police always knew that I probably wasn't going to set bail for a nonviolent crime unless there were some extenuating and unusual circumstances. Experienced police officers were in agreement with that, to the best of my knowledge, because they realized that everything is relative. They knew that my thinking was pretty much - No Blood, No Bail.

At this time of year most people were still finishing up their Christmas shopping, but as the defendant was leaving he said, "Sorry to inconvenience you Mr. Doherty. I was just out doing a little Christmas shoplifting!"

There are thousands of outstanding warrants, some for serious felonies and others for minor offenses, which remain active in Massachusetts and ready for potential service every day. A Revere Police Officer, for example, might arrest someone in that city on a warrant issued by a court other than the Chelsea District Court. Laws and procedures governing the release of criminal defendants have evolved and changed over the years with courts now much better equipped to deal with out of district arrests. Younger police officers probably aren't as familiar with the geography of the state outside of their town as their older colleagues were because back in the day there was a whole different procedure. A common assignment for a police officer reporting for duty at 8:00 AM on Monday would be to drive to some other police department to pick up a prisoner who had been arrested on a warrant. This might happen every day, but much more frequently on Monday as a result of weekend arrests with police cruisers crisscrossing the state and passing each other from every direction. Bail authority rested with the home court, but amendments to the controlling statute have basically, in effect, created one big state wide court for the purposes of bail determinations and some other significant events.

Long before those laws changed, I received a call from a very courteous and professional captain on the Quincy Police Department who began the conversation by apologizing because one of his rookie officers had made an arrest on a bad check warrant that I had issued. The rookie officer was at the hospital to interview a patient who had been in a motor vehicle accident as part of an investigation. During the interview a pregnant woman was brought into the hospital screaming in pain and ready to deliver a baby very soon. She was accompanied by her husband who was doing the best he could to comfort and calm her. Somehow the officer recognized the husband and ran him for outstanding warrants! The husband came back a hit on a default warrant for a bad check and was placed under arrest by the officer which did nothing to sooth the nerves of the screaming wife!

The experienced captain knew that a potential release could not come from the Quincy Court and back in those days could not officially come from anybody else as the defendant was arrested on a default warrant. The captain told me that the wife was continuing to scream and yell that she wanted her husband back. He was on the phone with the hospital and could hear her cries of agony himself as she wanted her husband to be the one to tell her to push and nobody else. He asked me if I would consider making an exception and I quickly ordered the defendant's release on the phone so that he could care for his wife. I don't remember the name, but that baby is now about 40 years old so I hope that he or she has had a good life.

The Foxborough Public Safety Building is a clean and modern facility of which the town can be very proud, but the old police station was a decrepit run-down quarters with old holding cells. The police did the best that they could under the circumstances, but there was one cell that reminded me of a civil war prison where people who had been arrested at concerts or sporting events were crammed together into an area so small that defendants could be heard yelling and begging to get out. One guy tried to kiss my hand when I released him. I told him thanks, but I only accept cash.

The police had a staging area at Gillette Stadium to begin the process of prisoner transport directly to the police station. Sometimes a concert would produce so many arrests that a Foxborough School Bus had to be used for the trip to the lock up with the prisoners handcuffed and seated on the bus in the police station parking lot until they could be booked inside. There weren't enough cells to hold the prisoners waiting to be booked and processed so they were kept in the school bus until room became available. The large black letters on the side of the yellow bus spelling out FOXBOROUGH PUBLIC SCHOOLS seemed to present a humorous paradox to me one night with armed police officers guarding both exits of the vehicle. The occupants of this bus were far different than the usual precious cargo of young impressionable children on their way to and from school. This was now a temporary prison for a crowd of handcuffed adults in varying states of mind and degrees of sobriety including many who were swearing, drunk, screaming, singing, vomiting and angry. It was 2:00AM so the extremely loud group prompted me to think that I was glad that I didn't live across the street from this place.

An officer opened the bus door so that I could address the crowd in an effort to expedite the process. I stood up front as the moaning and yelling continued while the officer announced, "Listen up! This is Clerk-Magistrate Doherty. Pay attention to what he has to say. Class is now in session!" It was convenient for me to be able to explain the need for them to begin thinking about who they could call for cash and a sober ride, amount of release fee and other information only once instead of 50 times. It was important that phone calls be made ASAP because sometimes a defendant's release money would be coming from hours away. I finished speaking and exited the vehicle as it became loud once again when the officer smiled at me and said, "I don't think there are too many honor students on that school bus!"

I released a young woman who had been arrested at one of the Foxborough concerts for public drinking. She was pleasant and seemed genuinely grateful that I was sending her on her way to freedom. She thanked me and left the police station as I started to fill out the recognizance form for the next defendant that was being brought to me by the officer in charge of the cell block. The police kept bringing in more arrests from the concert so I was still there a couple of hours later when the officer working the front desk approached and presented me with a very large sheet cake that said, "Thank You Clerk-Magistrate Doherty," handwritten in frosting on top! The cake had been brought to the police station by the young woman that I had released earlier. She dropped it off for me at the front desk and told the officer how appreciative she was that I had let her out. It was extremely nice of her, but I was just doing my job and you never know what some people are really thinking so the police were the only ones who enjoyed eating that cake.

Steven F. Crogan was one of the very best federal agents that I have ever known. The Special Agent served as the Group Supervisor of Criminal Investigations for United States Customs in Boston when the name of the agency was changed to United States Immigration & Customs Enforcement creating the acronym ICE. Steve, a hardworking great guy, took some good-natured ribbing from some of us when we said that now he was going to have to point his gun and say, "Freeze ICE!"

The officer gave the defendant a pen and paper and asked him to write down what happened. The defendant asked if he should print and the officer responded by telling him that he could print or use cursive, whatever he wanted. The defendant, apparently confused about the meaning of the word cursive, told the officer that he wasn't going to write down any swears!

Sometimes concerts would produce well over one hundred arrests and could be very lucrative for my assistants and myself. I spent the first half of my career in the ADC which had Great Woods in its jurisdiction and the second half in the WDC which handled the arrests from Gillette Stadium. Each of these venues had different names at one time or another.

I didn't mind missing sleep because arrests from Guns N' Roses were putting my kids through college and on this weekend they were playing on back to back nights. I had never heard Guns N' Roses play, but I really loved that band! I released a 25-year old guy from the Mansfield lockup who had been arrested during one of their concerts at Great Woods for selling balloons filled with nitrous oxide on a Friday night. He was so happy that I think he had been sampling his own product. As he left the room the cooperative young fellow smiled at me and said, "Thanks, see you tomorrow night man!" Sure enough, he was arrested again on Saturday night!

I was releasing prisoners at the State Police Barracks in Foxborough after a Patriots' game where I had set $5,000.00 bail on one out of state defendant who was alleged to have beaten a victim severely. He knew that he couldn't come up with the cash to post the bail so he realized that he would be staying in his cell. Since he was spending the night he asked me if he could have a king size bed! I told him he was in a State Police Barracks, not the Holiday Inn!

There is a comical sign dealing with a serious subject on display in some of the local tackle shops and other businesses along the Cape Cod Canal. The Bourne Police Department gave the signs out to local merchants to hopefully make a thief think twice. It starts off by making you think there is a contest with prizes. In varying sizes of lettering the sign reads, "FREE RIDE IN A POLICE CAR IF YOU SHOPLIFT FROM THIS STORE COMPLIMENTS OF THE BOURNE POLICE DEPARTMENT."

Great Woods, as the concert venue was previously called, is located in a section of Mansfield that is situated very close to the Mansfield/Norton town line on Route 140. Arrests from this concert facility are taken to the Mansfield Police Station, but some revelers make it as far as Norton before succumbing to the long arm of the law. Concerts would sometimes produce well over a dozen arrests in the Norton Police lock-up and many more in Mansfield. I had just released a long line of prisoners from Norton on a sold-out Friday night when I was reviewing the police report for a young man from Boston seated in front of me. He was too intoxicated and couldn't get a ride so I told him to sleep it off at the station and I would release him in the morning for court on Monday. He was a happy drunk so he agreed as he listened to the officer tell him that he could make one phone call. He asked the officer for the phone number to Papa Gino's so he could order a pizza and have it delivered to his cell!

Sergeant Joseph E. Cheevers is a fantastic bagpiper with the Boston Police Gaelic Column of Pipes & Drums. Joe was always extremely generous with his time and played the bagpipes for our Law Day Ceremony every year at the WDC. The talented piper was always one of the highlights as the crowd enjoyed his unique and inspiring notes that filled the courthouse air. Joe would bring his uniform so I told him that he could change in my private bathroom. He is a big guy so he probably had to maneuver slowly to get dressed in that tiny room, but he never complained and was always there when needed.

Joe was also very helpful to me one day when I was with J. Do in Boston. We had been invited to the groundbreaking of a new hotel in the Seaport District by our friend George K. Regan Jr. as the Regan Communications Group continues to be involved in so many newsworthy events. George is very active in the Boston Police Foundation, has been recognized by the Boston Police Detective Benevolent Society for his ongoing support and was instrumental in bringing the mounted police unit back to the city of Boston. George leads an extremely dedicated team of experienced, talented and innovative professionals including President Ashley Boiardi, Senior Vice President Sean Martin and many more.

Intercontinental Real Estate Corporation and Harbinger Development were breaking ground on the new $176 million dollar hotel project at the Boston Seaport within the Raymond L. Flynn Marine Park. It was a magnificent event with complimentary food trucks on site and interesting speeches. J. Do and I had a nice conversation with Eliza P. Dushku, the talented actress/producer well known for her movies like *Bring It On*, *True Lies* and many more. She was very cordial and told us that she was engaged to Peter Palandjian, the CEO of Intercontinental. I have listened to my share of speeches from Boston to Washington, but Palandjian is definitely one of the most powerful and dynamic speakers that I have ever had the privilege to hear. Mayor Martin J. Walsh

J. Do & Eliza Dushku

and other dignitaries including City Councilor Michael F. Flaherty Jr., a smart lawyer with Adler Pollock & Sheehan P. C., took part in the traditional groundbreaking with ceremonial shovels full of dirt. It was good to see the great Boston City Councilor again so I mentioned to Mike that he looked just as majestic with a shovel in his hand as with a microphone. We also got to have a few laughs with some of the folks from Suffolk Construction, the general contractor on the project, including former Senator Linda Dorcena Forry and others.

We may never have made it to this function without the welcome help of Joe Cheevers. Joe also served as the Harbormaster for the Boston Police Harbor Unit which is located on Drydock Avenue not far from our destination on Summer Street. I didn't even know where his unit was situated and it wouldn't have helped if I did as I could never be a cab driver in Boston due to my inability to master some of the oldest roads in the nation. We were trying in vain to find a parking space within a reasonable walking distance of the event and I was getting sick of trying to navigate one-way streets when we just happened to spot Joe walking into his headquarters. I called out and Joe smiled as he came over to our car. He told us to leave the car in the space marked NO PARKING - BOSTON POLICE. Joe came through with the kindness he is known for and we had an outstanding day.

Once in a while I worked in courts other than my own so J. Do and I were staying in Nantucket for a few days as I had been assigned by Chief Justice Paul C. Dawley to work at the island's District Court. Don Hart is the great Clerk-Magistrate there who was appointed by Governor Deval L. Patrick and again later by Governor Charlie D. Baker. Don is a talented lawyer, carpenter, musician, song writer and a real good guy who genuinely cares for others. I had just finished some hearings at the court and was walking outside the building on my way to lunch with J. Do when I heard my name called. Not knowing many people on Nantucket, I turned around to happily see Joe Cheevers and his family who were vacationing on the island. Joe was surprised to see me coming out of another court as we kidded about rendering justice everywhere.

The death of a young Black man while in police custody in 2015 resulted in civil unrest and riots in the streets of Baltimore. The Baltimore Police were working hard to stem the tide of violence and investigate murders happening at an alarming rate. Joe Cheevers and other Boston Police Officers wanted to provide a little relief for their brothers and sisters in blue so they drove to Baltimore and hosted a catered BBQ for the weary guardians of Maryland's largest city. The Baltimore Police appreciated the kindness, enjoying smoked ribs, chicken and pork with all the sides compliments of the Boston Police during a short break from the chaos and senseless destruction. Many of the officers had to leave to respond to the second homicide of the day, but some got to hear Joe and his band mates fill the air with sweet music. Unfortunately, Baltimore crime statistics have gotten worse as the annual per capita homicide number reached a new high of 342 murders with only a few days left in 2019. The Boston Police, just like all departments, quietly do a lot of nice things for the local community and in other venues as well without ever seeking fanfare or recognition so let us hope and pray for their safe return from every shift.

I first met Daniel J. Coyle when he was a patrolman on the North Attleborough Police Department although he would rise up quickly through the ranks and eventually be promoted to the high rank of captain before his young life would tragically come to an end. Dan served as the DARE Officer and gave good advice to hundreds of kids along the way including our daughters Kaitlin and Christine who were both graduates of his program. I worked with Dan's wife Carole and was overjoyed to see her promoted to Assistant Clerk-Magistrate of the ADC. Dan's father was the Chief of Police, his uncle was the Detective Sergeant Prosecutor and Carole's father was the First Assistant Clerk-Magistrate so she used to joke that she needed extra space to list all of her relatives on her annual State Ethics Commission Report!

    Two women in their 30's were arrested for shoplifting by the North Attleborough Police at the Emerald Square Mall. They had a five-year old boy with them so the officers separated the three of them to prevent alignment of stories before interrogation. Lieutenant Dan Coyle took the young boy aside to ask him some questions out of earshot of the two women. The boy said that one of the women was his aunt so when Lieutenant Coyle asked him what her name was the five-year old, obviously already well-schooled in criminal activity and taught to limit answers, spoke in a cool and deliberate tone asking Coyle, "What did she say her name was?"

    V.H. Blackinton & Co., Inc. in North Attleborough is widely recognized for manufacturing top quality badges and uniform insignia for law enforcement. They produced a large advertising poster featuring Lieutenant Dan Coyle of the North Attleborough Police Department along with samples of their badges. Carole Coyle hung the majestic color poster with her husband's handsome face on display just above her desk at the ADC. The attractive poster was visible to a lot of foot traffic in the office so people would often stop to admire it. I knew that Carole was proud that Dan had been selected for the ad as well she should have been.

    Before heading for court one morning, I stopped at the North Attleborough Police Department at 6 AM to accommodate a prisoner so he could go home and get cleaned up for his appearance before a judge. I only released one defendant because the other three drunks in the lockup were uncontrollably rattling the cell door while screaming and swearing at Dan Coyle who was one of the best all-around police officers that I have ever known.

    After I released the prisoner, I exchanged pleasantries with Dan who was a squared away professional and just a really nice guy. The three screaming nitwits had calmed down long enough to have a conversation with him for a few minutes. I said good bye to Dan when they resumed yelling insults like imbeciles and stuck around just long enough to hear Dan tell them that it was time to take their breakfast order. Dan announced that the special today was blueberry pancakes and that the bacon and eggs came with extra bacon. The prisoners couldn't see me laughing as I watched Dan pretend to write down the breakfast order being yelled out by the three dopes. "I want the special with extra sausages," demanded one idiot as the other two were insisting on orange juice and English muffins before the main course. "OK," Dan said, "I'll get this order in right away." He winked at me as I left for court. I'm told that the day shift came in at 8 AM when the three belligerent buffoons were served the usual lockup breakfast of a single donut. Cries of dissatisfaction could be heard coming from the cell block proclaiming that the food was mixed up and that they had ordered sausages, bacon and eggs!

Our two daughters were shopping with J. Do at the Emerald Square Mall in North Attleborough. Five-year old Chrissy and seven-year old Kait loved going into the pet shop there and on this day they both fell in love immediately with a beautiful golden retriever puppy. I was on the couch after a long night of thieves, drunks and violence when I got a call from my bride saying that the kids really wanted to take this cute puppy home. I could hear our girls in the background saying "Please dad, please, please!" as J. Do suggested that we put the dog on MasterCard. It was an easy sell as I am a dog guy myself so they came home with a new member of the family that we named Champ.

Champ joined me as the only other male in the house and quickly became an integral part of our everyday life. He would take turns sleeping with the kids and accompanied me to police stations so often that the police would ask me where he was if he had stayed at home. Sometimes I would tell the police that Champ takes Thursdays off, or whatever day it was, and we would all have a good laugh.

Champ would happily greet people with his tail wagging so fast that we called it the 90 MPH tail. Police officers, witnesses, victims, and defendants all loved the friendly golden retriever with the powerful tail sweeping anything in its path. Even violent hardened criminals were known to soften and find a smile for my four legged partner.

My canine companion would sit on the floor next to the desk as I filled out the recog forms. One time, at the North Attleborough Police Station, Champ climbed under the desk and laid down next to my feet. There was a foot of space between the floor and the bottom of the desk which left an opening exposed, but the dog was not visible to someone walking by. A police officer brought out the next prisoner who sat down next to me.

I told the 65-year old woman that I had to fill out the recog and that I would be right with her. She was charged with OUI and had just blown a .37 on the breath machine so she was pretty well lit as I was almost catching a buzz off of her breath. Every department does things a little differently with North Attleborough giving property back after release so she was sitting there barefoot. The woman had no idea that there was a dog under the desk as her head swayed back and forth in a drunken stupor. Champ spotted those bare feet inches away and started licking her toes through the opening under the desk. His long tongue would dart out, take a lick, and then disappear. The woman's eyes shot wide open as she told me that there was some guy under the desk licking her feet. The officer told her that she had been drinking heavily and not to worry as her sober ride was here to take her home. She kept insisting, but eventually signed the recog and went on her way.

I was filling out the recog for the next defendant as he sat down next to me wearing socks that were full of holes. I wasn't surprised to learn that the intoxicated 23-year old was still single when he said, "I've got to find a woman who will darn my socks!"

The North Attleborough Police arrested three shoplifters who tried to flee in an unusual vehicle. They had gone on a larceny spree at a Route 1 shopping plaza and stolen items from Marshalls, TJ Maxx, Spencer Gifts, and Dick's Sporting Goods including bags full of Nike and Adidas clothing. They were using so called "booster bags" which prevent security system alarms from going off and they were also in possession of a tool that is commonly used by thieves to free up clothing from anti-theft devices. I used to see these types of arrests all the time which is why honest people pay so much for clothing as stores have to compensate and factor the "stolen merchandise element" into the price equation. This activity is more common than some people think, but the thing that made these particular arrests unusual was the getaway car. The shoplifters were arrested after hiring a ride from a Lift driver! The police determined that the Lift driver was not involved and took the three backseat passengers into custody.

NAPD Detective Lieutenant Michael P. Gould Sr. is a nice man with powerful and obvious leadership qualities that would eventually carry him up the ranks to the position of Chief of Police. He is a very smart man who used his superior intellect to be able to calm people who wouldn't listen to anyone else. I personally saw a handcuffed defendant being escorted into the booking room while screaming, swearing, threatening, kicking and trying to bite the arresting officer. This guy was acting like a petulant four-year old after finding out that his brother had taken the last donut. The officer gave a double take when Detective Lieutenant Gould instructed that the handcuffs be removed, but followed orders and immediately freed the well-built maniac. The detective lieutenant stuck his right hand out, looked in his eyes and said, "I'm Mike. What's your name?" The guy shook his hand, calmed down and became a different person in a flash. I only wish that this had been on film because it remains the most impressive act of tension reduction and peaceful persuasion that I have ever seen.

On another occasion Mike Gould quelled a potentially deadly situation when responding to a noise complaint that turned out to be a marital dispute. Domestic difficulties can be some of the most perilous events for police officers and this was no exception. An extremely aggravated husband was cutting the stairs in half with a chainsaw. He told Mike that his wife wanted a divorce so he was cutting the house in half! The man would not put the chainsaw down at first, but after some professional persuasion by Mike the powerful weapon was surrendered without any injuries.

The sworn officers of the North Attleborough Police Department were always a very highly skilled and dedicated group of trained professionals who didn't sit around and let crime come to them. On a slow night they would get on the phone and call people who had outstanding criminal warrants to tell them to bring the release fee and surrender to the police station by 8:00 PM. I would walk in at 8 and sometimes release about 20 people for a variety of minor non-violent crimes. This helped the police and courts clear up outstanding warrants and put cash in my pocket.

One night, when the police were making calls to ask defendants to surrender on warrants, I got a call from Detective Lieutenant Gould on an unusual case. Mike had called a young woman on a bad check warrant who lived right across the street from the police station and she had agreed to turn herself in with the release fee, but the only problem was that she was almost nine months pregnant and ready to have the baby any minute. Mike was trying to prevent the station from becoming a delivery room so he asked me if it would be OK if she stayed in her apartment and came across the street as soon as I got there instead of waiting in a cell. I said that was an excellent idea so as soon as I got there, I released her first. No handcuffs, no shoe removal - she was out of there faster than a federal worker at closing time! I told Detective Lieutenant Gould that if the baby is a boy, they should name it Mike!

I was releasing prisoners on a busy night at the NAPD. Sometimes the police would let a relative wait with a nonviolent defendant as I released a line of arrestees. A 60-year woman was seated nearby next to her husband who was under arrest for drunk driving. The release fee at the time was $25.00, I was working on a recog for another defendant when the drunk driver asked me how much it cost to get released. I told him it was $25.00 to get out prompting his wife to say, "How much to keep him in!"

Tony was a one-man crime wave in the city of Attleboro. He would get arrested frequently, but with the exception of his earlier life it was usually for something minor and nonviolent. He got arrested three times in one weekend for minor offenses that I think entailed shoplifting, public drinking and disorderly. After releasing him for the second time, Attleboro Police Lieutenant Richard J. Pierce called me to say that they had him under arrest again. I had to go to the station for some other prisoners anyway so I told Rick that we would speak then.

Rick is a squared away, honest and down to earth guy who would eventually be appointed Chief of the department. I was honored to attend his swearing in ceremony with J. Do and always enjoyed our conversations because he is a straight shooter. He was concerned that the system was becoming a joke for the defendant, but I didn't want to put bail on him as everything was so minor. We talked for a while and agreed that Tony would be put under house arrest. Tony was brought out of his cell and a unique system was immediately created just for him. I told him that I was releasing him, but he was going to have to remain under house arrest until going to court on Monday morning. Tony, who was once described as being a few cookies short of a dozen, wanted to know if he could leave his apartment to buy some cigarettes and beer to which I replied no. Somehow, he had gotten the impression that I wanted him to stay in his bedroom so he asked if he could come out to go to the bathroom. I told him that was OK, but then to get back in the bedroom. He started pressing for details such as going to the kitchen to make a sandwich when I told him that I better not see him again until Monday morning in the courtroom!

Another one-man crime wave was in court so often that he decided to represent himself sometimes and file his own motions. He eventually moved to California so a local police officer told me, "Now that he's gone, we're going to have to lay off three cops!"

I had just released a few prisoners from the Attleboro Police lockup and directed the next defendant to put his $25.00 release fee on the table. He said that he didn't have any money, but the officer stated that his mother had dropped off the cash earlier and that it had been given to him in his cell. The man then told me that he ripped up the cash and flushed it down the toilet because he was bad and didn't deserve to get out of jail! He got his wish!

Our daughters Kaitlin and Christine were introduced to the criminal justice system at an early age as they each started accompanying me to police stations when they were very young, usually on weekend mornings when defendants were too hung over to cause a problem. They observed my transactions with so many defendants that they probably could have done the job themselves. The kids would go in the back room with an officer if I had to speak with an unruly subject so I probably owe Detective Lieutenant Kenneth D. Collins babysitting money, but for the most part I wanted them to see that not everybody who gets arrested is a bad guy. They learned early on that there is a difference between a bad guy and a good guy who had made a bad mistake.

Police departments had just begun to increase their security by installing keypads with numbered codes required for access through the employee entrance. My girls were about 6 and 4 years old when they quickly memorized the four-digit codes for all of the area police lockups. As soon as I pulled into the parking lot of another police station, they would each start saying that they wanted to press the buttons on the keypad and I would have to keep the peace by trying to remember whose turn it was this time!

The Attleboro Police station was usually a busy place and this Sunday morning was no different. My girls were seated at a desk right near me as we waited for the next prisoner to be brought out of the cell block. He was 50 years old with broken English and a bad hangover. His head hurt so badly that he almost started crying from the sound of a slammed door. The release fee back in those days was $25.00 and he had a 5 dollar bill in one hand and a 20 in the other. My girls listened intently as he tried to negotiate with me through the language barrier. He wanted to keep the 5 to buy a six pack for his hangover so he moved the hand with the 20 toward me and said, "You get 20, I keep 5?" Before I could say anything 6-year old Kaitlin demanded, "No, my mother wants it all!" The guy immediately knew that he had lost that battle and surrendered both the 20 and the 5!

We used to call our girls Pete and Repeat because Kaitlin would tell a story as Christine would repeat the same story on about a three-second delay as it was coming out of Kait's mouth! It was actually pretty impressive as Kaitlin would be talking to a police officer and then Chrissy would join in with her talent. I remember Kenny Collins laughing and getting a big kick out of this act.

My girls are now both married with children of their own, but they still have fond memories of the street smart criminal justice education that they received in their youth. They were just reminiscing recently about the time that they were shown the inside of a holding cell by an officer and told that's where kids go who don't keep their bedroom clean!

Detective Lieutenant Collins was leading a group of Attleboro Police Officers into a rooming house to serve a warrant on one of the occupants. The detectives and uniformed officers had their weapons drawn as they slowly made their way through the hallway as they looked for the defendant's room number. One of the tenants opened the door to his room, stuck his head out and asked what was going on. Kenny immediately ordered the guy to get back in his room so the man quickly complied. They opened the door to the defendant's room and found him seated at a table under a low hanging overhead ceiling fan that was going full blast. Kenny pointed his gun at him and told him to stand up and raise his hands. The guy stood up and as soon as he raised his hands his fingers went into the fan spinning above. He screamed and pulled his hands down as Kenny ordered them back up so the guy's fingers went back into the fan! Kenny knew that this couldn't continue so he ordered the man to move away from the fan and cuffed him. They seated the defendant in the back of a cruiser and brought him to the police station for booking. Kenny was still at the station about three hours later when a call came in from the rooming house. The guy who had stuck his head out into the hall and was ordered back in by Kenny was on the phone wondering if it was OK to come out of his room now!

Kenny Collins is one of the best natured police officers that I have ever known possessing the self-confidence necessary to poke fun at himself. He went to K Mart in response to an advertising flyer announcing that outdoor folding chairs were on sale. Kenny showed the photo of the chair in the flyer to a K Mart employee and asked where he could find them. Kenny is a big guy, maybe 230 pounds, but not huge so he was surprised when the store clerk told him what isle they were in, but also said, "The chair won't hold you. They're only for people under 250 pounds!" Some guys would have had their feelings hurt, but Kenny just laughed.

Kenny came to the court to present me with an affidavit for a search warrant for a drug house in Attleboro. The ace detective had plenty of probable cause so I signed the warrant and wished him luck. I was surprised to receive a call a few hours later at home that he needed another search warrant. Another case had developed as he was working on the drug case so I asked him to come to my house. It was extremely cold as I think the temperature had dropped below 0 on that bitter winter night. I opened the front door and quickly told Kenny to come in, but he handed me the paperwork and said that he would wait in the cruiser while I read the affidavit. He told me that his shoes were covered in cockroach eggs from the drug house that they just raided so he didn't want to infest our house with future visitors come spring.

The target of the second search warrant was a convicted criminal who had broken into the ADC and stolen insignificant items like a jackknife and bottle of mouthwash from my desk. I flashed the front lights for Kenny and handed him the warrant. I had to go to the station later that night for a prisoner so Kenny asked me to go upstairs to the detective division. The floor was covered with items stolen from the court that were being catalogued into evidence. They already had enough on the guy so Kenny told me to take anything that was mine. I picked up my jack knife, but Kenny and I both laughed when I said that I was leaving the Listerine there just in case the thief had already taken a swig! This guy apparently didn't like the halls of justice as he had already set a courthouse on fire in Suffolk County.

I will never forget the kindness of the easygoing APD detective lieutenant with a heart as big as Capron Park. A less considerate police officer may have come right into my home to escape the cold and left a disgusting mess for my family. I'm glad that J. Do and I were able to make it to Kenny's retirement party which was a very well attended event as people came from near and far to pay tribute to the big guy with the easy laugh.

A North Attleborough Police dispatcher called and woke me to say that they had a defendant under arrest for possession of an under sized lobster! Sometimes I wake up out a deep sleep pretty slowly so my brain machinations were trying to determine if I had heard correctly. I already knew that obviously the lobster had not come from Falls Pond when the dispatcher told me that the arrest had been made on a warrant. The defendant had been given a citation in Bourne and ignored the instructions which had resulted in the Barnstable District Court issuing a warrant for his arrest. He was then stopped for speeding by a North Attleborough Police Officer and came back a hit on the warrant. As the defendant handed me the cash for the release fee he said, "This is the most expensive lobster I've ever had!"

Paul J. Maher is a former Massachusetts State Trooper who later started his own business called Muni-Tech, repairing municipal property that has been damaged mostly by motor vehicle accidents as well as providing Accident Recovery Services to the Commonwealth DOT. Paul is one of the most honorable men that I have ever known as he genuinely cares about people and always tries to do the right thing. His quick Irish wit has served him well over the years while speaking at many prominent functions and serving as a highly sought-after master of ceremonies. Paul, who always accentuates the positive, mentioned to someone at the Cops for Kids with Cancer fundraiser that he had grown up in a three-decker in Brookline. Retired BPD Superintendent Robert Faherty who already knew Paul, heard the conversation and responded with his own Irish wit. Bob told Paul, "You don't have to tell everyone that you grew up in a three-decker" to which Paul responded, "Why not, you grew up in a three-decker didn't you?" The retired superintendent with a twinkle in his eye stated, "Yes I did, but sometimes I tell people I grew up in a twenty-one room house with three bathrooms, on the way to the Cape, I just leave out Dorchester!"

I was playing in a golf tournament with the rest of the foursome comprised of Paul, Plainville Police Chief Edward M. "Ned" Merrick and Kenneth W. Kaiser who, at the time, was the Special Agent in Charge of the Boston Field Office of the FBI. Leadership qualities run deep in the Merrick family as Ned's brother Brian was appointed to a judgeship by Governor Michael S. Dukakis and eventually served as the outstanding First Justice of the Orleans District Court. We were having a lot of laughs and even hitting the ball straight once in a while when Ned, who was a terrific guy with the slowest backswing in America, hooked his ball into the woods. We all went into the forest, as Ned always called it, to look for his ball. Ken was the one who found the errant sphere and called out the good news to Ned. Paul served as the MC for the tournament dinner after we finished playing and went through a litany of jokes and funny stories that had the audience roaring in comical hysterics. He then told the story of the FBI SAC finding the golf ball belonging to the Chief of Police earlier that day and said, "Ladies and gentlemen, this is the first time in the history of law enforcement that the FBI has ever shared pertinent information with a local police department!"

Paul also had the audience laughing from his story about the man from Charlestown who was speaking to his son. The father told the young man that if you remember these three little words you will never go hungry and always be able to support your family – "stick em up!"

I put high bail on an alleged car thief from Boston who took a swing at the police officer who had pulled him over for speeding and driving erratically. He had a record of violence and defaults to go along with some other serious character flaws. Most car thieves drive stolen cars carefully and don't exceed the speed limit!

A police officer pulled a car over suspecting the driver of being intoxicated. The driver, soon to be known as the defendant, knew that he had consumed too many beers so he didn't want the officer to be able to smell his breath. The officer approached the driver's window which remained closed. The officer observed the man's face turn red as he held his breath while opening the sunroof and handed his license and registration up through the opening!

When my family arrived at Ellis Island they were not greeted with open arms. I am a descendent of Irish immigrants who came to America with pockets that were nearly empty, but with dreams full of hope for the promise of a better life in a new land. Family stories that I grew up hearing recalled the cruel prejudice of signs reading HELP WANTED - IRISH NEED NOT APPLY and had a deep, lasting impact on me as a young kid. Thus, I have always been sympathetic to the plight of all immigrants trying to provide a safe life for their family in the greatest country on the face of the earth.

Just the other day I was reading *The Sun Chronicle* newspaper when I came across an advertisement in the General Services section directing potential customers to call Eamon at a phone number. The headline for the ad was IRISH CARPENTER/PAINTER. After many generations having experienced pain and rejection, now people publicize their Irish ancestry and continue to shine in the melting pot of American life, so how times have changed.

Immigrants from across the globe, just like every other group, are comprised of good and bad individuals, but with most being hardworking, nice, honest people. Championship soccer games brought huge crowds to Gillette Stadium with fans travelling great distances to watch their favorite teams and players. They may very well have a higher level of devotion to the game of soccer than many other fans have for their sport so their enthusiasm was admirable. A young man from Brazil was celebrating his team's victory when he decided to run out onto the field after the game so he was arrested for trespassing by the Foxborough Police. His anger was apparent as he entered the room and sat down in front of me. He was about 25 years old, well built with tense muscles upon muscles and a set of dark colored eyes that were fixated upon me like I had just killed his pet hamster! I explained to him that I was filling out his recog form and that he needed $40.00 for a release fee. He leaned in toward me, pointed a finger at my face and arrogantly proclaimed, "In my country we can run on the field!" I told him to put his finger away and said, "Well, in this country you need $40.00, welcome to America!"

It was a busy night at the Mansfield Police Department as I released about 40 people who had been arrested at a Great Woods concert. An officer stood next to me and handed defendants their belongings after each release. The officer brought out the very last kid, a 20-year old who sat down next to me. The officer had to leave as I filled out the recog form and spoke with the highly intoxicated defendant. I finished my transaction and was ready to go, but the officer had not returned so I didn't want to leave the defendant alone. I made small talk with him and told him that the officer should be back in a minute to give him his property. This kid was really drunk and becoming more impatient by the minute. He was also tired and wanted to go to sleep so he finally got up and started walking back to the cell block as he said, "Tell the police that I'll be back in my old cell!"

Another busy night of Great Woods arrests had produced mostly happy drunks. I told a young man that he had to report to the ADC the next morning to which he replied, "Attleboro!? Don't I have to go to court in Worcester?" Upon being told that he had been at a concert in Mansfield and that Attleboro handles those arrests he appeared dumbfounded as he stated, "Son of a bitch! I was wondering why there was no roof over the Centrum!"

After a concert the Mansfield Police Department parking lot would sometimes be full of cars, including limos, with dozens of people waiting for me to show up and release their relatives or friends. I would get out of my car to be greeted with inquiries being yelled my way like, "Are you the bail guy?" or "Are you the man from the courthouse?" As soon as I confirmed that I was the one they were waiting for a rousing applause would erupt with cheering and one guy even breaking into a drunken celebratory dance.

The first defendants that I would always attempt to release were those who had moms and dads waiting so that they could all leave together and be on their way home as quickly as possible. I tried to accommodate parents as best that I could because it was going to be a tough night for their family. I used an area in close proximity to the cell block so on this night I brought the first mom and dad into the room and asked them the name of their son. They had already told me that they had enough cash for his release so I asked an officer to escort the young man from the cell and he set off to find him.

This was an old police station that sometimes had dozens of people crammed into a few cells, unlike the huge holding cell that was built in Mansfield long after the initial opening of Great Woods. The officer was yelling out this kid's name and that his money was here into a loud and unruly group of agitated prisoners as he walked along the cellblock outside of the iron bars. Arms were hanging out in a sea of disrupted humanity and captured chaos. The officer went back and forth a couple of times before a kid said, "That's me." The officer got the other prisoners to move over enough to get the kid out and brought him into the room with us. I said his name, the kid said yes and the mother said, "That's not my son!" The officer put the imposter back in the cell and eventually found the real kid passed out. The first guy didn't have enough cash for the release fee so he tried to pull a fast one not knowing that the mom and dad would be in the room.

The Grateful Dead brought in huge audiences to Great Woods with their tie-dyed clothing and laid-back attitude temporarily making the town of Mansfield resemble a smaller version of Woodstock. Drugs were rampant as this nonviolent crowd were joyous and carefree, but after the concerts many of them would just camp out on resident's lawns and sleep off their narcotic-induced state. An elderly man looked out the window in the morning and called out to his wife, "Marge, there's a bunch of hippies sleeping on the front lawn!"

Our personalities, values and thought process are primarily shaped by the home life in which we are raised as children. We learn more from our parents than any other component of our environment. I was fortunate enough to be raised in a home where the sound of a siren from a police cruiser was something positive because it meant that the good guys were on the way.

The ADC is located on Route 152 which is a very busy street. It is not unusual for police cruisers to go by with blue lights flashing and sirens blaring. The sirens can be heard through closed courtroom windows and were quite often picked up on the tape recordings of trials and other court proceedings. A more modern recording system has replaced the old, but I used to process cassette tape requests for attorneys and anyone else who placed an order so I would frequently hear police sirens on the tapes.

I was heading for the courtroom on a very busy morning as I slowly made my way through the overflow crowd of defendants in the hallway who were waiting to be arraigned. A young woman was leaning up against the wall while waiting for the court session to begin with her four year old daughter standing next to her. A police cruiser's siren went off and started blaring just as I walked by the mother and daughter. I could see the little girl's face suddenly full of fear with her eyes darting left and right as she heard the police siren. She immediately sought security by grabbing hold of her mother's leg and menacingly said one word, "Cops!"

Bruce P. Gordon retired as a major after having been involved in many celebrated cases and making some interesting arrests during a long and distinguished career with the Massachusetts State Police. I was honored to be the main speaker at his sold-out retirement party that was held at Lombardo's in Randolph. Bruce is always quick with a joke or funny story and his lovely wife Rena is as interesting as she is humorous. Rena holds the extremely unusual distinction of having won the Miss Massachusetts Pageant and of later being voted Mrs. Massachusetts. Rena and Bruce are the proud parents of two sons – Nicholas who was an assistant district attorney, now an excellent attorney in private practice and Anthony, a squared away detective sergeant on the Connecticut State Police who could make a very good living as a standup comic if he wanted.

Rena and Bruce were at our house when he got a call on the Gary Lee Sampson case. At the time, Bruce was the detective lieutenant in charge of the Plymouth County Crime Prevention and Control (CPAC) unit. I could almost see Bruce's mind working when the phone conversation ended because the defendant had gone on a crime spree in two different states, with a stolen car from Massachusetts recovered at a homicide scene in New Hampshire, eventually resulting in three murder charges. After a top-notch investigation by Bruce and others as well as a dynamic prosecution, Sampson was sentenced to death and died in prison while awaiting appeal.

Bruce was working a detail at a New England Patriots game when he had to take an intoxicated middle-aged man into protective custody. The man had gone to the game compliments of his friend who was a season ticket holder. Not knowing if he was about to be arrested and out of concern that his detainment might trigger the revocation of his friend's season tickets, he put the ticket in his mouth and swallowed it as Bruce was approaching. Bruce told me he had to admire the guy's loyalty!

The Gordons have been married a long time so Bruce told a story about how he was asked to explain the secret to having a lengthy successful marriage. With tongue firmly planted in cheek, Bruce explained that their recipe for a long happy marriage is that they go out for a nice romantic candle light dinner once a week, she goes on Tuesdays and he goes on Thursdays!

Some of my most memorable and enjoyable hearings at the ADC were with Anthony Gordon when he was working security at the Emerald Square Mall prior to becoming a police officer. Tony was prosecuting cases, mostly against shoplifters, which were at the show cause hearing stage. I would try to keep a straight face while it felt like a Saturday Night Live skit was being performed as Tony called one case after another. Tony was always respectful, but had a creative way of injecting humor into almost every circumstance.

Another time Tony was involved in something deadly serious. He assisted in the capture of a well-known child molester who was caught on film stalking a young girl in the mall. The defendant was brought to the North Attleborough Police Station where he told the booking sergeant that he knew where his kids went to school! The sergeant exhibited great restraint, continuing with the booking procedure and Tony, ever the honest warrior, turned down 50 thousand dollars from a national TV show that wanted a copy of the film. I was glad to send letters of recommendation for Tony as he is an outstanding young man of enormous integrity and physical ability, plus I always figured that in the unlikely event that he couldn't overpower a bad guy, he could make him laugh until surrendering!

Tony became a North Attleborough Police Officer, serving with class and distinction in a very busy department. Tradition dictates that his badge be pinned on his uniform by someone close so Tony chose his father for the ceremony. Tony, with badge in hand in front of a huge crowd, was told by Bruce to put it away. The proud father took out another badge and pinned it on his son while telling him, "This belonged to my father, your grandfather. He never tarnished this badge so don't you either."

Bruce was happy that his son had followed him into law enforcement and held local police in high esteem, but facetiously told Tony that he couldn't use the front door as that was reserved only for state police! When Tony started dating a beautiful girl named Lisa, he felt like he had hit the lottery and knew that she was the one. Lisa had already met Tony's mother Rena, but not his father so Tony packed a cooler full of food and drinks for a cookout at the North Attleborough home of his parents and looked forward to Lisa meeting his dad. As they walked around the side of the house, they spotted Bruce in the backyard sitting on a poolside chair. Tony yelled that they had arrived and Bruce returned the greeting by saying, "OK, make sure you use the side door." When Lisa asked Tony why they couldn't use the front door he had to tell her it was because he wasn't a trooper!

Tony went on to graduate from the Connecticut State Police Academy where they conducted a similar badge pinning ceremony. Bruce proudly pinned the Connecticut State Police badge on Tony's uniform and told him, "There, now you can use the front door!"

J. Do and I were honored to attend Lisa and Tony's wedding where everyone thoroughly enjoyed a terrific day of great food, drink and fun. The long guest list included some Connecticut State Police, North Attleborough Police and others from near and far. It was a beautiful ceremony and we were glad to be a part of it.

My bride and I were planning a little mini vacation at the Mohegan Sun casino so I called our favorite Connecticut State Trooper to let him know we were heading for the Nutmeg State. Tony hooked us up with Stu Friedman, a terrific professional poker player who is a retired detective sergeant from the New York City Transit Police. Stu took us into a complimentary buffet for heavy hitters and could not have been nicer or more accommodating. Stu survived three shootings and was still carrying a bullet in his chest when he was so kind to us at the casino. He was assigned to Bronx Homicide and received many awards and commendations during a brilliant career including the Combat Cross. The Transit Police would eventually merge with the NYPD where Stu's brother Ralph survived fifteen shootings while killing four perpetrators and making over 2,000 arrests while assigned to the famous 41st Precinct in the South Bronx which came to be known as Fort Apache. Ralph is the most decorated detective in the history of the NYPD. Later, after returning home I was flicking the channels around on TV when I came across a police story all about Stu and his brother Ralph. The program was an episode of *Top Cops* showing the Friedman brothers saving the day and solving a crime in progress while they were off duty.

Tony was promoted to detective sergeant and put in charge of two Connecticut State Police Units - the Statewide Organized Crime Task Force and the Northwest Field Office of the Statewide Narcotics Task Force. Part of his responsibilities required undercover work so he grew a scruffy beard and went to work in his new role. Tony was seated at the bar in Mohegan Sun when he noticed a man a few stools down who was wearing a Fort Myers Country Club golf shirt. Tony and his parents own condos in that vacation mecca so he struck up a conversation with the gentleman. Tony had Mike laughing so hard that he asked if he was a comedian, but Tony, being undercover, said he was a landscaper. Mike was disappointed because he owned a comedy club nearby and one of the comics had called in sick so he was looking for a fill in for that night. Tony quickly said he could do it, but Mike suddenly became skeptical and asked Tony to make him laugh again. A very short impromptu routine left Mike laughing so hard that he immediately offered Tony the job for that night. Tony walked into Comix Roadhouse and jotted some jokes down on a cocktail napkin to prepare for his maiden show. He was introduced to a lively full house as Tony G., going on to entertain the comedy club crowd and keep them laughing hysterically for close to fifteen minutes. Mike was very happy with Tony's performance, but said that he must be a professional as his act was just too good! When Mike tried to pay Tony, he explained that he was an undercover State Police Detective Sergeant so he couldn't take the money and asked that it be donated to charity. Keep an eye out for Tony G., headlining somewhere close to you in the near future!

A guy well-known to the Attleboro Police had been given the nickname "Rocks in the Head" and the family legacy continued when his son was dubbed with the moniker "Pebbles."

An old school police officer had worked his way up to become Chief of the department. He was a throwback to a different era who set a no-nonsense gruff tone with his officers, holding them to an elevated standard of policing, thus providing the general population with a remarkably high level of professionalism in public safety.

The day shift had just begun as the usual arrangements were being made to bring some food to the prisoners locked up from the previous evening. A young police officer was walking by the female cells when a 21-year old defendant whispered through the bars asking if she could speak with him. She told the officer that it was her time of the month and asked if he could get her a tampon. Unsure if they had those at the station, he told her that he would ask the Chief and get right back to her. He proceeded to the Chief's office, knocked on door and wasn't surprised to hear a loud and unhappy voice direct him to come in. Apparently, the Chief may have thought that a tampon was a special breakfast treat or some other kind of food item. "Chief", the young officer began, "the female prisoner in cell two is asking for a tampon." The Chief pointed his finger and stated, "Bullshit! You tell her that she's going to get a plain donut just like all the rest of them!"

The 40-year old drunk driver fell asleep at the wheel while navigating a winding country road in a snowstorm. The car safely drifted off to the side of the road coming to rest up against a snow bank without damage to the vehicle or injury to the driver. When the trooper approached the driver's window, he observed the man sleeping with his head resting on the steering wheel, the engine still running and headlights illuminating a large snow bank that had caused the vehicle to come to a stop. The trooper tapped his flashlight on the window while running in place causing the panicked drunk driver to wake up and think he was being chased by the state police on foot. The trooper kept running in place while yelling, "Slow down, slow down!" The soon-to-be defendant kept hitting the brakes and turning his head toward the trooper with a facial expression from a horror movie.

Christmas season was always a busy time at the Emerald Square Mall in North Attleborough. Police Officers worked details directing incredibly long lines of vehicular traffic from Route One into the mall parking lots. Holiday music could be heard as stores became bustling places full of Christmas shoppers and shoplifters. I was seated at the NAPD releasing prisoners as a 40-year old female alleged thief was being booked for stealing an enormous amount of clothing and jewelry from the mall. There was so much stolen merchandise that two officers were working the case to catalog and inventory all of the evidence. Dozens of stolen items were laid out on the floor covering most of the carpet from the female cell block all the way back to the windows. The booking process continued as she watched the officers remove more items from her bags. One of the officers snapped a photo of a winter jacket causing the woman to yell, "No! I didn't steal that one. I bought that coat a long time ago. It's really mine!"

Arthur Collins was one of the first police officers to welcome me to my new job at the ADC. He was a squared away professional and one of the nicest guys that I would ever meet. Art was extremely helpful to me and treated everybody with courtesy and respect.

One night a very unhappy defendant was being held on a default warrant in a cell at the NAPD lockup. The rude reprobate was screaming insults at the top of his lungs while rattling the metal bars and climbing them like the inhabitant of a metropolitan zoo. Based on this guy's derision of so many different classes of people it was no surprise that he also hated the police.

His fellow lock up mates were now yelling at him to shut up and Art Collins was getting a headache. The good officer removed everything clipped on his dark blue uniform shirt including his badge and took off his gun belt. He rigged a white piece of cardboard into the collar of his shirt so that he now looked like a priest. Art walked into the cell block, approached the angry degenerate, looked into his eyes and sympathetically asked, "What's troubling you my son?"

Richard C. DesLauriers was the Special Agent in Charge of the Boston Field Office of the Federal Bureau of Investigation at the time of the horrific Marathon Bombings. The first time I met Rick was when I was invited by United States Attorney Carmen M. Ortiz to a Massachusetts Anti-Terrorism Advisory Council (ATAC) meeting at the Moakley Courthouse in Boston. He is a very intelligent, personable and engaging man who projects a no-nonsense aura of professionalism. Rick had a long, distinguished career in the FBI with his name and face on TV screens throughout the world every day during the Marathon Bombing investigation. He became the reassuring face of the good guys during the fight against evil in the pursuit of justice and was universally praised for his tremendous leadership skills when those responsible were finally taken down and held accountable, one in death and the other in prison.

I was honored to speak at his retirement party in Boston where I presented him with the American Justice Award. The best presentation of the night came from Boston Police Superintendent in Chief Daniel P. Linskey who spoke before I did. The United States Marine Corps veteran served as the Incident Commander for the Marathon and is the recipient of numerous commendations including the Boston Police Medal of Honor. He addressed many of Rick's positive attributes in his speech and also remarked that, "My 84-year old mother was seeing press briefings with Rick on TV all the time and refers to him as that tall, handsome man from the FBI, so Rick I just want you to know that you're a big hit with the over 80 crowd!"

Bay State Lodge #30 of the Fraternal Order of Police put together an annual chicken wing competition where local restaurants deliver their best fare to be consumed by celebrity judges. They must have been short on celebrities as they asked me to be a judge several times and I was honored to participate. Huge

Chicken Wing Judging Panel, L-R Chief Brian Clark, Chief Rick Pierce, Senator Jim Timilty, author, 5x NFL All Pro Fred Smerlas

crowds turn out to cheer the judges on as they ingest samples of different kinds of chicken wings. I had a nice conversation with Rob Gronkowski who was eating wings next to me before most people recognized the future 4 time Super Bowl Champion. Five-time NFL All Pro Fred Smerlas kept me laughing so long I could hardly eat any wings! Fred, a funny man who I had met before in Boston, is a gifted story teller who could do well as a standup comic with hilarious anecdotes from his NFL career. Some of these wings were too spicy for my Irish American stomach so Fred said I was in the lightweight division! Later, a police officer smiled and told me, "I always knew you would become a judge!"

Captain Robert A. Enos was a good friend to me and countless others. After completing a distinguished career with the Massachusetts State Police Bob retired and became head of security for Leach & Garner Company, a jewelry manufacturer in Attleboro. We would get together for lunch with as many as a dozen other guys sometimes where the conversation was always interesting, current and funny.

Bob's Christmas parties at Benjamin's restaurant were legendary lavish affairs with everything from soup to nuts. They were always well attended with many interesting guests including Bob's lovely wife Paula, his assistant Ken Cote, Senator James E. Timilty, Massachusetts State Police Captain Brian L. McKenna, US Postal Inspector Daryl Diotte, Attleboro Police Detective Lieutenants Ken Collins and Art Brillon as well as all of their lovely wives and many, many more.

Everyone enjoys eating to some degree, but I think when God made me, he turned up my appetite quotient a couple of notches because I seem to look forward to having a good meal more than most people. Bob knew this and sometimes kidded around with me about my food consumption. I called him to RSVP with the dinner choices for J. Do and I for one of his elaborate Christmas parties in Taunton. I told Bob to put us down for two prime ribs to which he replied, "OK, what does your wife want?"

Cape & Islands District Attorney Michael D. O'Keefe, before retiring, was reviewing a criminal case with one of his ADAs when he realized he had to leave. He told his assistant that he was meeting Bob Enos for lunch so they would continue their discussion when he returned. The young ADA asked, "Who's Bob Enos?" The surprised district attorney proclaimed, "You don't know who Bob Enos is! Bob Enos is the Babe Ruth of law enforcement!" After that high praise it wasn't uncommon for one of us to refer to Bob as Babe Ruth!

Bob is mentioned in four different books including *AN APPOINTED TIME* by retired Massachusetts State Police Lieutenant James G. Redfearn, a smart guy, outstanding author and squared away trooper who I knew from the Foxborough Barracks.

One of the places we would frequent was the Chieftain Pub in Plainville which was owned by Tom and Mary Cahill from Ireland. The Chieftain resembles an authentic Irish Pub and many of the waitresses still speak with an Irish brogue. Bob was a practical joker so one time he tried to pay the bill with one of those Stop & Shop check cashing cards that look like a real credit card. The poor Irish waitress kept running the card through and getting rejected every time until Mary put a stop to Bob's shenanigans.

There was almost a problem on another occasion, although quite accidentally. People who order cocktails are sometimes particular about their certain drink. Bob had an affinity for Manhattans and wanted to be sure that it was going to be made correctly. He asked the waitress, again an Irish lass with a brogue, if she knew how to make a good Manhattan. The shock on her face was evident when she scurried away quickly as Bob asked, "What just happened here?" Mary came to the table and told Bob that the poor girl was very upset and Bob repeated that all he wanted to know was if she could make a good Manhattan. Mary let out a chuckle and said that with the slight language inflection that the waitress thought that Bob had said, "Do you know how to make a good man happy!"

Jim Timilty is a trusted friend, honorable public servant and devoted family man who simply lived to help his constituents. Jim had previously been elected to the Massachusetts State Senate where he served with great distinction for many years. The multi-talented Senator could analyze and handicap a political race with such precision detail that it resembled a prime-time interview on CNN! He was seated with Bob Enos, Governor's Councilor Joe Ferreira, myself and a few other guys having a good time at a clambake on a nice summer day. Just before the steamed clams came out a huge Budweiser truck happened to pull into the parking lot behind us to make a delivery. The driver parked so that the side of the trailer sat right in our view displaying enormous advertising lettering on the side that spelled out BUD LIGHT. Bob knew that it was Jimmy's favorite beer so without missing a beat he said, "Jimmy, your ride's here!"

The Enos contingent were enjoying lunch and laughing at the Brook Manor in North Attleborough as Bob kept telling one humorous story after another. Everyone listened as Bob finished telling a funny, but what would have to be described as a dirty joke. Bob's back was to the next table which, unbeknownst to him, was occupied by three nuns who could hear every word coming from him. They had finished their lunch and just happened to be leaving as Bob finished his next joke. He suddenly realized that they had heard him and felt badly so as they walked by the table, he told them that he was sorry and apologized for his language. One of the nuns said, "Are you kidding! You were great. We're coming back here again tomorrow for more!"

Bob had been assigned to the district attorney's office back when the jurisdiction extended past the Cape & Islands into North Attleborough and beyond. Bob would jump on one of the small commercial airplanes flying out of Hyannis if he had to conduct an investigation on one of the islands. He had to go to Nantucket for a murder so he climbed on board a plane and sat in the co-pilot's seat to make more room for the other passengers. Bob had a tradition of always blessing himself with a sign of the cross just before takeoff. The passengers didn't know that Bob, dressed in plain clothes, was a detective captain with the Massachusetts State Police. Everybody on the plane except the pilot thought that Bob must be the co-pilot so the man behind him got his nerves rattled when he observed the sign of the cross being administered by the co-pilot!

Artie Brillon, myself, and some other guys joined Bob for lunch at Luciano's in Wrentham on his last day on the job when he retired from the security business. We had a lot of laughs with the solid Navy veteran as we all wished him well on his second retirement. Later, at the end of that day, when it was time for Bob to leave the building for the last time, his colleagues did their best to simulate a military Honor Guard holding crossed swords over head as the newlyweds or honored guest walked under the blades. They didn't have swords so they used snow shovels and umbrellas to form an arc that Bob walked under and out into history. A truly great man left the facility that day and will never ever be replaced or forgotten.

I was signing books at a fishing show at the Taunton Holiday Inn when I was pleasantly surprised to see off-duty Trooper Adam J. Emond of the Massachusetts State Police walk up to my table with two of his friends. Adam, a real good guy assigned to the Middleborough Barracks, truly makes a positive difference in representing his department as the State Police Prosecutor for the Brockton District Court. He is included in my first book with reference to his father and grandfather giving him good fishing tips when he was a kid. Adam has the admirable quality of being able to laugh at himself which comes from self-confidence as he takes his job, but not himself seriously. The burly squared away trooper introduced me to his two buddies who all use the same gym as Adam inside the Holiday Inn. K-9 Officer Joe O'Brien of the Department of Correction and Officer Steve Rose, retired from DOC are both nice guys who I enjoyed speaking with that day. I told them they should be very proud of Adam because their friend is now famous and prominently mentioned in my book. All guys, especially those in law enforcement it seems, like to kid around and bust chops so it came as no surprise when Joe said, "If Adam is in a book, it must be a coloring book!"

Clerk-magistrates and assistant clerk-magistrates make decisions, many times well after midnight, based on information from police officers and dispatchers on the phone or at the station. I took bail sometimes while working at the WDC, but the vast majority of my time in police stations occurred while I was employed in Attleboro. Each police department has an officer assigned to prosecute court cases for the entire department. I would be remiss if I didn't express my appreciation for the assistance given to me by so many during hearings, on call at night and on other occasions. I have a high regard for those in law enforcement listed below and on other pages so at the risk and almost certainty of omitting the names of some outstanding individuals, I am grateful for the professionalism and dedication of those on the following partial list, which may not include those in law enforcement mentioned elsewhere;

Amtrak Police - Sergeant Stephen McGovern.

Attleboro PD - Chief Howard M. Cruff Jr.; Lieutenants Steven A. Bennette, Thomas E. Dion, John A. Otrando, James J. Keane, Scott W. Killough & Stephen Pitas Jr.; Sergeants Steven Beaudet, Thomas L. Birch, Thomas A. Brillon, Robert E. Dion, Walter H. Errington Jr., Raymond Gazzola, Donald G. Hebert, Richard P. Campion, Brian J. Witherell & John P. Parkinson; Detectives Paul J. Berard, Timothy D. Cook Sr., James Cote, Robert N. Palmer & Joseph W. Sproul; Officers Henry J. DeArruda,

Norman E. Lyle, James R. Malley, Robert P. Messier, Berryman P. Minah, Thomas P. O'Brien, Carl E. Otto & Donald L. Witherell.

Boston PD - Commissioner William G. Gross; Detective Mary McInness; Officer Paul Sullivan; Principal Administrative Assistant Dana McGillicuddy.

Bourne PD - Lieutenant Richard Tavares; Sergeant James Nelson; Officer Jared P. MacDonald.

Barnstable County Sheriff's Department - Sheriff James M. Cummings; Major Barney Murphy.

Connecticut State Police - Trooper First Class Randy S. Silvestri.

FBI - Special Agents in Charge, Warren Bamford, Harold H. Shaw & Vincent B. Lisi; Assistant Special Agent in Charge Kevin R. White; Supervisory Special Agent Kevin L. Swindon; Special Agents John F. "Fred" Roberson, David L. Clark & Lawrence S. Ferreira.

Foxborough PD - Chiefs Edward T. O'Leary & Michael A. Grace; Deputy Chief Richard H. Noonan; Lieutenant John Chamberlin; Detective Sergeant Thomas A. Kirrane; Sergeants David Foscaldo, Timothy O'Leary & John Thibedeau; Detectives Patrick Morrison & Charles Gallagher; Officers Frank Azevedo, Kerry Kilroy, & Paul Shields.

Franklin PD - Chiefs Lawrence P. Benedetto, Thomas J. Lynch, Stephan H. Semerjian & Stephen T. Williams; Deputy Chief James A. Mill; Sergeant Daniel R. Aiello; Detectives Paul F. Padula & Timothy Nagle; Prosecutor Edward Clifford.

Holliston PD - Lieutenant James Barrett.

Mansfield PD - Chief Arthur M. O'Neill; Acting Chief Michael Ellsworth; Lieutenants George Figueredo & Walter Crickard; Sergeants Lawrence G. Crosman, Roger Miller & Earl W. Weeman; Detective Peter Vargas; Officers Robert L. Giroux, Walter P. Langley Jr., Natalie E. Rammel & John T. Simpson; Dispatcher Paul A. Copparini.

Massachusetts State Police - Colonels Timothy P. Alben, John DiFava, Thomas J. Foley, Kerry A. Gilpin & Christopher S. Mason; Lieutenant Colonel Thomas D. Grenham; Majors Timothy J. Curtin & Thomas R. McGilvray; Detective Lieutenants Curtis T. Cinelli & Fred Morse; Lieutenants Michael A. Ahern, Paul F. Baker, William Cederquist, Robert H. Friend, Martin Fay, Michael George, Herbert Harding, Richard W. Seguin & J. Jeff Stuart; Sergeants John H. McGillvray, Dermot P. Moriarty, Lynne F. Mulkerrin, Robert J. McKeon, Jeffrey Gonsalves, Byron L. Rizos, Timothy R. Whelan, Peter Littlefield & Richard F. White; Troopers Joseph G.

Evans, Jason F. Morse, James O'Donnell, Robert Tryon & Christopher Roy; Program Coordinator Lisa Botka; Administrative Secretary II Sarah K. Lefebvre.

Medway PD - Chiefs Allen Tingley, William Kingsbury Jr., W. David Lambirth; Detective Donald Grimes; Officers David McRoberts & John Rojee.

Millis PD - Chiefs Albert J. Baima, Peter McGowan & Christopher J. Soffayer; Detective Sergeant Dave C. Egy.

New Bedford PD - Sergeant Gary Sarmento.

Norfolk County Sheriff's Department - Lieutenants David C. Sheehan & Patrick F. Weir.

Norfolk PD - Chief Charles H. Stone Jr.; Deputy Chief Michelle Palladini; Lieutenants John W. Holmes & Eric S. Van Ness; Sergeants David J. Eberle & Glen R. Eykel.

North Attleborough PD - Chiefs John D. "Jack" Coyle Jr. & Richard K. McQuade; Captains Joseph P. DiRenzo & Jason Roy; Lieutenants Gary Flood, Frank M. Gookin Jr., Michael P. Gould Jr., Thomas McCafferty, David Neal, Charles Nicholas & Frank Pfefferle; Sergeants Michael Bunker, Christopher Ciccio, Denis Donovan, Bart Folan, David Gould, John Grim, Shane McKenna, John Panchuk & Kevin Silvestri; Detective Kevin J. McKeon; Officers Ted Barrett, Lawrence P. Birch, James Brennan, Pamela Brown, Craig Chapman, David Cullen, Steve Doucette, Kevin LaCasse, Michael Shepard & Pamela St. John.

Norton PD - Chief Brian M. Clark; Deputy Chiefs Thomas J. Petersen Jr. & Todd M. Jackson; Detective Sergeant Stephen R. Desfosses; Sergeants Jacob Dennett & Richard H. Spicer; Detective Todd A. Bramwell; Officers Timothy P. Gariepy, Marc Robichaud & Michael J. Smith.

Plainville PD - Sergeant Scott Gallerani; Detective James Moses; Officers Julie A. Barrett & William Lamb.

United States Secret Service - Special Agents Michael Pickett & Vincent Crossman.

Walpole PD - Chiefs Joseph Betro, Richard B. Stillman & Richard M. Kelleher; Deputy Chiefs Scott Bushway & Robert Kilroy; Detective Sergeants Robert Anderson & Jacklyn B. Hazeldine; Sergeant David P. Smolinsky; Detectives Mark D. Dalton & Timothy W. Songin; Officer Richard R. Ryan; Director of Communications William Fitzpatrick.

Wrentham PD - Chiefs James Anderson & Joseph E. Collamati Jr.; Deputy Chief George Labonte; Detective Sergeants Barry McGrath, James Boucher & Stephen Hearon; Sergeant Jeffrey Smith; Detective Stephen Saulnier; Officer Kristine Crosman.

*MSP Detective Lieutenant Curt Cinelli (in background)
watching my ball head for the woods!*

6. Breaking News

There were many other details, twists and turns to some of the cases reported in this chapter as this is only a brief synopsis of some of the issues including my sometimes minor involvement.

I read a couple of newspapers every day and have always considered the vast majority of reporters and others in the print media to be honest, diligent and hardworking. Newspapers are a prestigious, honorable, indispensable and vital form of our communication as well as an important hallmark in the elements that have made America the greatest country on the face of the earth. Freedom of the press, without fear of reprisal, has contributed significantly to the transparency that has kept our nation strong and provided inspiration for our citizenry during periods of crisis and duress.

The six o'clock news is a regular part of our day so I have the utmost respect and admiration for Channel 4 WBZ-TV CBS Boston News Anchor Lisa Hughes who was generous enough to interrupt her busy schedule to address the standing room only crowd at our Courthouse Speaker Series. Hughes, the recipient of the Edward R. Murrow Award, Emmy Awards and other notable honors regaled our grateful audience with captivating stories from her time in front of the camera. She is a hardworking professional, taking the time to pose for photos with our audience and exhibiting genuine kindness in every conversation.

Emmy Award Winning WCVB-TV ABC Boston Anchor/Reporter Rhondella Richardson once interviewed me for Channel 5 in my office in Wrentham. She is a true professional who is always fair with a thought provoking style and an instinctive drive for accuracy. Rhondella would sometimes call me to get the scoop on a breaking story so I would always help her as best I could. One time she was driving her daughter and other kids to school in the morning while I gave her information about a criminal case on the phone. After we finished our conversation, she thanked me and we hung up. A few minutes later I picked up the phone in my office to make a call and was surprised that I could hear Rhondella speaking with her daughter in the car. She must have thought that she had hung up the phone, but missed the button. I started yelling her name into the receiver, but she couldn't hear me. I kept yelling, but to no avail which meant that I could not make any calls. I didn't mean to ease drop, but I was hearing a lot of family conversation going on in that car. I remember thinking her daughter must be a smart girl because she got a B+ on a test, but Rhondella thought that it should have been an A. I hung up my phone and after about 15 minutes I was relieved to find that the line was clear and ready for use. I was just hoping that Rhondella's daughter would get an A on the next test, but it turns out that she kept on achieving exemplary grades and really benefited from her mother's guidance in setting a high bar. Years later, that little girl grew up and was accepted at Brown University!

It was always nice to see Jack Harper from WCVB Channel 5 at our counter as the old school reporter was always polite, dignified and congenial. The long time intrepid newsman worked hard and treated everyone with respect, but always got the job done. My feelings of happiness for Jack and his family upon his retirement announcement were coupled with the realization that we were losing a voice of reason who had become a solid institution in the delivery of breaking news. One of the funniest lines from Jack involved giving rides to his kids, "I like to say I am an unpaid Uber driver! Round and round I go and my passengers get out of the car asking for money instead of paying!"

I appreciate TV reporting, but I guess that I'm an old fashioned newspaper guy as I know that my news cycle is only complete once I can see black ink stains on my fingertips! I always admired the impressive stories written by the highly esteemed William J. Cole of the Associated Press and was proud that he lived in my district.

I consider myself lucky to be able to read *The Boston Globe* every day. I enjoy it so much that there would always be a stack of newspapers waiting when we returned from vacation so it was a significant benefit when I could start reading online while away! I never miss the outstanding columns of Renée Graham, Joan Vennochi, Renée Loth, Jeff Jacoby and Scot Lehigh. I usually agree with their positions, but even when I don't it is always a pleasure to read their well-reasoned arguments and dynamic points of view on the issues facing our country.

The Sun Chronicle, our dynamic local newspaper, continues to cover important events and deliver insightful opinions through the leadership of Executive Editor & General Manager Craig Borges and Managing Editor Jessica Zandan, a couple of real professionals. I will always remain grateful to Editor Mike Kirby for publishing a baseball story that I had written about my dad. I always enjoyed reading the interesting *Sun Chronicle* columns written by esteemed News Editor Larry Kessler who was once honored by throwing out the first pitch at a Pawtucket Red Sox game. Larry was also presented with a Sandra C. Labaree Volunteer Values Award by the American Cancer Society for his vast efforts with the Greater Attleboro Relay for Life. Special Political Correspondent Jim Hand always had the story behind the story and was mentioned in the *Washington Post* as one of the best political reporters in the nation!

The courthouse was covered by some great old fashioned crime beat reporters like the legendary staff writer Rick Foster of *The Sun Chronicle* who was honored as Reporter of the Year by the New England Newspaper & Press Association which also recognized *Sun Chronicle* Photo Editor Mark Stockwell in the Best Sports photo category. I always enjoyed speaking with dedicated *Pawtucket Times* scribe Dale King who was a daily presence at the counter.

Hank "Scoop" Reiley was the outstanding crime beat reporter for *The Sun Chronicle* in Attleboro for many years until retiring after a distinguished career of chasing down stories and their ancillary components so that he could always produce an accurate account of the facts. Scoop was honored many times including by his colleagues when the New

England Newspaper Association voted him the First Place Economic Reporting News Award and a share in the First Place Spot News Award.

Intrepid crime beat reporter David Linton carries on that tradition of excellence for that same newspaper today by writing stories with an infusion of creativity that continue to spark the interest of his loyal readers. I enjoyed my interactions with "Scoop" early in my career and provided court documents for David as he covered crime while I worked in Attleboro and later in Wrentham. David has developed an incredible network of high level sources everywhere so it wasn't unusual for him to be able to answer a question that I might have about some riveting breaking news prior to publication. I remember being at a local police station when a detective was going to call Dave to ask him for information! He has received well deserved recognition with Awards by the New England Press Association and the New England Associated Press Newspaper Association for Spot News Coverage as well as other honors.

Peter M. Gay does as outstanding job as the Executive Director of North Attleboro Community Television where he serves as the anchor for election coverage and hosts several other programs on the popular award-winning local channel. The busy Bryant University grad also writes a weekly column for *The Sun Chronicle* where he shares his opinions on important issues of the day. Peter is a terrific writer with a superior intellect and the courage to speak the truth on topics that have divided our nation so I always enjoy his commentary.

David M. Wedge, another of the very talented writers who covered the crime beat for *The Sun Chronicle*, was an inexperienced cub reporter when we first met. We quickly developed a good working relationship as I admired his attention to detail and nose for the real guts of a story. Dave always had a nice way about him and learned very quickly. We were all excited for him when he moved on to a better opportunity as a reporter for the *Boston Herald*. Dave later became a celebrity writer and two time *New York Times* bestselling author.

I always enjoyed reading Mark Flanagan's stories in *The Sun Chronicle* as he has a nice way of presenting a narrative balanced with creativity and hard facts. Mark has been recognized for his outstanding talent including having won the First Place Editorial Writing Award from the New England Associated Press. The retired Opinion Page Editor wrote a beautiful tribute on the passing of David Hardt, one of the best, if not the greatest, athlete to ever graduate from Attleboro High School. Dave later played for the New England Patriots, sustaining a career ending injury in his very first game against the New York Giants which was also the first tilt played at Schaefer Stadium. Superior athleticism ran in the Hardt family where Dave and his brothers were all big guys. Whenever I went to their childhood home on Bishop Street it was like walking into an Olympic training site! I played high school ball with Dave's younger brother Gregory whose constant smile belied his toughness and competitive nature. Eventually, Dave worked as a court officer in the ADC where he kept order in the courtroom and the staff safe in the building. I would be calling cases as fast as I could in Courtroom One on some incredibly busy days and Dave would often make me laugh by whispering a funny story to me!

My wife J. Do, our youngest daughter Chrissy as well as my two brothers Brendan and Chris all graduated from Bishop Feehan High School. The Catholic school was a cross town rival of AHS which inspired many well attended, hard fought games over the years. Dave Hardt was a dominant force for the Attleboro High School football team so Mark Flanagan captured the spirit of those contests when he reminded readers of the wording on a 1965 banner proclaiming AHS superiority - "Feehan has God but we've got Hardt."

Henry Maxim writes about Greyhound Racing and has witnessed some of the most significant pari-mutuel events in the history of the sport. He is a brilliant writer who is able to capture the action and make you feel as though you were standing at the rail as the dogs sprint by to the finish line.

Unfortunately, it seems as though the repeated attacks on the press, as well as other myriad complex contributing factors, may have served to diminish a portion of the shiny luster and reputation for the integrity of the Fourth Estate in the eyes of some. Deanna Pan wrote a story about rowdy beach behavior occurring at M Street Beach in South Boston that appeared in the August 24, 2019 edition of *The Boston Globe*. A woman was quoted by Pan, but only offered her first name for the story. "…Chrissy, 56, who grew up in Southie had declined to give her last name because she didn't want her friends to know she'd spoken to the Globe."

The Honorable Edward A. Lee, appointed by Governor Foster Furcolo, was the First Justice of the ADC when I was sworn in as Assistant Clerk-Magistrate in late January of 1980. The kind hearted jurist, son of Irish immigrants, was very helpful to me and always cordial to court staff as well as everyone he encountered. We would both cross the street and head over to the Attleboro YMCA after court for a workout. Judge Lee, an outstanding athlete when he was younger, played professional baseball for a minor league affiliate of the Boston Braves and had regional scouts evaluating his talent before World War II sidetracked what probably would have been a call up to the major leagues. The erstwhile second baseman defended our country during the war as a member of the 315th Antiaircraft Division of the 9th Army in the European Theater. His daughter Anne, one of the nicest kids in our high school class, married the Honorable Anthony R. Nesi, First Justice of the Bristol County Probate & Family Court who was appointed by Governor Jane M. Swift. Thus, her father and husband were both distinguished judges. Tragically, Anne lost her battle with brain cancer at the young age of 48.

Courts were open for business on Saturday mornings until noon when I entered the system. No court cases were scheduled for these weekends as a skeleton crew processed only new business including arrests from the previous night. There was one judge who would drive his station wagon into the courthouse parking lot on Saturday morning and leave the engine running with his family in it as he raced onto the bench to do the arraignments from Friday night. He would zip through the cases and then jump back in the car to head for the Bourne Bridge! These sessions were generally considered to be an inconvenient waste of time because everything on Saturday could have waited until Monday and the on-call clerk-magistrate or assistant could have handled any other pressing issues. First Assistant Clerk-Magistrate Antonio J. Casale had worked more Saturdays than he probably cared to remember. He was a former police officer with a gruff exterior, but the heart of a good devoted family man. He was teaching me my job and it was plain to see that, as the low man on the totem pole, I was being groomed to inherit the Saturday morning duties from Mr. Casale. He had expressed as much to me in a declaration that he was soon going to be free!

I worked hard every day trying to absorb as much information as possible for my new job. I constantly asked questions and read everything that I could at night to facilitate and hasten the learning curve. I stood next to Mr. Casale in the courtroom and watched him every day to learn the important task of becoming a session clerk and eventually would run the session by myself, but he was always within earshot if I needed help. Finally, I was given the blessing from Mr. Casale that I could handle the job and was ready to work on my own.

Saturday, May 10, 1980 was my first weekend in the courthouse as the person in charge of the Clerk-Magistrate's Office and also the first time as a session clerk in the courtroom without help nearby. I was on call with the police that week, but went to bed Friday night without getting a single call from the police, which was unusual. I was kind of nervous as I closed my 25-year old eyes that night in anticipation of my big day on Saturday, but somewhat comforted by the knowledge that the police hadn't called so it looked to be an easy first day for my maiden weekend court session. What I didn't know was that the North Attleborough Police had arrested Peter Kane charging him with assault with intent to murder his girlfriend's 22-month old baby boy and would be transporting him to court for arraignment. The seldom used process of bail having been set by someone else prior to arrest had obviated the need for the police to call me.

I was still living at home, only a couple of weeks from getting my own apartment, so my mother prepared a huge breakfast as always. I finished the veritable feast, kissed my mom good bye and headed down Route 152 for the courthouse. I was enjoying the fresh air during the ride with my car windows down on a beautiful spring day without a cloud in the sky. I was relaxed and ready for a slow easy day of justice as I pulled into the courthouse parking lot.

Describing my mind set as surprised would be an understatement as I immediately saw TV news trucks, cameras, reporters with microphones and dozens of other people milling around the prisoner's entrance and in between vehicles! I parked my car and maneuvered through the crowd toward the entrance as a reporter, who somehow knew my name, shoved a microphone in my face and asked a question that I couldn't answer. So much for a slow first day on my own!

Judge Lee and I entered Courtroom One, which unlike most Saturdays, was almost full to capacity. I called the criminal case of Commonwealth vs. Peter Kane and read the charge of assault with intent to murder to the defendant. After listening to both sides on the bail hearing, Judge Lee set bail at $50,000.00 cash and I gave the defendant another date.

Kane had lived in a North Attleborough apartment with his girlfriend and her two young sons, one of whom was the victim. The child's mother and one of her sisters left to go to the store at about 6:15PM on May 8, 1980 and returned to the apartment about a half hour later where she found the unconscious, severely bruised victim not breathing on the floor of his bedroom. The baby was pronounced dead on May 15, 1980 at Rhode Island Hospital having lapsed into a coma seven days earlier. There was irreversible brain damage and the cause of death was determined to be severe blunt force.

I had the honor of meeting Attorney Phillip L. Weiner when he was a Bristol County Assistant District Attorney. Phil conducted seminars for the Commonwealth and I can honestly say that I learned much more about search & seizure issues from him than anyone else. His valuable instruction and innate ability to communicate effectively provided essential educational components throughout my career. When judges, attorneys, police and clerk-magistrates needed an answer the most common refrain was, "Call Phil Weiner!" Phil's resume is so impressive that the details could fill the pages of an entire book.

He served in a leadership capacity as a prosecutor at the International Criminal Tribunal for the former Yugoslavia (Den Haag, Netherlands) and was appointed as an International Judge at the Court of Bosnia and Herzegovina where he also served as an Appellate Judge, hearing cases of war crimes, crimes against humanity and genocide. Phil was responsible for overseeing investigations of crimes resulting from the Khmer Rouge regime at the Extraordinary Chambers in the Courts of Cambodia where he was "Knighted" for his efforts in training judges, attorneys, and police officers.

Phil is a graduate of Boston College Law School where he later taught Criminal Law and Criminal Procedure. He has spent over three decades lecturing on legal topics on four different continents and most recently has devoted himself to the training of judges in Ukraine.

Phil assisted ADA Patricia O. Ellis, the lead prosecutor who argued the appeal on the Kane matter before the SJC. He was kind enough to take time out of his extremely busy law practice to provide me with his summary of the case. The following are Judge Weiner's words;

"The Peter Kane case has a long and complex history. He was convicted in 1981 of Murder in the Second Degree which was affirmed by the Supreme Judicial Court of Massachusetts. The case, however, did not end and in December of 2000, a Superior Court Judge ordered a new trial ruling that the trial Judge's instructions given to the jury back in 1981 were erroneous. This decision was affirmed on appeal in 2003. Later that same year, an agreement was reached between the Prosecution and the Defense resulting in Mr. Kane pleading guilty to the crime of Manslaughter which is a lesser form of the crime of murder. He was given a sentence of 19 to 20 years imprisonment. Since, he had already served over 20 years in prison on this case, the sentence was deemed to have been served and his case was completed."

The House and Senate passed a bill that was signed by the Governor ordering the closure of courthouses on Saturdays in the Commonwealth. It took effect on June 26, 1980, not long after my first Saturday on the job so the timing of the legislation could not have been any better. There were no complaints from me or the rest of the staff about the closure legislation, but I'll never forget that first Saturday court session on my own!

Trooper Paul Landry is now retired from the Massachusetts State Police, but I knew him when he was assigned to the Foxborough Barracks and I was at the ADC. He is a squared away honest man who found himself in the middle of a chaotic shootout on an early dark cold February morning in 1982. Trooper Landry had pulled into the rest area off of Route 95 South in North Attleborough a couple of hours after midnight for a routine check of vehicles. Landry rolled up to a parked green station wagon and used his high beams to illuminate part of the inside of the vehicle where he observed two occupants in the front seat. The trooper approached the driver's side and had a conversation with the driver and occupant of the front passenger seat. Trooper Landry observed a bag on the floor near the passenger's feet and a large dog moving about in the rear of the car. Both occupants seemed nervous and produced IDs just after the trooper noticed the passenger move his right hand inside his jacket near the waist and keep it in there. The driver said that the car was owned by his girlfriend who he had known for two years, but that he couldn't remember her phone number.

Landry was now getting suspicious as he returned to his cruiser and repositioned it before calling in the IDs. His observations and instincts caused him to sense danger so he called for backup and was soon joined by Trooper Michael Crosby, who would later reach the rank of sergeant before retirement. Trooper Crosby had been heading home after an overtime shift targeting drunk drivers when he heard the radio transmission from Trooper Landry inquiring if anyone was in the area. I always enjoyed Trooper Crosby's humor when he represented the State Police at hearings as he is a natural born comedian who would entertain the court staff with funny anecdotes and other quick stories.

After parking next to Landry's cruiser, the troopers had a brief conversation before walking to the passenger window of the station wagon. Landry noticed that the bag was gone as he tapped on the window with his flashlight and ordered the passenger to get out. The trooper asked what was inside of the jacket as he attempted to put his hand in which was knocked away by the passenger and resulted in Landry ordering him to put his hands on his head as he felt a bulletproof vest. Landry then called out for Crosby to watch the driver as the passenger moved his hand inside of his jacket and Landry drew his service revolver.

The driver exited the vehicle and crouched along the station wagon until getting to the rear right bumper where he opened fire with a pistol in the direction of the troopers. Landry, who by now had the passenger by the back collar, returned fire and eventually brought the passenger to the ground. Crosby took cover behind a rest area dumpster and, while taking fire himself, dived into his cruiser to radio for help.

The driver escaped into the woods and became the subject of an intense manhunt involving police officers from many surrounding communities. Law enforcement from near and far joined in the search including my brother, Trooper Brendan P. Doherty of the Rhode Island State Police, who had been on the job for less than two years, but was very familiar with the terrain as we had all grown up in Attleboro. Notwithstanding the incredible all-out effort and extensive search by the Massachusetts State Police, Rhode Island State Police, North Attleborough Police and many others - the vehicle's driver had escaped and would remain at large for over two more years.

A search of the station wagon yielded a duffle bag containing a .45 caliber machine gun, an extended magazine shotgun and ammunition. Trooper Landry had taken a 9 millimeter semi-automatic pistol off of the passenger who was transported under arrest to the Foxborough State Police Barracks and eventually to the ADC. I assisted in the preparation of the criminal complaints for the passenger and the arrest warrant for the shooter, which was under the old tri fold system requiring a separate complaint for each criminal offense. The stoic faced defendant was arraigned on two counts of assault with intent to murder and twelve other charges before being ordered held without bail by Judge John J. Dolan. Trooper William J. Coulter, a nice guy and a true professional who would go on to reach the rank of detective lieutenant, signed the complaints against the shooter for two counts of assault with intent to murder and the warrant was entered into the system. Assistant District Attorney James Perkoski nol prossed the district court cases against the passenger a few weeks later on the Attleboro return date once the defendant had been indicted and arraigned in Superior Court.

Both of these individuals were members of a radical group that had formed out of another militant organization. Members of the group were being sought for bombings including a courthouse, bank robbery and the murder of highly decorated Trooper II Philip J. Lamonaco of the New Jersey State Police who was gunned down during a traffic stop on Interstate 80 in Knowlton Township, 6 weeks prior to the rest area gunfight in Massachusetts. Trooper Lamonaco, who was awarded the distinction of Trooper of the Year in 1979, had his life taken only four days before Christmas in 1981 and left a wife and three children.

John Markey, now retired, was an FBI Special Agent assigned to the Task Force that was created to investigate and capture this group, known as the United Freedom Front. He confirmed, during an interview with me, that the passenger arrested in the Massachusetts rest area shootout, the shooter who escaped and the murderers of NJSP Trooper Lamonaco were all members of the United Freedom Front. Retired Special Agent Markey also confirmed that the UFF was a radical left wing group, part of whose mission was to cause disruption by bombing government and other facilities, financing their misguided quest through bank robberies.

Some members of the United Freedom Front, including the rest area shooter, were eventually arrested in a predawn raid in an area of Ohio near Cleveland in November of 1984 and two others were taken into custody a few months later in Norfolk, Virginia.

Eventually, the rest area shooter and others were convicted and given long prison sentences including the murderers of Trooper Lamonaco who both died in prison.

Detective Sergeant Luigi Reali, who was my brother's boss, was one of the participants in the well-coordinated raid that brought down and captured the majority of the fugitives in Ohio. Brendan, a detective corporal at the time, called the courthouse to inform me of the arrest of the shooter which meant that the warrant could be recalled from an already overburdened system with the sometimes slow wheels of justice continuing to turn.

Soon after the rest area shootout Troopers Crosby and Landry were recognized for their performance in the highest tradition of law enforcement in the protection and safety of the citizens of the Commonwealth. Both troopers were presented with the Award of Distinction by Governor Edward J. King during a ceremony at the State House in Boston.

Many years later I was flicking the TV channels around when I came across a very interesting movie about the manhunt in the Trooper Lamonaco murder case. *In the Line of Duty: Hunt for Justice* is described as being based on a true story featuring an all-star cast of Melissa Leo, Adam Arkin, Dean Norris and others including Nicholas Turturro who plays a New Jersey state police detective and best friend of the murdered trooper. One of the most powerful and poignant segments of the film occurs during the arrests toward the end of the movie. An actor playing an FBI Special Agent and Turturro in character approach one of the already handcuffed fugitives. Turturro introduces himself, looks him right in the eyes and says, "…, New Jersey State Police, you remember them, right?"

Michael Lamonaco was only four years old when his father was brutally murdered in 1981. He went on to graduate from the same State Police Academy as his dad in 2001 and was eventually promoted to lieutenant. Today Lieutenant Lamonaco continues the family tradition of excellence while proudly wearing the uniform of the New Jersey State Police.

Trooper Thomas W. Summers responded late in the evening of May 20, 1990 to the Emerald Square Mall in North Attleborough after being notified of a female body in a vehicle where the area had been secured by the North Attleborough Police. The victim, later identified as 36-year old Cheryl Kosilek of 10 Concetta Circle in Mansfield, was found lying on her back in the rear of the vehicle with triple strand wire and rope wrapped around her neck. The autopsy performed the next day determined the cause of death to be strangulation.

I knew Tom Summers to be a hardworking and diligent investigator with the Massachusetts State Police assigned to the Bristol County DA's Office. The investigation continued a few hours later at approximately 3:00AM on May 21 for a threshold consensual viewing of the victim's home by Detective Lieutenant Michael Gould Sr., who would later become Chief, Detective Sergeant David Dawes, who would later be promoted to lieutenant and Officer James Carey of the North Attleborough Police Department accompanied by Trooper Summers and Trooper Daniel Clark, later promoted to sergeant, also from the Massachusetts State Police assigned to the DA's Office. Trooper Summers returned to the home later in the day to make further observations along with Detective

Raymond Maigret, later promoted to sergeant and Detective Sergeant Robert Martin of the Mansfield Police Department.

Dan Clark is a squared-away guy who I would get to know much better when he sang at the 19th Hole St. Patrick's Day party hosted by Dave Cronan and my brother Chris. Dan also did a terrific job of singing the National Anthem at our Courthouse Law Day Ceremony where the crowd loved his powerful rendition and patriotic commentary delivered from his thundering, professional voice.

The next night I received a call from Detective Lieutenant Gould requesting the issuance of a search warrant for the purpose of collecting evidence at the victim's house in Mansfield. I asked them to come to my home in North Attleborough where I was presented with the affidavit for the search warrant. The detectives were seated in our living room as I reviewed the affidavit which had been produced based on the observations made inside the home, numerous inconsistencies in statements made by the victim's 41-year old husband Robert Kosilek and other information. This was an excellent search warrant affidavit except for a minor oversight on the home address of the murder victim which was listed as having the correct street, but with the town as North Attleborough. She lived in Mansfield, but her body was discovered in North Attleborough so I drew a line through North Attleborough and printed Mansfield next to it in least a couple of places which was initialed by myself and Trooper Summers. I found that the Commonwealth had sustained its burden in the demonstration of Probable Cause and issued the search warrant allowing the police to enter the home for the collection of evidence including rope and wire that was similar to the murder weapon.

The search warrant was executed with evidence taken into custody and inventoried in the presence of Detective Lieutenant Gould, Detective Sergeant Dawes and Detective Sergeant Martin. Also present were Trooper Summers, Trooper Maryann Dill who retired as a detective lieutenant and Trooper Jose Gonsalves who retired as a lieutenant of the Massachusetts State Police.

Robert Kosilek was charged with the murder of his wife and arraigned on May 30 when he was ordered held without bail. The trial began on January 14, 1993 in New Bedford Superior Court. It is extremely unusual for an assistant clerk-magistrate like myself at the time or a clerk-magistrate to be called to testify in any kind of pending criminal or civil case, but I was subpoenaed by the defendant's lawyer, Attorney Bruce E. Ferg. Detective Lieutenant Gould was also going to testify that day so he was kind enough to pick me up in his unmarked car along with Detective Sergeant Dawes for the ride to New Bedford. I happened to see Attorney Ferg before court was called into session where he told me that he just wanted to go over the parts of the affidavit that I had amended and initialed with Detective Summers. Ferg is a smart lawyer and a nice guy who I had known from other cases. He later questioned me on the witness stand about the affidavit and I explained what had transpired. He was doing the best that he could for his client in a difficult case, but I wasn't on the stand that long as I don't think that the ADA even felt the need to cross examine me.

Kosilek was convicted of first degree murder and sentenced to life in prison without parole. He legally changed his first name to Michelle three years after killing his wife and has been diagnosed with gender identity disorder. Kosilek has been fighting for sex reassignment surgery through the filing of lawsuits over the years which have ultimately been unsuccessful. Kosilek wore a beard at the time of the murder and the victim's 15-year old son had testified during the murder trial that his stepfather had shaved the beard off on the day that his mother went missing. The young man also stated that Kosilek cooked a steak for them that night. The poor kid didn't realize at the time that he was having dinner with the person who had brutally murdered his mother earlier that same day.

Irene Kennedy and her husband Thomas set off for one of their frequent walks through Bird Park in Walpole on the first day of December in 1998. The couple, who had celebrated their 50th wedding anniversary the previous June, were almost inseparable, but they took different paths through the park on this day as was their custom. They would always meet up afterwards in the parking lot, but when Mr. Kennedy's bride, as he still called her, didn't show later he went looking for her and found her bludgeoned lifeless body on the ground just off of one of the paths. The 75-year old mother of four and grandmother of 12 had been strangled, stabbed over two dozen times and had both of her breasts bitten.

Within hours of the murder a Massachusetts State Police K-9 Unit comprised of Trooper Kevin P. O'Neil, who would later retire as a detective lieutenant, and his dog Shane followed a circuitous trail with the canine leading investigators to a nearby home where Edmund Burke lived with his mother and 32 cats. Edmund Burke's brother had married one of the victim's daughters. Neighbors and others described Edmund Burke with some level of eccentricity that made it easy for some to believe that he had committed this unspeakable crime. For instance, it was rumored that he had become so close to and attached to his cats that he was reluctant to bury them after they died. There were dead cats in the refrigerator and the freezer!

During part of the investigation Burke had agreed to accompany Massachusetts State Police Detective Sergeant Kevin P. Shea, who would later retire as a detective lieutenant, and Walpole Police Detective William F. Bausch to the Walpole Police station where he voluntarily submitted to giving an impression of his teeth that was taken by forensic dentist Dr. Kate Crowley of the Chief Medical Examiner's Office. Massachusetts State Police Trooper Scott C. Jennings, one of the detectives assigned to the Norfolk County District Attorney's Office, was working diligently on this gruesome case. Jennings would later be promoted to sergeant and tragically lose his life to the coronavirus at age 67. I knew all of these detectives to be honest dedicated police officers who always tried to do the right thing and follow the evidence wherever it took them.

I brought Trooper Jennings into my office at the WDC to review his affidavit with the accompanying request for a search warrant. The warrant sought my authorization to search the Burke home for evidence of the crime of murder. Trooper Jennings, who was the affiant, had done an outstanding job of documenting facts in a lengthy affidavit detailing multiple aspects of the continuing investigation. The affable trooper and I agreed that a statement made by Dr. Lowell Levine from the New York State Police Crime Lab was the most powerful and critical evidence against the defendant. Dr. Levine, a forensic dentist, had identified the skeletal remains of Nazi war criminal Dr. Josef Mengele on behalf of the Department of Justice, participated in the Ted Bundy serial murder investigation and many other celebrated cases. He examined photos showing the bite marks on the victim's breasts as well as the dental impressions of the defendant as presented to him at a meeting with Trooper Jennings, Dr. Crowley and Walpole Police Detective James J. Dolan, later promoted to sergeant, who I would come to know over the years as a smart, squared away detective. This meeting took place in the Doctor's home in Albany, New York on December 6. Dr. Levine observed and pointed out particular similarities and indicated that he would like to examine more closely enhanced photographs for assistance in his determination. Massachusetts State Police Trooper Steven M. McDonald, later promoted to captain, told Trooper Jennings on December 10 that he had spoken with Dr. Levine. The content of that conversation was memorialized by Trooper Jennings in the affidavit presented to me stating that Dr. Levine, with the following quote from the affidavit and not directly quoting the Doctor, "…was of the opinion to a reasonable degree of scientific certainty that the bite marks found on the body of Irene Kennedy were caused by Edmund Burke." At the time some considered bite marks to be extremely strong evidence as they were being assigned the same evidentiary value and weight as fingerprints. There was other evidence including, upon examination that Burke's hands, pants, coat, hat and sneakers tested positive for blood, but the examination results of Doctor Levine finally persuaded me to a finding of probable cause. I issued the search warrant and wished Trooper Jennings good luck.

Judge Daniel W. O'Malley was sitting in Courtroom One at the WDC when Edmund Burke was brought into the lockup under arrest for murder and then arraigned prior to a bail hearing. Judge O'Malley listened to both sides before issuing his decision with the defendant remaining in custody and being given a date for his next appearance.

Although I had already spent eighteen years working in another court, this was my first year in Wrentham so I was still getting used to having state prisons in my district as Attleboro, like most district courts, had none. I had gotten to know Assistant DA Gerald C. Pudolsky who was very helpful as I explored and researched different ways to address inmate's requests for criminal complaints and civil actions. Some inmate requests were legitimate, but many were not.

There are four state prisons, including MCI Cedar Junction formerly known as MCI Walpole, located within the territorial jurisdiction of the WDC. Walpole was the prison where Albert DeSalvo, identified as the Boston Strangler, was stabbed to death. If a defendant is convicted of first degree murder in Springfield, for instance, he may be spending the rest of his life in Walpole. The WDC has jurisdiction and the responsibility to address legal issues that arise during that lifetime even though those four prisons house inmates that have been convicted of committing crimes from all over the Commonwealth.

I had to learn about a whole new set of rules and procedures in Wrentham to handle requests from inmates. Similar or identical issues would arise from inmate litigation so I created some forms to handle the volume of requests to be of assistance to my staff and myself. The most commonly used were form WDC 830 which encompassed small claims and form WDC 822 that addressed criminal complaint applications. Because the three digit numbers were higher than 800 it probably caused some people to think that we used hundreds of forms, but the reality was that we only had a few. I had assigned the numbers 822 and 830 because they are the birthdays of two Hall of Famers. Carl Yastrzemski was born on August 22 and Ted Williams celebrated his birthday on August 30!

I listened to testimony from and about convicted murderers and rapists while conducting show cause hearings either in person or on video through closed circuit TV from prison. Michael G. Bellotti was the Norfolk County Sheriff at the time and remains one of the truly great public servants in the Commonwealth. He also just happens to be one of the funniest people I know so meeting with him was always a pleasure. Mike was thoughtful enough to pay for the audio visual equipment so that hearings could be conducted in the courthouse while the inmate remained secure at the facility. There were many benefits to this technology including the cost savings of not having to transport inmates and the obvious security concerns. There was also the personal benefit that if a shoe happened to be thrown by an inmate it would hit the TV screen and not me!

Eventually I was able to design a system that, in effect, eliminated private citizen complaints. Case law was taken from *Victory Distributors, Inc. v. Ayer Division of the District Court Department, 435 Mass. 136 (2001)* and used to fashion a manageable system for inmate requests and others in compliance with the law. I was grateful that my procedure survived scrutiny when a petition under Chapter 211, Section 3 was denied by a single justice of the Supreme Judicial Court in 2003.

Jerry Pudolsky is a nice guy who had devoted a good part of his career working on prison litigation which gave him a unique perspective as an extremely knowledgeable assistant district attorney. He used to kid around and joke that he had spent so much time working in prisons that if he were ever convicted of a crime he would be "deemed time served!"

Edmund Burke was being held in custody as the case moved through the system. It had been 41 days since the arraignment when Jerry Pudolsky came to court to see me. Jerry walked into my office and handed me a document as he said, "I am now doing something that I have never had to do before in a murder case." The document was an entry of nolle prosequi in the Edmund Burke case as the DNA evidence taken from the bites on the victim had excluded him. Burke was about to be set free.

Decisions made by me in this case were guided by testimony taken under oath and an affidavit sworn to and signed under the penalties of perjury presented by honest police officers who were trying to do the right thing. Regardless of the outcome of civil suits, Edmund Burke can never get those 41 days and nights of his life back. Our system of justice is based on the acceptance of having a lot of bad guys go free to hopefully ensure that an innocent man is never incarcerated. A finding of Not Guilty is a far cry from a declaration of innocence, but when a truly innocent man has his freedom taken away, the best system in the world has failed.

William R. Keating was the newly elected District Attorney of Norfolk County and had inherited the Burke case from his predecessor. Almost five more years would pass before the real killer was identified through the DNA database as 44-year old Martin Guy who was already serving a life sentence for stabbing his neighbor to death. I issued an arrest warrant for Guy in late June of 2003 charging him with the crime of murder after being presented with evidence including sworn testimony from Massachusetts State Police Trooper David McSweeney who would later retire as a lieutenant. McSweeney, whom I had known from other cases as a good guy and conscientious investigator, presented me with the DNA Crime Lab report results signed by Administrator Robert E. Pino.

A few days after issuing the warrant for Guy I was having lunch with Chief Probation Officer Al Pizzi at Nicky's Restaurant in Wrentham. I told Al that I had issued the murder warrant and that I was so happy for the victim's family that at least part of their ordeal could be brought to an end. Al agreed that they would hopefully get some much needed closure to this horrific incident. Al and I would never discuss any court business outside of a secure setting unless it was, like the subject of this conversation, in the realm of open public information. Thus, it wasn't a problem when a woman in the next booth overheard our conversation and turned around to ask if we were talking about the Irene Kennedy case. After acknowledging such she told us that she was Mrs. Kennedy's daughter. She was very nice as Al and I expressed our condolences on her family's terrible loss. I told her that the District Attorney's Office would be contacting her soon and wished her well.

Assistant District Attorney John P. Stapleton is a great guy who I had gotten to know through some conversations we had about state prison inmate litigation, but I had already heard that he was a good person and outstanding ADA from then practicing Attorney John D. Casey who, as mentioned previously, would go on to serve with great distinction as the Chief Justice of the Probate and Family Court of Massachusetts. John had conferenced cases with Jack Stapleton and had said such nice things about him that I was happy to have finally met him. A nolle prosequi is frequently filed by the prosecution in District Court essentially ending the case at that level when a defendant has been indicted by a grand jury and arraigned in Superior Court. Martin Guy was already doing life for another murder so ADA Stapleton simply cited that, "… a grand jury presentation has been scheduled…" as reason for his filing a nolle prosequi in the case. Jack Stapleton would go on to have his talent, congeniality and legal acumen universally recognized when he was appointed to a District Court judgeship by Governor Deval L. Patrick. He sat in the WDC quite a bit while doing an outstanding job on some busy days and always exhibited the humility, intelligence and grace that Chief Justice Casey had spoken of so long ago.

Martin Guy, who had been previously represented by Attorney Robert L. Jubinville, was eventually convicted of first degree murder for the slaying of Irene Kennedy and sentenced to life in prison without parole, which hopefully brought some degree of closure to her family. District Attorney Keating pointed out that this was the very first time for a first degree murder conviction based on evidence from the Massachusetts DNA Registry to which all convicted felons must submit. The Convicted Offender Database continues to be used by law enforcement as a powerful and sophisticated tool in the never-ending battle against serious violent crime. Keating joined the court in praising the outstanding performance of the prosecutor in the case - Assistant District Attorney Robert Nelson.

I have had the privilege to know many talented and honorable government employees, but I can say without a doubt that Bill Keating is an honest man of enormous intellect and integrity, one of the most hardworking and devoted public servants that I have ever known. He knew that an injustice had been done to Edmund Burke and that his release from jail had not stopped some of the continued taunting insults that were still directed at the innocent man years later. The district attorney was quoted by the Associated Press after the Guy conviction by making two noteworthy points that really showed how much he cares about people and the service of justice. "It is my hope that this will bring some measure of release for the Kennedy family," Keating said. "But it is also my fervent hope that this conviction will make clear to any who still doubt that Ed Burke did not murder Irene Kennedy."

Later that year I was asked and immediately accepted an invitation from Bill Keating to join and serve on his Norfolk County District Attorney's Anti-Crime Council. Bill brought a diverse group of stakeholders together in a unified cause while recruiting outstanding speakers who were both educational and enjoyable. Bill, who would later be kind enough to write the magnificent Foreword in my first book, went on to win election to the United States Congress representing Cape Cod, the Islands and southeastern Massachusetts. Bill Keating is a man of the people who is able to bridge gaps in ideology and compromise when appropriate for the good of our country. We are lucky to have him in Washington where I know he will always continue to stand up for what is right just as he did as district attorney in helping to bring some measure of solace to so many victims.

J. Do and I were honored to fly to Washington for the swearing in ceremony for Congressman Keating where we met up with Sally Bruno Linton, her husband Dave, Attorney Glen Hannington, Anne Keating and others. The administration of the oath of office is much more than a perfunctory ceremony as it serves as a symbolic signal to our country as well as the entire world that our democracy is alive and well. Congressional Offices are located in three different buildings so J. Do and I entered the Cannon House Office Building on Independence Avenue SE and proceeded to Room 241 so I could show her where I did my LBJ Internship for Congressman James A. Burke all of those years ago. Bill's office is now located in Room 2351 of the Rayburn House Office Building, but at this time was still in Room 315 of the Cannon so we made our way there where we were greeted by many of his friends and supporters. Ambling through any part of DC has always given me a genuine sense of appreciation and feel for American history in thinking about all of the trailblazers who had walked on that same ground before us. That sense was never more evident and palatable than the moment we were told that Bill's office had once been occupied by a fellow son of Massachusetts. Room 315 had been the office of another Bay State Congressman before being elected President of the United States - John F. Kennedy.

A United States Congressman is one of the busiest people in the world, yet Bill took time out of his hectic schedule to pay respects at the funeral for my brother Chris and I was even more appreciative for his call to me expressing his condolences in an extremely long conversation during that terrible time in my life. J. Do and I both retired to an area of the state that we truly enjoy for many reasons, and we are grateful that one of the benefits of living in the Ninth Congressional District of Massachusetts is having the opportunity to cast a vote for Congressman Bill Keating.

US Congressman Bill Keating swearing in, Washington

Gillette Stadium in Foxborough, home of the New England Patriots, sits in the territorial jurisdiction of the WDC so many Patriots players and their families live in the surrounding community. Unfortunately, just like others, sometimes professional football players are the victims of crime. I ordered a criminal complaint to issue for two counts of larceny, one of which was a felony, against a 19-year old. The victim was Stephen Gostkowski, placekicker for the New England Patriots. He reported to police that his backpack containing his iPad had been stolen from his truck and forwarded several photos of people that were saved to his ICloud account that had been taken after the theft. Gostkowski, who is well known for his off the field acts of kindness, utilized his app that locates a missing iPad and provided an address of the location of the stolen item for the police. An investigation by Wrentham Police Detective Robert O'Connell, a nice guy and hard-working police officer, resulted in a successful prosecution and the return of the stolen property.

Michael W. Morrissey succeeded Bill Keating as the District Attorney of Norfolk County. Mike is a gregarious yet hardworking man who never leaves a stone unturned whether in his campaigns for public office or in the pursuit of justice for the victims of crime. Prior to being elected Norfolk County Sheriff, Patrick W. McDermott was assisting in then Senator Morrissey's reelection campaign by securing commitments for lawn signs for advertising in the district. Patrick had worked the phones and gone door to door in an exhausting all-out effort to accomplish this crucial task. He was pretty well satisfied and pleased with the results until Mike analyzed the list and went on by pointing out other potential spots including that he knew that Mrs. so and so would take a sign and that her neighbor across the street was a sure thing! Some folks graciously and affectionately refer to Mike Morrissey as the Energizer Bunny because he never stops interacting with people and uses that energy for the good of the Commonwealth every day.

The first time I put together our Law Day Ceremony we were honored to have Mike serve as our Keynote Speaker. He held everyone's attention with an interesting and humorous speech that was perfectly tailored for the occasion. Mike is always quick with a funny comment or story. The long time former civil attorney noticed that my bride was wearing a cast on her foot and asked if there was "anybody we can sue?"

Mike took me out on his boat along with ADAs, staff and some of the Massachusetts State Police assigned to his office. One of those troopers was Bruce J. Tobin, who would later be promoted to sergeant and is the son of Arthur H. Tobin, the great Clerk-Magistrate of the Quincy District Court who was appointed by Governor Edward J. King. The Tobin family's commitment to public service runs deep, Bruce's brother Mark is a highly thought of Assistant Clerk-Magistrate in Norfolk County Juvenile Court. We had a fabulous time as Mike skippered us around Boston Harbor and beyond, but as hard as I tried I just could not stump Bruce Tobin with any Red Sox trivia questions. Bruce is a nice guy, but I think his addiction to the home town team may be just as severe as mine!

The lifeless body of Odin Lloyd was discovered on June 17, 2013 in an industrial park in North Attleborough. There were .45 caliber shell casings found at the crime scene which was located about a mile from the home of Aaron Hernandez who had signed a $40 million dollar contract to play football for the New England Patriots. Lloyd had been dating the sister of Hernandez's fiancée and police were gathering evidence that pointed to the star tight end as the killer.

The big receiver with the soft hands, who was also valued for his blocking skill, had been an All-American at the University of Florida and had combined for 24 touchdowns in his second year in the NFL with fellow tight end Rob Gronkowski. Hernandez, who had been a 4th round draft choice, was a tremendous athlete with a brilliant future ahead of him.

North Attleborough and state police detectives searched Hernandez's home which was in a very nice section of town and described by some as a mansion. It took a while for the police, including now retired North Attleborough Police Detective Michael J. Elliott, to go through the large palatial estate in the hunt for evidence from the nearby murder. Hernandez, with apparent nerves of steel and an untroubled conscience, had decided to take a nap on his couch as police were rummaging throughout his home. After an extensive search there was only one place left to look so Detective Elliott had to shake Hernandez's shoulder to wake him up so that the couch could be examined! Most people, guilty or innocent, probably wouldn't be able to take a nap with a house full of law enforcement in addition to the sound of news helicopters that had been flying over his house for about a week in anticipation of a story. I think court psychologists and psychiatrists would have found some interest in documenting a conclusion on that state of mind.

Mike Elliott is a good friend, fellow AHS grad, was a crackerjack detective and a solid all-around police officer. I had nominated Mike, many years earlier, for the Rotary Club's Distinguished Service Award and was ecstatic when he was chosen as the Outstanding Public Employee out of a pool of candidates taken from two adjoining towns. J. Do and I were honored to attend the ceremony with Mike and his family including his beautiful wife Judy who would later tragically lose her courageous battle with cancer. Judy was a Registered Nurse at Massachusetts General Hospital and one of the nicest people that we have ever known. Their son Kyle, who was Grounds Superintendent at TPC Sawgrass Golf Course in Ponte Vedra Beach, Florida, and is now the Course Superintendent at TPC Boston was also there along with their daughter Jen, a DNA Analyst who had security clearance working with our armed forces in a civilian capacity overseas. Years later Jen, who knew that I was very appreciative for the service of veterans and doing whatever I could to help them, was extremely thoughtful in having an American Flag flown in my honor over Camp Leatherneck in the Helmand Province of Afghanistan on the Fourth of July in 2011 during Operation Enduring Freedom. Leatherneck served as the home base for most of the operations of the United States Marines there so her kindness really meant a lot to me and the flag is still proudly displayed in our home.

Many years before the Hernandez case, I had just released a prisoner a few hours after midnight at the NAPD who was well built and angry. This guy had muscles growing out of muscles and looked like he could choke a horse to death! He had kept his mouth shut long enough to pay me and sign a recog, but upon putting the pen down started acting up with the mistaken belief that his new found freedom granted him immunity from further arrest. I handed him his copy and turned to walk away with his release fee still in my hand. I wouldn't normally turn my back on an angry defendant, but Detective Elliott happened to be standing right next to me as I headed for the door. Suddenly I could hear the defendant behind me scream all kinds of disgusting insults at Detective Elliott and myself as I looked over my shoulder to see him reaching for the money in my hand. I took a step back as he got up close in the good natured detective's face. The detective exhibited great restraint and didn't lay a hand on the rude reprobate until the defendant quickly moved toward me shouting, "F*** you. You got no right to take my money." It looked like Mr. Muscles was hell bent on assaulting me and reclaiming his release fee, but his forward progress was stopped immediately by Detective Elliott's prompt reaction. Remember, this is inside of the police station, Mike quickly grabbed the guy's shirt just under his chin and lifted him in the air with one hand! I had to rub my tired eyes to make sure that I was in fact seeing space between the big guy's feet and the floor! Mike had a little chat with the guy while airborne which, combined with the fist lift, caused a remarkable attitude transformation. I will always remain grateful that Mike Elliott, literally, had my back that night!

Hernandez was arrested on June 26, 2013 and escorted out of his house in the custody of North Attleborough Police Detective Daniel B. Arrighi and Massachusetts State Police Trooper Eric J. Benson who was later promoted to detective lieutenant. He was arraigned on the murder charge in the ADC, long after I had worked there. The New England Patriots announced Hernandez's release less than two hours after his arrest and soon corporate sponsors started to end their relationship with the 245 pound NFL star who possessed the speed of a wide receiver.

The case would make its way through the judicial system in Bristol County eventually under the leadership and direction of Acting District Attorney Thomas M. Quinn III. Quinn had been appointed by Governor Deval L. Patrick to fill the vacancy created by former District Attorney C. Samuel Sutter when he was elected Mayor of Fall River. Sam, a real nice guy, was a zealous, but fair-minded Assistant DA when we worked together at the ADC. Quinn has won every election since and continues to prosecute crime and protect the people of Bristol County.

Hernandez owned the house in North Attleborough, but had also rented what was described by some as a "flop house" in Franklin which is located in Norfolk County within the territorial jurisdiction of the WDC. A search warrant was issued for his less publicized abode at the Ledgewood Apartments on the same day as the North Attleborough arrest. I administered the oath to Trooper Michael B. Bates, later retiring as a sergeant, when making the return on the search warrant about a week later. The inventory listed various types of ammunition including a Glock .45 caliber loaded magazine clip and 22 other lines of items that were seized as evidence. I congratulated Trooper Bates on a successful search as I signed my name to the search warrant return.

The inventory of the seized items was made in the presence of Trooper Christopher J. Dumont, later promoted to lieutenant, of the Bristol County District Attorney's Office who, only a few months prior according to the September 29, 2013 *Taunton Daily Gazette* story written by Brian Fraga, had been on the tarmac at Logan International Airport to work a security detail escorting President Barack Obama. The President had come to Boston for a prayer service to honor the victims of the Marathon bombing. Dumont had just finished when news broke that MIT Police Officer Sean A. Collier had been shot. The detective immediately drove to the scene of the tragic murder of Officer Collier and then to Watertown where the two Marathon bombers were engaging police in a ferocious gun battle.

MBTA Police Officer Richard H. Donohue Jr. was lying in a driveway while rapidly losing blood after having been shot in the femoral artery. Dumont, a New Bedford native, returned fire during the shootout before going to assist Officer Donohue. The detective, who is a trained, experienced paramedic, went to work on Dic Donohue and is one of the officers credited with helping to save his life. Dumont and others rode in the ambulance rendering aid to Donohue while enroute to Mt. Auburn Hospital. Detective Dumont was presented with the Massachusetts State Police Medal of Honor for his actions during the Watertown shootout.

Officer Donohue, who retired from the force as a sergeant, would survive his close brush with death and work hard on his rehabilitation during the long path to recovery. I called Officer Donohue to ask him to come to our Law Day Ceremony the following year where I had requested that United States Congressman Joseph P. Kennedy III introduce him to our audience. The crowd reacted with thunderous applause for Dic Donohue - a true hero standing before us. I was also honored that Congressman Kennedy was able to take time out of his busy schedule and come to our court. He is a man of his word who I first laid eyes on when he was a little kid running around on the grass with his brother at a birthday party for his father at the Kennedy Compound in Hyannis Port. Congressman Joseph P. Kennedy II, whose birthday we had been celebrating, represented the Eighth Congressional District in continuing the excellence in leadership provided from that legendary section of Massachusetts. Joe's Uncle John F. Kennedy had represented the same hallowed ground in Congress prior to his eventual election to the Presidency of the United States and was succeeded by United States Congressman Thomas P. "Tip" O'Neill Jr. who was elected to the same seat and later became Speaker of the House.

Hernandez was indicted in May of 2014 by a Suffolk County Grand Jury in connection with two murders related to a 2012 drive by shooting in Boston. He was tried in Fall River Superior Court and convicted of first degree murder in the Odin Lloyd case in April of 2015 and sentenced to life in prison without parole by the Honorable Susan E. Garsh who had been appointed by Governor William F. Weld. In 2017 Hernandez was tried and acquitted of the charges stemming from the drive by shooting murders in Suffolk County. His troubled existence would end within days of that acquittal when he took his own life in his jail cell at the Sousa-Baranowski Correctional Center. Pursuant to the legal principle of abatement ab initio, the Hernandez murder conviction was vacated in accordance with law that calls for convictions to be vacated if a defendant dies before an appeal can be heard. The prosecutors from the Bristol County District Attorney's Office appealed that decision and approximately two years after Hernandez's suicide, the Supreme Judicial Court of Massachusetts overturned that legal doctrine thereby reinstating the original murder conviction.

Aaron Hernandez was a talented athlete who had achieved financial independence as a multi-millionaire. He could have continued to make a living catching footballs, but instead chose a path of violence that led to him catching a life sentence before taking his own life.

People have often asked me about the worst case that I have seen over the course of my career in the court system. Just so that there is no misunderstanding, obviously I have never had to undertake the terrible task of having to respond to a fatal auto accident or process a brutal homicide crime scene like a police officer. I have been up close and personal with some horrific tragedies, but the fresh blood observed by a police officer is usually dry by the time I get involved. That's an important distinction because a police officer's job is becoming much more difficult, demanding and dangerous every day.

I will probably never forget the 25-year old man who was arrested for rape after a thorough investigation by some outstanding detectives. Any rape falls into the category of a heinous and disgusting crime, but this case seemed to somehow raise the bar to define a new and repulsive definition of a bad guy. The 40-year old paraplegic victim was assaulted, terrorized and raped repeatedly while confined to her wheelchair. Those facts alone are bad enough to put this animal in select company, but it gets worse. The poor lady in the wheelchair - she was the mother of the defendant!

7. Family

We lived on Bedford Road in Montreal when I was a young kid while my dad was attending McGill University Dental School. My most vivid memory is of my mom taking me out to play in the snow and there was plenty of it! One of my father's friends was Phil Samis who graduated from dental school a year before my dad. Phil Samis played hockey for the Toronto Maple Leafs in their Championship 1947-48 campaign and later practiced dentistry until retiring. He is now 93 years old and still living in Canada.

Dr. Samis' name was engraved on the Stanley Cup with his Maple Leafs teammates and of course he was very proud of his Championship ring that every professional athlete dreams of. Anyone who watches the game of hockey knows that it is not uncommon for a fight to break out between players so there is nothing unusual about men with missing teeth in the National Hockey League. Dr. Samis' daughter, Attorney Jill McCutcheon, is a lawyer in Toronto. She was telling me about some of her father's missing teeth from the fights the left handed defenseman had been in. It's kind of ironic that a man with missing teeth who played a game with so many guys with missing teeth eventually became a dentist!

I have loved the Florida Keys ever since my first trip there as a teenager where I slept on the beach without a care in the world, but when I took my bride there many years later I figured it was time to spring for a hotel! It was J. Do's first trip to the famous island chain so I wanted her to see it the same way that I had many years before - from the passenger seat of a vehicle travelling down Route A1A. We flew into Miami and rented a car so that she could eventually take in the entire 125 mile stretch of tropical paradise all the way south to Key West. It was my first time back since my high school teammate Gary Joubert and I did some diving off the Atlantic side of Marathon while on college break. Joub is a good friend and a real nice guy so it was great to be able to explore the ocean together.

J. Do and I thoroughly enjoyed ourselves for a week at a beautiful resort right on the water and were still smiling as we headed to the hotel parking lot after checking out on our last day. My wife is well known for getting the absolute most out of every single day and this was no exception. I always try to get to an airport early whereas she is quite content to stay on the beach until the last minute and board the plane just before takeoff! I'm usually saying that we have to leave and J. Do wants to see one more wave break!

J. Do was taking in every last bit of beautiful scenery as we left our little Garden of Eden and made our way to the car. Her eyes were being massaged by the soothing sight of the magnificent palm tree fronds being gently lifted by the light on shore breeze. Pacifying trade winds carrying a mist of salt spray from the ocean encouraged an atmosphere of relaxation.

J. Do didn't notice the hole in the paved macadam in front of her as we continued our walk toward the car. She was still admiring the majestic beauty of our surroundings and looking around at the scenery while walking in high heel flip flops as she stepped into the hole and broke a bone in her left foot. The intense pain caused her to let out a loud blood-curdling scream as I quickly grabbed hold of her and carefully got her seated in the car. Poor J. Do was in terrible pain, but she didn't want me to call an ambulance or to drive her to a hospital. She kept saying no and that all that she wanted was some ice for her foot. I quickly turned around to assess which part of the hotel would have ice and the fastest route to run. Suddenly five or six maintenance workers were in front of me in response to J. Do's loud screams. These guys spoke limited English, but were kind enough to respond and it was obvious that they wanted to help. They didn't seem to understand when I told them that she needed some ice, so not thinking clearly myself and probably out of a hurried concern for my wife, I then foolishly tried to cure the language barrier by raising my voice. It wasn't as if they were hard of hearing, but I started yelling ICE, ICE, ICE! I'm guessing from their facial expressions of sudden fear that the poor guys were here illegally and mistook me for a federal agent from ICE on an immigration sweep. One guy jumped through the bushes and the rest were last seen running down A1A.

J. Do, Islamorada, Florida Keys

J. Do was still experiencing some intense pain when we returned home from Florida. Our family alternated holiday celebrations between our home and my brother Brendan's so it was J. Do's turn to cook Easter Dinner which was only a few days after our return home from the Keys. I told her that our family would certainly understand her discomfort and that I would pick up a delicious catered meal from Morin's Restaurant in Attleboro, but my persistent bride insisted on cooking her usual culinary masterpiece of scrumptious food. She had finished the preparations, retrieved a bag frozen peas from the freezer, rested her leg on the couch and applied the sack of cold vegetables to her swollen foot.

Chris was the first of our family to arrive so he walked in the living room, observed the patient and expressed sympathy for her condition. Our kids, just like everyone, loved their Uncle Chris so his presence always created a joyous and festive occasion as his big smile would light up our home. After a while Chis asked J. Do what we were having for dinner to which she replied that she had made strawberry cheesecake for dessert, but that the main course will feature dinner rolls, baked Virginia ham, mashed potatoes & gravy, buttered carrots and peas. Chris looked over at the bag of frozen peas on her left foot and smiled when he said, "I'll skip the peas!"

To say that my mother was practical, ingenious and resourceful would be a vast understatement. My brother Chris had just finished school and had an apartment in a somewhat undesirable neighborhood before he moved to a nice place on Cape Cod. We were seated at our family's Thanksgiving dinner table when Chris mentioned that he had an old mattress that he wanted to get rid of and was going to purchase an annual dump sticker because the mattress was too big for the city rubbish truck. Mom immediately told Chris not to buy a dump sticker because they were too expensive when considering that he would only be using it once. I'll never forget the next words out of my pragmatic mother's mouth, "Chris - you live in a rough neighborhood. Just leave the mattress on the sidewalk and somebody will steal it!" He did and the mattress was gone that night!

J. Do and I would rent a vacation cottage in Hyannis sometimes and always take our young daughters to see their Uncle Chris at the 19th Hole for our first stop on the Cape. He would serve them pizza and soda in the empty pub prior to opening so it became an enjoyable tradition.

Chris was truly a gentle giant, described by some as a big teddy bear. He was always in control of his emotions which is a good thing because he was a big guy. Chris helped everybody who needed it and probably almost felt bad if he had to kill a mosquito! The Cape is full of college kids from Ireland working summer jobs who haven't spoken with their parents back home for a while. It wasn't unusual for my generous brother to hand the 19th Hole phone to one of them and have them call home on him.

Sometimes after dinner we would stop to see Chris standing on the sidewalk working the door to the Hole. Chris was an experienced bartender, but he liked to work the door as his theory was that it was easier to keep trouble out than to put it out. He had a nose for potential problems, could read people like a poker player and made up excuses to keep undesirables out. I was standing next to him on the sidewalk one night when he told a guy that he couldn't come into the pub. Chris said, "Sorry, no brown pants on Thursday night!" The guy just walked away mumbling to himself!

Another night we had finished dinner at the Roadhouse Cafe and stopped by to see Chris before heading back to the cottage. J. Do, our two daughters and I were having some laughs with Chris on the sidewalk as he carded patrons at the door. Chris had to tell one guy that he couldn't come in because he was intoxicated. The guy exploded in anger and went from being a slow moving drunk to getting in Chris' face in a hurry. I pulled J. Do and our daughters out of harm's way as Chris said, "Excuse me girls!" Chris got the rude fool between himself and the outside wall, leaning into him causing the guy to stop swearing and start screaming!

Chris was working the door on a busy night when the line to get in extended around the block. He had to turn away a drunken celebrity who became upset at being denied admittance to the bar. The incensed luminary loudly asked Chris, "Do you know who I am?" Chris then turned to the patrons in line outside of the Hole and was just as loud when he asked the crowd, "Got a man here who doesn't know who he is! Does anybody know this guy?"

On yet another night a foul mouthed iniquitous low life spit in my brother's face. This vile and disgusting act would inspire a return of unbridled violence from almost everyone and a homicide from some, but not Chris. Chris wiped his face, turned down his anger a notch and instead of punching the bejeezus out of the despicable miscreant he slapped him one time in the face knocking him unconscious. Chris had big, powerful paws so one open hand took the guy out in a hurry. Years later I happened to be in the judge's lobby shooting the breeze with Judge Dan O'Malley who as I previously mentioned was a professional boxer before donning the robe. I related this story and he answered in the negative when I asked if he had ever heard of a guy getting knocked out from a slap!

Three brothers playing Chris' favorite game.

Chris was invited to a golf tournament by one of the beer company representatives so he asked me to come. We had a terrific time as the highlight of the day was to play a hole with Celtic great Larry Bird. Larry was very cordial as he greeted us warmly with some

Carol Doherty & her three boys

funny stories and interesting anecdotes. It is not unusual for a professional athlete to be proficient in her or his sport in addition to also being an outstanding golfer and Larry Bird is no exception as we played a beautiful par 3 where he made a nice shot from the tee and scored a birdie. Chris hit the ball well, but mine found a pine tree deep in the woods where it remains today. Larry just smiled and changed the subject so that I wouldn't feel bad as he really is a nice guy who genuinely cares about others.

J. Do was working in the Academic Lab at Foxborough High School when a student became disorderly and disruptive. J. Do has a soothing way about her with a kind and sympathetic approach to chaos, but even she couldn't convince this young man to calm down. He ran out of the room into the hallway so J. Do called the principal to alert her to the situation. When all else failed, Sergeant Scott Austin from the Foxborough Police Department responded to the scene and tried to restore order with the goal of a peaceful resolution. Scott, who would later retire as a lieutenant, is a class guy with vast experience in defusing problems from calls laden with volatile and deteriorating conditions, but this kid was just so arrogant that he had to be arrested. Foxborough is one of the towns in the territorial jurisdiction of the WDC so the defendant was transported to the court lock up for arraignment just as I was finishing some criminal hearings. I have known Scott and his lovely wife Jeanette for years and we have a mutual friend in Attorney Nicholas J. Riccio who now serves as the building commissioner for the town of Foxborough. Nick is an outstanding lawyer and a terrific guy who was introduced to me by my brother Chris years ago so it was my pleasure to have previously administered the oath to him in my office at the WDC so that he could also practice law in the state of Florida. When Nick heard about the arrest that Scott had to make he said, "That kid couldn't behave himself in Mrs. Doherty's class so Scott had to take him to Mr. Doherty's class!"

Jack Riccio and his lovely wife Barbara put on fabulous cookouts at their summer home in Hyannis where we always enjoy the festive atmosphere with a multitude of guests including their son Nick and his lovely wife Pam. Chris and I were visiting Jack, Nick and some other guys in Fort Lauderdale. I always said that Jack should write a book on how to have a perfect life with restaurants, golf courses and racetracks rounding out many days. We were having fun playing the horses at Gulfstream Park in Hallandale Beach and decided to bet one more race before leaving for one of Jack's favorite Italian restaurants. Chris put his money on the 5 horse to win along with some other combinations that all had the 5 on top. Jack, Nick and I all played pathetic nags that ended up looking like they were going to roll over and take a nap on the backstretch, but Chris' #5 looked terrific as he galloped toward the finish line. He was leading the whole race so it looked like some cash was headed for Chris' pocket until the very end when another horse seemed to beat him at the wire. Poor Chris went from being happy and excited to disappointed in an instant as he threw his tickets to the ground. We started to walk out toward the exit when I noticed that the "Objection" sign was lit up which meant that the judges had to rule on an objection for some alleged violation before determining the winner. Chris made a bee line back to our seats to try to find his discarded tickets. He had to run about 50 yards, but Chris could always move pretty fast for a big guy so those who saw him coming jumped out of the way like a running back trying to avoid a nose tackle. Chris finally got by the crowd and searched through the rubbish covered floor at our seats until he luckily found his tickets. He scuffled back to where we were waiting with a big smile on his face which grew even bigger when the judges turned off the Objection light and put the 5 horse up in the Win position! We all cheered when Chris' horse won the objection and he picked up over $400 dollars! Chris said that even though he's not a lawyer it was the best objection ever!

As previously mentioned, Bourne Police Detective John Doble, before retiring, was part of the Cape Cod Drug Task Force. This elite unit, responsible for putting a huge dent in the drug trade, was headed by well-respected Massachusetts State Police Detective Lieutenant John J. Allen. They made numerous narcotics arrests and celebrated success in Hyannis at the 19th Hole Tavern. Chris had served cold beverages to members of the Task Force on many nights after their undercover operations and clandestine raids. Chris was exceeding the posted limit while driving through the town of Bourne when he was pulled over for speeding by a local police officer. Chris was hoping that it might be helpful if he dropped Doble's name so when the officer approached to ask for his license and registration he said that he was good friends with Detective John Doble. Chris then asked the officer if he knew Detective Doble to which Officer Brian Doble replied, "Oh yea, I know him real well. He's my father!"

Chris, Boston Red Sox four-time All Star Bill Monbouquette, author at Ted Tomasone time (Bill Grassia photo)

Chris and I were long time baseball fans so I encouraged him to become a sponsor of the Hyannis Mets of the Cape Cod Baseball League which features the best college players in the country. The Cape League produces an incredible number of future stars with approximately 1 out of 6 Major Leaguers having played on the prestigious Cape Cod fields. Chris and his business partner David Cronan got involved and hosted the kids, coaches and others for an alcohol free luncheon every year and had a huge advertising banner displayed on the centerfield fence at McKeon Park. The team later became the Hyannis Harbor Hawks with Barnstable Police Detective Brian Guiney as their General Manager. I met Brian through Chris so we ended up in the same golf foursome sometimes where it was always fun to watch the Worcester native tee off and absolutely crush the ball down the middle of the fairway. Brian, a guy you can count on who also served on the Cape Cod

Drug Task Force, actually designed the beautiful 19th Hole logo on a cocktail napkin while sitting at the bar one night. The American and Irish flags crossed above a green shamrock became the veritable symbol of the famous Hyannis pub.

Chris and David hosted a golf tournament for the 19th Hole Tavern which was well attended and a lot of fun. We would play 18 holes at the Hyannis Golf Course and then head to the "Hole" for a feast which included vats of delicious piping hot clam chowder delivered from Captain Parker's Pub in West Yarmouth. Gerry Manning owns the landmark restaurant which continues to produce award winning chowder and was a big hit at the Hole. Gerry, who is OFD - originally from Dorchester, is a great man who was always upbeat, never forgot where he came from and took pride in delivering the famous chowder to his mother in Boston.

I was in Chris' foursome joined by David Cronan and Matt Bulman, a former court officer and great guy who would go on to become a Barnstable Police Officer. Chris and David had been friends since kindergarten so we used to kid around that they had been together longer than most marriages! We had all reached the green on one of the first holes in the early morning and took out our putters for the dance floor. My ball was so far away on the edge of the rough that Chris kidded that I should get out my driver! It had rained hard the night before the tournament so my put had water shooting off the ball as it left a long trail on the green and stopped about five feet short. Chris tried to get a feel for speed by looking at my mess as he leaned over his ball with putter in hand and took a couple of practice swings. Just as he was about to hit the ball a frog jumped out of the water filled cup and sat on the green right next to the hole while staring at Chris. My youngest brother, with a heart as big as Cape Cod, said that we better wait until the frog moves so that he doesn't get hurt from the moving ball. David immediately came back with, "Don't worry Chris - with you putting that frog is in the safest place in Hyannis!"

I was playing golf another time in the same foursome on a nice day on the Cape. I have more trouble chipping the ball than most golfers so instead of using a chipping wedge I will take out my putter whenever possible regardless of the distance. Other guys usually do a double take, but I am actually able to get closest to the pin quite often which always amazes the rest of the foursome. The first hole had a flat fairway that edged up nicely next to the green without many bumps or obstructions so I pulled out my trusty putter and did my best to line up a 40 yard put! It's hard to judge speed at that distance, but I got lucky and hit this one perfectly as the ball travelled down the fairway, rolled along the green and dropped right into the cup! Chris and David let out a roar while Matt was laughing so hard that he actually fell down on the fairway!

It was a busy night at the 19th Hole Tavern with many of the regular patrons enjoying themselves including Joe Lally and his lovely wife Diane, Maureen Murphy, Billy Concha, Brian Dubuc, Tom Ryshavy, Jim McLaughlin and his lovely wife Maureen, their son Matt and others. Craig Bentley is a pilot for Cape Air and worked as a part time bartender at the popular watering hole. Craig is a real good guy and also a patron sometimes when off duty so this night he was sitting on a stool nursing a cold beer. Chris had just walked into the Hole to start his shift without really noticing who was present. He called Craig on the phone and was engaged in a nice conversation when he started laughing after noticing Craig speaking to him on his cellphone at the end of the bar!

Chris was working security at the Cape Cod Hospital in Hyannis where he was beloved by doctors, nurses and everyone else. A well-built angry man whose physique resembled that of a body builder had been evaluated by a doctor at the hospital. It had been determined that the man should be put under observation with the hope that he would calm down and later qualify for release. It was well known throughout the hospital that Chris could handle himself so he was assigned to stay with the muscle bound madman all night. Chris spent hours listening and speaking as the man took an instant liking to Chris while they developed a bond based on sports and other common interests. Chris always had a terrific memory for sports trivia so he rattled off previous Red Sox lineups and details of legendary Celtics' games as the guy became calmer by the hour. Finally, after a long night a nurse came in and stated that the doctor was going to discharge the gentleman so Chris could go home now. The guy, who by this time thought of himself as Chris' best friend, was suddenly concerned that his discharge would mean some loss of income for his new buddy. He wanted to help Chris increase his paycheck with a unique offer. "Chris", he stated, "Do you want me to punch somebody in the face so you can keep watching me and work some overtime?"

Judge Frank Crimmins, Chris, Mayor Ray Flynn, author

When a bartender reaches for a ringing phone it is common to see a dozen or so negative head shakes and waving arms go up at the bar in the universal sign meaning "I'm not here!" Chris told me about a bar in South Boston called the Quencher Tavern where the bartender will say that you're not there if you give him $1.00 and for $5.00 he will say that he's never heard of you!

One time Chris mentioned a new bar in Boston named Church. He said guys were telling their wives, "Honey, I'm going to church and it might be a long sermon!"

Chris told me about another bar with a sign outside that read, "Come on in and meet your future ex-wife!"

Chris and I attended the 2000 Baseball Hall of Fame Induction Ceremony in Cooperstown, New York. We had been there before as kids, but it was always a thrill to return and walk on that hallowed ground. We had a lot of fun along with thousands of other fans listening to the speeches of Carlton Fisk, Tony Perez, Sparky Anderson and other inductees honored that day. Fisk received thunderous applause after being introduced to the crowd by Commissioner Bud Selig. Fans will never forget Game 6 of the 1975 World Series against the Cincinnati Reds where Fisk drove a 12th inning Pat Darcy right-handed offering to left field in Fenway Park. The iconic image of Fisk waving the ball fair until it hit the left field foul pole for a home run became an integral component of celebrated Boston lore. The legendary catcher was very interesting and thanked a multitude of people which was extremely classy, but his speech seemed to go on forever, even longer than my retirement party speech. He was talking about players in the 1970s when Chris said he had to hit the men's room. Chris came back from the portable facility and the first thing he said was, "Eddie, is Fisk out of the 70s yet?"

Chris used to call me frequently to settle bar bets and disagreements about our national pastime. Patrons of the 19th Hole would need some issue settled and although I wouldn't always know the answer, I would be happy to help if I could. For some strange reason an uncanny number of these requests came while I was in the shower. Shortly after returning from our honeymoon I can vividly recall J. Do coming into the bathroom and speaking loud enough for me to hear her under the din of the surrounding shower water. She said that Chris was on the phone and wanted to know how many lifetime home runs had been hit by Joe DiMaggio (361) and a few weeks later the lifetime batting average of Jimmy Foxx (.325). I remember J. Do standing outside of the shower telling Chris on the phone that Rico Petrocelli hit 40 home runs in 1969. Not that I minded these calls because Chris and I would talk at least once and usually several times each day, but I finally gave my kind-hearted brother what every American pub needs - a new crisp copy of the heaviest book I have ever owned - *The Baseball Encyclopedia.*

I was having dinner with J. Do and our two daughters at Lindsey's Family Restaurant in East Wareham where they served the best fish chowder and most delicious baked stuffed haddock in America! I noticed a sign hanging on the wall in the bar that caught my attention so I asked our daughter Chrissy to duplicate it for her Uncle Chris' pub. She did a nice job of adding shamrocks to surround the slogan and presented it to Chris who loved it and hung it up in the 19th Hole where it remains to this day. The sign reads, IT'S BETTER TO LISTEN TO YOUR BARTENDER AT NIGHT, THAN TO A JUDGE IN THE MORNING!

I enjoyed reading the colorful sports stories of the great Dan Shaughnessy even before he became a famous award winning columnist for *The Boston Globe*. Boston has been blessed with some outstanding writers in the world of sports and otherwise, but Shaughnessy is, without a doubt, the most courageous, creative, thorough and interesting of them all. Dan took a seat at the bar with his daughter to watch the baseball All Star Game in the 19th Hole. He was instantly recognized by my brother Chris who was tending bar that night so they struck up a nice conversation. Chris knew how highly I thought of the accomplished wordsmith so he asked him to inscribe a book to me. As soon as Dan graciously agreed, Chris reached under the bar and pulled out a fresh copy of THE CURSE OF THE BAMBINO which Dan had written about the epic failures of the Boston Red Sox. A surprised Dan Shaughnessy smiled, wrote a very nice inscription to me and told Chris, "This place is great. You've got baseball on TV, cold beer and my book under the bar!"

Every year a publication is distributed categorizing businesses and restaurants on Cape Cod. One time the 19th Hole Tavern was mistakenly included in the Fine Dining Section for Hyannis restaurants. The Hole is noted for a lot of positive things, but gourmet dining is not one of them. At one time or another, except for special events, patrons could get a pizza, burger, hot dog and stuffed quahog, but not much else to go with their cocktails, wine or cold beer. Several tourists called Chris to ask for reservations thinking the Hole was a fine dining establishment. I was standing next to him when he started getting tired of these interruptions as somebody else called and asked him for the specials! Chris went right into a spontaneous comedy routine telling the caller that tonight they were featuring veal parmigiana on a bed of spaghetti with garlic bread and a complimentary glass of red wine! Before Chris could say that he was only kidding the guy hung up. I guess he didn't like the special!

John McDermott, formerly of the Irish Tenors, is a world famous singer and a humorous guy who was friends with Chris. We all went to one of his terrific concerts in Hyannis and reconvened later at the 19th Hole Tavern to quench our thirst. Chris introduced J. Do and I to John who is not only an inspiring vocalist, but also a very funny man. Earlier when he was on stage that night he had told the audience, "I'm half Irish and half Scottish which means that I like to drink, but I don't like to pay for it!"

My brothers Brendan and Chris both thought very highly of Sister Patricia Harrington, one of their nuns from Bishop Feehan High School. Chris would host Sister Pat at the 19th Hole St. Patrick's Day party every year. I had gotten to know the cheerful nun through my brothers over the years and always enjoyed her company at the Hole as well as parties at Brendan's house. She was a truly magnificent person who was helpful and loyal to my brothers until the day she went to heaven. I was in Boston watching a playoff game between the Bishop Feehan Shamrocks and the Bishop Stang Spartans with Chris' team down by a few points and only about a minute left to play when I noticed Sister Pat standing near me behind one of the baskets. Realizing that Feehan was in trouble, I said, "Sister Pat, I think you better start working the rosary beads," but the level-headed disciple of faith didn't miss a beat in quickly correcting me with the knowledge that God doesn't play favorites between Catholic schools, when she replied, "I can't! We're playing Stang!"

Both of my brothers and I were enjoying a ballgame in Boston as we rooted for the Red Sox at Fenway Park. I was seated between my brothers on the 3rd base side with Brendan on my left and Chris on the right before we all stood up for the 7th inning stretch. Brendan and Chris began talking about leaving the game early and beating the traffic, but I wanted to stay for the full nine innings. I was standing between my two brothers with my folded arms interlocked across my chest when Brendan picked me up by my left elbow and Chris did the same with my right! We all had a good laugh as my brothers, much bigger than me, started walking out of the ballpark with me hanging between them as my feet dangled in the air!

The Lee family lived a few blocks from our childhood home in Attleboro. The Lees, Dohertys and other neighborhood kids would play sports together and be in and out of each other's homes quite frequently. Mark Sturdy is absolutely one of the smartest, most well rounded and nicest guys in the system. He did a terrific job as an ADA in the ADC and, as previously mentioned, would later become an Assistant Clerk-Magistrate before being appointed Clerk-Magistrate. You will never hear a bad word about Mark as he continues to serve justice fairly with compassion, intellect and grace. Mark married Kerry Lee and in the process of moving her belongings out of her home he came across something belonging to my brother Chris. Mark approached me at a recess in Courtroom One in Attleboro and gave me a Bob Gibson model baseball glove that had Chris Doherty written on the side! This was probably about 20 years after it had been lost so we both had a good laugh when I called my brother. Bob Gibson was one of the greatest pitchers in history, breaking the hearts of Red Sox fans with three complete game wins for the St. Louis Cardinals in the 1967 World Series. Perfect authenticity though is sometimes trumped by money and commercialism. Apparently, Spaulding made Gibson model gloves for right handers as well as left handers. Bob Gibson was right handed, but my brother's glove was made for a southpaw - Chris was left handed!

Chris got to know several members of the famous Kennedy family very well. John F. Kennedy Jr. stopped by the 19th Hole to pick up some gum not long before he perished in the heartbreaking plane crash off the coast. Chris would sometimes volunteer to drive Joan Kennedy, the former wife of Senator Ted Kennedy, to various events around the Commonwealth. He would select a vehicle from the Kennedy fleet of cars and pick her up at Logan airport or some other location. She is a very nice lady so Chris enjoyed their conversations, but one time he just couldn't get away from work to drive her from the airport as she was flying in on the Concorde Turbojet from France. Mrs. Kennedy insisted on Chris so he got a call from somebody in the Kennedy office in Chicago inquiring about the problem. He reminded the guy that he was a volunteer, but Chris told me that the man was being extremely persistent as Mrs. Kennedy didn't want anyone else.

Congressman Joseph P. Kennedy II warmly welcomed J. Do and I to his birthday party where we had a terrific time. As previously mentioned, his son, Joseph P. Kennedy III, was enjoying himself running around on the huge lawn with some of the other kids. Young Joe would later follow his father, serving in the United States Congress and take time out his busy schedule to speak at our Law Day ceremony. He is currently the United States Special Envoy for Northern Ireland.

One time Chris picked up United States Senator Christopher J. Dodd from Connecticut and drove him to the Kennedy Compound for a little get together. The Kennedy's home workers, landscapers, and cleaning staff all knew my brother from drinking at the 19th Hole so they were thrilled to see him drive up with Senator Dodd. Dodd was greeted by a jubilant Ted Kennedy yelling from the front porch, "Chris, good to see you. Thanks for coming Chris." The workers were very impressed because, not knowing who Dodd was, they thought that the Chris that Senator Kennedy was talking to was my brother.

US Congressman Joseph P. Kennedy II, Kennedy Compound, Hyannisport

Chris used to jokingly say that he had his own bedroom in the main house at the Kennedy Compound and he did sleep there sometimes after parties. Ethel Kennedy was having some remodeling done so a sliding glass door was destined for the dumpster until Chris got permission to have it installed in his condo. He would even pick up my daughters and drive them around in one of the Kennedy vehicles while explaining a history lesson about the family who owned the car.

I was having a beer at the 19th Hole when Chris introduced me to Paul Hill who I would get to know pretty well. Paul is a nice guy who, along with three others known as the Guildford Four, were convicted of bombing a pub in England and sentenced to life in prison where he remained for 15 years until being freed for a crime that he didn't commit. The story of the grave injustice is portrayed in the movie *In the Name of the Father* as a brutal tale of mistreatment and torture. Daniel Day-Lewis stars in the film with John Lynch playing the part of Paul. The Belfast born Hill would eventually receive an apology from the British government and marry Courtney Kennedy, daughter of Ethel and United States Senator Robert F. Kennedy.

Paul Hill

Paul is an interesting guy so I enjoyed his company and listened intently to his stories while feeling like I was tuned into the History Channel. The authorities were convinced that he and the others were members of the Irish Republican Army so he was moved to different prisons over 50 times during his incarceration, sometimes in the middle of the night, so that the IRA would have trouble keeping track of his location thereby reducing the chance for a jail break. He wasn't able to convince them that he wasn't with the IRA and told me how he had a pistol shoved into his mouth and on another occasion had the beginning of a root canal done by a dentist and was then thrown back into a cell without the tooth being sealed with filing material.

Paul drinks Heineken so I once told him that he clearly has a lot of those to catch up on to make up for lost time. I met his wife Courtney for the first time when Chris and I went with Paul to the Kennedy Compound. She was very nice and gave me a beautiful gift which I still have prominently displayed in our home. The magnificent clear acrylic paperweight encompasses a salient portion of a powerful speech given by her father during the monumental campaign year of 1968.

The Kennedy family has endured such unspeakable horror with the loss of so many lives through devastating assassinations and terrible accidents, but yet another tragedy struck when Courtney and Paul had to bury their beautiful daughter Saoirse who died at the compound in Hyannis. No one should have to endure the tragedy, horror and loss experienced by Courtney and Paul. They are no longer together so I hope that they can somehow find solace, peace and happiness in the midst of such unspeakable pain.

Chris called Paul Hill to get himself, Brendan and I into the Robert F. Kennedy Human Rights Annual Golf Tournament at the Hyannisport Club. I had played there before with Chris so I knew it was a beautiful layout with ocean views, but one of the most fascinating aspects that he and I had spoken of that morning as we were walking up to the first green, was that we were following in the giant footsteps of legends. We had seen photos of many dignitaries including President John F. Kennedy playing this course and we had just stood in the same tee box where our 35th President had swung a driver!

Brendan, Chris and I met a lot of interesting people that day including Celtic greats John Havlicek and Tom Heinsohn, both having played on 8 NBA World Championship teams. Heinsohn, who also won 2 NBA World Championships as a coach, had autographed my Celtics program after a game on the sidewalk outside of the Garden when I was nine years old and he was just as nice then - "What's your name kid?" - as he was at the RFK Tournament. Later we met the immortal Bill Russell, arguably the greatest team player in history. Russell became an integral part of the civil rights movement displaying courage and grace to the world. After winning 11 NBA World Championships Russell didn't have enough fingers for all the rings he had won! The first time I saw Havlicek up close and personal was during an exhibition game at Bishop Feehan High School in Attleboro many years before. He was also very gracious at the golf course where we all shared some laughs and stories. It's hard to look at John Havlicek without hearing Johnny Most in your ear yelling, "Havlicek stole the ball!"

Boston Celtic legend Tom Heinsohn

Chris, Boston Celtic all-time great John Havlicek, author

Havlicek, Heinsohn and Russell are true champions who emptied their bucket on the parquet floor every night and entertained fans in arenas throughout the NBA. They played on some remarkable teams and instilled fans with the concept of Celtic Pride. As I stood next to them I actually let my mind envision how frustrating it must have been for an opponent to be in that close trying to guard the immortal Hall of Famers! If a Mount Rushmore of Boston Celtics were constructed, Havlicek, Heinsohn and Russell would be unanimous choices by anyone who has ever seen them play and if they ever build one for bartenders our brother Chris would be smiling from the top of the mountain!

Tom Heinsohn & Brendan

Brendan, his lovely wife Michele, their children Shelby and Matt, our girls Kait and Chrissy, J. Do and I all met Natalie Sands for the first time at our brother Chris' bedside in Cape Cod Hospital a few days before we lost him from a fatal heart attack. She is a beautiful girl inside and out so I'm sure that Chris was ready to introduce her to our family when tragedy struck. The three brothers had lunch together in Mattapoisett exactly one week before Chris was hospitalized where we enjoyed each other's company, had a lot of laughs and heard Chris speak glowingly of Natalie. He spoke of her in a loving way like I had never heard him profess before about any other girl. We were all glad to meet Natalie, but unfortunately, God took our brother way too soon.

Brendan could always handle himself and, as previously mentioned, did some boxing out of Grundy's Gym. I didn't know how far he would go in this brutal sport, but I wanted to be there for him even though the only thing that I knew about boxing was from watching it on TV. Brendan didn't ask me to, but I wanted to learn at least enough about the business end of boxing to be of some assistance to my brother in case he needed it.

I have always tried to live my life by what I describe as the Mickey Mantle Theory. A home run is the best result a batter can achieve in the game of baseball, but the big stroke increases the chance of swinging and missing the ball which sometimes results in failure - a strikeout - when swinging for the fence. Mantle, one of the all-time great ball players, led the league in strikeouts five times on his way to slugging 536 home runs. I was never afraid of failure or rejection for long shot ventures as it was a small price to pay for occasional success in achieving a goal that may have initially seemed out of reach. It wasn't a problem for me to make cold calls to someone I didn't know seeking information, a job or something else. I had nothing to lose as the worst thing that could happen from my perspective was to hear a dial tone when the other person immediately hung up.

I didn't know Angelo Dundee, but I cold called the renowned boxing trainer at his gym in Miami seeking advice. He was training a boxer in Europe, but I spoke to some others who were somewhat helpful. I worked Brendan's corner which involved putting the stool in the ring between rounds, taking his mouthpiece out and giving him water. I was single at the time so I was speaking with some girl in the stands during one fight when the bell rang and I should have been quicker to the corner. Brendan, of course, couldn't take the mouthpiece out himself with boxing gloves on so he was understandably unhappy!

I sparred with Brendan in our garage in Attleboro. We didn't have a bell so a song on the radio would be one round. He wore oversized gloves so that he wouldn't do too much damage to me and I wore head gear. He didn't need head gear as I don't know if I ever even hit him once except on the gloves. Even with big gloves his jabs hurt and one time he delivered a half powered hook that turned my head gear around so I couldn't see.

Boxing is part of the program at the Rhode Island State Police Academy as it probably is at most. I think all state police departments are somewhat quasi-military organizations and Rhode Island is no exception. J. Do and I would bring clean clothes to Brendan at the academy sometimes feeling like we had just entered a United States Marine boot camp!

I got lucky and won a Rodman Ford football contest by coming closest to predicting the Super Bowl teams and score prior to the beginning of the season. This was long before I had gotten to know Don Rodman and he was extremely generous by providing his personal limo, driver and four terrific Celtics tickets as the Grand Prize. We invited my two brothers to meet us in Boston and J. Do and I were picked up at our home in Don's limo.

Johnny Most was the legendary play by play radio announcer for the Boston Celtics, calling many of their historic championship victories from "high above courtside" as he always proclaimed from his roost at the old Boston Garden. Don provided premium seats that night with the parquet floor right in front of us as the crowd cheered on the Celts to beat the Chicago Bulls. Brendan and Chris noticed that Johnny Most was sitting a few seats to our left, but I don't know why he wasn't in his usual elevated perch looking down on the action because he had not yet retired. The raspy voiced icon had an oxygen tank on the floor in front of him with tubing running up to his face as he smoked cigarette after cigarette! There were huge, well lighted NO SMOKING signs all over the building so just for the heck of it Brendan asked an usher, "I thought you couldn't smoke in here?" The usher smiled and said, "Except for Johnny Most!"

L-R Kait, Chrissy & Shelby

Laughter and sweet Celtic music filled the air at the annual St. Patrick's Day party at the 19th Hole Tavern. Chris and Dave always put together a tremendous event so a good time was being had by all. Brendan happened to be standing near the entrance when a couple of rugged guys 30 years younger than him walked in the door. Brendan's years of experience with the state police immediately kicked in as he sensed something about these guys that wasn't right. My niece, Brendan's beautiful daughter Shelby, is a very nice girl who was mingling in the crowd while listening to the music as one of these morons came up and grabbed her from behind, put her in kind of a half nelson while trying to force a kiss upon her as Shelby tried to fight him off! Brendan's sixth sense was correct and fortunately for Shelby he was close by which was bad luck for moron #1. Brendan quickly took the loser's beer out of his hand and placed it on the bar as he tore the guy off of his daughter, grabbed him by the throat and spun him around into the wall near the door. This guy had no idea what just happened as he suddenly found himself in a death grip with his feet dangling in the air. His flight to the wall, hard landing and up close view of Brendan's determined face may have caused him to need an immediate change of underwear! Knowing that this reprobate had come in with a friend Brendan was cautiously on the lookout for moron #2 while #1 was hung up like a Christmas tree ornament. When

Brendan's peripheral vision picked up the second dope moving toward him he pointed at the door and told him to leave now or his teeth would be all over the floor. Moron #2 instantly acquired enough intelligence to do the smart thing and promptly sprinted out the exit. Brendan had a little chat with moron #1 and told him to get out and not come back. Instant justice!

I would usually be on call with the ADC police departments for a full seven straight days and nights. Answering the phone at all hours and travelling to busy police stations would start to become more difficult as the week wore on so by day 5 or 6 banking a few hours of sleep was like hitting the lottery.

As previously mentioned, J. Do would take the kids out of the house for a couple of hours on weekends so I could get an afternoon nap in before heading out again. You can imagine how disappointing it was to have valuable sleep interrupted by a salesman ringing the doorbell so I made a sign to protect my slumber time. I used a black marker to write on a bright yellow small claims folder that read - QUIET MAN SLEEPING! DO NOT RING. DO NOT KNOCK. PLEASE GO AWAY NOW! I hung this on the front door before hitting the couch and never had a problem.

My mother always loved watching *The Quiet Man* with an all-star cast including Maureen O'Hara and John Wayne in the title role. My sign had QUIET written above MAN SLEEPING obviating the need for punctuation after QUIET. The first time my mother dropped by when the sign was up, however, she intentionally interpreted the three words together as QUIET MAN SLEEPING! She used her key to let herself in and, always the comedienne, she waited until I woke up and began yelling down the hall, "Where's John Wayne and why is he sleeping in your house? Wake him up and tell him I want to meet him! Get John Wayne out here!"

If anyone phoned our mother on Sunday morning it had better not have been when NBC's Meet the Press was on TV. Our mom simply loved Tim Russert, the multi-talented host of the legendary news program. Russert's superior intellect and direct interview skills combined with an engaging personality provided for a very informative as well as entertaining presentation. He just seemed to have a nice way about him as he educated his viewers on the issues facing the world. He was a down to earth guy who we lost much too young, but he left his positive mark on an appreciative audience who will never

Tim Russert, NBC - Meet the Press

forget his wisdom. The smile on his face seemed to be accompanied by a twinkle in his eye when I told him that my mom was his biggest fan!

Domenic DiMaggio was an outstanding center fielder for the Boston Red Sox. DiMaggio was my dad's favorite ballplayer, but he retired the year before I was born so I never got to him play. Our family would be watching a ballgame on TV as our dad regaled us with stories of the baseball greats he had seen growing up. If a major league outfielder committed an error by misjudging a fly ball dad would always say the same thing, "Domenic DiMaggio would have had that in his back pocket!" Hearing dad's repeated praise of Joe DiMaggio's younger brother became such a tradition in our family that upon seeing an outfield blunder, even long after we had lost our father, my brothers and I would proclaim that, "Domenic DiMaggio would have had that in his back pocket." I had the high honor and incredible privilege of meeting Dom DiMaggio at a baseball function where I sat next to The Little Professor, as he was called, and told him the story about our dad. The baseball legend seemed genuinely touched as he thanked me for the memory while his friend came close to tears which triggered my emotions with thoughts of my dad, almost causing my own waterworks to flow.

Jim Corsi was a terrific major league pitcher, including for the Boston Red Sox. He was an even better person who was taken from us much too young so J. Do and I enjoyed our conversations with the fan favorite who was courteous, kind, funny, outgoing and extremely generous with his time.

World Series Champion Jim Corsi (Barry Okun photo)

My bride strapped our one-year old Kaitlin into the stroller on a beautiful summer day. We started walking from our three-decker on Peck Street and headed for downtown

Attleboro to enjoy the nice weather on a Sunday afternoon. As we were walking by the Attleboro Public Library I noticed a career criminal on the other side of the street who must have taken a hiatus from his illegal endeavors as I hadn't seen him in a while. He had previously told me that alcohol was the root of all of his problems so I was happy to hear that he was trying to beat his addiction as he yelled across the street, "Mr. Doherty, I haven't had a drink in four months!" "That's terrific," I said, "Keep at it and hang in there. Good for you!" J. Do smiled at me and said what we both already knew, "You really do work 24/7 in this job don't you!"

Joseph L. Currier, J. Do's father, owned a string of service stations and an auto parts store. He was a hardworking, generous guy who always put his family first. We had a lot of good times together when he skippered his boat the *RIPTIDE* 25 miles out into the Atlantic for bottom fishing. J. Do first started pumping gas at one of his stations when she was only about 14 years old. She learned a lot about repairing cars from watching her dad and his other mechanics which gave her the ability to fix problems with our cars including a remarkable transmission job she did on my vehicle. We kid around sometimes that J. Do is the second coming of Joe Pesci's character's girlfriend played by Marisa Tomei in the movie *My Cousin Vinny*. J. Do may not be quite as knowledgeable about engines as Mona Lisa Vito, but she is definitely the best-looking mechanic to ever work on my car!

Authors Note: I wrote the following, many years after our youngest daughter was a little girl, which was published after editing in the "Ideas" section for the June 2, 2019 issue of *The Boston Globe*.

> My wife Joanne and I were headed out to the backyard, but we wanted our three-year-old daughter Chrissy to stay in the house and keep playing. I guess television really does have an influence on kids. "We'll be right back," I told Chrissy. "Right after these messages!" she quickly replied."

Kaitlin was about six years old when she decided to have a funeral for a fish that she had caught. She tried to make it a formal affair with her sister Chrissy and the neighborhood kids including the Bray sisters - Sheila and Meghan serving as flower girls and pall bearers in a solemn procession that started near the swing set. Before the fish was buried in the backyard, Kait stood up on top of a cooler and gave the eulogy. She spoke of how it was a wonderful fish and everybody loved him and amongst other respectful declarations Kait proclaimed that, "This fish gave his life for a worm!"

We were having a yard sale before selling our home and moving from North Attleborough so I helped J. Do and our two daughters move an incredible amount of clothing, furniture and other items to the front lawn. The girls had various goods organized and spread out between aisles that resembled a department store as well as dresses hanging on a portable closet with a bar to hold coat hangers. My wife and kids were stationed out front making sales and having a fun time as always while I was reading the newspaper in the living room, which had windows looking out onto all of the activity with the hordes of shoppers milling through the merchandise. After a while Chrissy came in through the front door and walked by me while holding a dress on a coat hanger. She said that a lady wanted the dress in the same color, but wanted to see if we had it in a size 10! I told Chrissy to tell her it is a yard sale, not Filene's Basement!

Kevin Eagan was a star soccer player at the University of South Florida. I don't remember having any classes with him, but we got to know each other from celebrations at the Copper Top Pub and at parties on campus. I graduated in 1977 which was the same year that Kevin was drafted in the first round by the Tampa Bay Rowdies so he got to play professionally in the same city where he went to school. The defensive standout later signed as a free agent with the New York Cosmos and also played for the Tulsa Roughnecks during a very impressive soccer career.

I never played soccer as growing up in New England didn't lend itself to being a fan, but everybody liked Kevin as he is a humble guy with an easy laugh and a genuine appreciation for the important aspects of life. The St. Louis native was kind enough to leave a couple of tickets for me when he came north with the Tampa Bay Rowdies to play the New England Tea Men in Foxborough at what was then called Schaefer Stadium. I asked my brother Brendan to go to the game, but he looked at me like I had just offered him some used dental floss. I don't blame him because none of us were soccer fans, but I really wanted to see Kevin. Finally, Brendan reluctantly agreed to go with me, but most of the state and many people from around the country were celebrating another event on the same day as the soccer game. It was John Havlicek Day in Boston in honor of the Celtic great who we had watched since we were kids. This made the timing even worse for my basketball minded sibling Brendan, but he is a good brother who didn't complain too much.

I introduced Brendan to Kevin when he came over to the seats before the game to say hello. It was nice to see the talented soccer star who told us that he was surprised that anyone was in the stands as he had heard all about Havlicek Day on the plane ride with the team which caused Brendan's head to snap toward me with a glance that just about said, "See, why are we here?"

Kevin Eagan is a class guy so I was appreciative of his courtesy and glad that we were able to see each other. I had just driven the car out of the stadium parking lot onto Route One South for our ride home after the game when Brendan looked over at me and rhetorically asked, "Kevin is a nice guy, but why couldn't you be friends with John Havlicek!"

I was at a function at Anthony's Pier 4 when Brendan called inviting me to an impromptu dinner with a few other guys including Boston Bruins immortal Derek Sanderson. I hustled out of Boston and drove to a small restaurant in Cumberland, RI where my brother introduced me to the 2x Stanley Cup Champion. I think there were five of us at the table as Derek regaled us with exciting stories that had never been in print while we all enjoyed listening to his take on some historic events in the world of sports. Turk is an extremely down to earth, nice guy who has continued to help others after becoming a Boston legend on the Garden ice. Derek is revered wherever he goes with his grace and incredible talent recognized and respected by everyone including hockey fans throughout the league.

Boston Bruins' legend Derek Sanderson

Our youngest daughter Chrissy and her husband Dan both graduated from my alma mater - the University of South Florida in Tampa. I told her that she could go anywhere, but I was happy when she chose my school and enrolled in their highly rated nursing program. She called me during her freshman year and asked for some money to buy a second hand watch so I immediately told her that we would buy her a new watch. Chrissy was such a good kid who studied hard and always tried to do the right thing. I appreciated her attempt at frugality, but I told her that no kid of mine would be wearing a second hand watch and that she deserved a new watch to which she replied, "No dad, you don't understand. In nursing school we have to take a pulse so I need to have a watch that has a second hand!"

My great Uncle Gabby Doherty was co-owner of a barroom in Taunton called the Parker House. His partner in this lively enterprise was Frank Roster and they both looked over my dad as he spent time mastering card games like Seven Card Stud and High Low Jack long before becoming a teenager.

I had only been working a short time at the ADC when I met Taunton Attorney Edward A. Roster whose uncle was partners with my great uncle. I got to know Ed very well over the years when he would come to court on behalf of a client so we would sometimes swap family stories culminating in a good laugh. I always had an enormous amount of genuine respect and admiration for the Silver City advocate as we enjoyed each other's company during breaks in the court session.

Many years later after I had moved on from the ADC, our youngest daughter Chrissy graduated from the School of Nursing at the University of South Florida in Tampa. Chrissy had done very well so we were extremely proud to attend the graduation ceremony where she received the Spirit of Nursing Award from my alma mater. The enthusiastic Registered Nurse eventually headed back north to live with us and began to look for a job in the field of nursing.

Chrissy is a sweet, caring and talented professional, but nursing jobs were hard to come by with very few openings. I armed myself with a supply of her resumes and started looking for familiar names because almost everybody needs a little help sometimes. Chrissy had applied at Morton Hospital in Taunton where my mother had worked as an

RN and I had been born. My mother's connections were long gone, but I scanned through upper management listings to see what I could find and discovered that Attorney Ed Roster was the Chairman of the Board of Directors for Morton Hospital!

I called Ed and told him that Chrissy had applied to Morton, but did not immediately request his assistance as I was going to ask for his help later in the call. We had a nice conversation as he listened to me say many great things about Chrissy and I then asked him to please consider helping her to get a job at Morton Hospital. The usual drill is that the contact takes the applicant's resume and says to call him next week or something along those lines, but after I asked for help he just said OK. I wasn't quite sure what he meant when he said OK as I would usually mail a resume in this type of situation. A resume not only provides information for the contact to use with others if any persuasion is necessary, but it also serves as a simple physical reminder for the contact to act.

Everyone does things just a little differently than the next so I asked Ed if he wanted me to send him Chrissy's resumé. "Resumé", he said, "Why do I need a resumé? She's your daughter so she's got the job." Wow! Chrissy's interview had lasted ten minutes and she wasn't even present! I thanked him profusely while recognizing to myself that, although I had been in this circumstance many times before, this was the easiest conversation of my life regarding employment.

As it turned out, Chrissy found her true calling working with young kids as a Registered Nurse at Boston Children's Hospital where she worked part time for many years while raising her own three daughters with her husband Dan. Chrissy is now enjoying her job as a school nurse for the Freetown-Lakeville school district, but I shall never forget the innate kindness, class and dignity of my good friend from Taunton who never forgot where he came from and spelled Loyalty with a capital L!

I had mentioned that my father had played Seven Card Stud and High Low Jack to help pay his way through dental school and that he started playing cards at a very young age in the Parker House. My dad was great with numbers and could make a deck of cards almost dance across the table. The nimble and talented fingers that produced incredible sleight of hand card tricks like Three-Card Monte would later be used to take away the pain of patients in his dental chair. Dad taught me to never draw to an inside straight and sit with my back to a wall whenever possible. People loved my father and confided in him during his entire life. He had many friends and taught me that it was OK to have faith in people, but even though there was trust - you should always cut the cards!

Grandpa Doherty's brother Johnnie, who looked just like him, was a fun loving character who passed away when I was about seven years old. He was my father's uncle so it was the first Irish wake and funeral for my young eyes. I sat in the front seat after the funeral as my dad drove us to the collation while thinking about how this was going to be a very sad day as my imagination started picturing women crying, a dead body and elderly relatives hugging in consolation. I asked dad and he said that it wasn't going to be anything like that as the Irish celebrate death like it's an accomplishment!

The familiar sounds of Celtic music permeated the air as we got out of the car and headed inside. Dad opened the door and we walked into the middle of a serious party! Nobody was crying as backs were slapped and funny stories swapped as Irish whiskey flowed like Niagara Falls! A young guy was doing a jig in the corner as an older gentleman was keeping in time with the music. A nice lady said that Johnnie looked good and asked me if I wanted a soda. I have been to a lot of Irish wakes and funerals since then, but I'm glad my dad was with me for my first.

Sometimes our family would accompany our dad on some of his card playing trips at conventions and tournaments in New York and beyond. We were getting ready to pack for one of these sojourns when dad showed me a small suitcase that he had just purchased which had a locked latch with a three digit combination. Dad said that the combination could be created by registering three digits significant to the owner which he had just done and said that I would never guess the number. I thought for only a couple of seconds before saying 1-3-9 which caused my dad's jaw to drop in absolute amazement! He said I was correct, but how did I ever figure it out? I told him that it was the months of his three son's birthdays - Chris was born in January, Brendan in March and my birthday was in September, 1-3-9. He was even more surprised at my explanation as he called my mom into the room to hear what he was about to tell me. He said that I had the right answer for the wrong reason. He was born on School Street in Taunton and the address of the house was 139!

My cousin Thomas F. Doherty Jr., his lovely wife Mary, J. Do and I were having a lot of laughs while enjoying dinner at Luciano's in Wrentham where I have never had a bad meal. There is a long line of Thomas F. Dohertys including Mary and Tom's son. Tom's late father was Ted William's dentist, which is the source of a plethora of interesting stories about the greatest hitter who ever lived. Right after swallowing a juicy bite of mouthwatering sirloin steak, I was asked by Mary about my recent operation where a stent was placed near my heart. I mentioned that I now had heart doctor, but Mary thought I said that I had a "hot doctor!"

J. Do and I met Jerry Trupiano and his gregarious wife Donna at a house party where Al Pizzi and his lovely wife Carol were hosting a tremendous Christmas celebration. I had always enjoyed listening to Jerry broadcast Red Sox games alongside his radio play by play partner Joe Castiglione. Trupe was kind enough to take time out of his busy schedule to participate in our Law Day ceremony by providing audience introductions for Foxborough Police Officer Val Collins and her husband Jeremy, a Cambridge Firefighter. Val is now a sergeant and they were both in the cast of the TV show *Survivor* with Jeremy coming out the winner of a later *Survivor* episode and the one million dollar prize!

An ad in the newspaper announced that American League Cy Young Award Winner and World Series MVP Frank Viola was going to be making a celebrity appearance soon at a local car dealership so my bride had mentioned that she was going to stop by to meet him. The next day I was listening to the Red Sox game on the radio as they took on Minnesota at Fenway Park in Boston. Viola was on the mound for the Twins, baffling the home town team with his masterful finesse and sweet left handed offerings. J. Do was kind of half listening and hearing part of the broadcast from another room when Viola induced his fourth consecutive out from Sox batters. Trupiano proclaimed on the radio that Viola has now retired four in a row. J. Do, upon hearing the word "retired" said, "Hey, he can't retire. I'm going to see him tomorrow!"

I inherited my love of baseball from my dad who told colorful stories of Hall of Famers and took me to my first major league game at Fenway Park. Carl Yastrzemski, who wore #8, quickly became one of my childhood heroes making the summer of 1967 an exciting and memorable part of my youth. Everyone knew that #8 belonged to Yaz so that digit became almost magical in Boston. Long after his historic Triple Crown season and retirement Yaz had a grandson performing on the diamond for the San Francisco Giants so J. Do and I got tickets to see Mike Yastrzemski play the Sox at Fenway. The following year the talented outfielder with the famous last name came in 8th in the National League MVP vote. That number 8 sounds familiar!

A father and son had never played together on the same major league baseball team until the Seattle Mariners signed Ken Griffey Sr. to join future Hall of Famer Ken Griffey Jr. in the outfield. J. Do and I were seated behind home plate in the second row on a beautiful fall night to watch the Griffeys play against the home town team at Fenway Park. Right handed pitcher Mike Boddicker started the game for the Sox and induced the first batter to ground out bringing up the second man in the lineup, Ken Griffey Sr. to the left handed batter's box. The two-time World Series Champion connected with the 0-1 pitch driving the ball deep to right center field into the Red Sox bullpen for a home run. Baseball tradition dictates that the man crossing home plate is always greeted with congratulations from the on deck batter. Griffey Sr. was very familiar with the man giving him high fives as I told my bride that we were witnessing hardball history. There seemed to be a poignant aura of deep sentimental and heartfelt family emotion in the air as the elder Griffey was warmly greeted at the plate by the proud on-deck batter - his own son!

At the risk of sounding shallow and superficial, guys know that if you want to see what your girlfriend will look like when she gets older, just take a look at her mother. J. Do's mother Marie Currier is still a stunningly beautiful woman just like the first time I met her so right then I knew that the future looked real good!

J. Do asked me to stop at the store and pick up some diapers on the way home from making my rounds at the police stations. I knew from experience that the diaper size on the side of the package was listed by the weight of the baby. It reads, "Holds up to 10 pounds," or "Holds up to 20 pounds," etc. The poor guy next to me in the diaper aisle must have been a new father because he thought the pounds were the payload! He was serious when he asked me, "How can a baby shit out 20 pounds?"

J. Do's nephew Joe Currier is a true patriot having completed four tours of duty in Iraq and one in Afghanistan. The Army Sergeant First Class was traveling in the lead with his unit about 20 clicks south of Samarra in central Iraq when an IED exploded under the vehicle causing severe shrapnel wounds mostly to his face and left foot. The brave soldier was medevac'd to Germany, transferred to Walter Reed Hospital and completed most of his rehab at his home base of Fort Stewart, Georgia.

Upon his honorable discharge from the military Joe eventually landed a job with the Army Corps of Engineers as a Construction Control Representative and was looking forward to meeting the Chief of Construction for the New England District. The wounded warrior sat down in the Chief's office where they engaged in a lively conversation about different topics. Joe noticed that my book *SEVEN MILES AFTER SUNDOWN* was sitting on the boss' desk so when the discussion turned to striped bass fishing Joe pointed out that the book had been written by his uncle. The Chief wasn't sure if he heard correctly as it would seem to be a longshot that my book would be in the Concord Headquarters while my nephew was in the same room! Joe smiled and replied in the affirmative when the surprised Chief asked if his uncle was East End Eddie Doherty. Sometimes the world is smaller than we think!

J. Do talks to herself in the kitchen quite frequently. Sometimes it seems as though there is a full blown conversation going on in there so I never want to interrupt. I'm not really sure when she is talking to me so it is sometimes a guessing game as to if I should participate, but I have the best wife in the world so who cares if it sounds like there's a party going on in there!

J. Do used to take our two young daughters to doctor's appointments together at the same time for convenience sake. Six-year old Kaitlin and four-year old Chrissy were waiting with J. Do in the examination room for a new doctor that they had never met. Kaitlin was a good kid, but she grew up with the devil in her eye and always seemed to be up to something. The doctor walked in, introduced himself and asked Chrissy if she was Kaitlin to which Chrissy replied, "No, I'm Christine. I'm the good child!"

I guess that I have to plead guilty to being old fashioned. Our daughter Kaitlin was holding her cell phone and talking about getting a new app. I thought she was about to order an appetizer.

J. Do worked as a Speech & Language Assistant at Burrell and Igo Elementary Schools in Foxborough. A second grader was eating a cookie during the lunch break at Igo so J.

Do commented that it was such a big delicious looking cookie and asked if the chocolate chip treat had been baked by his mother. The little boy turned the cookie over, looked at the bottom and said, "No, if my mother made this it would be burned on the bottom!"

A 1st grader at the Igo School proudly told J. Do that her father was a firefighter. "That's great," she responded, "You should be very proud of him. What's your father's name?" The little girl said that her father's name was, "Daddy."

J. Do wanted to reward a 4th grade girl for doing something positive so she asked the little girl if she would like to have a sticker. The kid said, "No, I want a tattoo!"

On the first day of school Foxborough 3rd graders were in line waiting to buy lunch. One kid had a check from his mother to cover meal payment for the whole month. The little boy next to him was suddenly upset because his mother forgot to give him money for lunch. The 3rd grader with the check said, "That's OK, I've got a check. It's on me!"

One of the teachers told J. Do that her nails looked great and asked where she had them done to which J. Do replied, "I did them myself on the way to work this morning at a red light!"

My bride was doing some Christmas shopping at Walmart with her sister Cathy McNamara. The store telephone hanging on a post next to them started ringing, but there were no employees in the area to answer the call. The two sisters continued to have fun together as always, but the incessant ringing was becoming annoying so J. Do walked over and answered the phone by saying, "Walmart, may I help you?" It was an outside call from a woman who was looking for a certain kind of Barbie Doll for her daughter. Cathy was almost falling down laughing as J. Do told the woman that she had the doll in her hand and would leave it at customer service for her to pick up. She wrote the woman's name down and left it with the doll at customer service where she told the Walmart supervisor to save it for the customer. The supervisor wasn't quite sure if J. Do was a new employee or what to make of her!

My brother-in-law Gene McNamara and his lovely wife Cathy have a daughter named Jennifer, a Registered Nurse who is married to John Sanderson. John and Jennifer's oldest son Johnny, is a terrific young hockey player. He is no relation to the legendary former Bruins player Derek Sanderson, but that didn't stop Gene from having a little fun. Johnny was playing his heart out in a game outside of Boston when a man approached Gene to compliment him on the outstanding talent of his grandson. The guy was going on and on about how good he was and then asked if he had inherited his skating ability from any relatives to which Gene replied, "Well, his name is Sanderson!"

Gene and Cathy's son Jason is a union plumber who was working on a job in Boston where he appeared to be moving quickly and rushing his work. Another plumber saw this and said, "Hey Jason. Why so fast? Why are you rushin'?" to which Jason facetiously replied, "I'm not Russian, I'm Irish!"

J. Do came out of the Super Market and began to put the groceries in the car for the Thanksgiving Day Dinner. The back seat quickly filled up with bags so she placed the 27-pound turkey on the front passenger seat. As soon as she started the car the passenger seat belt warning buzzer went off so J. Do did the only thing that she could to silence the alarm. She clicked the seat belt in and fastened it around the turkey!

Celebrating Wedding Anniversary with 30,000 Red Sox fans

J. Do and I were coming home from a cookout when she asked me to stop at a Cumberland Farms. I pulled into the parking lot and parked a few spaces away from the convenience store's entrance. I remained outside as she went into the store to buy some milk. Another vehicle drove in and parked right next me. The 80-year old driver stayed behind the wheel as his wife, I presume, got out and went into the store. It was the exact same color and make as my car so when my bride walked out of the store she headed right for the wrong vehicle. J. Do opened the passenger door and sat down next to the elderly gentleman as he let out a scream like he was thwarting a potential carjacking! She quickly jumped out of the car, apologized and darted into our vehicle saying, "Let's get out of here before the police show up!"

We hadn't used the grill in the backyard for a few weeks so J. Do got a sudden surprise when she turned on the gas and opened the lid. A mouse had decided to build a nest and create a little rodent habitat inside the metal walls. J. Do freaked out and ran in the house while I went outside to turn off the gas. I left the grill cover up to encourage a voluntary exodus before an intense cleaning which prompted my bride to quickly say that if that mouse closes that grill cover tonight we're moving!

I had just issued a search warrant at the ADC when I received a call from NAPD Detective Dan Arrighi that my J. Do had been in a motor vehicle accident. Our daughter Chrissy had forgotten to bring her lunch to school so J. Do dropped it off and was returning home when she was rear ended by a driver on a cell phone. It was welcome news to hear the Detective say that my bride was not seriously injured. However, in her haste to deliver the lunch she had left the house without her usual cosmetic applications. As J. Do was being carefully put into the ambulance Detective Arrighi told her that he would call me so she thanked him and asked that he relay an important message. When the Detective called he said that, "Your wife is OK, but she asked me to tell you bring her red lipstick to the hospital!"

J. Do took my green car to work one day because she said that it matched her outfit!

My mother always had the quick witted timing of a standup comic. I was about 12 years old and very sick so I was standing with my head over the toilet and my hands on my knees. I was seconds away from becoming violently ill when my mother opened the bathroom door. I turned my head to look at her then quickly vomited into the toilet causing her to say, "Oh Jeez, I look that bad! I better put on some makeup!"

College dorm rooms are so small that many students build a wooden loft to increase living space. My roommate Roberto Santiago and I wanted to accomplish this by elevating our beds to somewhat resemble a second floor when we were freshmen. We had some lumber, but we needed a saw so I called my mother in Massachusetts and asked her to mail us the saw that was hanging up in the garage. My mom took the saw to the post office where the postal employee was kind enough to wrap it for her. She told the guy that she was mailing it to her son to which the man replied, "So where is he - in prison?"

I have always had a terrible snoring problem. In fact, it was so bad in college that guys in my dorm could hear me in the next room through the heavy cinder block wall. J. Do is a saint who will someday go right to heaven after suffering through a marriage of earth shattering decibels. One night, before she had cooked dinner, we were watching the evening news when a story came on about how people who snore can sustain very serious memory loss resulting in a failure to recall even recent events. A wry smile came over J. Do's face as she turned toward me and said, "I don't know if you remember, but I already cooked dinner and you really enjoyed it!"

The entire minor league baseball season was cancelled in 2020 as a result of the coronavirus so the loyal PawSox fans were unable to attend games in what would have been the last year in McCoy Stadium before the team moved from Pawtucket to their new ballpark in Worcester.

J. Do and I attended many games there with our kids and friends over the years in an inexpensive family-oriented atmosphere. Attorney Peter F. Murphy was thoughtful enough to invite us to his tailgate party in the parking lot before one of the games. Pete is a brilliant lawyer with a frequent smile on his face so we had a fantastic time at the cookout, but our seven-year old Kaitlin insisted on standing beyond the left field fence to try to catch a batting practice home run. Older children would rush in front of her to snag balls that seemed headed her way so the poor kid was starting to get a little frustrated. I tried to coax her over to Pete's party for a hot dog, but she was determined to catch a souvenir. It was a muggy day so Kaitlin took off her baseball cap and wiped the perspiration from her forehead. Her hand was clutched onto the bill of the baseball cap which was momentarily being held upside down as suddenly a baseball came sailing over the fence and landed right in her hat! She was elated at what looked to be a gift from heaven and we were relieved that she could now have something to eat, but instead of enjoying a burger she said that she wanted to go back to the fence to catch another ball for her sister Chrissy!

We had finished unpacking after moving into our retirement condo, but the large bathroom mirror that J. Do had ordered had not yet been delivered. Kaitlin stopped by and went into the bathroom to brush her hair, but when she couldn't find a mirror she said, "What are you people doing - sitting Shiva!"

Kait & husband Jon (S. Campbell photo)

The Honorable Francis T. Crimmins Jr. was sitting in Attleboro at the time and I was his session clerk so I took the judge to a PawSox game one night after work. First we stopped at my house on Stanson Drive in North Attleborough for a change of clothes and it would be years before our young daughters stopped referring to him as, "the nice judge who gets changed in the bedroom." This was Frank's very first minor league game so when we were half way to Pawtucket I popped in a cassette by the band Alabama. I told Frank that he should listen carefully to the next song as it described the minor league experience to perfection. Frank loved the song "Cheap Seats" so much that we both started singing it in my car. He later had it played at his daughter Melissa's wedding and came over to our table to say, "That was for you!"

I always looked forward to attending PawSox games with my brother Chris who shared my enthusiasm for America's Pastime. We saw future Hall of Famers Jim Rice, Carlton Fisk, Wade Boggs and other great players like Bruce Hurst before they became millionaires as well as a young right handed pitcher fresh out of college named Roger Clemens. Chris really liked slugger Mo Vaughn, but I thought that Carlos Quintana would eventually make a better first baseman so we would go back and forth debating the positive attributes of each player, but Chris was proven to be the better judge of talent as Vaughn would go on to win the American League MVP Award.

Chris and I would also see players who were established stars who had been sent to the minor league team for physical rehab or to fine tune their games. We were two of the 9,389 standing room only fans who were lucky enough to be there on a July summer night in 1982 when a couple of former American League Rookies of the Year toed the rubber at McCoy Stadium. Dave Righetti, Rookie of the Year for the New York Yankees the previous season was pitching for the Columbus Clippers against Mark "The Bird" Fidrych and the PawSox. Fidrych, a Northborough native, had become an overnight sensation as a rookie in 1976 when he won 19 games for the Detroit Tigers and led the major leagues in ERA. I worked at Foxborough Raceway with Joe Hebert who said he had coached Fidrych as a kid and was the first to tell me that he talked to the ball while standing on the mound, although Fidrych's daughter Jessica told me many years later that her father talked to himself and not the ball. The hype surrounding this matchup was incredibly intense as evidenced by the official attendance count that almost doubled the actual number of available seats. Righetti pitched terrific that night, allowing two earned runs and striking out a dozen PawSox before leaving the game after six innings. Pawtucket won the game 7-5, however, as the Sox rallied twice and battled back with Fidrych working his way out of trouble while throwing a nine-inning complete game.

Joe Morgan managed the PawSox in the longest professional game in baseball history which was played in Pawtucket. The PawSox took the field in this historic contest against the Rochester Red Wings, the Triple A affiliate of the Baltimore Orioles on a cold windy night in April of 1981. The score was still tied up when the game was called off at around 4AM after 32 innings. The following quote of Joe's late wife Dottie is from Kevin Cullen of *The Boston Globe*, " 'Dottie Morgan was at home in Walpole preparing Easter dinner after midnight when she realized her husband should be home. She called the stadium and couldn't believe the game was still going. "Joe could have come home a lot earlier," she said. "He got thrown out in the 22d inning.'" The game resumed in June with the PawSox winning on a Dave Koza single over the head of future Hall of Famer Cal Ripken that drove in future 1986 ALCS MVP Marty Barrett in the 33rd inning!

Oliva's Market in Milford has been serving cold and piping hot quality food to an ever expanding loyal customer base since I was a kid. Their specialty is the BOG which stands for Babe Oliva Grinder and is one of the best subs that I have ever eaten. I got to know Babe's son Nick as they did a terrific job of catering the annual clambake for the Association of Clerk-Magistrates and Assistants. They also catered the post-game meal for the Boston Red Sox so it was nice to have a conversation with Nick one time on Van Ness Street as he was making his way into the clubhouse at Fenway Park. Nick is a charismatic guy who enjoys making people happy with his delicious cooking so he got to know Joe Morgan during his preparations of the after game spread. Al Pizzi, Carmine M. Simonelli, Franklin Auto Body owner Dick DeMarzi and I attended the induction ceremony at McCoy Stadium when Morgan was inducted into the PawSox Hall of Fame in 2017. Carmine, who is the very capable First Assistant Clerk-Magistrate of the Westborough District Court, brought a BOG for Joe as he knew that the guest of honor would enjoy the

Boston Red Sox Manager Joe Morgan (Barry Okun photo)

famous product of Oliva's. Joe was asked by one of the reporters at the ceremony if he thought Roger Clemens should be in the Hall of Fame to which he replied, "Oh yeah, he made lots of money for me!"

Joe Morgan is one of the nicest guys with whom I have ever had the pleasure of sharing a golf cart. Both of his parents were born in Ireland and his stories of some of the all-time great ballplayers he played with and against are veritable legends so it was an honor to play 18 on more than one occasion with the pride of Walpole. I have always thought that the Board of Selectmen should promote the town with an oversized sign displaying Joe's famous quote, "If you don't live in Walpole, you're just camping out!"

Joe would be promoted to the big league club and begin the 1988 season as the 3rd Base Coach of the Boston Red Sox before being named Manager at the All-Star break. The former Boston College standout knows baseball inside and out with his classy down to earth approach to problem solving supplementing his well thought out superior diamond strategies. The blue collar off season snow plow driver, behind the wheel for the blizzard of '78, inspired the team to win his first dozen games and 19 of the initial 20 with him at the helm! A new slogan came off the presses as Morgan Magic became the talk of the town and the entire baseball world. Morgan and the Boston Red Sox eventually won the American League East, but were defeated in ALCS by a tough Athletics team with future Hall of Famer Dennis Eckersley saving all four games for Oakland. Joe Morgan would lead the team to winning the Division again in 1990 and become a local legend who will never be forgotten by the fans of the Boston Red Sox.

World Series in Boston

It is only natural that married couples become familiar with their spouse's job and this was especially true for my bride who answered our home phone so often for bail and search warrant requests from police officers as well as notification of prisoner status. It wasn't unusual for J. Do to take a call and then yell to me in the shower that the Norton PD has six ready to go.

I actually used to get a kick out of how much criminal procedure J. Do had acquired simply by hearing my phone conversations and she knew that the release fee was $40.00 at this time. The Celtics had just won another championship so the Boston Police were trying to keep the peace and maintain civility with the crowd in front of the Boston Garden when they arrested two guys who were acting up. We were watching the TV news which showed the two handcuffed defendants being put in a cruiser. As soon as J. Do saw that she said, "There's $80 bucks!"

Grandmothers are known as nana, grandma or various other monikers and my bride is called Grammie Jo. Her steadfast devotion to our family results in her driving our five grandchildren around so I put a bumper sticker on the back of her car that reads - GRAMMIE JO TAXI SERVICE. J. Do was in a line of cars at the Dunkin' drive thru when the vehicles in front of her moved up, but she didn't because her attention was focused on her mirror and the reapplication of a fresh coat of lipstick. The guy in the car behind her beeped the horn and, seeing the bumper sticker, yelled, "Let's go Grammie Jo!" Another time, after seeing the bumper sticker, a woman actually tried to hire J. Do asking how much it would cost to get to New Bedford because she thought that she was really a cab driver.

My massive eyebrows have long been a source of humor, described by one friend as being so bushy they look like two caterpillars mating on my forehead and my barber once said he was going to have to use a hedge trimmer to cut through the hairy appendages!
My daughter Chrissy and I were at a function back when people were still wearing covid masks when I spotted an old friend across the room. I waved to Doug Forbes who I served with on the Homeland Security Task Force, but hadn't seen in years due to covid and retirement. Doug, who was the southeastern Massachusetts coordinator for the Massachusetts Emergency Management Agency, came over and greeted me with an enthusiastic, "Hi Eddie, how are you?". We had a nice conversation, but after he walked away I mentioned to Chrissy that I was surprised that Doug recognized me after all this time, even while I was wearing a mask. Chrissy just smiled and said that Doug probably knew it was me because I have the biggest eyebrows in the Commonwealth!

J. Do and I were at home when we received one of the worst phone calls imaginable. Our ten-year old daughter Chrissy had been playing in the garage at her friend's house when she somehow became impaled on the sharp blade of a rototiller. The large blade had pierced her foot and calf leaving the poor kid in intense pain and anguish. North Attleborough Fire Department personnel quickly responded and dismantled the machine by disassembling the blade while leaving it in her leg. Chrissy was transported by ambulance to Sturdy Memorial Hospital where the huge blade was removed, our prayers were answered and she was set on the path to a full recovery. Our family will always be grateful to the outstanding doctors & compassionate nurses at Sturdy and for the swift response, calming professionalism and quick thinking of EMTs Dale Collard & Michael Fulton; Paramedic John Underhill, John Cooper & Chris Coleman from the Rescue Squad; Firefighters John Devlin & Scott Forbes and Lieutenant Ronald Meyer as well as the dedication of off duty Captain Peter Cullen who had responded to the horrific scene from his own home.

After Chrissy graduated from college I was attending a Trial Court educational seminar with hundreds of other employees in a huge conference room when I received a call from her that she had passed her nursing boards and that she would now have a license to work as a Registered Nurse. I was so proud and overjoyed that I suddenly announced the good news to the entire audience who were kind enough to recognize my pride with thunderous applause.

There is nothing that can stop the dedication of a nurse. Our daughter Chrissy was walking into Boston Children's Hospital on a day that was so cold that her eyelashes froze to her face during the short walk between her car and the hospital!

Chrissy was working her shift at Boston Children's Hospital where one of her young patients had some chest pain. Chrissy gave the five-year old girl some pain medication as well as some orange pajamas to wear for the night. When Chrissy stopped back latter in a few minutes to check on the patient's pain she found the poor kid crying. Chrissy asked what the matter was and if the pain was still bad to which the fashion conscious little girl wiped away her tears while telling Chrissy, "It doesn't hurt anymore, but I just can't wear this color!" Chrissy explained that the sizes are color coded and that she can get her blue pajamas, but they will be too big for her. Chrissy retrieved some blue pajamas, rolled up the sleeves and put a smile on the little diva's face!

Chrissy & husband Dan

Tom Brady became the Greatest Of All Time playing quarterback for the New England Patriots while leading his team to six Super Bowl victories and then another in his first year with the Tampa Bay Buccaneers. Our family was watching Brady carve up the Chicago Bears' defense on TV during his second season in Tampa when the conversation turned to age. We all agreed that it was simply amazing that Brady could continue to compete at such a high level with his body seeming to defy conventional age limitations. We were wondering just how many years he could play when my son-in-law Dan said, "Someday Brady might be the first professional quarterback on Medicare!"

My two brothers and I were flying to Dublin for the first time when Brendan noticed that the big guy sitting a few rows in front of us on the plane was former heavyweight boxer George Chuvalo who had fought Ali, Frazier, Quarry, Ellis, Patterson, Terrell and Foreman. We struck up a nice conversation with the man who was never knocked down in 93 professional fights and of whom, after their first brawl for the Heavyweight Title, Muhammad Ali stated, "He's the toughest guy I ever fought." George was managing boxers and was kind enough to invite us to the fights in Dublin, but we were anxious to see our Irish cousins. It was very considerate and thoughtful, however, of the good natured heavyweight who had knocked out 63 opponents in his 73 wins before retiring.

Heavyweight George Chuvalo

Day one of our first journey had been memorable just for being there. My brothers and I were seated at a table celebrating our heritage and quenching our thirst in a small pub in Dublin. The friendly patrons made us feel so welcome that I almost forgot that we were in a foreign land. I made my way to the bar to purchase three more pints for us and stood behind a gentleman who was drinking a beer while the bartender prepared the rest of his order. He turned his smiling face toward me and said, "Lad, don't forget to have your Vitamin G," as he held up a perfectly poured pint of Guinness!

We took a tour of the Guinness factory at St. James Gate in Dublin which culminates in a beautiful bar where you can sample the cold dark colored product. It is very common to see signs in Ireland advertising Guinness. They often will read, "Guinness, it's good for you!" After seeing enough of these signs you almost begin to think of it as a medical issue and drink it for your good health!

Two brothers singing at cousin's pub in Ballyjamesduff, Ireland

At least some and probably all of my great-grandparents were born in Ireland. After my brothers and I travelled to visit our cousins there for the first time in 1994 we came back to Dublin and celebrated in Ballyjamesduff which is the home town of our mother's family. The three of us returned the next time with our mother and enjoyed a reunion with our cousins in the family homestead where they still live today. We all watched with great pride as the Irish family matriarch May Lynch and our mom embraced in an emotional hug that seemed to shorten the distance across the sea.

Three brothers with cousin May Lynch, Ballyjamesduff, Ireland

I returned to Ireland for a third time in 2002, this time with J. Do and our daughters, 13-year old Christine and Kaitlin who had just turned 15. It was a ten-day trip so naturally they each packed enough outfits for a two month stay! Many of the narrow winding roads in Ireland seem to be created for a horse and buggy so the best car you can get is a very small one, but unfortunately an economy size vehicle wasn't big enough to hold the

Ladies Clothing Department that we were hauling around! I had to rent a large Mercedes with just enough interior space to be able to squeeze all the suitcases in between the kids. I looked in the rear view mirror to see two little faces peering out between the luggage piled to the roof. Driving an oversized vehicle on tightly constricted cow paths requires intense concentration to avoid an accident. I had to say no when the girls wanted the radio on as it was stressful enough trying to concentrate on the wrong side of the road and in the rotaries which the Irish call roundabouts. My brother Brendan had done a superior job of driving on our first two trips so I wish that we had him behind the wheel for this one. One time we just barely avoided a collision with a rambling Guinness truck that came speeding at us from the opposite direction and another time I had to slam on the brakes for a couple of wandering cows.

We had a terrific time visiting J. Do's cousins in Galway and my mother's family in Ballyjamesduff. Kaitlin had been assigned a summer reading tally from school and one of the books on the list was *Angela's Ashes* by Frank McCourt so we headed for Limerick which was the setting for the memoir. I think that I can say with a very high degree of certainty that our Kaitlin was the only kid in her class who had her photo taken that summer standing off the road next to the sign that reads, WELCOME TO LIMERICK.

Back when I was single, I owned a brand new BMW which was long before most people had ever even heard of them, but as I grew older my priorities shifted as I lost my fascination with top end vehicles. Now, a car has everything I need if it starts every time and keeps running safely.

The new law in Massachusetts prohibits cell phone use while driving unless hands free. I have an older model vehicle so I was looking into getting it modified so that the phone could be operated in hands free mode. I mentioned this to my brothers as we were having lunch at The Inn on Shipyard Park in Mattapoisett. My brother Brendan said not to worry because my car will be all set as long as it has Bluetooth. I told him that my 17-year old Honda Accord doesn't have Bluetooth, as a matter of fact, it's so old that it probably doesn't have any teeth!

J. Do and I were watching an episode of the TV show *Blue Bloods* when the defendant's lawyer entered the police station. The attorney was actually a real lawyer playing himself - the famous Bruce Cutler who had represented Gambino crime family boss John Gotti and had become a household name in American jurisprudence. J. Do smiled, immediately looked at me and said, "Maybe they could use a real Clerk-Magistrate on this show!"

Even after retirement, J. Do stays in touch with her friends from the North Attleborough area including those she worked with in the school department-celebrating birthdays and enjoying trips to different places in New England. Any given outing may include Patty Bray, Cathy Pizzuto, Anne Keating, Fran Sonis, Cathy Mulcahy, Jackie Buckner, Kristen Siddle, Connie McLaughlin, and Fran Stilwell. They are all lovely ladies that I have come to know who have an outstanding sense of humor just like my bride.

A birthday celebration was held for J. Do at Kelly's Place in Norton where they enjoyed the delicious food and outstanding service. She received a beautiful oversized coffee mug from Jackie which she loved so much she showed it to me as soon as she got home. She had her coffee in it while remarking about how perfect it was and how much she liked the colorful red design featuring a heart over an X & O. Notwithstanding their agreement to forgo gifts, Jackie had told J. Do that she had to buy the mug because, "it is so you!" Unfortunately, after a few days it fell out of her hand onto the kitchen floor resulting in the handle breaking off the cherished gift. This was about as close to depression as I have ever seen my happy soulmate because of her affinity for the mug. She even kept using it without the handle while carefully avoiding the jagged sharp edges protruding from the break. She turned down my offer to sand it smooth as she mentally powered her way through the acceptance of her disabled caffeine comrade. Our daughter Kait secretly helped get me a new one online so while J. Do was out I replaced the broken cup with a brand new identical mug. She spotted it as soon as she came home and started screaming to me from the kitchen. Her mind was racing as she considered all kinds of possibilities while I told her that maybe the mug had grown a new handle, but I then quickly confessed for fear of her losing her mind! J. Do smiled as she said, "I thought I had dementia!"

J. Do and I had the genuine pleasure of meeting actors Chazz Palminteri & Joe Pantoliano at an event in Providence. The well-respected actors are easily recognized mostly from their appearances in movies and on TV as well as ancillary endeavors in the world of entertainment. Both have reached out to help others and received numerous awards for their work as they are admired by colleagues in the industry as well as by an enormous fan base. They were very gracious, interesting, and outgoing as we enjoyed the conversation with the two legends of Hollywood.

Actors Chazz Palminteri & Joe Pantoliano

8. Grandkids

Our first grandchild was a beautiful little girl named Adalyn. One day our daughter Chrissy was giving her breakfast as the infant kept saying Da, but not Ma, causing the mother to say, "Hey Addie, don't forget who's feeding you!"

Grandchildren at Sabrina & cousin Brendan's wedding. L-R Addie, Joe, Rose, Molly, Lucy (Chrissy Ehlers photo)

We were babysitting for our youngest grandchild one day at our condo. J. Do placed Molly on a blanket on the floor next to me as I went through my exercise routine. Part of my regiment includes holding one leg at a time straight up to stretch muscles and relieve lower back pain. As soon as I stuck my right leg up in the air 5 month old Molly smiled and did the same with her right leg!

Chrissy's husband Dan was trying his best to say Grace while leaning over the dining room table next to one-year old Rose who was screaming during the prayer. Dan would say, "We thank you Lord…" as Rose yelled louder so he would raise his voice a few decibels and she would follow suit. They went back and forth until we were all glad to hear Dan say "Amen."

Not long after her first birthday, our granddaughter Lucy became interested in cell phones. Someone would leave a phone on a table and Lucy would pick it up and say hello as if there were someone on the other end. We taught her to swipe with her finger so she could look at photos. Somehow Lucy got the impression that she had to actually say the word "swipe" as her finger moved across the screen. She would sit there swiping her finger and saying, "swipe, swipe, swipe!"

Sometimes J. Do takes our two-year old grandson Joe with her to the bank. She goes to the drive thru where they always give Joe a lollipop during the transaction so he associates the financial institution with a sweet treat. J. Do tries to teach Joe new words so as she was approaching the lane for the drive up window she slowly emphasized the word bank to try to get Joe to say it. Joe was sitting in his car seat in the back listening to Grammie Jo so as soon as she said bank he said, "Pop."

Right about the time when our granddaughter Rose turned one she started giving long speeches of baby talk babble. She would try very hard to formulate words as she would just go on and on with long sentences of incoherent baby talk. Rose would keep on going like a marathon filibuster on the Senate Floor. Come to think of it, Rose seemed to make more sense than some United States Senators!

Our daughter Chrissy and son-in-law Dan were nice enough to invite us over to their house for dinner. Chrissy was with our granddaughter Lucy at the supermarket that morning food shopping for the evening meal. Just like most kids, Lucy loves ice cream so she quickly cooked up a scheme to convince her mother to buy some as Chrissy pushed the shopping cart down the frozen foods aisle. The two-year old spotted ice cream in the freezer section and quickly said to her mother, "Grampy and Grammie are coming tonight so we should get some ice cream for them!"

Kait and our 20 month old granddaughter Molly were visiting their neighbor Liza Grosso who has a beautiful brown lab named Brady. Molly absolutely adores Brady, named after Tom, whose tail starts going as soon as he spots the cheerful toddler. Liza's son has long outgrown a highchair, but she is such a good friend that she keeps one in the kitchen just for Molly's visits. Molly sat in the highchair eating white powdered donuts while Brady sat on the floor close by waiting for a crumb to fall with his eyes trained on her every move. Kait told Molly not to feed the dog and turned away to speak with Liza. Molly's love for Brady was just too strong so when Kait looked again the evidence was clear - notwithstanding the little girl's innocent smile, Brady had white donut powder smudged all over his nose!

J. Do purchased a talking doll for our 18 month old granddaughter Rose and brought it back to our condo about three weeks before Christmas. The motion-activated Baby Kisses by Playzone blows kisses and giggles so realistically that it sounds just like a real baby. The doll would start laughing every time we walked by it in the living room so my bride decided to keep it in a bag in the basement until Christmas.

Tom Cook, a nice guy who works for Alarm New England, came to our home to install an upgrade on our alarm panel. He went down to the basement and happened to walk by the bag containing Baby Kisses which set off the real life sounding giggles coming from a dark corner of the cellar. The poor guy was startled and probably concerned for a moment until J. Do told him it was only a doll!

I read at least two newspapers per day so it is common for young kids to remember their surroundings more than we sometimes think as they are very impressionable. J. Do was reading a book to our three-year old grandson Joe that featured pictures to be associated with words. Grammie Jo pointed to a picture of a newspaper in the book which caused Joe to say, "Grampy!"

Sometimes we all see someone driving erratically, acting counter productively or basically doing something that causes us to think that the world would be a better place if the person had stayed home and never left the house. When I see something like this I have a habit of saying out loud inside my own car, as if I were speaking directly to the miscreant, "Get back on the couch!"

Kids hear things and never forget. J. Do and I were bringing our four-year old granddaughter Addie back home after her swimming lesson at the Middleborough YMCA. She was in the car seat in the back when a crazy driver laid down some rubber and sped by our vehicle with a roaring loud muffler. J. Do and I both had a good laugh when we heard the young four-year old little voice coming from the back say, "Get back on the couch!"

An unseasonably warm winter day produced a unique opportunity for our three-year old grandson Joe to play on the slide and swings at the Mattapoisett Town Beach. Our daughter Kaitlin met us there and dropped Joe off before leaving to do some errands. Joe was having a good time as J. Do and I pushed him on the swings and had a lot of laughs. Tim Seeberger, a dynamic writer and photographer for *Sippican Week*, showed up and started snapping photos of Joe as he was coming down the slide. The next issue had a beautiful photo on the front page of our smiling grandson as he zipped down the slide to the beach. The same issue also had a short story announcing some details about my upcoming surfcasting seminars at Bass Pro Shops in Foxborough and the RI Convention Center listed deep inside the paper, far away from the front page. I was never happier to be on page 20 when our grandson made page 1!

J. Do was visiting her mother in Florida so I decided to take our daughters and three youngest grandchildren out to breakfast at Jake's Diner in Fairhaven. The kids were feasting on their chocolate chip pancakes as we were enjoying the delicious food with smiles all around. Suddenly, 22-month old Molly lifted a huge pancake off the plate with her fork and power flipped the breakfast disk off the utensil straight up in the air high above our heads. I was sitting right across from her and couldn't believe how far the pancake traveled before coming straight down and landing right back on her plate. We all laughed and Molly couldn't stop giggling at what almost seemed like a successful circus trick!

During the coronavirus outbreak J. Do and I would visit our family in their yard allowing for interaction without getting too close. I was speaking on the phone with our four-year old granddaughter Addie and told her that we were coming to her house when she declared, "The Governor said to stay home!"

A couple of weeks later our daughter Chrissy offered some of her lunch to Addie's sister Lucy to which the three-year old replied, "The Governor said not to share food!" These girls may be the only young kids in America quoting Governor Charlie D. Baker!

9. Politics

George K. Regan Jr. was hired as a reporter for *The Boston Globe* at the young age of 17 and was rewarded with his first byline when he was only 18. He served as Press Secretary for Boston Mayor Kevin H. White and went on to found his own Public Relations firm located on the historic Union Wharf in the capital city. Regan Communications Group represents many famous clients and has become the largest privately owned PR firm in New England. George always has his ear to the ground and is one of the sharpest, nicest, funniest, most generous and creative professionals that I have ever known.

J. Do and I always have a terrific time at the poolside cookouts at his beautiful Willowbend home in Mashpee and enjoy listening to the famous James Montgomery Blues Band playing from the second floor at the legendary Christmas parties at his Marina Bay condo in Quincy! I have had some interesting conversations there with James who still plays to sold out venues as a highly sought-after musician, but continues to bend sweet notes out of his blues harp right in George's house!

James Montgomery before playing at Elizabeth & George Regan's Willowbend home

George had a beautiful Pekingese named Brother Bailey who made an appearance at every event and was the star of the show. J. Do and I even attended a birthday party for the dog at George's office in Boston. The guests included former Mayor Ray Flynn, City Councilor Mike Flaherty, former Boston Police Deputy Superintendent Gerry McHale and many others. George happened to have been engaged in an ongoing yet long forgotten argument with *Boston Globe* columnist Steve Bailey at the time he was deciding on a name for the good-natured canine. He told Steve that the dog looked just like him so he was naming it Brother Bailey! The cuddly pooch never ate dog food so he would excitedly greet

George when he came home with leftovers from Davio's, Ninety Nine Restaurant & Pub and Legal Sea Foods! When the time came, George couldn't bring himself to say that his loyal companion had died after living more than 17 years so he announced to his friends that Brother Bailey had retired. Brother Bailey was the oldest dog of his breed in the Commonwealth so maybe the secret to his longevity was that his master had fed him nothing but human food!

Former Governor William F. Weld was running to unseat President Trump in the Republican Primary. Weld hired Regan Communications Group for the campaign as was reported in the November 26, 2019 edition of *The Boston Globe* by Jon Chesto. George was responsible for a lot of smiling faces as Chesto quoted him for the story. "There's no comparison between the brainpower of Bill Weld and Donald Trump," Regan says. "Bill Weld speaks six languages fluently and Donald Trump has trouble with the English language."

J. Do and I were honored to attend the lavish wedding of George and his beautiful bride Elizabeth. The first night of the magnificent three day event kicked off with legendary comedian Steve Sweeney performing at their Willowbend home. Celebrity guests from many vocations enjoyed the festivities as Governor Charlie D. Baker officiated the marriage ceremony the next afternoon at Nauticus Marina in Osterville on a memorable day that will never be forgotten.

Norfolk County Treasurer Mike Bellotti, author, Boston City Council President Ed Flynn at Elizabeth & George Regan's wedding

Once nominated as a clerk-magistrate or judge by the governor, a hearing is scheduled at the State House before the Governor's Council which is also known as the Executive Council. This body is an assembly of eight elected councilors from districts throughout the Commonwealth who take turns questioning the nominee and usually vote on his or her candidacy the following week. Tradition dictates that the hearing be chaired by the councilor who represents the district where the nominee lives so Kelly A. Timilty did a terrific job as the chair of my hearing. The kind hearted councilor from District 2 went out of her way to make me feel comfortable and provided extensive background intelligence for my benefit. Kelly was the daughter of former Senator Joe Timilty and the sister of Senator Jim Timilty who would become a frequent lunch companion of mine.

Governor A. Paul Cellucci's legal team suggested that the nominee produce character witnesses from different walks of life to testify so I was grateful that a judge, former congressional aide, attorney and a senator agreed to take time out of their busy lives to say nice things about me.

I also needed someone from the private sector to round out my group so I asked Greg Murphy who has never worked for any government agency. When it was Murph's time to testify he told the story of my very first golf tournament which had been organized at Ballymeade Country Club by Attorney Peter S. Mrowka, an outstanding lawyer and great baseball agent. Murph, who is a very good golfer, explained to the councilors how I had called him after the tournament and told him how I had enjoyed myself and had fun notwithstanding my terrible golf score of 136! Murph then went on to testify that he really didn't know much about what it takes to be a clerk-magistrate, but that he would imagine that honesty is an important quality to have in the court system, so that any guy who admits to shooting a 136 has to be an honest man! The Governor's Councilors burst out laughing and voted unanimously to confirm my nomination a week later.

Governor's Councilor Dr. David F. Constantine was a very sociable, engaging and decent man as well as being an accomplished golfer. He represented southeastern Massachusetts in District 1 and would later jokingly tell me that he felt obligated to vote in my favor to make me a clerk-magistrate because it was obvious that I wasn't going to be able to make a living playing golf!

Attorney Christopher A. Iannella Jr. represented District 4 on the Governor's Council and still does to this day. I used to enjoy speaking with him later at Somerville Court Clerk-Magistrate Teddy Tomasone's times in the North End as Chris is an outstanding Governor's Councilor, great guy and the only one still serving who voted for me.

Some people, like Governor's Councilor Edward M. O'Brien, spelled the word Loyalty with a capital L. His very talented and extremely capable daughter Shannon O'Brien was Treasurer of the Commonwealth and the Democratic Nominee for Governor in 2002. The great District 8 Councilor had been hospitalized with a serious illness that prevented him from attending my hearing and vote. The passionate political legend from western Massachusetts called me from his hospital bed to assure me that I had the necessary votes for confirmation, but that if it appeared, for any unknown reason, that a successful vote was in jeopardy, he asked me to call him so that he could travel to Boston in an ambulance to cast a vote in my favor at the State House. There aren't very many of those old school guys left so that kind of Loyalty is never forgotten!

Governor's Council Administrative Secretary George F. Cronin Jr. and Executive Secretary Valerie McCarthy were very helpful to me with Valerie continuing the tradition of excellence while now serving as the Administrative Secretary. The vote on my nomination was scheduled for the following Wednesday which just happened to fall on April Fool's Day, thus providing a bit of comical material for some of my friends. "You got confirmed, no you didn't!"

J. Do and I raised our family in her hometown of North Attleborough where public service is considered to be a sacred honor. Marie Clarner, a nice person who chairs the Planning Board, does a terrific job in a complex field.

Jo Ann Cathcart, who has helped me and countless others over the years, served with distinction as Civilian Assistant to the Police Chief prior to being elected to a seat on the Town Council.

I was unanimously appointed by the North Attleborough Board of Selectmen in 1996 to be a Charter Member of the Advisory Committee of the Human Rights Commission. It was an honor to serve with a terrific group of sincere individuals who were all dedicated to a righteous and worthy cause. Congressional Aide Rick Leco, a terrific guy, did an outstanding job as the Vice Chair and would later testify on my behalf before the Governor's Council. They were all nice people and one lady had a particularly funny sense of humor. At one of the meetings somebody mentioned that a product was supposed to be "user friendly." Rene Araujo got a big laugh with her response of, "I've been used before and there was nothing friendly about it!"

Attorney Christopher P. DiOrio is an exceptionally bright lawyer and a very funny guy who has no trouble employing self-deprecating humor. It takes a lot of guts to say some of the things that Chris says about himself which makes him a strong person defined with an easy laugh. Just like many of us he has fought to keep his weight down, but has always been a bit on the heavy side which contributed to one of his many humorous stories. After graduating from law school and passing the bar exam Chris was working as a public defender in a Bronx courthouse in New York City. Unbeknownst to him, there was a deranged criminal aiming a rifle out of an open window directly across the street from the court. He didn't like attorneys so as Chris exited the courthouse and started to walk down the stairs to the sidewalk the disturbed sniper took a shot and wounded the jocular lawyer with the bullet piercing his hand. Chris' remarkable sense of humor served him well when he told me later that, "The guy was a lousy shot. He took aim at 350 pounds of lawyer and all he could hit was my hand!"

United States Congressman Stephen F. Lynch is a Democrat from South Boston who represents the Massachusetts Eighth Congressional District in Washington. Attorney DiOrio, who now has an office in Hingham, and Congressman Lynch know each other because they shared an apartment while attending Boston College Law School. I remain grateful for the American Flag that the great Congressman had flown over the United States Capitol in my honor to celebrate my retirement. Congressman Lynch was kind enough to agree to take time out of his busy schedule to present the Spirit of American Justice Award to then Norfolk County Register of Probate and now Sheriff Patrick W. McDermott at the WDC, but unfortunately he lost his mother whose funeral was on the same day as our Law Day Ceremony. I served as the MC for the event and asked the audience for a moment of silence to honor the legendary Congressman's mother.

US Congressman Stephen F. Lynch

J. Do cooks a huge corned beef and cabbage dinner for our family on St. Patrick's Day that just somehow seems to get better every year. I used to go to the annual St. Patrick's Day Breakfast in South Boston, usually with J. Do. This is truly the event of the year providing a bit of history, comedy and political jabs all in good natured fun. Tradition calls for the State Senator from the South Boston District to serve as host of the breakfast so then Senator Lynch followed in the storied footsteps of Massachusetts Senate President Bill Bulger and was immediately followed in that capacity by Senator Jack Hart, Senator Linda Dorcena Forry and Boston City Council President Bill Linehan with Senator Nick Collins currently hosting the proceedings. This televised event was later held in the Convention Center, but when I first started attending everyone squeezed into the Local 7 Ironworkers Hall. It was a nice facility, but was practically bursting at the seams to hold the overflowing crowd celebrating the High Holiday of the Irish. Long tables held traditional Irish cuisine with chairs so close together that once seated you were really trapped in place for the long haul. Your chair couldn't be backed up more than an inch to get out so experience would dictate a trip to the men's room just before going to the table.

One time I was squeezed into an area near the center of the room and Chris DiOrio was a few tables over to the right of the stage. We had already finished eating and were about two hours into the program as speakers continued to regale the audience with humor and sharp elbows. United States Congressman Joe Moakley, the great Representative from South Boston, was at the podium entertaining the crowd with his Irish wit when all of a sudden Chris needed a bathroom break. He couldn't back his chair up enough to get through the crowd so he did the only thing that he could - he climbed up on top of the relatively narrow table and tried to gingerly tip toe around the empty plates. The people surrounding me immediately talked of hoping that the table would hold the big guy and not break under him. Congressman Moakley, without missing a beat, saw Chris maneuvering down the table to his left and said something very close to, "Oh great, right in the middle of my act they bring out the belly dancer!"

South Boston Breakfast

Congressman Lynch always delivered funny lines while hosting the St. Patrick's Day Breakfast including his mention of Mayor Tom Menino who was seated close by. A 78-year old grandmother was arrested for selling drugs in the projects of South Boston so Congressman Lynch facetiously quoted Mayor Menino as saying, "Where were the parents?"

Mayor Menino served five terms as Mayor and was elected President of the United States Conference of Mayors. The legendary public servant was famous for his devoted constituency work and became the longest serving mayor in Boston history.

CPO Al Pizzi and I went in together for the Grand Opening of the John Joseph Moakley United States Courthouse in the Seaport District of Boston. This is a magnificent building in a beautiful location. I think they have 27 courtrooms

Mayor Tom Menino

equipped with all the latest technology and modern amenities. The huge glass wall facing the ocean is several stories high which allows for a spectacular view of Boston Harbor. Al and I were honored to listen to the list of dignitaries speak at the dedication for the new facility including Congressman Joe Moakley himself. The Congressman kept the audience laughing with his funny stories and self-deprecating humor before continuing with a reference to the huge glass wall by saying something close to, "Look at all that glass. I hope we included some money in the federal budget to pay for a crew of window washers!"

One of the many interesting people that I had the pleasure of meeting during my LBJ Internship was Congressman Joe Moakley. I was introduced to him by Congressman Jim Burke along with some others in the House Dining Room. The very next day when Congressman Moakley and I passed each other in the hallway of the Cannon House Office building I said, "Good morning Congressman Moakley," and he replied, "Hey Eddie, how's it going?" I was absolutely stunned that with all the constituents that he represents and all of the people that he meets in the course of a day - he remembered the name of a college intern! I am still amazed to this day - what a guy!

I have always been a big fan of anyone who uses self-deprecating humor as I believe it shows sincere humility, courage and a mundane outlook on life. Speaking on the issue of foreign policy Congressman Moakley declared, "I may not have been a foreign policy expert - in fact, my idea of a foreign affair used to be driving from South Boston to East Boston for an Italian sub."

I have long admired our 16th President for his courage, intellect and keen sense of humor. Before being elected to the Presidency Abraham Lincoln was a trial lawyer in Illinois where he was defending 70-year old Melissa Goings on a murder charge for killing her abusive husband. Her $1,000.00 bail had been posted before the trial which was heard in Metamora outside of Peoria in 1857. Huge crowds gathered at the courthouse which was covered by the press from near and far. This of course was long before the recognition of the horrors of domestic violence and 63 years before women would even be granted the right to vote. Women were considered second class citizens so under these circumstances the evidence against the defendant was strong and things weren't looking good for her even from the beginning. Judge James Harriott granted Attorney Lincoln's request for a recess and when the court session resumed the defendant was nowhere to be found after having fled. Upon questioning by the judge, Lincoln denied telling his client to flee the jurisdiction, but told the judge, "Your Honor, she said she was thirsty and asked me where she could get a drink of water. I told her that I hear that the water is really good in Tennessee."

The world could use more self-deprecating humor. Abraham Lincoln was once accused by his political opponent Stephen Douglas of being two faced to which he replied, "Honestly, if I had two faces, would I be showing you this one?"

Occasionally committees tend to overanalyze some issues. I have been appointed to enough committees to admire the logic of Ross Perot as he had some down to earth, common sense expressions that would have been helpful in Washington today like, "If you see a snake, just kill it. Don't appoint a committee on snakes."

My brothers and I were raised in a home devoid of any kind of prejudice. We were taught to respect everyone regardless of color, religion or nationality. I remember my dad paraphrasing Attorney General Robert F. Kennedy who had said something like, "Imagine how much your world would change if you woke up one morning and your skin was black!" I have always remembered the thrust of that statement in trying to see the world through the eyes of another. One of our dinner table discussions involved assessing the chances that a Black person could be elected President of the United States. The general consensus was that this could not happen with the overwhelming level of extreme prejudice and racial unrest in our nation.

Our dad died in 1983 so he didn't live long enough to see Barack Obama win election to our country's highest office, becoming our first Black President. My mom called me at the courthouse the next day and said, "Well, this proves that there are no phones in heaven because your father would have called me on this one!"

Attorney Gerard F. Doherty was very good friends with the three most famous of the Kennedy brothers. Although we were not related, I had been reading about the Charlestown native's close association with the Kennedy clan in newspapers and magazines for many years. He wrote a book entitled *They Were My Friends - JACK, BOB AND TED: My Life In and out of Politics* which came out a few months before my first book. We were both doing book signings and author talks when we coincidentally ended up being scheduled for different events in the same small town of Acushnet on the same night.

My friend Darcy H. Lee is a former senatorial aide who worked for Senator Ted Kennedy and is the author of *Ghosts of Plymouth, Massachusetts*. Darcy is a terrific writer and a very nice person who was extremely helpful to me when my first book came out. She enjoyed hearing Attorney Doherty speak at the Acushnet Council on Aging while I was addressing another crowd at the same time just down the street at the Acushnet Public Library. I made it a point to begin my presentation by informing the audience that if they had come to hear about the Kennedys that they were in the wrong place. What are the odds on two guys named Doherty speaking at the same time in the same small town on the very same night!

Paul Flanagan was, until his retirement, the First Assistant Clerk-Magistrate in the Plymouth County Juvenile Court, where he helped people every day and invoked laughter with his good natured sense of humor. I used to work with his brother John at the racetrack in Foxborough when we were both in college. After wrapping up his illustrious collegiate hockey career, John graduated from New England School of Law and after a successful law practice is now employed by the Massachusetts Trial Court. Their brother Jim, who also works for the Massachusetts Trial Court, is one of the nicest and most helpful guys in the system. Their father is the famous former District Attorney of Suffolk County - the legendary Newman A. Flanagan. Whenever Mr. Flanagan starts telling a story he has my undivided attention immediately as his words are a veritable history lesson on law and politics. One day at one of Paul and his lovely wife Kathy's cookouts Mr. Flanagan related the story of a 60-year old convicted armed robber who had a lengthy criminal record so it was time for the judge to issue a long period of incarceration. The judge gave him 30 years committed causing the defendant to plead for a lighter sentence. "Judge, 30 years!" he exclaimed, "I'll never be able to do 30 years!" The judge then declared, "Just do the best you can!"

My bride and I, at one time or another, had some interesting conversations with Boston Mayor Michelle Wu, United States Senator Ed Markey, Vice President Dan Quale and United States Congressman Barney Frank. They are all noted for their effective constituency work, faithful service and honest devotion to doing what is right regardless of intense political pressure. They are true patriots who have always worked hard to fulfill the duties of their office as they each have exhibited great courage in challenging situations for the good of the people.

Boston Mayor Michelle Wu

US Senator Ed Markey

Vice President Dan Quale

US Congressman Barney Frank

    The First Session at the ADC was in recess as I was about to leave my session clerk's position to get a coffee. A well-dressed smiling young man offered me his hand and business card as he introduced himself as the Lawyer of the Day for the Bar Advocates program. His name was Paul F. Walsh Jr. and that would eventually become a household name after his election to the position of District Attorney of Bristol County.

    Paul is the son of my mentor and sponsor, Dr. Paul F. Walsh who had been so kind to me when I was in school and was later appointed to be the great Clerk-Magistrate of the Wareham District Court by Governor Edward J. King. The younger Walsh, who had been a terrific basketball player and great all-around athlete, ran one of the best newspaper campaign ads that I have ever seen. The intended message was that he could reduce crime by keeping kids involved with sports. A full page photo showed him standing on a basketball court in gym shorts with a ball under his arm speaking to a bunch of young kids who were sitting down on the blacktop in front of him. The brilliant caption read, "HALF COURT, NOT JUVENILE COURT!"

    Bristol County has a significant Portuguese population so it didn't hurt Paul's election chances that he could speak that language fluently. Some would say that if you closed your eyes while Paul was speaking that you could almost imagine that you were standing in Lisbon. His successful campaign against the incumbent District Attorney proclaimed that it was, "Time for a Change." When Paul ran for reelection, however, his slogan became, "Keep the Change!"

My grandfather, Thomas F. Doherty, came to live with us in Attleboro toward the end of his years. I learned a lot of baseball strategy when I would stop by his bedroom and find him smoking a Winston in the dark with the Red Sox game on the radio. I loved hearing about our family and listening to his colorful stories of a bygone era. Grandpa Doherty was proud of our Irish heritage and I think was the first to tell me that, "If you're lucky enough to be Irish, you're lucky enough!" He once showed me a gray spot the size of a dime on his left ankle where skin had grown over a bullet after he was shot while heroically rescuing his younger brother from the backyard of a madman. The doctor said it would be best to leave the slug alone so Grandpa carried it with him for the rest of his life.

He and my grandmother raised their family, including my dad, in Taunton where they owned a small market at 52 Adams Street at the corner of Grove Street near the center of the city. The edifice has been renovated and updated since the 1930s, but the building structure owned by my grandparents still remains there today at the same address according to Samantha Mills, Principal Clerk of the Taunton Building Department. During Prohibition, Grandpa Doherty had a speak easy set up in the back to serve liquor which was hidden from the rest of the store by a long wall. Grandpa was only providing a thirsty country with what would soon become legal anyway so he would close the shop at five o'clock and go home as his assistant would come in to run the illegal bar. Grandpa had been caught once and put on probation, but for some reason there would be no probation violation as long as he wasn't on the premises while liquor was being served.

Business was going fine until Grandpa came home from work one day and was greeted with a dangerous request from my grandmother, his wife Mabel Doherty, nee Hollihan. She told him that she had forgotten to mention earlier that she needed some bread and milk and asked him to go back to the store for the items. He reminded her that he was still on probation and couldn't step foot inside while the speak easy was open. Not recognizing the gravity of the situation she insisted so he relented and set off back to the market. The timing could not have been worse, as soon as Grandpa walked in the front door federal agents came through the back and arrested him immediately after serving a search warrant.

Grandpa's probation was revoked and he was sentenced in US District Court in Boston to a commitment of incarceration to be served at the Plymouth County House of Correction even though he was a federal prisoner. Grandpa was a well-liked guy who had friends in high and low places. It was many years later that I received a copy of the Petition for Executive Clemency that was filed with my grandfather's case in Washington, DC along with letters of support including one from Congressman Joseph W. Martin Jr. who would go on to later become Speaker of the House. After investigation by the United States Department of Justice and others, the Petition eventually landed at 1600 Pennsylvania Avenue on the Oval Office desk of the most influential man in the world. An order was signed in the White House to commute my grandfather's sentence by President Herbert C. Hoover. Our family was saved and a good man was set free by Executive Order of the President of the United States of America!

Francis W. O'Brien was Chairman of the Norfolk County Commissioners. The Commissioners are in charge of the county owned buildings so they were essentially the landlord for the WDC. Fran's incredible contributions to the success of our Law Day program can't be overstated. The two other Commissioners, Attorney Peter H. Collins and John M. Gillis always treated me right and were always there when needed. Fran had a terrific sense of humor and used to kiddingly refer to the Superintendent of Buildings as the SOB!

I was proud to serve in state government with many honorable and hardworking people who make sacrifices every day on behalf of the taxpayers and the entire Commonwealth. Budget cuts, attrition and a reordering of some priorities has caused a reduction in the state workforce resulting in overworked staffers and supervisors. These dedicated individuals continue to make our state run and get the job done every day.

There was a time, however, way back in the day, when an argument could be made by some that various levels of state government were actually overstaffed.

A seasoned political reporter asked a veteran State Representative how many people work at the State House to which the Rep replied, "Oh, about half of them!"

Then there was the experienced state employee who was elated that the Governor had just appointed his son to a high level post, but advised him not to look out the window in the morning. When his son asked why the father explained, "Because, if you look out the window in the morning you won't have anything to do in the afternoon!"

A veteran State Representative had risen up through the ranks to become Chairman of a very influential committee in the House of Representatives. He told me one time that he loved working in the State House and said that it was the only job in America where you leave on Wednesday and say, "Have a nice weekend."

My mother could crack wise with the best of them. I had called her from the courthouse and mentioned that I was going to be on vacation next week to which she replied, "How can you tell?"

Attorney John H. Rogers from Norwood represents the people of the Twelfth Norfolk District in the Massachusetts House of Representatives. The beloved House Majority Leader was always a big hit at our Law Day Ceremonies where he regaled the crowd with unforgettable stories and had people laughing like it was a sold out comedy club. John did a tremendous job of introducing New England Patriots' Hall of Fame Quarterback Steve Grogan to our audience in such colorful detail that it almost sounded like an ESPN documentary. Grogan later said to me, "Rogers knows more about me than I know myself!"

Another year I asked John to present the American Ambassador of Philanthropy Award to Teddy Cutler and he was scheduled at the following Law Day to introduce our Keynote Speaker - US Olympic Gold Medal Hockey Champion Jim Craig of "Miracle on Ice" fame. John called me and had to cancel as a very important bill that he had co-sponsored was coming up that day for a vote in the House Chamber. The ever upbeat State Representative said that he had been speaking with his colleagues about it so much that it quickly became known as the Rogers' Bill so he definitely had to be present for the vote. I certainly understood and was just grateful for all the times that John was able speak at our events because everyone always enjoyed listening to him.

One time John told the story about teaching his three young daughters about the potential danger of strangers and instructed them to run away if approached. He then wanted to be sure that they understood so he asked five-year old Abby what she would do if a stranger approached her and asked if she wanted a toy, candy or money to which Abby responded, "I'll take the money!"

John had some tickets to a Boston Bruins game one night so he gave them to a couple of State House staffers and told the young ladies to have fun. They told John that they had a real good time when they saw him at the State House the next day and were genuinely impressed with the terrific location of the seats. John agreed that the seats were great and said, "Yea, they're right on the blue line." One of the girls, who had never before been to a hockey game, then stated, "No, we didn't take the subway. I drove my car."

WDC 2002 Capital Improvements Ceremony L-R SJC Associate Justice Robert J. Cordy, author, Chief Justice for Administration & Management Barbara A. Dortch-Okara, House Ways & Means Chairman John H. Rogers, First Justice Daniel B. Winslow (Vin Igo photo)

Doug Larson was quoted with a funny line about politics - "Instead of giving a politician the keys to the city, it might be better to change the locks."

Unfortunately, I have never been able to positively identify the State Representative in the following story although it was related to me by a very reliable source.

An incumbent State Representative was out campaigning for reelection to the State House in his hometown, greeting people and shaking hands in pursuit of another term in office. He walked through a local watering hole as he spoke with patrons and asked for their consideration. A young man named Billy who had recently completed a period of incarceration was seated on a barstool as the politician made his way through the pub. Even though Billy's sentence had ended, to some degree, he considered prison to be his home away from home. He had just been released from jail and was having a beer as the veteran solon approached him, stuck out his hand and introduced himself by stating his name and his job, "House of Representatives", to which Billy responded, "Billy, House of Correction!"

We were lucky enough to be represented by United States Congressman James P. McGovern prior to redistricting. He is a smart, down to earth guy with a big heart and the courage of a lion who was always very helpful to me. Attorney General Francis X. Bellotti, United States Senator Paul G. Kirk Jr., United States Congressmen Martin T. Meehan, William D. Delahunt, Seth W. Moulton, United States Congresswoman Lori A. Trahan, Worcester Superior Court Clerk of Courts Dennis P. McManus, Braintree Mayor Joseph C. Sullivan, RMV Supervisor Lillian Laro, Baker Administration Secretary of Public Safety Daniel J. Bennett, Attleboro City Councilor Carolyn J. Tedino, Plymouth County Assistant Register Timothy H. White, Representative Steven S. Howitt, Plymouth County District Attorneys Timothy J. Cruz and Michael J. Sullivan who was later appointed United States Attorney were all very supportive and kind to me at one time or another as was Plymouth County Probate Register Matthew J. McDonough.

Attorney General Francis X. Bellotti, District Attorney Michael W. Morrissey
(Eric Adler photo, courtesy of The Sun Chronicle*)*

I have always been a big fan of President Ronald W. Reagan and enjoy his quotations to this day such as, "One way to make sure that crime doesn't pay would be to let the government run it."

Michael J. Callahan served in different state agencies and was one of the best natured and funniest guys I have ever known. I worked the race track circuit when I was in school, mostly in pari-mutuels, when Mike worked for the Massachusetts State Racing Commission. I was a 19-year old kid taking action on the main line at the old Foxborough Raceway with hundreds of hard core gamblers milling around in front of me trying to pick the winner of the next race. Cigarettes wedged between lips burned down close to flesh as regulars marked up the racing program to chase a dream with a deuce. You could drop a quarter in that crowd and it would never hit the floor. Mike walked up to my window, shook my hand and thanked me for coming in. He wasn't even my boss, but he acted like he owned the place and everyone loved him.

I was eating lunch with Mike and some other guys much later in life after he had been elected to the Governor's Council from the same district that is currently represented by famed Attorney Terry Kennedy, another great guy. I have a habit of eating kind of fast so

Mike watched me hurriedly consume my lunch for a while before announcing that, "Eddie eats like the Russians are coming at us from around the corner two blocks away!"

Mike and the Honorable Paul C. Dawley, who would go on to receive many significant appointments in the court system including Chief Justice of the Massachusetts District Court Department, are both alumni of Kelly's Roast Beef in Revere. They worked there as young men and kept pace in the fast moving environment of the bustling legendary seaside institution. The food is so good that I can't drive through Revere without stopping for one of their famous roast beef sandwiches. Chief Justice Dawley told me that he and all the other employees were told upon being hired that they could eat anything that they wanted, but to go easy on the lobster!

Sometime after Mike Callahan was elected to the Governor's Council his brother secured a new job with the Massachusetts State Racing Commission. Mike was in the State House when a TV reporter who was investigating allegations of nepotism put a microphone in his face after asking him about his brother getting a plum job with the state. Mike just looked at the reporter with an expression of shock and disbelief as he stated, "Whaaat! I have a brother?"

Boston Globe columnist Scot Lehigh wrote an interesting story after former Massachusetts Governor William F. Weld became a registered lobbyist. Lobbyists are usually very personable, intelligent and high energy professionals, but there is a negative reputation associated with at least a portion of their activities by some members of the general public. A lobbyist might tell you that it is better to have his family think he is doing almost anything other than lobbying. Lehigh made reference to this by stating that, "…even paid-to-persuade professionals are known to joke: Please don't tell my mother I'm a lobbyist. She thinks I play piano in a brothel."

US Capitol, Washington

When Governor William F. Weld arrived for the inauguration of Governor Deval L. Patrick he was asked about memories of his own ceremony by an Associated Press Reporter. He reminisced that, "'My recollection is that I forgot to raise my right hand (for the oath of office), and so Paul Cellucci, ever the loyalist, who went immediately after me, also did not raise his hand so I wouldn't look stupid. That's loyalty."

Attorney James E. Vallee is an outstanding lawyer with the law firm of Nixon Peabody LLP, but I first got to know him when he was the State Representative from Franklin representing the Tenth Norfolk District. Jim, who served as the House Majority Leader, is a very nice guy who is as cordial as he is down to earth so I always enjoyed his company. We were playing golf on the Cape when Jim received a phone call as he was getting out of the cart. It was from Richard J. Egan who is the E in EMC and a supporter of Jim calling to inquire about a bill before the legislature. Egan's son Christopher is the President of Carruth Capital, LLC, a real smart guy who I would get to know later.

I had already been to Ireland twice so now J. Do and our two daughters were coming with me to enjoy the Emerald Isle for the first time. By now Dick Egan had been appointed United States Ambassador to Ireland by President George W. Bush. I had never met the famous businessman who had become a well-respected symbol of American success so Jim Vallee was kind enough to contact him on our behalf. We had a terrific time with the charismatic Ambassador in his office at the United States Embassy in Dublin. Egan was a very charming and engaging man so even our teenaged girls really enjoyed listening to him. Kids that age don't pay much attention to anybody over 20, but they were enthralled by his stories and almost mesmerized by his dynamic personality.

We were there on July 3 and the Ambassador had invited Neil Diamond to the embassy for the next day to perform a private concert. Ambassador Egan graciously invited our whole family to the concert for a private Fourth of July celebration, but unfortunately our airline reservations were booked for the trip home so we had to decline. The Ambassador told us that he had asked Diamond to sing Coming to America so we expressed our appreciation for what must have been a patriotic and momentous occasion.

His Excellency, Deval L. Patrick served two outstanding terms as Governor of the Commonwealth. I don't know him personally, but have always admired his intellect, sense of humor and powerful leadership ability. J. Do and I were seated close to the stage when Governor Patrick was called to the microphone at the St. Patrick's Day Breakfast in South Boston. The charismatic Governor had the huge crowd laughing at his funny comments and humorous remarks including when he said something close to, "I'm also from Southie - South Chicago!"

Governor Patrick had been criticized in some newspapers for alleged lavish spending on new drapes and furniture for the corner office. The governor represents our state to constituents, dignitaries and visitors from across the globe so upgraded appearances are important. Governor Patrick is an honest man so if he thought that improvements were necessary that was good enough for me.

Maryann Pozzessere served with distinction as the First Assistant Clerk-Magistrate of the Westborough District Court. Her honesty, fairness, integrity and kindness earned her a reputation as a smart, thoughtful, dependable go to person. Maryann was a little nervous, as we all are, when she went to the State House to be interviewed for the position of clerk-magistrate. She was greeted warmly by Governor Patrick in his office and made to feel comfortable immediately. The Governor having been slammed in the press for his interior decorating choices was not foremost in her mind as Maryann made complimentary small talk stating, "I love your window treatments, drapes and décor!" The good natured Governor just smiled and offered her a seat. Governor Deval L. Patrick did the right thing, as always, making a terrific appointment as Maryann Pozzessere soon became the great Clerk-Magistrate of the Westborough District Court.

10. Race Tracks & more

I spent many hours of my youth listening to the Sports Huddle on the radio broadcasting lively, entertaining discussions mostly about the Red Sox, Patriots, Celtics, and Bruins between Eddie Andelman, Attorney Mark J. Witkin and Jim McCarthy. I always enjoyed the funny antics and humorous stories so I was very happy to learn that Eddie Andelman had bought Foxborough Raceway. I met him there one night before going to my window and enjoyed a fun conversation with the legend of sports radio.

After getting my feet wet and learning the ropes at Foxborough Raceway, I would eventually land jobs in the pari-mutuels department at Raynham Park, Suffolk Downs, Taunton Dog Track, Lincoln Downs and the Marshfield Fair. All of these jobs were only part time as the legislature determines the number of racing dates allotted to each track every year, but I worked as much as possible to earn college tuition money. Sometimes I would be selling tickets at one track in the afternoon and cashing them at another facility that night.

The race tracks were full of colorful characters including professional gamblers, handicappers, thieves, touts, ticket splicers and con artists as well as nice people just out for a night of entertainment. Sometimes I felt like I was living in the middle of a Damon Runyon story that never ended. Everybody went by first names and nicknames so I immediately inherited the moniker "Fast Eddie" from some cashiers who named me after the Paul Newman character in the movie *The Hustler*. I think that every guy named Eddie working at a track or casino had the prefix Fast automatically attached to his name. I was the youngest of two at Foxborough so I was sometimes called "Little Fast"!

I got to know some heavy hitters and regulars at the different tracks in Rhode Island and Massachusetts. Nobody had a last name and most guys were known by colorful labels like Joe the Roofer, White Shoes, Minty, Bullshit (it's what he said every time his horse got beat), Stinky, Blue Eyes, Big Wad, Elvis, Shrimp Boy, Bubba, Rockefeller, Tipper, Walnuts, Scooter, Bad Breath, Loopy, Big Billy, Little Chip, Whistler (a missing front tooth caused a whistle when he exhaled), Green Shorts, Black Jack, Pokey, Screwball, Cookie, Black Socks and Hawaii Five-0 who wore the same bright flowered Hawaiian shirt every day at Taunton Dog Track. He had hit a trifecta for 10 grand in the spring while wearing the Hawaiian shirt which instantaneously became his lucky garment so he kept wearing it all summer and never wanted to take it off or wash it! By the time July turned into the humidity of August we had a different name for him!

Inexperienced gamblers would often discard winning tickets by dropping them on the floor because they thought they were losers. They would bet a horse to show, for instance, and throw the ticket away when the horse won the race because they thought that it had to come in third. Every track has a multitude of live good tickets sitting on the floor mixed in with thousands of losing ducats.

Sammy the Stooper worked the huge floor in front of the Main Line at Suffolk Downs where he had a paper clip stuck into the inside front sole of his right shoe. Sammy would walk along very slowly with his head down as his eyes scanned for winning tickets that had landed face up on the floor which was littered with all kinds of trash. He used the paper clip as a sixth toe to flip over tickets that were face down and sometimes had to do an about face to be able to read the numbers. Sammy's paper clip trick allowed him to continue walking in an upright position and only stoop over for a winner. His head, however, was always facing down with his chin resting on his chest so we all hoped that Sammy found enough winners to pay a chiropractor for some neck therapy!

I was a cashier on my first night at Foxborough Raceway, but I would also work as a runner sometimes which involved hand carrying test tickets and paperwork to supervisors in other sections of the track. This was a nice job that took me all over the facility and let me get to know some of the other employees like Ray Hill who was a nice guy and a music teacher at King Philip Regional High School. Jimmy Morse was a terrific guy who was always in a good mood. One of his clients was Charlie Finley, the flamboyant owner of the Oakland A's baseball team and the hockey team from the same city - the California Golden Seals. Finley was a showman who tried to introduce orange pucks into the game and had given one to Jimmy. Pari-mutuel staff would always be told of any shortages from the night before when checking in for nightly work assignments. If you took a bad ticket or lost a change game to a con man the outage would have to be paid to the track out of your own pocket. A thief beat Jimmy with an old ticket for about $300 bucks one night so Gerry Purro took up a collection to help him out by walking around holding out an envelope and telling guys that Jimmy had taken a pigeon. Jimmy was nice to everybody so it was good to see a lot of cash coming out of wallets for the kind hearted gentleman.

Many years later J. Do and I first met the ever-endearing Joanne M. Vitale during a festive Christmas party at the Community House hosted by Attorney John P. Gibbons and Attorney Diane M. Jeffers, both highly skilled, experienced advocates and genuinely nice people. Joanne worked in the Clerk-Magistrate's Office of the Dedham District Court and is the proud mother of two sons, Rob is the Chief Court Officer of the Supreme Judicial Court and Steve is a corrections officer at the Norfolk County House of Correction. Her brother Peter, who is an author, is a terrific writer. Little did I know, when we first started speaking with Joanne that she was the daughter of a stand-up guy who I knew very well as we had worked together many years before.

Phil Vitale was a 50-year old hustler from Mission Hill who worked on the main line at Foxborough Raceway and sold all kinds of products on the side. I always enjoyed listening to Phil as he seemed to be a real life character cut out of a 1930s novel. I'd walk by his cashier window and he would hold up some socks and yell, "Doherty you need some new socks," or he might have some bottles of CHANEL No 5 PARFUM and say. "Doherty Christmas is coming. You need to get some Channel 5 for your girlfriend!" That's not a typo as Phil really called it Channel 5 just like the TV network! One night, when I was still new and hadn't yet mastered all the track lingo, Phil wanted to play a trifecta, but he couldn't leave his post to get to the ticket seller. I was a runner that night so he knew that I would be walking by the right place. "Doherty", he said as he handed me some cash, "Go around the corner and box the 2-5-8 tri for me." I hadn't been there long enough to realize that he wanted to play every combination of those three numbers such as 2-5-8, 2-8-5 and so on in a trifecta, thus producing a winner if those three horses finished in any order for Win, Place & Show. My reply of, "Huh!" was probably accompanied by a deer caught in the headlights expression so Phil emphatically raised his voice, as if my hearing was the problem, and told me, "Box it kid, box it!" and then simplified his request by saying, "Give that cash to Dusty, tell him Phil wants the 2-5-8 trifecta and to put it in a f***in box!" At least I was smart enough to realize that Dusty wouldn't be putting Phil's bet in a cardboard box!

People were pouring into Taunton Dog Track for the prestigious $25,000 American Greyhound Derby in 1977. Everyone was talking about a greyhound named Downing that was constantly winning and looked to be the closest thing in history to a sure bet. I was taking action on the main line as the growing crowd moved about while studying the "book" AKA the racing program. A well-dressed 35-year old man came up to my window and placed a black leather briefcase in front of me. I had gotten to know many gamblers and recognized faces from one track to another, but I had never seen this guy before which probably meant that this was his first time in the door. He opened the briefcase and started stacking bundles of money on the counter in a very precise and orderly fashion. After I counted the cash and confirmed that it was $5,000.00 he said that he wanted to bet it all on Downing to Show, thus producing a winner if the dog finished in the top three. Massachusetts guarantees a minimum winning payoff of 10% so that if a dog finishes in the money a $2.00 bet will produce a payoff of at least $2.20 even in the event of a minus pool. I processed the gentleman's bet and never saw him again. Downing, who was always quick out of the box, broke on top out of the 5 hole, sprinting around the track while sometimes almost touching the rail and won the race by two lengths. The Red Brindle speedster paid $2.20 on the bottom so the mystery man took home a $500.00 profit for a few minutes investment.

I was still working at Taunton Dog Track when the handle dropped so significantly that I wasn't needed by the track itself so Doc Walsh gave me a job with the State Racing Commission as a testing assistant. A plastic cup was dropped into a slot holding it in place at the end of a long pole. The lead out boy would hand me the leash of a greyhound after the race and I would walk the dog, sometimes around a fake fire hydrant, until urinating. I would catch some urine, snap a cover on the cup, affix a label and seal the edge with glue before relinquishing it to a Massachusetts State Trooper who would drive all the samples into Boston for drug testing. The dogs finishing first and second always had their urine collected for testing, but sometimes the judge would call and tell us to spot the 3, for example, if that dog had run out of form and had come in last after going off as a 6-5 favorite, for instance. I always enjoyed conversations with Walter Dermody, a commission judge and a great guy who I spoke with frequently. I only had to do this job at the dog tracks and never had to collect urine from the horses thank God, but there was an interesting story that came out of Foxborough as horses usually take longer to begin urinating than dogs. Sometimes the horses would have to be walked for more than 20 minutes before producing a sample. A guy was walking a horse after the race while smoking a cigar and handicapping the program for the next set of trotters. The horse showed no sign of wanting to urinate so the guy was getting nervous that he might get shut out at the betting window, which to a hard core gambler is just about one click below having a fatal accident! He kept trying to coax the standardbred to hurry up, but to no avail as the horse just wouldn't go notwithstanding his sweet talking pleas for pee. Finally, with nobody looking, the guy urinated into the cup himself and turned it over to the State Police before running over to the betting window. After the urine was analyzed in the lab the chemist called the Racing Commission Office and said, "There were tobacco traces in that urine. I guess that horse must have been out having a cigar after the race!"

The Marshfield Fair was granted about 10 afternoon racing dates every year toward the end of August. The fair is a wonderful event featuring various booths, rides, food vendors, agricultural contests, horticultural displays, 4H animal exhibits and when I worked there- live horse racing. I used to park in the infield and walk through the huge crowds over to my cashier's window. There was a lemonade stand not far from the front of my window so the owner used to bring me an ice cold delicious lemonade every day. It even had a half a lemon sitting on top of the ice so I really looked forward to that tasty treat, but the generous guy would never allow me to pay for it.

I loved working at Marshfield because, in general, there were fewer thieves and happier people, many of whom had never before been to a race track, but it wasn't what you would characterize as a major league operation. Some guys would complain that the horses were rated at a low quality level and kiddingly say that they had just been pulling a plow yesterday or that the horse was really just a 4H exhibit. The Tote machine that produces the tickets for the bettors is always electronically aligned with the starting gate so that the machines automatically shut off when the gate opens for the horses at the beginning of the race. It was rumored that the machine coordination wasn't so perfect at Marshfield so that tickets would still pop out sometimes for 2 seconds after the gate opened. An advantage might be gained if a guy watching the race could yell the number of the horse that broke on top fast enough to a ticket seller who could then punch that number until the machine shut down. Even the announcer would call the race by the horse's number instead of his name, but that was all part of the fun in the dynamic atmosphere of an old fashioned country fair. Ray Fitzgerald, the late great colorful *Boston Globe* sports columnist, wrote a beautiful column about his interesting experience one day at Marshfield and I'm pretty sure that he mentioned that one of the horses had winked at him before the race!

George L. Carney Sr. and Russ Murray wanted to build a dog track in Raynham many years ago, but it had to be approved by voter referendum as any kind of gambling venture is always somewhat controversial. My grandfather, Thomas F. Doherty, was hired to spearhead the campaign to convince the townspeople of the employment and economic benefits of having a track on Route 138. Grandpa was a well-spoken man with a memory full of funny Irish tales so he worked every room, pub, assembly and meeting hall in Raynham. His efforts were successful as the measure passed and Raynham Park opened in 1941. Grandpa Doherty received a check from the owners of Raynham Park until the day that he died and as luck would have it, his grandson, would be earning paychecks many years later from that very same Massasoit Greyhound Association.

George L. Carney Jr. would work his way up and eventually acquire Raynham Park. He introduced a unique spirit of creativity with promotions like "Chinese Food Night" and other innovations including the installment of color TVs when most of the rest of the world still had black & white. His brother Joe had a reserved parking space next to his which would continue to remain reserved even after his death as a sign of respect from one brother to another. George Carney is one of those guys who spells Loyalty with a capital L and was always good to me.

Mr. Carney introduced me to his son Christopher at the track when he was only about 10 years old. Chris would grow up to be one of the nicest and most generous people that I have ever known as the apple doesn't fall far from the tree. There is a big water tower at the top of a hill at Woods Hole Golf Club in Falmouth which I used for navigation purposes when I was a kid, but I had never gotten close to it until Chris invited me to play golf there. Going by the massive structure, which rises up behind the 4th green, in a golf cart made me feel as though I had come full circle from my youth. Most golfers take at least ten seconds or so addressing the ball when teeing off, but Chris just walks up, winds up and crushes the ball right down the middle. He is as unpretentious on the golf course as he is in every aspect of his life.

He and his dad would get into some business ventures together and succeed in real estate and other opportunities. One time they bought a house and turned it over for a quick profit, but Chris had done all of the work on what had been his idea so when his father commented that "we" had done well on the deal Chris kiddingly responded, " What's this WE shit!"

Doc Walsh, my sponsor, had called Mr. Carney on my behalf when I applied for a job there. I was scheduled for an interview along with two New Bedford schoolteachers who I did not know. As I previously mentioned, Doc was not only the Chairman of the State Racing Commission, but also served as the Chairman of the New Bedford School Committee so he was always getting track jobs for school teachers who would earn extra income and qualify for social security at the same time. Doc was a great guy whose campaign committee never asked me for a political donation until after I had graduated from college.

This was not what would be characterized as a traditional job interview as the three of us were brought into an office together on the main line. Mr. Carney was seated on the side of a table with a tall athletic looking man standing behind him who he introduced as Ripper Reagan. Richard "Ripper" Reagan, a former Boston College football star, looked to be a no nonsense type of guy with biceps bursting out of a tight fitting golf shirt. I would get to know a lot of former athletes that worked there who could handle themselves just like Mr. Carney including Paul Pender who had been the Middleweight Champion of the World.

I had heard that Mr. Carney was an honest and hardworking man who cared about the facility and his employees in it so it was a common sight to see him bending over himself to pick up discarded pieces of trash on the floor of the grandstand. This was kind of a go through the motions interview though because Mr. Carney was almost definitely going to hire us as we were all Doc Walsh guys. Even though I was a young 21-year old kid I already had experience in the pari-mutuel department at a few other tracks, but the school teachers had never worked at any racetrack. Mr. Carney asked the first teacher what he could do and the guy just shrugged his shoulders and sadly said he didn't know. Mr. Carney looked a little disappointed as he asked the same question to teacher number two and got an almost identical response. George Carney is a very positive gentleman who would go through a brick wall for a friend so he was visibly downhearted at what he had just heard. He then turned to me, almost out of desperation and asked me what I could do at the track to which I responded, "Mr. Carney, I can do whatever you need including calculating odds and sweeping the floor." Mr. Carney's face lit up with a big smile as he excitedly burst out, "Jesus Christ kid, that's great. Ripper take this kid up to Clubhouse Two and get him squared away!"

After that propitious beginning, it wasn't unusual for Mr. Carney to stop by my window just to say hello so some of the other pari-mutuel clerks thought that I must be some distant cousin, but the reality was that he took a liking to me that started with a good answer that was made to look even better by the two guys from New Bedford who were not having their best day.

I was working in an outdoor section on the day in 1976 when Raynham Park hosted the first matinee dog racing card in the history of Massachusetts pari-mutuel gambling. Raynham quickly became my favorite track for many reasons including being protected by the best security staff in the business. Mr. Carney cherished a crime free environment so if anybody raised hell or got out of line by bothering his employees - look out! Donny Walsh was a nice, genial and down to earth guy who headed a security team of former boxers, federal agents and other athletes. A combination for these guys had nothing to do with gambling - it was defined by which fist was thrown first. There were so many guys with broken noses that the track resembled a boxing gym. Louie Assad, who would be seen on TV safeguarding the New England Patriots' Head Coach, would stand near me looking over the crowd and Paul Pender used to stand in front of my trifecta window in the Clubhouse so I guess you could say that we were pretty well protected!

Sometimes I would work a ticket selling machine in the Mezzanine where the Supervisor was Charlie Dansereau. Charlie was a thin man with long narrow feet that looked to be a size 12A so we used to tell him that his shoes could be used for water skis. He was a nice guy who would bet on the outcome of a little league game so he always wanted to split a bet with everybody. He'd walk by my window and say, "Give me a buck kid and I'll make you a millionaire!" If Charlie bet on the 7 dog, for instance, and it finished out of the money you would hear him sadly proclaim, "The 7 shit the bed!" The Mezz was full of all kinds of characters including a heavy set gambler who would loudly continue to root for his dog as he watched the instant replay on closed circuit TV! The dog had lost and would definitely lose again on the replay!

Many of my regular customers were of Asian descent. Chinese gamblers always knew what they were doing and never ever made a mathematical mistake. I would be punching in combinations as they called out numbers finally resulting in them knowing exactly how much they had bet at the end of the transaction. For some reason the Chinese culture has trouble pronouncing the numeral 6 so I got used to hearing "sick" when bets were coming in on the 6 dog. They were always polite, reserved and respectful.

There are eight different dogs that run in each of about 12-15 races per day or night. The same eight different colorful numbered blankets are used in every race, but of course the greyhounds are all different as each one only runs once per card. One night the 4 won three races in a row and of course they were all three different dogs, but an inexperienced rail bird thought that the same eight greyhounds ran all night so he bet on the 5 dog in the next race because he said that the 4 must be really tired after winning three races in a row!

It was convenient that Taunton Dog Track and Raynham Park were located close to each other as I would often work at one in the afternoon and the other at night. Rather than drive home to Attleboro after the day card and then come back again in a few hours, I would have dinner quite often at Farrell's Café in Taunton. I could sit at a table in the bar section and watch the news on TV while enjoying a delicious home cooked meal. Sometimes I would be joined by Joe Cook and some of the other great guys who worked at the tracks. A group of about ten heavy hitters would sometimes take me to Ann's Place on Bay Road in Norton where we all sat at a huge round table and consumed family style portions of terrific food. I think that I was the only one looking at the menu as everybody else was studying the racing form and dog program in a gathering of happy guys with no last names!

Judges and clerk-magistrates are prohibited from political involvement so my daughter Kaitlin and her husband Jon were kind enough to hold signs, which I would have done if I could, on Election Day in 2008 in support of the continuation of live dog racing in Massachusetts. Loyalty is a transferable trait in my world so Kait and Jon held a sign because of what Mr. Carney did for me so long ago. The sign asked people to Vote No on Question 3, but unfortunately the referendum passed thus prohibiting greyhound racing in the state after the next year which ultimately put a lot of good people out of work in the Commonwealth. Raynham Park, which still handles simulcasting action, ran its last live card in December of 2009.

The campaign to ban dog racing was spear headed by Attorney Christine A. Dorchak who is the co-founder, President and General Counsel of GREY2K USA Worldwide. The proclaimed mission of this group is to promote adoption and rescue as well as to end the cruelty of dog racing. I have never met Attorney Dorchak so she and her group are probably well intentioned kind hearted people, but I respectfully disagree with the premise that dogs were being mistreated at the tracks where I worked. I never saw anything close to cruelty and only witnessed dog trainers and owners exhibiting love and affection toward these gentle animals. Some owners and trainers would come up to my window and bet on their dog in races where the competition was so fierce that their entry didn't stand a chance, but they handed me their cash out of some sense of loyalty.

I not only worked in pari-mutuels, but my job as a testing assistant for the State Racing Commission put me in close proximity to lead outs, trainers, owners, veterinarians and the dogs themselves. All I can say is that I only saw good people caring for happy dogs.

George. L. Carney Jr. sits as a Trustee of the New England School of Law and has been very generous in providing financial assistance for scholarships at that institution. Attorney Dorchak is a graduate of the New England School of Law where she was the recipient of a scholarship. Ironically, the scholarship that provided assistance for her education was funded by none other than George Carney!

The nuns at Dominican Academy in Plainville were all wonderful teachers who guided my spirituality and other essential components of young thinking in my formative years. It was an excellent school that produced innovative titans of business like Attorney Gerard C. Lorusso and many other successful people from various walks of life. I would come to appreciate the nun's instruction of fair play as well as their inspired love and devotion even more so later in life.

My classmate Jon stuttered at the beginning of the first grade, but spent the rest of the school year speaking without delay after being taken under the ingenious guidance of Sister Bernard Marie. I don't know what she did, but he spoke perfectly as a result of her love and care. Sister Bernard Marie taught grades 1 & 4 so Jon went back to stuttering in grades 2 & 3 and stopped in 4. He started stuttering again in grade 5 and continued until the last time I saw him in grade 8. I have thought about him from time to time with the hope that he finally beat this arduous affliction.

It was just about a decade earlier than my first grade year when another young man was going through the same speaking difficulties as Jon. He was a student at another Catholic academy, St. Paul's Elementary School in the blue collar city of Scranton, Pennsylvania. He endured ridicule and was mocked by some of the other kids in this hardscrabble spot just over 100 miles outside of New York City. The boy worked hard to overcome his stuttering and with the loving support of his family was determined to not let this temporary imperfection define his life. He learned to speak freely and left his stutter behind, eventually being elected 46th President of the United States of America!

President Joseph R. Biden Jr. is living testament that huge obstacles can be overcome through hard work and perseverance. He has dedicated his life to public service and been there for those in need. If Sister Bernard Marie is still with us after all this time and President Biden needs someone to spear head an effort to combat stuttering he would do well to look no farther than the kind and gracious nun who worked her magic on another young boy all those years ago.

My friends and I would make the trip to Dorchester for lunch at the Eire Pub whenever we could. Owner John Stenson runs a top-shelf establishment with outstanding food and lively conversation. John Curran pours a perfect pint and greets patrons in his beautiful Sligo accent. Martin Nicholson was another friendly bartender who always treated us like family. We enjoyed our delicious hot pastrami sandwiches as the banter would go back and forth between Martin and our table. He is a very nice guy who started working in bars as a young man in Ireland and eventually became part owner of the famous pub in Adams Corner. When Martin retired there was talk that he might write a book about a life of serving drinks and I hope he is working on it because the title was supposed to be *45 Years Behind Bars*!

I have had the distinct privilege of meeting and getting to know some United States Navy SEALs including Tommy Maher, who was the nephew of my friend Paul Maher. Dana Perino is a best-selling author and outstanding American political commentator who served as White House Press Secretary under President George W. Bush. I have always enjoyed her interesting interviews as well as her enlightening commentary because she asks pertinent questions without being rude and never interrupts.

One time she interviewed a Navy SEAL in a memorable exchange with one of America's best. These are the incredibly well trained brave patriots who are put in harm's way all over the globe to perform enormously difficult missions, save lives and initiate precision timed tasks to avert almost certain tragedy. After discussing the different countries that these courageous warriors had been sent to, she asked if they had to learn several languages. His humble response was as powerful as it was understated. The reply from the Navy SEAL was, "Oh no ma'am, we don't go there to talk."

I never did very much shopping, but now that I'm retired I sometimes accompany J. Do to the store. We were heading down an aisle in Walmart when a five-year old boy and his mother walked by in front of us. Apparently she was not in contention for Parent of the Year because when the little boy asked if he could have a candy bar the mother loudly replied, "Youuuu? You ain't gettin shit!" The screaming young man was not pleased.

Peter Marciano & author in front of Rocky Marciano statue, Brockton

Baseball, boxing and horse racing were king when our father was growing up. Dad spoke often about a local kid from Brockton who grew up to be the Heavyweight Champion of the World. Rocky Marciano, AKA the "Brockton Blockbuster", fought his way to an undefeated record of 49-0 with 43 of those wins by knockout! Dad said Marciano was the greatest fighter to ever enter the ring, superior punching power and a determined spirit his trademark. Marciano's undefeated record is usually the most talked about aspect of his boxing career, but I have always felt that there was another, less famous yet extremely impressive tally. His 43 knockouts meant that out of 49 fights - only 6 guys were left standing at the end!

I was sitting at a table for a book signing when a 35-year old gentleman picked up my book and started thumbing through it. We had a pleasant conversation as I told him that I would be happy to inscribe and sign the book if he wanted one. The poor guy said that he had already read three books in his life and just didn't have time to read another one!

Many of the fans of the New England Patriots were unhappy with the ruling of NFL Commissioner Roger Goodell regarding popular Quarterback Tom Brady. One guy was selling T shirts outside of the Patriots' game that read, "There is no good in Goodell."

Another guy had a sign at a Pat's game declaring, "Gronkowski is Polish for touchdown!"

I played in a golf league years ago which was a lot of fun because I just wanted to hit the ball, have some laughs and didn't care about my score, but some golfers throw clubs or swear loudly upon making an errant shot, as their blood pressure rises quicker than a Nolan Ryan fastball! I was told that I had a pretty good swing so that I should have a better score, but the only way to improve your golf game is to play much more than I wanted. Luck was my constant companion one summer, however, as good fortune followed me around like a loyal golden retriever. It seemed like almost every time I hooked a bad shot into the woods the ball would hit a tree and bounce back onto the fairway! This happened so often that guys started calling it my Irish Bounce. Apparently this was a topic of discussion on the course and just like any story talked about from one foursome to another, details became exaggerated. One golfer thought that I could make trick shots and cause my ball to strike a tree perfectly and land safely. He actually asked me if I could teach him how to hit an Irish Bounce!

I got to know Harvey Nasuti through our mutual friend John "The Master" Padula. Harvey was a funny guy who was always quick with a joke until the day that he left us for the big golf course in the sky. The first time we played golf together Harvey asked me if I wanted a snack as he reached into his golf bag and pulled out a bag of hot peppers. One time we were playing at Franklin Country Club on a perfect day for golf as Harvey regaled us with funny stories and kept the whole foursome laughing. I placed my ball on the tee and lined up my driver to get ready to hit on a long straightaway. I was just about to tee off when a large deer walked out onto the middle of the fairway about 250 yards away. I backed up and told the guys that I had better wait until the deer takes off which caused

Harvey to say, "Don't worry Eddie, with you hitting that deer is in the safest place in America!"

Harvey was driving home one night from a party where he may have had a little too much to drink. A police officer happened to be behind him as he swerved slightly over the yellow line and quickly back into his own lane. Harvey pulled over when the blue lights and siren came on and waited for the officer to approach his window. The officer asked Harvey if he had been drinking to which he replied, "Of course I've been drinking! Do you think I'd drive like this if I was sober?" The officer couldn't stop laughing so Harvey dodged a bullet!

When Harvey was a kid he was in the school food line with other students when they got to the table holding a big bowl of apples. A nun had made a sign which read - ONLY TAKE ONE APPLE. REMEMBER, GOD IS WATCHING! Right next to the apples was an enormous platter of cookies so Harvey made his own sign which read - TAKE ALL THE COOKIES YOU WANT. GOD'S WATCHING THE APPLES!

I was playing with Harvey, the Master and Attorney Peter Padula in a tournament at a golf course on the Cape. A very nice priest with a terrific sense of humor, who happened to be a friend of Harvey's, was in the foursome directly behind us so they were following us all day. We had finished playing and were walking off the course after 18 holes when the priest told Harvey, "Nice game today Harvey", to which Harvey responded, "Well not really Father, my short game was kind of off today." The priest then stated, "No Harvey, I meant you only said the F word three times all day!"

Harvey told me that some guy had stolen his wife's credit card, but that he wasn't going to call the police. When I asked him why he wasn't going to report it stolen Harvey said, "I'm going to leave well enough alone. The guy is spending less per month than my wife does!"

Sally Bruno Linton grew up in Mansfield where she and her husband Dave still live today. Her loving parents always wanted to treat their two children equally so if Sally's sister received $200.00 worth of Christmas presents and they ended up spending $198.50 on Sally, they would then level the playing field by writing a check for $1.50 to Sally.

The first time that I had a doctor's appointment after receiving my Medicare card made me realize how much the world has changed. I called and had a pleasant conversation with a nice lady who took my new insurance information. I answered in the affirmative when she told me that they had me listed as a man and wanted to know if that was correct. She was just doing her job, but I must admit that I really wasn't prepared for the next question as she wanted to know if I identified as a man! I couldn't believe what I was hearing so I guess my silence caused her to think that I may have been confused. The nice lady tried to simplify the process by asking me if I thought of myself as a man!

I am in favor of equal treatment for all people regardless of gender, race, sexual orientation, religion or anything else, but I guess that I am just old fashioned and continue to be grateful and happy that God made me a man!

My physician at Brigham & Women's in Foxborough is a remarkable guy and an outstanding doctor. We always have a good time swapping stories and laughing during my checkups. One day I mentioned how I always visit Five Guys to get a delicious burger after my medical appointments as the restaurant is only a short walk away. My doctor emphatically told me to stay out of there as I had already had a stent placed near my heart to open a blockage and if I ate too many more burgers I would find myself right back in the operating room again. I will admit that my daughter Christine, who is a Registered Nurse, has sometimes described me as an "uncooperative patient" so as soon as I left my doctor's office, of course, I headed straight for Five Guys! My doctor always gives me good advice, but I could hear those burgers calling my name!

I had just taken a bite out of my hot juicy burger as a long line of hungry customers was forming from the cash register all the way back to the door. I was trying not to dwell on having a guilty conscience as I tried to keep the image of my kind-hearted physician out of my thoughts. I looked up from my feast and low and behold my very own doctor who had just examined me was standing in line to get his own burger! We both smiled as we had caught each other in the act red-handed!

When you walk into Five Guys at Patriot Place in Foxborough one of the employees loudly announces something in Spanish to the rest of the staff. It turns out to be a simple yet effective management tool used to stay ahead of orders and keep up with the number of burgers cooking on the grill. It was later explained to me that if three customers walk in, for instance, an employee will call out "three in the door" so the chef can then drop the correct number of hamburgers on the grill. It can be a little unsettling if, like me, you don't speak Spanish so I hadn't known what they were saying, but was relieved to find out that they weren't proclaiming, "Here comes that jerk from the courthouse again!"

I made some lifelong friends at the University of South Florida in Tampa including the Terrio brothers - Ralph and Ken from New Jersey, Jim Mittenzwei, Kit Whitehurst and Mitch Manday from the Miami area, Ken Albert from Pittsburgh and Tim Mahoney from Connecticut. Some of us used to drive from USF to the Florida Keys during spring break where we would dive, fish and have the time of our lives cooking our catch on an open roaring bonfire. We were all students without extra money for lodging, but that was OK because we really didn't mind sleeping on desolate beaches surrounded by scattered coral under enormous palm trees. This beautiful long stretch of islands connected by Route A1A is a veritable tropical paradise that will lower your blood pressure better than any prescribed medication. Marathon is located toward the middle of the island chain and is one of the larger Keys where you can dine on delicious food at a busy restaurant called The Wooden Spoon. Cookie and other friendly waitresses serve outstanding fare in the legendary dining destination that has a clock on the wall without the numbers 1-12. Instead

author at USF

of numbers there are just a couple of words on the clock that perfectly sum up the easy laid back feeling of the festive relaxing atmosphere and enduring spirit of the Florida Keys. The two words on the clock are - Who Cares!

Getting friends and family to help move furniture when relocating from one place to another when we were younger would sometimes involve the exercise of brute strength in a party atmosphere. I was older with a barking back when we moved to our last single family home so I wanted to hire a moving company to transport a washer, dryer and other heavy items. I had heard good things about Mucker's Delivery Service, AKA Mucker the Trucker, but I wasn't sure if they only did commercial accounts or if they also moved residents from homes. I called and asked the gentleman who answered the phone if they also moved residential customers and he answered, "Oh sure, we move everything except your bowels!"

Stephen Newman was one of my high school teachers, but he had a much greater impact on me as my track coach. Teenagers get reprimanded by adults, but the lessons don't always hit home. Coach Newman, however, had a way of communicating with kids who may have been slightly off course like myself and some of my teammates. Many years later I told Lesley Hines, one of the nicest girls in our class, that Coach Newman had saved my life. Lesley was astonished because she had also heard that from others. I may have been the happiest guy in town when the track surrounding the football field at Attleboro High School was named the Steve Newman Track.

I became fast friends with Bob Walker at Attleboro High School. We were teammates on the track team and he was a talented shooting guard on the basketball team as well as a speedy multi tool outfielder in baseball. The fleet footed athlete came in first in the long jump as well as the 100 yard dash in every dual meet and sprinted to fifth place in the state finals. We had great times as teenagers learning about life together and have remained friends throughout the years. He is one of the best people that I have ever known so I am lucky to call him friend.

Bob's family moved away from the Attleboro area as his dad had a job that required extensive mobility. Bob graduated from Texas Tech and while a student there during one summer he came back to visit me at my parents' house while I was on college break myself. He was accompanied by two of his friends from school so we all had a good time together for about a week. Kirby Johnson and Mike Haygood were both from Texas where they had very little familiarity with trees. Mike told us that the only trees on the campus of Texas Tech in Lubbock had been transported from elsewhere and planted there so these guys were staring at the woods like it was a magic show. They were absolutely fascinated to be travelling in a car under large tree branches that hung over the street and blocked out the sky. New England forests provided a Disney World type of fascination for this crew.

Anyone who has oak trees growing in the yard like we did knows what a chore it is to rake up the leaves and acorns off the lawn in the fall. The boys from Texas wanted to take some souvenirs home so on their last day with us Kirby asked my mother if it would be OK to take some of the leaves and acorns with them. My mom quickly replied, "Sure, take them all with you back to Texas!"

An attorney was in the middle of a work out at his gym when he noticed a very large man lifting weights on the bench press. The guy looked like he weighed over 400 pounds and was wearing a t-shirt that read I BEAT ANOREXIA!

John T. Carroll is the talented businessman behind the Carroll Advertising Company and is the owner of the Red Rooster Bar & Grill on Route One South in Wrentham as well as many electronic advertising billboards. John is smart, funny and generous with a level of courtesy that is only exceeded by his genuine kindness. He turned the Rooster, as it is called by regular patrons, into an exact replica of an old fashioned Irish pub. The food is absolutely delicious with the drinks, service and atmosphere all top shelf. My first pint of fresh cold Guinness, perfectly poured with a head to admire, took my mind back to my cousin's pub in Ballyjamesduff just west of Dublin. The remarkable attention to detail in the Rooster is not surprising as John and his lovely wife Jen own a house in Connemara which is not far from J. Do's family homestead in Galway.

It is not unusual to find the Rooster full of people from all walks of life including courthouse personnel, litigants, witnesses, lawyers and jurors enjoying food from the extensive menu along with a refreshing beverage. John had a very successful book signing there for me while Attorney James M. Brady entertained the crowd with his precision guitar play and strong Celtic voice while accompanied by the very talented Jack Glennon. Jim, an excellent lawyer, put his way through law school singing Irish songs and now it could be said that he sings to the judge and jury!

Jim even performed at The Dubliner in DC and recommended the delicious shepherd's pie when J. Do and I travelled to Washington for the swearing in of Congressman Bill Keating. I was honored that he and some fellow musicians played at my retirement party where the sound of Jimmy's voice quickly brought back Celtic memories from a favorite pub. Jim's robust singing is still just as powerful as his persuasive legal arguments!

I'm happy that John Carroll is doing well because he is one of the nicest guys around. We lived an hour away from Wrentham at the time of my retirement party so John

Look who just retired
from the Wrentham District Court.
Eddie Doherty
FISHING WITH HIS YOUNG GRANDCHILDREN
Life is
STRIPERS & DIAPERS!

Route One retirement billboard

surprised me and other drivers on Route One with a farewell humorous message about my work in the court which was displayed on a huge electronic billboard not far from Gillette Stadium.

The day after my retirement party my wife J. Do took what was left of the huge beautiful cake and brought it to the Veterans' Transition House in New Bedford where they were all very happy and extremely appreciative. My bride accomplished two things that day - she put a smile on the face of many veterans and she kept the cake away from her husband!

That week the Environmental Police seized 500 lobsters in New Bedford that were taken illegally from Georges Bank by an offshore fishing trawler and donated the tasty crustaceans to the same group of veterans.

It doesn't get any better than free cake and lobster for the brave veterans who have kept us safe by defending the greatest country on the face of the earth.

One of the most underrated municipal jobs is that of a crossing guard. These devoted public servants stand in the middle of busy streets to stop speeding traffic so that children can cross safely. When we were kids there was a very nice crossing guard named Mrs. Pye who worked the busy intersection of North Main and West Streets in Attleboro. Mrs. Pye's first name was Theresa, but when I was a little kid I called her Apple Pie and she always got a kick out of it. She cared about and protected every kid crossing that street like it was her own child. Mrs. Pye was a sweet, kind lady who reminded me of Aunt Bee on the *Andy Griffith Show*.

Fast forward many years and Mrs. Pye was at the counter of the ADC where she asked for me. She was crying and told me that she knew that I worked at the court from the newspaper. Tears were falling as she said, "Do you remember me? You used to call me Apple Pie when you were a little boy!" I told her that of course I remembered her and gave her a hug as I felt the poor lady trembling. I brought her into my office where she told me that a car was traveling north very fast and ignored her command to slow down. She had to grab a young kid out of the road to avoid a tragedy and was yelled at by the occupants of the vehicle. She said that they had called her names, said some very bad words and almost hit her.

I was outraged and felt terrible for this wonderful woman who absolutely lived for helping children. This story was getting worse until I heard the magic words - she got the license plate number! I made a phone call and before Mrs. Pye left the court she was wearing a smile and the offending driver was wearing handcuffs! Nobody messes with my Apple Pye!

Nicky's Restaurant in Wrentham is a first-rate place run by Mickey Scouras and his father Pete who serve delicious food and warm hospitality. I used to volunteer there a few days before every Thanksgiving to help put together hot turkey dinners with all the fixings for busloads of needy people. The Scouras family are very generous with their time and money so I was honored to participate.

It is easy to get a true sense of how lucky we are on a day like this. An elderly woman told me that the last time that she had a hot meal was the last time she had seen me just before the previous Thanksgiving and an elderly man's hand was shaking as he tried to give me a dollar bill. Everything is free of charge thanks to the kindness of the Scouras family, but the poor man was just trying to do the right thing.

I was part of an assembly line in the kitchen where we would place a serving of one item and then pass the plate to the next guy. I started out as the stuffing man and eventually got promoted to turkey! A homeless man heard that I was the stuffing guy and told me that it was the best that he had ever tasted so I thanked him, but told him that I couldn't take the credit as I only scooped it and that the real culinary genius was Mickey who created and cooked everything.

Many of the volunteers for this magnificent event are kids from nearby King Philip Regional High School so it is nice to be surrounded by youth doing a good thing and making a positive difference in the community. Most of them serve as wait staff and bring the food to the seated guests. A teenaged boy was the cranberry guy next to me and his older sister was one of the waitresses. They were both good kids who had just received their report cards from school. The girl brought home a report card with a C in every subject which caused her parents to be extremely upset resulting in her crying all the way to her room. She was still crying when her brother, the cranberry scooper, came home with all Ds on his report card causing the parents to go to console the daughter and tell her, "We're sorry, we're very proud of you for those Cs!"

The Attleboro YMCA is almost directly across the street from the courthouse so I would walk over there almost every day after work. Retired Attleboro Fire Chief Benjamin R. "Bob" Livesey and I would finish our workouts and usually end up in the steam bath at the same time. His son Glenn retired as the Assistant Chief of the Attleboro Fire Department and son Gary was one of the best athletes in the history of Attleboro High School. Bob was an interesting man and a World War II Marine combat veteran of Tinian and Iwo Jima and was awarded the Navy Cross for courageous action on Saipan. The former tank commander only talked about the horrors of those invasions upon prompting by myself. I loved listening to his stories as it was like sitting in the steam room in the middle of a living History Channel documentary. Bob left the service as a Staff Sergeant and was a humble American hero who I always admired.

Chief Ronald Churchill was another great leader from the same department. Chief Churchill gave CPR classes at the Attleboro Public Library so J. Do and I signed up shortly after getting married. He taught us to practice on each other so when my bride was on the floor playing the role of the unconscious victim I would have to shake her shoulder, eventually open her mouth and lock my lips onto hers'. The only problem was that every time I lowered my face and got close to J. Do she would burst out in uncontrollable laughter! Laughter is contagious so the whole class would soon be roaring! I kept telling her that she was supposed to be unconscious and if she didn't stop giggling we weren't going to pass the test! The good natured Chief just stood over us while shaking his head and J. Do eventually stopped laughing just long enough for him to give us our certification!

I played high school football with a nice guy who wasn't the brightest student in school. He said that his favorite classes were homeroom, gym and lunch!

Some of my family and friends have commented that my salt intake is so high that I am lucky to be alive. It's true that I shake salt on top of salt and use more of it than anyone has ever seen so the joke is that when the DPW runs out of road salt for a snowstorm they call me!

A bunch of guys went to lunch at Café Assisi in Wrentham where you will never get a bad meal from the delicious homemade menu offerings of owner Dereck DiBiase, a terrific host who always takes care of us and treats us like royalty. We were all laughing and having a good time when Carmine Simonelli noticed that the salt shaker on the table was so tiny that he picked it up and said, "Eddie's in trouble! He's going to need a lot more salt than this!"

Paul Perry is a dear friend who is tough as nails. We used to have slap fights in high school which entailed one guy holding his hands together, as if in prayer, but straight out, and the other guy facing him with hands at his side. The one with the praying hands tried to move quickly to avoid being slapped. Paul was the undisputed champion of this mindless exercise that used to leave the skin on my hands as red as a ripe tomato! Paul was not a very big guy, but had a solid build with hands like lightning. He was probably the smallest bouncer in history, but always got the job done at the local establishments he protected.

Paul was also a terrific tennis player who always had a funny line ready. We were making our way into the gym to watch an AHS basketball game just after Christmas when we found ourselves next to a kid named Tommy. He had been in and out of trouble frequently and always carried a knife. Paul smiled as we walked by and said, "Hi Tommy, what'd you get for Christmas - a new knife!"

My dad gave me an old station wagon, but I wasn't a very handy guy so I asked Paul to install an 8 track player under the dashboard so that I could listen to musical tapes. After Paul finished the job I chose a J. Geils Band tape for my first selection. I pushed the tape in, but instead of music the windshield wipers started flapping at full speed! Paul came over and fixed the problem and we had a good laugh!

As previously mentioned, Donald E. Rodman, who had helped thousands of children and adults in need, was the recipient of our American Ambassador of Philanthropy Award at my very last Law Day Ceremony. Don was one of the most humble and nicest guys that I have ever known so I really had to twist his arm to get him to accept an award honoring him and not somebody else. He was a giant amongst successful businessmen with the heart of a lion and the kindness of Mother Teresa. He is missed as much today as the day that we lost him.

Don was sick in bed when somebody ordered flowers to be delivered to his home in Canton. Kristen Orlando's father, Frank Richardson, was the delivery man who rang the doorbell with the flowers in hand. He didn't know Don, but was mistaken for one of his friends and invited right into the house. Frank was told to go directly upstairs to the bedroom as Don will be happy to see him. Don was propped up with pillows and asked him to come into the bedroom and have a seat next to the bed. Don and Frank spoke for a while with Don being as friendly and outgoing as always, but after a few laughs Don said, "So, please refresh my memory. How do I know you anyway?" "You don't," Frank answered, "I'm just the delivery man!"

Greg Murphy and I met while coaching our seven-year old daughters who played together on the same softball team. Meghan Murphy and my daughter Kaitlin had fun meeting new kids and learning a team sport as Murph and I became fast friends. Murph's son David grew up to be a successful attorney, worked in the Commissioner's Office of Major League Baseball and won election as Chairman of the Attleboro School Committee.

After earning his undergraduate degree at Fordham University in the Bronx, David moved into a different apartment and began working at his baseball job. Greg and his lovely wife Sharon helped David get settled in his new place which was not located in a bad area of New York, but was far from the nicest neighborhood that the Murphy's had ever visited. Having already felt a sense of relief that David had survived four years in the Bronx, Sharon was understandably nervous with continued concerns about violent crime where her son was now living. She continued to express her unease and apprehension to her husband during the drive back to Massachusetts.

Greg and Sharon were watching *Law & Order* on TV when they got home to Attleboro. Anyone familiar with that series knows that the printed address where some scenes are taking place is displayed at the bottom of the TV screen during the beginning of each segment. If the prosecutors or police are walking into a building, for instance, the New York street address will sometimes be shown at the bottom of the TV. In this particular episode the police had just entered an apartment to investigate a murder. The detectives worked around the body on the floor to process the crime scene as the address for the homicide appeared on the TV. The address shown on the TV screen for the murder happened to be the same street as David's new apartment in New York where they had just left their son! Needless to say, this did nothing to calm the already frayed nerves of a concerned mother!

Murph and I are both die-hard baseball fans so it is always a pleasure to discuss our National Pastime with him. Murph knows that I am a serious Red Sox fan so he realized that I would be disappointed as the 2011 baseball season came to an end. Boston was up by nine games on Tampa Bay in the American League Wild Card race on September 3, but the Sox lost 18 of their last 24 games and were eliminated from playoff contention. Murph sensed the inevitable collapse and knew that I wouldn't be happy so with two games left to the season he sent an email to J. Do and stated, "Might be a good idea to use plastic knives around your husband the next 48 hours."

Murph graduated from my father's alma mater, Stonehill College, which is referred to as the Notre Dame of the east. I stayed there at O'Hara Hall for high school football camp and have fond memories of the camp's director Val Muscato kidding around with us while eating off my plate at lunch! Coach Muscato was the legendary coach and athletic director at Oliver Ames High School, an acclaimed guy who we all looked up to. He held the record for the 440 at Notre Dame, but by this time had put on a little weight and may have even liked to eat as much as I did!

Murph's roommate at Stonehill, Herb Morrison Jr., was the oldest of four boys from an old fashioned Irish Catholic family. Herb's father, Herb Sr., a real practical joker, sold communications equipment. One morning Herb Jr. and his brothers were walking to catch the bus for grade school as their dad was leaving for work with a suitcase. When asked where he was going the father facetiously replied that he was going to be away for a few days as he was headed for the hospital to have brain surgery. Herb Jr. thought that his dad was serious so he told a nun about the sudden calamity when he got to school. Every one of the school's eight grades prayed for Mr. Morrison daily for the entire week as word of the brain surgery quickly spread around town. The whole family attended church that Sunday, as always, with Mr. Morrison upstairs in the choir and his wife and kids seated together in the front pew when they heard the priest make a request from the altar. No one was more surprised than Herb Sr. when the priest addressed the congregation and asked, "Let us pray and please keep Herb Morrison in your prayers for a swift recovery from his brain operation."

Jackie Buckner is one of J. Do's friends and a very nice person. Her mother had valeted her car at Brigham & Women's in Foxborough to take Jackie's daughter, her granddaughter, to physical therapy. Once finished they came outside where Jackie's mom held out the ticket to a guy wearing sunglasses who she thought was the parking attendant as she was ready for her car. The man politely told her that he was not the valet as he kept on walking. Jackie's daughter quickly rhetorically asked her grandmother, "You know who that was don't you?" It was New England Patriots wide receiver Julian Edelman!

One of my all-time favorite baseball managers was Dick Williams who brought the 1967 Red Sox of my youth all the way to the seventh game of the World Series. He said some funny stuff like, "I was a low ball hitter and a high ball drinker."

J. Do and I have had the pleasure of meeting some interesting professional athletes. Jason Varitek, Luis Tiant, Boog Powell, Julian Edelman and Danny Amendola have all become iconic names in the world of sports. Their willingness to help others, superior athletic skill, clutch play, dedication to craft and passionate determination have made them incredibly accomplished heroes who will never be forgotten by an adoring public.

Two-time World Series Champion, AL MVP Boog Powell, Camden Yards

Boston Red Sox two-time World Series Champion Jason Varitek, caught 4 no hitters

Boston Red Sox three-time All Star, two-time ERA leader Luis Tiant (Barry Okun photo)

NE Patriots two-time Super Bowl Champion Danny Amendola

NE Patriots Super Bowl MVP, three-time Super Bowl Champion Julian Edelman

11. Canal Rats, et al

I have enjoyed fishing ever since I was very young when Grandpa Flynn took me to the storied banks of the historic Cape Cod Canal. Anglers' rods bent toward the raging current with striped bass breaking the surface introduced me to the thrill of surfcasting and had me hooked for life! Much later, I would rise at 2 AM to head for the Canal and fish until sunrise, then hustle back home to take a shower and be at the courthouse in time for work, but now that I'm retired I can keep casting after sunup!

My great-grandfather John T. Brady came to America from Ireland as a young man with very few possessions. He did carry some fishing gear across the sea, including his reed lined creel, which is now proudly displayed in our living room. He passed before I ever knew him, but his daughters told me that he loved to fish and suggested that his DNA was the likely source of my addiction to surfcasting!

John T. Brady

Experienced fishermen who surf cast the Cape Cod Canal are affectionately referred to as Canal Rats. Legendary anglers like Stan Gibbs, John Doble, Bill "On the Grill" Prodouz, "Breakin' Bob" Weir, "New Hampshire Bob" Szwyd, Bill Walsh, Kenny Nevens, "Paulie the Painter" Gravina, Tony McCann, Zak Baker, Fred Creager, Tim "Hollywood" Petracca, Hiep "Henry" Nguyen, Al Mazeiko, Mark Beckford, Pat Denno, Joe Gray, Josh Douglas, Steve & Rob Dewar, Vinny Rosata, Jimmy Kelly, Bill Jenkinson, Dr. Johan Frenje, David & Ray Barros, Bob Abreau, Bob Dermody, Lou Dupiton, Bill "Costy" Costello, Bob "Bull" MacKinnon, Rob Ebert, Joe Eufrazio, Dwight Cochrane Sr., Dwight "D2" Cochrane Jr., Mike Allaire, Jeremy Louro, Marie's husband Steven Murray, Kevin Downs, Mike Deryck, Rob & Donnie "Hawkeye" Willis, Patrick Kearney, Todd Benedict, Greg McSharry, Captain Paul Sexton, "Mashpee Mike" LaRaia, Bob Dyer, "Taunton Teddy" Menard, Paul Sroczinski, Tim Sullivan, Mark "Preacher" MacNeill, Martin Souza, Ben Sivonen, Ron "Hollywood" Sivonen, Chuck Franks, Scott Ewell, Jo Jo Andrade, Anast & Nick Terezakis, Joe "The Reel" McCoy, Glenn Lindsey, "Timmy Tuna" Lendino and the brothers Keegan - Sean, George & Joe have contributed to making the Big Ditch a famous fishing destination.

Some great fishermen also happen to be dynamic lure makers like Harold Skelton - Skelton Lures, "Jumpin Joe" England, Phil Chorman - Bigdelicious Baits, Mike Webster - Striper Gear, Larry Welcome - Northbar Tackle, Wayne Hess - Guppy Lures, Dan & Matt Smalley - Gibbs Lures, Ron Arra - Strike Pro, "Pistol Pete" Freitas - 50# Plugs & Bill Hurley - Bill Hurley Lures, all highly skilled craftsmen who produce top quality lures for the surf.

Vito Marsico (Vinnie Marsico photo)

My favorite tackle shops like Canal Bait & Tackle, Maco's Bait & Tackle and Red Top Sporting Goods are located right near the Canal where they can outfit you with whatever fishing gear you need. These shops are staffed by experienced fishermen ready to assist novices and old salts alike. I have become very familiar with this work force over the years, but the absolute best in the business is Connor Swartz at Red Top Sporting Goods. Connor is extremely knowledgeable with a nice way about him and the ability to advise anglers with the most up to date information. He is a valued resource for boat guys and surfcasters like myself so you can't go wrong with Connor in your corner!

Vito Marsico is an experienced Canal Rat who makes the drive from his home on Long Island as often as possible with his father Vinnie. Just like all hard core fishermen, the easy going Sing Sing Corrections Officer forgoes sleep and other activities in pursuit of striped bass. Some may think we are crazy, but Vito expressed our surfcasting sentiments best when he said, "…a lot of sleep loss and of memories gained."

I was interviewed by the great Stan Grossfeld of *The Boston Globe* for a story about striped bass fishing on the Cape Cod Canal. Stan's beautifully written story as well as his extraordinary photography appeared on the front page of the sports section of the *Globe*. It was truly an honor for me as Stan has won so many noteworthy awards including back to back Pulitzer Prizes!

Stan first met his lovely wife Stacey, a Registered Nurse, when she was administering a domestic violence program at MCI Framingham prison for women. Stan was working on a story for the *Globe* about some of these women who were doing time after having been convicted of murdering their husbands during a marriage of horrendous domestic abuse. I asked Stan where he had met his wife and he wasn't kidding when he replied, "In prison!"

Stan had already interviewed me along the banks of the historic Cape Cod Canal for two days in the hope of getting a photograph of me catching a striped bass for his story, but the linesiders just weren't cooperating. The absence of small bait in the Canal had left stripers pursuing their prey in Buzzards Bay so I had been skunked on both occasions, but I actually felt worse for Stan than for myself. Stan, who is dedicated to his craft with the persistent determination of a warrior, came back for a third early morning foray to the dark edges of the big ditch. We spoke about all kinds of topics as I continued casting through the fog into the swift east flowing current. I mentioned that my friend Dave Linton is the terrific crime beat reporter and esteemed writer for *The Sun Chronicle* and had covered both of the courts where I had worked. Dave had recently told me that unfortunately some of his colleagues had lost their jobs due to layoffs at the newspaper. Stan facetiously shot back with, "If you don't catch a fish pretty soon I'm going to get laid off!" It wasn't long after that I was relieved to finally catch a striper for Stan's camera.

Sue Barlow is the multi-talented Access Coordinator for Bourne Community TV where she does an outstanding job as Host of *The Bourne Review* and *Cape House Cooking*. Sue asked me to shoot a monthly video fishing report for her viewers after hearing my name from Bill "On the Grill" so I was happy to oblige. She made me feel comfortable from the start with her warm personality, easy laugh and respectful listening ability. We shot the second segment on the Canal at the annual cookout for the Falmouth Fishermen's Association and Buzzard Bay Anglers Club. Bill lit the grill at 7AM which is lunch time on the body clock of surfcasters like myself who have been fishing since 2AM. The smell of delicious burgers and sauerkraut dogs permeated the salt air as guys put their rods down to eat. Sue finished filming me at about 7:30 so I asked her if she would like a piping hot cheeseburger, but the smiling professional declined stating, "Thanks Eddie, but it's a little early for me!"

I never shave before heading for the Canal unless I am shooting a video for Dave Anderson from *The Fisherman* magazine or for Sue and then I even apply cologne for the occasion. One morning, after Sue had filmed me, a guy walked by and said, "You smell good, but I don't think it will help you catch fish!"

J. Do hooks 'em & cooks 'em! (Kurt Gursky photo)

There has been a terrific quote in *The Fisherman* magazine attributed to the timeless Babe Ruth where he speaks of his future Hall of Fame teammate by saying, "Lou Gehrig would rather fish than eat." Ruth, arguably the best all-around baseball player in history, was a real character who caroused late into the night and even ate hot dogs in the dugout during the game. The immortal Ruth left a legacy of incredible statistics and although the lighthearted Babe's lifestyle could never be described as healthy, he never took illegal performance enhancing supplements. A guy was trying to make that point during the baseball steroid scandal by wearing a tee shirt on the Canal with an interesting slogan. The guy's shirt read, "THE BABE DID IT ON HOT DOGS & BEER!

Johnny Fernandes is an experienced fisherman and a terrific guy who I surf cast the Canal with, but he also owns a house on the east coast of Florida so he does a lot of fishing in the Sunshine State. Johnny, who is from New Bedford, started smoking marijuana when he was in the third grade so his mother sent him to live in Central Falls to get away from the drug scene. At the time at least, some would say that was like trying to lose weight by getting a job at an ice cream shack! Johnny is now married with two kids and doing very well as he sells and repairs scooters that he buys in bulk from Zhejiang, China which is just south of Shanghai. Johnny has an expression that he uses on everybody. I'll tell him a funny story while fishing next to him and he'll say, "You're killing me Eddie!" He says this to everyone so the woman that he speaks with on the phone in China when ordering scooters has heard this said a million times. Her name is Wuyi so Johnny has told her many times over the years, "You're killing me Wuyi!" Johnny has definitely rubbed off on her as she has heard it so frequently that recently she even told him, "You're killing me Johnny!"

I have also spent a lot of time on the Canal and elsewhere with Johnny's cousin Wayne Reis. Wayne also hails from the Whaling City and is one of the nicest guys that I have ever known. He is an accomplished surf caster who reels in quality fish on a consistent basis. He also knows people in all walks of life and uses his connections to help others as he is always there for those in need. The Air Force veteran is the unofficial Mayor of the Canal and can frequently be seen recruiting young kids, who are fishing with their families, to help him pick up trash along the service road and stone banks of the big ditch. I am proud to call him my friend because he lives to help others.

There were quite a few cars in line at Dunkin' after I finished a morning of surfcasting the Canal for striped bass. The guy in the vehicle in front of me finally made it up to the spot where you place the order. I'm no health nut, but when I heard him order a coffee with four creams and five sugars I suddenly felt a little better about that jelly donut I was about to order!

My brother-in-law Gene McNamara and his son, my nephew Jason, joined me to try our luck on an early morning tide near the east end. In between casts, Gene related a story about learning to use a firearm. The instructor told him to put a round in the target so Gene pointed the six-shot revolver and emptied the gun by pulling the trigger six times. The surprised instructor yelled that he had just told him to put a round in the target and that a round is only one shot to which Gene replied, "Oh, I'm sorry - I thought a round was like a round of drinks!"

People love eating sushi. The sushi craze has spread worldwide such that record levels are being consumed every day. To each his own, but I've never been a fan of eating sushi as we had a different name for it when we were kids. We called it bait!

Jack Barton is a finish carpenter who does all kinds of home renovations and surf casts the Canal as much as he can before heading to work in the morning. He is a good guy and a highly-skilled fisherman with a big heart. Brad O'Brien is a retired Berkley Police Officer and one of Jack's neighbors. One day, which happened to be a rain-soaked 4th of July, Brad found a young lhasa apso and contacted Jack thinking that maybe the dog belonged to him. It didn't, but Jack, his wife Michelle and their oldest daughter Rebekah Astle took the dog in and worked together in cleaning, drying and feeding the poor little guy. After an exhaustive search for the dog's owner which included handmade signs and social media site reviews, his master could not be identified and no one ever came forward to claim the happy puppy. The lucky canine had found plenty of love, however, and a new home on the Barton's sprawling farm. They had taken the pup into their family on Independence Day so Jack, being the patriotic guy that he is, named the dog Indie!

Just like most Canal Rats, Jack has a bike equipped with rod holders and baskets to hold fishing gear. His faithful dog Indie stays in the work truck while Jack fishes so after a morning of wetting a line he rides back to the truck to pick up the lovable canine. It is now the dog's turn to have fun as Jack puts the little guy in the front basket of the bike and pedals along the service road of the Canal as Indie takes in the view and enjoys the ride.

It's nice when people are able to recognize the truly important things in life. Jack's father John is recovering from open heart surgery and is slowly working his way back into fishing the Canal. Jack made a Canal chair for him complete with a rod holder for his transition back to good health.

Jack and his father returned to their vehicles about the same time as I did after a morning of surfcasting the Big Ditch. Jack's dad had landed a striped bass on the east tide and even though it was a small one he was the only one of the three of us to catch anything at all. I congratulated John in the parking lot as we were stowing our gear away and told him that maybe his next fish will be a monster. I felt a tug on my heart when he then told me that the size of the striper didn't even matter because the best part was that he got to spend a morning fishing with his son. Amen to that.

Canal bikes are designed to hold a lot of heavy fishing gear so a strong kickstand is a must. Wooden stakes, metal rods and even broken hockey sticks are just a few of the objects used as handmade kickstands to stabilize bikes. I was riding by the Herring Run when I had to admire one surfcaster's creativity. The angler was probably also a golfer as his kickstand was an old putter!

After spending a significant part of my life working in courtrooms as well as surfcasting the Atlantic coast, I am in agreement with something I heard from a fellow Canal Rat. I can say with a high degree of certainty that sometimes guys are like fish - they get in trouble when they open their mouth!

A golfer decided to try his hand at fishing. His first cast was terrible as the lure, with three treble hooks attached, flew through the air with the strong wind blowing it back into a crowd of startled anglers. The cast was so bad that he yelled, "Fore!"

I have heard or seen some fantastic names for boats in addition to Judge Patrick Hurley's *RECESS*.

IRISH AYES is creative and *SHE GOT THE HOUSE* says it all.

Walpole Police Detective Bill Madden named his boat *REEL AMERICAN* and one day fishing off of Block Island another boat went by with the home port listed on the stern as C.I. which caused Bill's friend to say it was from Castle Island not the Cayman Islands. I doubt it stood for Confidential Informant!

Gruffy's sister Maureen was a retired Massachusetts State Police Sergeant. She named her boat *NO CLUE* because that was her answer whenever she was asked what was wrong with the engine.

House Majority Leader John Rogers & Governor's Councilor Mike Callahan bought Maureen's boat and renamed it *PAIN IN THE AFT*.

Keith E. McDonough, the great Lawrence District Court Clerk-Magistrate appointed by Governor Michael S. Dukakis named his boat *FIGHTING IRISH*.

Legendary fisherman Charlie Murphy's boat is *TROPHY WIFE*.

Clerk-Magistrates collect an afterhours $40 fee for each prisoner released from lockup, hence the boat named *FOUR DIMES*.

Falmouth Defense Attorney Drew J. Segadelli is the Captain of *CRIME PAYS*.

Matt Davidson has *COOL HAND FLUKE* and Lisa Danforth skippers *FIN AND TONIC*.

Retired Franklin firefighter Mark Petitt is a Navy veteran who charters fishing trips out of Plymouth as Captain of the *FIRE ESCAPE*.

Then there was the guy who bought a boat previously owned by a plumber and decided to keep the boat's name - *FLUSH*.

Len DiCarlo is Captain of the *LOCAL BUOY*, Cindy & Sam Pappas own *ANGLER MANAGEMENT* and who could forget Lesley & Dick Swaylik's *YES DEAR*!

It's an easy guess that John Homa graduated from Holy Cross when seeing the name of the boat owned by he & his wife Amy - *CRUSADER*!

I've given a lot of breaks by finding people Not Responsible on speeding tickets over the years so if I ever buy a boat I will name it *KNOT RESPONSIBLE*!

My cousin John Cornish is a terrific guy who genuinely cares about his employees and others. As mentioned previously, we worked together at Gulf Hill as teenagers and had a lot of laughs together. John grew up to be a leader in the community as a man of great accomplishment and was kind enough to offer me my first book signing opportunity at the Open House for Atlantic Boats, his business in Wareham. The Open House was a well-attended event bringing in people from near and far featuring live on site broadcasts by COOL 102 FM & WCOD FM. I enjoyed being interviewed about my first book by legendary radio host and DJ Joe Rossetti who had the live microphone for the event. He is an interesting and talented guy who seems to know everyone so if you haven't met Joe it's probably because you must have just moved to the Cape!

Guests enjoy food, music and hopefully buy a boat after going for a test drive at John's other business Stonebridge Marina just down the street. During a phone call to Atlantic Boats you will hear a very creative expression if you are put on hold. John doesn't want you to hang up so the announcement says, "As the fisherman said to the fish - please remain on the line."

I was surfcasting for striped bass as the sun came up at pole #20 on the east end of the Canal. The fish weren't cooperating so I decided to take a short breakfast break. I had just taken a bite out of a peanut butter sandwich as another fisherman rode by on his bike. He noticed that I was eating as he laughed and said, "The fish aren't biting, but you are!"

My surfcasting day on the Canal was over so as I was travelling home in the middle lane on Route 25 West I noticed a car with roof racks holding fishing rods catching up to me at a high rate of speed in the left lane. As the vehicle passed me I saw the driver brushing his teeth with his knee on the wheel! It's time for him to loosen up his schedule so he can use the bathroom sink!

My father was my dentist until he became too ill and had to give up his dental practice. Dentists see each other's work, thus my dad knew that Dr. John Friedman was excellent so I became Dr. Friedman's patient until moving away in retirement. I am now happy to go to Dr. Charles P. Khoury who is also excellent. I should know because Dr. Khoury has done so much work on me that I now have more crowns than the Royal Family!

One of my favorite places to fish on the Canal is at pole 305 on the mainland side as I have landed some nice fish there, especially on an east dropping tide just before sunup. Brenda M. Andre, Dental Assistant for Dr. Khoury, is a really nice person and a true professional who I always look forward to seeing. By coincidence, Brenda vacations with her boyfriend Wayne Manchester at the Bourne Scenic Park which is located right behind my surfcasting spot!

There was a time when I had not yet emerged from my cave into the 21st century and chose not to participate in this modern invention called emails! My bride would use emails to communicate with her family, friends and even many of my friends. One day I was going fishing so J. Do put out a mass blast of emails to several of my buddies informing

Two-year old granddaughter Addie learning how to fillet a striper

them of my plan. Her email said, "Eddie's heading for the Canal. He's going for stripers." Unfortunately, the automatic built in word correction component added a "p" to the word stripers essentially announcing to the world that I was going for strippers! I got a call from a Boston lawyer who said, "Gee, your wife is very understanding!"

J. Do has almost always travelled with me when I have been a speaker at New England fishing shows from Plum Island to Mohegan Sun and many points between. I was walking into the Rhode Island Convention Center to give a surfcasting seminar at the New England Saltwater Fishing Show with J. Do helping to carry lures and other props that were needed. This is a busy three day event that is well attended by over 15,000 people and helps to take the chill off of the end of winter. Wall to wall vendors are selling rods, reels, lures and everything else imaginable that is fishing related. J. Do is a good sport who enjoys fishing to some extent, but certainly does not share my addiction to the surf and yet she was now suddenly surrounded by the world of angling. There was no shopping for dresses,

Keynote Speaker, NE Fishing Expo

pocketbooks or perfume as we slowly walked by an aisle of fishing vendors and maneuvered our way through the jam packed crowd of surfcasting fanatics. J. Do looked around at all the fishing gear and, not seeing any feminine products, smiled at me before saying, "I must really love you."

Massachusetts saltwater fishing licenses are free upon turning age 60, but there is a minor processing fee still applicable. My cousin Tom Bodge wasn't aware of the discount when he reached the magic age so he was surprised when the young clerk said that the price was only $1.34. He asked the young lady why it was so inexpensive and she told him it was because he was old!

Mike Morganelli is a nice guy who started boxing at the age of five. His pugilistic career had him fighting in rings all over the country while compiling an incredibly impressive amateur boxing record of 122-18 including a couple of national titles in Ohio! Mike eventually turned professional tallying a 2-0 record before hanging up the gloves for good. We were surfcasting side by side on the Canal, talking about how fishing equipment can be expensive so that it's not easy losing lures that are stuck behind a rock in the middle of the channel. It's all part of the game, but tough to see money go down the drain. The former welterweight cracked me up when he said, "Sometimes I feel like I just opened my wallet and dumped all my cash into the Canal!"

There is a terrific restaurant on the canal named the Fishermen's View in Sandwich, located on the Cape side close to the east end. Brothers Bob and Denny Colbert constructed the perfectly situated dining spot that also has a full beautiful bar and fish market all under one roof. I got to know Bob from Seafood Marketing Steering Committee Meetings, and other family members like his daughter Elizabeth also work there. The menu lists a wide variety of mouthwatering dishes including the freshest seafood from the nearby cold deep water of the North Atlantic. These siblings bring a wealth of seafood experience to the table as they are both local fishermen with their own commercial vessels. This is a fantastic place to enjoy a delicious meal with an outstanding view of the historic Cape Cod Canal.

Steve Colleran is a Vietnam-era United States Marine Corps veteran and a good guy who walks his dog on the Canal service road. Sometimes he fishes himself and other times will sit and speak with me as I am wetting a line. Jethro, his big lovable bloodhound, was always close by keeping us company. I discovered something about Jethro's diet the first time I caught a keeper while Steve was with me. The south wind was gently touching my face as I cast out 40 yards to a west bound breaking fish. After fighting and landing the 32 inch striper Steve asked if he could have it as Jethro loves poached striped bass! I happily gave it to him as he told me that sometimes he cooks it with a little chicken stock to add flavor for his longtime companion. Unfortunately, Jethro passed away after some difficult ailments, but Steve got another bloodhound, a puppy he named Boss Hogg who also enjoys a fresh plate of striped bass!

D.J. Muller is a dynamic speaker, author of several fishing books and a terrific surfcasting guide. The outgoing New Jersey angler introduced me to Janet Messineo on Martha's Vineyard when we all fished part of a tide with her on Chappaquiddick where seven foot swells were crashing up and down the sloped beach on a windy night. Janet is a very nice lady and an expert surfcaster who is a genuine legend on the island so it was an honor to be able to wet a line with her.

The next time I saw Janet was at the Wolves Den Sports Complex in Pembroke where we were both speaking at surfcasting seminars for the Sport Fishing Expo hosted by the Massachusetts Striped Bass Association. The well attended function is always in good hands with Expo Chairperson Captain George Doucette and MassBass President Ray West. Janet was speaking just before me so I was fortunate to be able to attend some of her talk and thoroughly enjoyed her presentation. You could hear a pin drop as the audience was extremely attentive listening to Janet who is an interesting speaker with the unique ability to make you feel as though you are part of the action and living the event along with her. She had finished writing a book entitled *CASTING INTO THE LIGHT* that was scheduled for release that summer which became an immediate priority on my reading list as J. Do gave it to me for my birthday. It is a wonderful book that is as enjoyable as it is informative and truly lives up to its name.

Janet related some portions of the book to the audience as she spoke about her experiences living in a vacation land off the coast of Massachusetts not far from the Elizabeth Islands chain. I found that the description of her daily routine was one of the most captivating and remarkable components of life on Martha's Vineyard. Janet would have her first lure in the ocean long before sunrise, surf cast along the dark sandy beaches and then sell the fish that she had caught to the local restaurants. She would race home to take a shower and then report back to the restaurant to work as a waitress. I thought that the most fascinating segment of her day was that Janet would sometimes serve patrons in the restaurant plates of fish that she had caught herself that very morning!

Attorney Jim Brady is a terrific advocate, guitar player, singer, MC and friend. Jimmy had a nephew who had just opened a tackle shop so he asked me to stop in and introduce myself. I dropped by a few times, but he was usually out taking customers on a fishing charter so I never had the pleasure of meeting him. The last time I went there with J. Do and asked a young man behind the counter if he was in. The young man told us that he was out because he and his wife had to go to their baby's autopsy. "Oh my God, that's terrible." I said, "Was it a car accident? What happened?" No, his wife is pregnant, we were told by the young man, so they went to the doctor to find out if it is a boy or a girl. "Do you mean an ultrasound?" J. Do asked. "Yea, that's it", the poor kid said, "An ultrasound and an autopsy is the same thing, right?"

There is no official striped bass record for the Cape Cod Canal, but after extensive research and with the help of great surfcaster Rob Curtis, I can confirm the largest catch with a very high degree of certainty. As far as I know, the largest striper ever caught on the Big Ditch was landed in 1956 by New Bedford angler Frank Machado with the fish weighing in at 63 pounds, 4 ounces!

I have been fortunate to have been able to get to know some of the best writers and others in the world of fishing like Mark Blazis of the *Worcester Telegram & Gazette;* Bill Hough of *The Falmouth Enterprise;* Chris Megan, Kevin Blinkoff, Jimmy Fee & Matt Haeffner of *On The Water* magazine; *The Fish Wrap Writer* Todd Corayer; Dave Anderson, Dale Nicholson, Joyce & Michael Caruso of *The Fisherman* magazine as well as Toby Lapinski who was with the same publication when he printed my first story. I was lucky enough to fish a couple of times with Charley Soares, a terrific angler and inspiring writer. It would seem that there are only so many ways to describe catching a fish, but the aforementioned scribes employ such creativity and imagination that their powerful words make you almost feel the salt spray in your face!

Captain Dave Monti, owner of No Fluke Charters, is a well-respected veteran columnist, Rhode Island based Charter Captain and a good friend. Dave operates the *Virginia Joan*, named for his lovely wife, out of Wickford where he consistently puts smiles on the faces of his customers with successful days on the water. He writes extremely interesting stories in magazines and other publications including a weekly fishing column that appears in several major newspapers. Dave asked me and some other stakeholders to accompany him to Washington a couple of times to assist in the effort in keeping the Magnuson-Stevens Act viable by visiting with Senators and Congressmen in the United States Capitol. We were sponsored by the generous folks at Ocean Conservancy and were told later that we had contributed to making a positive difference.

Anglers come from near and far to hire Dave for a half or full day of terrific fishing. He targets various species, but has become famous for his ability to put his customers on abundant schools of fluke. Dave mentioned a bait concoction that he had created himself in one of his columns. He combines squid, fluke belly and a horizontal minnow on a squid rig that is called - Captain Monti's Fluke Cocktail. Sounds like a fancy drink in a seaside pub!

Dave Monti was really the driving force behind the effort to bring us all together to enlist support in Congress for the values and benefits of keeping the Magnuson-Stevens Act intact. The legislation had been named after United States Senator Warren G. Magnuson of the state of Washington and United States Senator Theodore F. Stevens of Alaska. Their positive legacy in enacting enforceable laws and regulations to manage American fish stocks is still felt today by recreational and commercial fishermen on our oceans and beyond. It is somewhat ironic that Senator Magnuson would eventually be defeated on Election Day by the scion of a family made famous from fishing. The newly elected Senator was Slade Gorton of Gorton's of Gloucester!

Fishermen looking to hire a charter can't go wrong booking time on the ocean around Cape Cod and surrounding waters aboard the *Fish Bandit* with Captain Skip Bandini or with Captain Jason Colby on *Little Sister*. They are both experienced, talented, expert charter captains who consistently find fish for their clients.

Patrick Sebile at Red Top

Patrick Sebile is a prolific author, nice guy and an innovative award-winning lure designer. His latest venture is called A Band of Anglers with the remarkable sportsman holding over 300 fishing records including 34 IGFA World Records. My bride and I had a long conversation with him at Red Top Sporting Goods in Buzzards Bay and he has been very helpful to me on many occasions ever since.

George Osowick is one of the funniest surfcasters on the Canal. I always enjoy his quick wit, terrific sense of humor and innate kindness. George, whose real name is Gary, grew up in Brockton and spent a lot of time on his grandfather's farm in Easton. His grandfather had a brother named George who passed away when Gary was about six years old. The two brothers were extremely close and had been inseparable with the grandfather being so heartbroken at the loss of his sibling that he started referring to Gary as George. Gary's family picked up on it and eventually everybody was calling him George. Gary loved his grandfather and, even at a very young age, realized that by accepting the name George it helped to assuage his grandfather's pain. He didn't care what he was called as long as it helped his grief stricken grandfather cope so he has been called George throughout life and now in his 70's he still answers to George!

George can always be found fishing with his angling partner Bill "On the Grill" Prodouz, another great guy from the City of Champions. We are all members of the Buzzards Bay Anglers Club and Bill and George also belong to the Falmouth Fishermen's Association. Every summer Bill is instrumental in putting on the aforementioned fabulous cookout for a one day merger of both clubs together just off the banks of the storied Cape Cod Canal.

George Morani, retired from General Motors, and Boston Local 3 retired brick layer Dan McKay are just two of the pleasant people who walk along the Canal service road every day to complete an exercise regimen. They report their observations of fish activity along the Canal to surfcasters who appreciate the intelligence. Sometimes, after walking in the same direction as the current, they will stop on the service road behind me and let me know that there are fish riding the tide toward my position.

The same valuable information may come from amiable Anna Maher, friendly Lori Nelson, kind hearted Sue Driscoll walking her beautiful dog Bailey or upbeat Marie Murray who roller blades the entire length of the Canal every day from the west end and back for a total of 14 miles!

Dan stopped to speak with me before his morning walk and noticed that I had caught a 27-pound striper, but on my next cast I reeled in a huge clump of heavy seaweed. As soon as Dan saw the seaweed he smiled and said, "There, now you're all set. You've got a salad to go with the fish!"

Dan comes from a large family that includes many health care professionals including nine Registered Nurses and two nurse practitioners. If Dan even thinks about eating something that is unhealthy there is a whole crowd telling him "NO"! He tells me, "Eddie, I can't get away with anything!"

I'm always happy to see Linda and Paul Cormier, a loving couple with a terrific sense of humor, as they greet me on their early morning stroll along the service road. I told them how much I admired their routine of holding hands during their walk, even after 48 years of marriage. Linda had a back operation that causes her to sometimes veer off to the side as she is walking so Paul smiled when he told me that he holds her hand so that she won't stray off course. Linda calls Paul her "rudder"!

Gruffy, his son Patrick and I were fishing before sun up on the west end of the Canal. We were laughing and having a good time when I decided to sing a song that I had recently written for my J. Do. I'm not much a singer, but I wanted my friends to hear the words. Half way through the song an elderly man walking his dog stopped under a street light on the service road behind me to listen. He then resumed his walk as he told me, "Don't quit your day job sonny!" Gruffy and Patrick almost fell into the Canal laughing!

Some of my dearest friends have come from the world of fishing like Galen Locke, a class guy with an awesome sense of humor. Wetting a line next to octogenarian Larry

Silvestri is a sure way to hear some interesting stories and there are no better guys on the Canal than Dave Tworek, Jim Belcher, "Adirondack Jim" Cromme, Keith Dacey, Brian Crowley, Rob Stork and the multi-talented John Doble.

Surfcasters on the Canal need space between themselves to be able to avoid tangled fishing lines. Sometimes an inexperienced guy will come a little too close so I will politely point out the potential problems with crowding. Level-headed fishermen accept this and move on, but unfortunately not everyone is level headed.

I was fishing toward the east end with my good friend Bill "On the Grill" when he pointed out a weathered looking angler that he knew with a bushy gray beard who went by the handle "Wild Bill" Lytle. "Wild Bill" had to ask a guy to move as he was too close, but the space offender wasn't moving as he didn't seem to want to comply. The guy finally decided that the healthy thing to do was to abandon his position after "Wild Bill" said, "Don't make me go back to prison!"

J. Do off Islamorada, Florida Keys

J. Do hung a beautiful John Doble framed print in our kitchen. He had captured the sun going down over the bridges of the world famous Cape Cod Canal in an iconic photo that seems to take the chill off of winter every time I walk by. J. Do said that when I get too old to traverse the dangerous rocks along the canal she is going to seat me in front of his historic photo with a fishing rod in hand and tell me to pretend!

John Doble (Rob Willis photo)

Author's Note: The first time I was ever paid for a story was published after editing in the November 29, 2012 issue of the New England Edition of *The Fisherman*.

TACKLE SHOP TRIAGE

September 21, 2012 started out as a promising morning near the east end of the Cape Cod Canal. My first cast was made in the dark on a dropping west tide at 5:15AM. A fish was on my Daiwa Green Mackerel SP Minnow within five seconds. It was small so I wanted to get him off the hook and back into the ocean. I blindly reached down for the 30 lb. leader with my left hand, knowing that striped bass always, always, always hit the belly hook and so the hooks closest to my hand wouldn't be exposed because they would be in his mouth. Wrong! (more on this stupid theory later).

This striper had taken the tail hook. He zigged, I zagged and one of the points of the belly treble went into the tip of my middle finger and out the other side. I had just bought this lure at Red Top and sharpened the hooks the day before so it cut through flesh like butter. I was hooked good. The fish was flipping back and forth on the tail hook and I was on the belly. I quickly grabbed the top of the middle of the lure with my right hand so that the flopping linesider wouldn't rip the hook through my finger tip. My fishing pole was cradled between my right arm and chest as I tightly held the lure while wishing that I had a third hand to reach for the pliers on my hip.

An eternity seemed to pass during awkward attempts at trying to shake the fish off without doing any more damage to myself. Visions of a ride to the emergency room with a fish on my lap were interrupted when I heard a bike going by behind me. My cry for help was answered when the kind hearted angler stopped, navigated the Canal rocks and found my grateful face in the pitch black night. He released the fish, a few inches short of a keeper, and got it back in the water. Neither of us had cutting pliers, but he was nice enough to offer to carry my gear to the car. I politely declined so as not to take up any more of this great guy's fishing time. He said his name was Jim Turner and if he is reading this I would like to at least buy him a drink.

I carried my equipment with the lure attached to me, broke down two fishing poles with one hand, loaded everything and headed to Tobey Hospital in Wareham. I couldn't fasten my seat belt, but was never happier to have an automatic transmission that didn't need a hand to shift. Blood was now flowing onto my lap as I held my left hand high enough to reduce blood flow, but not so high as to hook an eyeball with the other treb. My good hand was on the steering wheel as I tried to be careful and avoid hooking my right wrist on a left turn. My daughter Kaitlin would later say that my pants looked like Curt Schilling's bloody sock after the second game of the World Series.

On my way to the hospital I noticed the lights on at Cape Cod Charlie's Bait & Tackle. After going around the rotary and pulling into the driveway, I was very lucky to meet Mike Peterson inside the shop. He put down paper towels on the counter so that I wouldn't bleed all over everything. Mike positioned cutting pliers on the hook and snapped it off very close to my finger. The barb was already showing so the rest came out easy. Some tight band aids after peroxide and I was a new man. Mike performed an outstanding operation. After thanking him repeatedly, I told him that from now on he will always be known as "Dr. Peterson".

I headed back to my spot, but the fish were already gone. A few more hours on the Big Ditch and I was headed home on 495 north. A texting nitwit swerved in front of my car causing hot coffee to land on my lap. My pants were now soaked in blood and coffee. I looked like I had just been in a knife fight at Dunkin' Donuts.

Now more on my "stupid theory." Even if the fish was on the belly hook, one of the points could have been in a dangerous position including the tail hook if the lure was upside down or if the fish moved. Worse yet, it could have been a bluefish like the one that took my uncle's finger off when I was a kid. I should have put my headlight on and been more careful. It was a dumb move so please learn from my mistake.

After I related this story to my startled daughter Christine, a Registered Nurse, she asked rhetorically, "Dad, you needed a medical procedure and you chose a bait shop over a hospital?" "Yes", I told her, "Dr. Peterson did a terrific job and there wasn't even a co-pay!"

J. Do, The Fisherman Statue, Buzzards Bay

12. Epilogue

I always enjoyed reading the articles in *The Sun Chronicle* that were written by creative Columnist Larry Kessler. The now retired News Editor employed his vast intellect, powerful writing skill, dynamic experiences and keen sense of humor to produce many outstanding newspaper columns over the years. We share a love for America's Pastime and for the fortunes of the Boston Red Sox in particular.

When I retired from the court system Larry congratulated me and wished me well. He said, "They ought to retire your number or at least one of your ties!"

Index

1967 World Series, 139, 240
1975 World Series, 238
1980 Gold Medal Olympic Hockey Team, 65
1986 World Series, 64
19th Hole Tavern, 9, 149, 231, 234, 236, 239, 246
2013 ALCS, 48
45 Years Behind Bars, 300
50# Plugs, 315
A Band of Anglers, 326
Ab Initio Elder Law Solutions, LLC, 90
Abany, Judge Stephen S., 122
Abascal, First Assistant Clerk-Magistrate Maria T., 72
Abreau, Bob, 315
Abruzzi Province, 83
Acerra, Officer Leo J., 162
Acevedo-Cotto, Assistant Clerk-Magistrate Darlene, 72
Ackerman, Ken, 12
Ackerman, Liz, 12
Acushnet Board of Selectmen, 105
Acushnet Council on Aging, 280
Acushnet Public Library, 280
Adams, CPO Sandra L., 83
Adams, Dr. David, 128
Adams, John, 29
Adamson, Chief Justice's Confidential Assistant Sarah M., 70
Adidas, 190
Adler, Eric, *61, 107, 289*
Adler Pollock & Sheehan P.C., 187
Afghanistan, 119, 226, 255
African American, 119, 167-8
Aguiar, Judge Antone S. Jr., 38-40
Ahern, Lieutenant Michael A., 206
Ahern, Officer Timothy B., 88, 101
Ahern, Taoiseach Bertie, (cover legend)
Aiello, Paulie, (back cover photo) 83
Aiello, Sergeant Daniel R., 206
Alabama (band), 260
Alabama (state), 16
Alarm New England, 270
Alben, Colonel Timothy P., 206

Albert, Ken, 303
Albertson, Judge Margaret F., 114, 122
Alcindor, Lew, 87
ALCS, 46, 261, 262
Alexander, Assistant Clerk-Magistrate Jean M., 72
Alfonse, Assistant Clerk-Magistrate Thomas W., 72
Ali, Muhammad, 265
All Star Game, 239
Allaire, Mike, 315
Allen, Detective Lieutenant John J., 234
Amaru, Chief Lillian, 84-5
Amaru, Sergeant at Arms Raymond J., 25
Amazon, 3
Amendola, Danny, 310, 313
America, 44, 51, 67, 83, 105, 119, 147, 176, 179, 195, 196, 209, 238, 272, 285, 286, 291, 299, 302, 314
American Airlines, 60
American Cancer Society, 210
American Embassy, 160, 161
American Flag, 48, 226, 277
American Greyhound Derby, 294
American Idol, 105
American League East, 262
American League Wild Card, 309
American League, 27, 64, 254, 260
American Legion Baseball, 163
American, 9, 27, 48, 52, 59, 60, 64, 65, 69, 83, 91, 96, 104, 105, 115, 119, 123, 147, 152, 160, 161, 163, 164, 168, 175, 177, 196, 202, 203, 210, 223, 226, 236, 238, 254, 260, 262, 267, 277, 286, 291, 294, 300, 307–9, 319, 325
Amrhein, Judge Mary L., 129
Amtrak Police, 205
AN APPOINTED TIME, 203
Anastos, Judge C. George, 113
Andelman, Eddie, 292
Anderson & Kreiger LLP, (cover legend)
Anderson, Assistant Chief Ken, 161
Anderson, Chief James, 207
Anderson, Dave, 316, 325
Anderson, Detective Sergeant Robert, 207
Anderson, Sparky, 238
Andrade, Jo Jo, 315
Andre, Brenda M., 321

Andrea Doria, 83
Andruzzi, Jen, 49
Andruzzi, Joe, 49, 50, *145*
Andy Griffith Show, 306
Angel, 57, 58
Angela's Ashes, 267
ANGLER MANAGEMENT, *320*
Ann's Place, 298
Apgar, Trooper William R. "Grumpy", 94
Aponte, Sergeant Alex L., 167
Appeals Court, 104, 129
Aramis, 24
Araujo, Rene, 276
Ardennes Forest, 91
Ardito, Clerk-Magistrate Charles J. III "Chuck", 71
Arena, Clerk-Magistrate Robert F., 37, 70
Arkin, Adam, 217
Arlington National Cemetery, 48
Armani, 87
Army Corps of Engineers, 255
Arra, Ron, 315
Arrighi, Detective Daniel B., 159-60, 226, 258
Arruda, Clerk-Magistrate Ronald C., 62
Assad, Louie, 297
Associated Press, 210, 211, 223, 290
Association of Clerk-Magistrate and Assistants, 61, 69, 261
Assumption College, 83
Astle, Rebekah, 318
Athletics, 262
Atlantic Boats, 320
Atlantic, 3, 144, 229, 249, 319, 320, 323
Attleboro District Court, 3, 6, 7, 28
Attleboro Elks, 164
Attleboro Falls, 169
Attleboro High School, 3, 11, 40, 112–13, 150, 152, 211, 212, 304
Attleboro Police Station, 167, 172, 182, 192
Attleboro Police, 6, 11, 112, 113, 151, 152, 154–57, 159, 164, 166, 170, 191-3, 200, 203, 205
Attleboro Public Library Reference Department, 6
Attleboro Public Library, 60, 249, 307
Attleboro School Committee, 3009

335

Attleboro YMCA, 212, 307
Attleboro, 99, 100, 104, 107, 109, 112-4, 122, 124, 127, 131, 150, 153, 155, 158, 163, 164, 171, 181, 182, 191, 193, 196, 203, 205, 210, 211, 216, 220, 231, 240, 242, 245, 249, 260, 285, 298, 304, 306, 309, 314
Atwood, Attorney Jack M., 131
Auerbach, Arnold "Red", 148
Austin, Jeanette, 234
Austin, Lieutenant Scott, 233-4
Azevedo, Officer Frank, 206

Babe Oliva Grinder, 261
Baby Kisses, 270, 271
Bailey (dog), 327
Bailey, Steve, 273
Baima, Chief Albert J., 207
Baker, Governor Charlie D., 25, 38, 46, 56, 69, 71, 74, 86, 96, 106, 113-14, 122, 129, 187, 272, 274
Baker, Lieutenant Paul F., 206
Baker, Zak, 315
Bakst, Attorney Arthur M., 131
Baler, Clerk-Magistrate Adam J., 96
Baler, Judge Gregory R., 129
Balfour, 9
Ball, Lieutenant Colonel Richard M., 27
Ballyjamesduff, 3, 24, 266, 267, 305
Ballymeade Country Club, 275
Baltimore Orioles, 260
Baltimore Police, 187
Bamford, SAC Warren, 206
Banana Republic, 87
Bandini, Captain Skip, 326
Barbie Doll, 256
Barker, Clerk-Magistrate William H. Jr., 20
Barlow, Coordinator Sue, 316
Barnett, Attorney Mark E., 131
Barnstable County Sheriff's Department, 206
Barnstable District Court, 194
Barnstable Police, 235, 236
Barrett, Judge Thomas S., 129
Barrett, Lieutenant James, 206
Barrett, Marty, 261
Barrett, Officer Julie A., 207

Barrett, Officer Ted, 207
Barros, David, 315
Barros, Ray, 315
Barton, Jack, 318-9
Barton, John, 319
Barton, Michelle, 318
Baseball Hall of Fame, 6, 10, 238
Bass Pro Shops, 43, 119, 271
Bass Shoes, 87
Bates, Sergeant Michael B., 227
Battle of Brandywine Creek, 115
Battle of the Bulge, 91
Bausch, Detective William F., 219
Bay State Lodge #30, Fraternal Order of Police, 202
Bay State Raceway, 13
Bear (dog), 133-5
Beatty, Attorney Bryan M., 131
Beaudet, Sergeant Steven, 205
Beckford, Mark, 315
Bee Gees, 34
Begley, Clerk-Magistrate Thomas J., 70
Beland, Attorney Mark J., 131
Beland, First Assistant District Attorney Lynn M., 131
Belanger, Trooper Stephen, 136
Belcher, Jim, 328
Belfast, 241
Belger, First Assistant Clerk-Magistrate David C., 72
Bellino, Joe, 62
Bellotti, Attorney Peter V., 131
Bellotti, Chief Patti, 27
Bellotti, General Francis X., 62, 288-9
Bellotti, Treasurer Michael G., 221, 274
Benedetto, Chief Lawrence P., 206
Benedict, Todd, 315
Benjamin's, 203
Bennett, Attorney Kelly Ann, 131
Bennett, Secretary Daniel J., 288
Bennette, Lieutenant Steven A., 205
Benoit, Joaquin, 48
Benson, Detective Lieutenant Eric J., 226
Bentley, Craig, 236
Berard, Detective Paul J., 205

Berkley Police Department, 318
Bermingham, First Assistant Clerk-Magistrate Felicita G., 72
Betro, Chief Joseph, 207
Bettencourt, Deputy Sheriff Ronald A., 166
Bianculli, PO Joseph, 83
Biden, President Joseph R. Jr., 129-30, 299
Big Ditch, 315, 316, 318, 319, 325, 330
Bigdelicious Baits, 315
Biggs, First Assistant Clerk David M., 96
Bill Hurley Lures, 315
bin Laden, Osama, 47, 142
Binghamton, Captain, 60
Birch, Officer Lawrence P., 207
Birch, Sergeant Thomas L., 205
Bird Park, Walpole, 219
Bird, Larry, 84, 148, 232-3
Birmingham, President Thomas F., 62
Birtwell, Attorney John G., 131
Bishop Feehan Athletic Hall of Fame, 9
Bishop Feehan High School, 9, 153, 212, 239, 242
Bishop Feehan Shamrocks, 239
Bishop Stang Spartans, 239
Bisio, Attorney Dennis P., 131
Black Mass, 166
Blais, Kenny, 12
Blake, Attorney Daniel T., 131
Blake, Eubie, 151
Blazis, Mark, 325
Blinkoff, Kevin, 325
Bliss, Attorney Robert C., 131
Block Island, 319
Bloom, First Assistant Clerk-Magistrate Robert, 72
Blue Bloods, 267
Blue Fin Lounge, 43
Blue Ribbon Commission, 168
Bluetooth, 267
BMW, 267
Bob Cousy Day, 149
Boddicker, Mike, 254
Bodge, Tom, 323
Boggs, Wade, 260
Boiardi, President Ashley, 186

Bombardier, Arthur, 40
Boone, Chief Troy, 136
Boozang, Attorney Steven C., 131
Borders, PO Gary, 83
Borges, Attorney Judith A., 131
Borges, Craig, 210
Borrelli, Assistant Clerk-Magistrate Damon J., 72
Boss Hogg (dog), 324
Boston, 21, 23, 26, 30, 43, 52, 61, 69, 81, 92, 107, 110, 111, 115, 118, 121, 126, 130, 133, 134, 135, 138, 139, 150, 153, 163, 169, 179, 184, 186, 187, 195, 202, 203, 217, 227, 228, 236, 238, 245, 250, 251, 254, 256, 257, 262, 273, 275, 278, 285, 294, 309, 322
Boston Braves, 212
Boston Bruins, 9, 62, 139, 250, *251*, 256, 287, 292
Boston Celtics, 6, 9, 38, 62, 104, 148-9, 232-3, 237, 242-3, 244-5, 250, 262, 292
Boston Children's Hospital, 11, 252, 264
Boston City Council, 105, *274*, 277
Boston City Hospital, 11
Boston College High School, 141
Boston College Law School, 214, 276
Boston College, 87, 262, 296
Boston Field Office, FBI, 153, 160, 195, 202
Boston Food Bank, 88
Boston Garden, 63, 139, 148, 149, 242, 245, 251, 263
Boston Harbor, 225, 279
Boston Herald, 56, 211
Boston Housing Court, 42, 59,
Boston Local 3,
Boston Marathon, 43, 166, 202, 227, 229
Boston Medical Center, 12
Boston Municipal Court, 29, 38, 43, 46, 57, 60, 64, 69, 70, 72, 114-5, 133, 138, 141, 168
Boston Phoenix, 56
Boston Police Gaelic Column of Pipes & Drums, 186
Boston Police Harbor Unit, 187
Boston Police Medal of Honor, 202
Boston Police, 47-8, 51, 133, 135, 156, 166, 178, 187, 202, 206, 262, 273
Boston Police Detective Benevolent Society, 186
Boston Police Foundation, 186
Boston Red Sox, 6, 9, 10, 23, 27, 28, 47, 48, 60, 62-64, 99, 107, 111, 163, 210, 225, 235, 237, 239, 240, 248, 253, 254, 257, 260-62, 285, 292, 309, 310, 312, 332
Boston University, 59
Botka, Coordinator Lisa, 207

Boucher, Detective Sergeant James, 207
Bourne Bridge, 213
Bourne Community TV, 316
Bourne National Cemetery, 10
Bourne Police, 140, 185, 206, 234
Bourne Scenic Park, 321
Bourne State Police Barracks, 142
Bouton, Father Thomas, 96
Bowers, Janice L., 70
Boyle, Attorney Eugene F., 131
Brackett, Judge Cynthia M., 129
Brady (dog), 270
Brady, Attorney James M., 305, 324
Brady, Clerk-Magistrate Marybeth, 71
Brady, John T., (cover legend), 149, 314
Brady, Tom, 49, 265, 301
Brais, Attorney Eliot T., 131
Bramwell, Detective Todd A., 207
Bratton, Commissioner William J., 166
Bray, Meghan, 249
Bray, Patty, 267
Bray, Sheila, 249
Brazil, 196
Brendemuehl, Judge Lynn Coffin, 136
Brennan Junior High, 151
Brennan, Officer James, 207
Brennick, Attorney William F., 131
Brennick, Christa, 157
Brennick, Sergeant Lawrence M. Jr., 157-8
Brewers, 163
Bridgewater State College, 21
Brigham & Women's Hospital, 59, 303, 310
Brighton Division, Boston Municipal Court, 168
Brillon, Detective Lieutenant Arthur J., (cover legend), 6, 153, 155, 167, 203, 204,
Brillon, Sergeant Thomas A., 205
Bring It On, 186
Bristol County CPAC, 149
Bristol County District Attorney's Office, 24, 103, 107, 160, 217, 227, 228, 284
Bristol County District Attorney's Office, SVU, 155
Bristol County Homeland Security Task Force, 166
Bristol County House of Correction, 108
Bristol County Juvenile Court, 62, 103, 106

340

Bristol County Probate & Family Court, 114, 212
Bristol County Savings Bank, 169
Bristol County Superior Court, 121
British, 115, 241
Britton, CPO Milton L. Jr., 96
Broadmeadow, Joe, 153
"Brockton Blockbuster", *300*
Brockton District Court, 36, 37, 46, 205
Brockton Police, 37, 176
Bronx Homicide, 199
Brook Manor, 204
Brookline District Court, 66
Brooks, Attorney John J. III, 131
Brophy, Assistant Clerk-Magistrate Thomas, 72
Brother Bailey (dog), 273-4
Brown University, 209
Brown, Ayla, 105
Brown, Officer Pamela, 207
Brown, Senator Scott P., 42, 47-8, 105
Bruno, Ann, 31
Bruno, Willie, 31
Bryant University, 211
Bryant, Deputy Roger C., 166
Buckner, Bill, 64
Buckner, Jackie, 267, 310
Bud Light, 134, 204
Budweiser, 204
Bulger, President William M., 62, 277
"Bullpen Cop", 48
Bulman, Officer Matthew R., 236
Bump, Judy A., (cover legend)
Bundy, Ted, 220
Bunk, ADA Diane M., 18
Bunker, Sergeant Michael, 207
Burberry, 87
Burbine, Attorney R. Andrew, 131
Burger Chef, 11
Burke, ADA Kevin J., 67
Burke, Assistant Clerk-Magistrate Andrew J., 72
Burke, Attorney John W., 131
Burke, Clerk-Magistrate Paul J., 70
Burke, Congressman James A., 123, 223, 279

Burke, Edmund, 219-233
Burlington Police Department, 154
Burrell Elementary School, 255
Bush, President George H. W., 168
Bush, President George W., 160, 161, 291, 300
Bushway, Deputy Chief Scott, 207
Bussiere, Captain George G., 154
Buzzards Bay Anglers Club, 3, 327
Buzzards Bay, 43, 80, 142, 316, 326, *331*

Café Assisi, 308
Caggiano, First Assistant Clerk-Magistrate Sandra, 64
Cahill, ADA Courtney J., 128,
Cahill, Mary, 203
Cahill, Tom, 203
Calagione, Judge Robert B., 71
Caldarelli, Armando, "Lefty", 65
California Golden Seals, 293
Callahan, Assistant Clerk-Magistrate Kevin F., 72
Callahan, Attorney Kevin D., 17-8, 60-1
Callahan, Councilor Michael J., 133, 289-90, 320
Callahan, Manager Pam, 83
Calvin Klein, 87
Cambridge District Court, 125
Camden Yards, 311
Camp Leatherneck, 226
Campbell, Glen, 49
Campbell, Susan, 89, *259*
Campion, Sergeant Richard P., 205
Canada, 160, 161, 162, 229
Canal Bait & Tackle, 315
Canal Sportsman's Club, 3
Canavan, Judge John A. III, 129
Candito, Clerk-Magistrate Kenneth F., 62
Cannon House Office Building, 223, 279
Cape Air, 236
Cape Cod 4 the Troops, 119
Cape Cod Baseball League, 44, 131, 235
Cape Cod Canal, 3, 110, 140, 181, 185, 314-6, 323, 325, 327-9
Cape Cod Charlie's Bait & Tackle, 330
Cape Cod Drug Task Force, 140, 234, 235-6
Cape Cod Hospital, 237, 244

Cape Cod Life, 3
Cape Cod Magazine, 3
Cape Cod Times, 3
Cape Cod, 8, 10, 45, 133, 223, 231, 235, 236, 239, 326
Cape House Cooking, 316
Capolupo, First Assistant Clerk-Magistrate Vincent F., 37, 64
Cappelletti, Gino, 62
Capron Park, 194
Captain Monti's Fluke Cocktail, 325
Captain Parker's Pub, 236
Caramanica, Attorney James M., 131
Carcieri, Governor Donald L., 9
Carey, Chief Justice Paula M., 46-7, 96, 112
Carey, Officer James, 217
Carlucci, Attorney Paul L., 28
Carlucci, Haley, 28
Carlucci, Robyn, 28
Carnegie Deli, 28
Carney, Attorney J.W. Jr., 131
Carney, Christopher L, 296
Carney, George L. Jr., 296-9
Carney, George L. Sr., 295
Carney, Joseph F., 296
Carney, J. W., 131
Carpenter, Judge Don L., 129,
Carr, First Assistant Clerk-Magistrate Rosemary T., 29
Carrigan, Clerk-Magistrate Thomas C., 70
Carroll Advertising Company, 305
Carroll, Chief John, 33
Carroll, Jen, 305
Carroll, Judge Jeanmarie, 129
Carroll, President John T., 305
Carruth Capital, LLC, 291
Caruso, Joyce, 325
Caruso, Michael, 325
Casale, First Assistant Clerk-Magistrate Antonio J., 33, 213
Casey, Attorney Edward J., 112
Casey, Attorney Jennifer M., 112
Casey, Chief Justice John D., 112-14, 222
Casey, First Assistant Clerk-Magistrate William P., 72
Casey, Jane, 112

Casey, Judge Edward F., 111-2
Cassidy, Attorney James M., 131
Castiglione, Joe, 253
CASTING INTO THE LIGHT, 324
Cataldo, Attorney Joseph P., 67, 181
Cataldo, Attorney Paul A., 181
Cathay Pacific, 167
Cathcart, Councilor Jo Ann, 276
Cayman Islands, 319
Cederquist, Lieutenant William, 206
Cellucci Committee, 21
Cellucci, Governor A. Paul, (copyright page), (cover legend), 3, 16-9, 21-25, 27, 33, 35, 42, 46, 56, 62, 69-71, 88, 104, 113, 119, 127, 129, 136, 152, 160-2, 275, 290
Cellucci, Jan, 160, *162*
Celtic, 10, 246, 253, 305
Celtics (see Boston Celtics)
Central Division, Boston Municipal Court, 29, 64, 69, 72
Centrum, 196
Cerda, Special Projects Coordinator Elizabeth R., 70
Cerrone, Attorney Louis F., 131
Chamberlain, Attorney Robert C., 131
Chamberlin, Lieutenant John, 206
Champ (dog), 189
Champagne, Detective Eugene, 6, 163
CHANEL No 5 PARFUM, 293
Channel 4 WBZ-TV CBS Boston, 47, 209
Channel 5 WCVB-TV ABC Boston, 6, 209-10
Chapman, Officer Craig, 207
Chappaquiddick, 3, 324
Chartrand, Clerk-Magistrate Omer R., 70
"Cheap Seats", 260
Cheevers, Sergeant Joseph E., 186-7
Chelsea District Court, 38, 183
Chelsea Yacht Club, 38
Chesto, Jon, 274
Chicago Bears, 265
Chicago Bulls, 245
Chief Medical Examiner's Office, 219
Chieftain Pub, 203
Chin, Judge Richard J., 46
China, 317
"Chinese Food Night", 296

Chorman, Phil, 315
Chretien, Prime Minister Jean, 161
Church, 111, 136, 166, 238, 310,
Churchill, Chief Ronald, 307
Chuvalo, George, 265
Ciampoli, Clerk-Magistrate Donna M., 72
Ciccio, Sergeant Christopher, 207
Cincinnati Reds, 238
Cinelli, Detective Lieutenant Curtis T., 206, *208*
City of Champions, 36, 96, 327
Civil Department, 31, 68, 80
Civil Motor Vehicle Infraction, 7, 8, 34
Clampett, Jed, 144
Clapp, Attorney Stephen D., 131
Clark, Chief Brian M., *202*, 207
Clark, Sergeant Daniel, 217-8
Clark, Special Agent David L., 206
Clarke, First Assistant Clerk-Magistrate Nancy E., 38-9, 117, 175, 179
Clarke, Lenny, 50-1
Clarke, Mike, 50-1
Clarner, Chair Marie, 276
Clemens, Roger, 260, 262
Clerk-Magistrate's Clambake, *37*
Clifford, Assistant Clerk-Magistrate Patrick J., 72
Clifford, Judge Paula J., 129
Clifford, Prosecutor Edward, 206
Clinton, Hillary, 153
Clinton, President Bill, 2, 22, 84, 104, 160
Clough, Assistant Clerk-Magistrate John J., 72
Coakley, General Martha M., 47-8
Coastal Angler Magazine, 3
Cochrane, Dwight "D2" Jr., 315
Cochrane, Dwight Sr., 315
Cohen, Attorney Harold, 131
Colbert, Bob, 323
Colbert, Denny, 323
Colbert, Elizabeth, 323
Colby, Captain Jason, 326
Cole Haan, 87
Cole, William J., 210
Coleman, First Assistant Clerk-Magistrate Sean P., 72

Coleman, Paramedic Chris, 263
Collamati, Chief Joseph E. Jr., 207
Collard, EMT Dale, 263
Collari, Judge Dennis L. 129
College of the Holy Cross, 87, 107, 115, 116, 320
Colleran, Steve, 323
Collier, Officer Sean A., 227
Collins, Chris, 62
Collins, Commissioner Peter H., 286
Collins, Detective Lieutenant Kenneth D., 192-3, 203
Collins, Firefighter Jeremy, 253
Collins, Officer Arthur, 201-2
Collins, Senator Nick, 277
Collins, Sergeant Val, 253
Collins, Trooper Kevin, 92-3
Colton, First Assistant Clerk-Magistrate John T., 72
Columbia Point, 38
Columbus Clippers, 260
Combat Cross, 199
Comerford, Assistant Clerk-Magistrate James, 138
Comix Roadhouse, 200
Commissioner's Office, Major League Baseball, 309
Commonwealth Coast Conference, 105
Community House, 293
Concannon, Assistant Clerk-Magistrate Mark, 72
Concannon, Judge John P., 129
Concha, Billy, 236
Concord District Court, 136
Concorde Turbojet, 240
Congressional Record, 3
Connecticut State Police Academy, 199
Connecticut State Police, 198, 199, 200, 206
Connecticut, 241, 303
Connell, Mike, 6
Connelly, Chief John J. "Boots", 87
Connemara, 305
Connolly, Chief Justice Lynda M., 119
Connolly, Director Thomas, 138
Connolly, John, 166
Connolly, District Courts Chief ADA Michael C., 131
Connor, Judge John P. Jr., 129
Connors, Clerk-Magistrate John J., 70

Connors, Deputy Court Administrator John M., 70
Constantine, Dr. David F., 105, 275
Convention Center, 277
Coogan Smith LLP, 131
Coogan, Attorney James Jerome, 131
Cook, Deputy Chief Timothy D. Jr., 155
Cook, Detective Timothy D. Sr., 205
Cook, Joe, 298
Cook, Tom, Alarm New England, 270
COOL 102 FM, 320
COOL HAND FLUKE, 320
Cooper, Appellate Division Clerk Brien M., 70
Cooper, Paramedic John, 263
Cooperstown, New York, 10, 238
"Copacabana", 53
Copparini, Dispatcher Paul A., 206
Copper Top Pub, 250
Coppola, Representative Michael J., 42
Cops for Kids with Cancer, 194
Corayer, Todd, 325
Cordy, Associate Justice Robert J., 42, 287
Cork, 104
Cormier, Linda, 327
Cormier, Paul, 327
Cornetta, Attorney Richard R. Jr., 131
Cornish, John, 13, 320
Corrib Pub, 106
Corsi, Jim, 248
Corso, Attorney Frank C., 131
Costa, Clerk-Magistrate Brian J., 71
Costello, Bill "Costy", 315
Costello, Attorney Robert M., 131
Cote, Detective James, 205
Cote, Ken, 203
Cotter, Officer Michael, 66
Coughlin, Administrator Catherine M., 73
Coulter, Detective Lieutenant William J., 216
Court Cards for Combat, 4, 119
Court of Bosnia, 214
Court of Herzegovina, 214
Courthouse Speaker Series, 47, 49, 76, 120, 153, 165, 209
Cousy, Bob, 148-9

Coven, Judge Mark S., 129
Cowens, Dave, 106
Cox, Assistant Clerk-Magistrate Douglas A., 72
Coyle, Assistant Clerk-Magistrate Carole A., 99, 100, 188
Coyle, Captain Daniel J., 188
Coyle, Chief John D. "Jack", 207
Coyle, Detective Sergeant Brian F., 178-9
Craig, Jim, 4-6, 47, 286
Crane, Sally, 137
Crawley, Melissa, 260
Creager, Fred, 315
Creedon, Assistant Clerk-Magistrate Brendan, 72
Creedon, Attorney John F. "Jake", 36
Creedon, Clerk Robert S. Jr., 36, 96
Creedon, Clerk-Magistrate Kevin P., 36-38
Creedon, First Assistant Clerk Patrick W., 96
Creedon, Judge Michael C., 36
Crescent Ridge Dairy, 91
Crickard, Lieutenant Walter, 206
CRIME PAYS, 43, 320
Criminal Show Cause Hearings, 8, 34, 46, 58, 75, 86, 88, 198, 221
Crimmins, Attorney Barry R., 125
Crimmins, Francis T. Sr., "Mike", 91
Crimmins, Janet, RN, 125
Crimmins, Joanne M., RN, 125
Crimmins, Judge Francis T. Jr., 6, 19, 20, 24, 88-92, 118, 125, 237, 260
Croce, Attorney Joseph A., 131
Crogan, Special Agent Steven F., 184
Croken, Clerk-Magistrate Joseph E., 70
Cromme, "Adirondack Jim", 328
Cronan, David, 9, 129, 164, 218, 235-6
Cronan, Judge Paul M., 129
Cronin, George F. Jr. 276
Crosby, Sergeant Michael, (cover legend), 215, 217
Crosman, Officer Kristine, 207
Crosman, Sergeant Lawrence G., 206
Crossman, Special Agent Vincent, 207
Crowley, Attorney David L. Jr., 131
Crowley, Brian, 328
Crowley, David, 13
Crowley, Dr. Kate, 219, 220
Crowley, Frank "Snacks", 139

Crown Royal, 26
Crudale, Attorney Jean N., 131
Cruff, Chief Howard M. Jr., 205
CRUSADER, 320
Crusaders, 107
Cruz, District Attorney Timothy J., 288
Cuba, 144
Cucinatti, Paul, 62
Cullen, Captain Peter, 264
Cullen, Kevin, 260
Cullen, Officer David, 207
Cumberland Farms, 257
Cumberland Police, 121
Cummings, Sheriff James M., 206
Cunis, Judge David W., 136
Cunningham, Assistant District Attorney Sheila, 103
Cunningham, Regional Administrative Justice Kevan J., 6, 101, 103-4
Curley, Attorney Kathleen V., 158
Curley, Mayor James Michael, 11
Curran, John, 300
Currier, Joseph L., 249
Currier, Marie, 254
Currier, Sergeant First Class Joseph, 255
Curse of the Bambino, 10, 64
Curtin, Major Timothy J., 206
Curtis, Rob, 325
Cutler, Attorney Bruce, 267
Cutler, Attorney Robert E. Jr., 131
Cutler, Teddy, 286

D'Andrea, Clerk-Magistrate Brian M., 71
D'Angelo, Attorney Paul, 50-1
D'Angelo, Judge Andrew M. 129
Dabrowski, Sheriff Edward K., 108
Dacey, Keith, 328
Daiwa SP Minnow, 329
Dalton, Detective Mark D., 207
Dana-Farber Cancer Institute, 135
Danforth, Lisa, 320
Dansereau, Charlie, 297-8
Darcy, Pat, 238
Darnbrough, Judge Douglas J., 122

Dave & Buster's, 96-7
Davidson, Matt, 320
Davio's, 45, 274
Davis, Attorney Willie J., 86
Davis, Commissioner Edward F. III, 166
Davoren, Speaker John F. X. "Jack", 131
Dawes, Lieutenant David, 217-8
Dawley, Chief Justice Paul C., (cover legend), 46-7, 70, 74, 104, 187, 290
Day, Assistant Clerk-Magistrate Daniel, 72
Day-Lewis, Daniel, 241
De Niro, Robert, 51
DEA, 168
DeArruda, Officer Henry J., 205
Decas, Attorney George C., 131
Decas, Clerk-Magistrate Charles N., 19, 37,
Declaration of Independence, 91
Dedham American Legion, Post 18, 96
Dedham District Court, 27, 293
Del Vecchio, Anne, 85
Del Vecchio, Attorney Daniel Jr., 85, 86
Delahunt, Congressman William D., 288
Delaney, Assistant Clerk Nancy J., 96
Deliverance, 144
DeLuca, Clerk-Magistrate John, 136
DeMarco, Tony, 63-4
DeMarzi, Dick, 6, 261
DeMeo, Attorney Elaine M., 131
Dennett, Sergeant Jacob, 207
Dennis, John "Dino", 56
Denniston, Chief Legal Counsel Brackett B. III, 18, 20
Denno, Pat, 315
DeNucci, Joe, 62
Department of Justice, 220, 285
Dermody, Bob, 315
Dermody, Judge Walter, 294
Deryck, Mike, 315
DeSalvo, Albert, 220
Desfosses, Detective Sergeant Stephen R., 207
DesLauriers, SAC Richard C., 202
Desperate Housewives, 82
Dever, Assistant Clerk-Magistrate Karen P., 72
Dever, Governor Paul A., 16,

Devine, Clerk-Magistrate John "Jack", 70
Devlin, Firefighter John, 263
Dewar, Steve, 315
Dewar, Rob, 315
Diamond, Neil, 291
DiBiase, Dereck, 308
DiCarlo, Ann, 142
DiCarlo, John, 144
DiCarlo, Leonard, 320
Dick's Sporting Goods, 190
DiFava, Colonel John, 206
DiGiorgio, Probation Officer David, 137
Dill, Detective Lieutenant Maryann, 218
Dillon, Joe, 148-9
DiMaggio, Domenick, 248
DiMaggio, Joe, 238
Dion, Lieutenant Thomas E., 205
Dion, Sergeant Robert E., 205
DiOrio, Attorney Christopher P., 276-7
Diotte, Inspector Daryl, 203
DiRenzo, Captain Joseph P., 207
Dirty Dancing, 22
Disney World, 304
District 1, 275
District 2, 275
District 4, 275
District 8, 275
Ditkoff, Judge Joseph M., 70, 129
Dixon, Charles, 156
DNA Crime Lab, 222
Doble, Detective John, 140, 234-5, 315, 328-9
Doble, Officer Brian, 235
Dodd, Senator Christopher J., 241
Doherty, Attorney Christine J., 131
Doherty, Attorney Gerard F., 280
Doherty, Attorney Michael P., 154
Doherty, Brendan Patrick, 269
Doherty, Carol F., RN, 10-16, 24, 26, 54-5, 128, 147, 227, 231, 233, 247, 251-2, 258, 266, 280, 286, 305
Doherty, Christopher J., 9-11, 23-4, 44, 105-6, 129, 164, 212, 218, 223, 231-3, 234-46, 253, 260, 265-7

351

Doherty, Colonel Brendan P., 9-11, 13, 56, 122-3, 153, 163, 212, 216-7, 230, 232-3, 239-40, 242, 244-7, 250, 253, 265-7

Doherty, Dr. Edward J., 10-1, 13-16, 24, 251-4

Doherty, Dr. Thomas F., 97, 253

Doherty, Eddie, author

Doherty, Gabby, 251

Doherty, Joanne "J. Do", (cover legend), 3, 4, 11, 17, 19-23, 26, 28-31, 34-5, 48-50, 52, 56, 63, 77, 85, 88-9, 97, 102-4, 110-2, 115-6, 122, 124-5, 133, 136, 139, 143, 153, 156-8, 164, 167, 181, 186-7, 189, 191, 194, 199, 203, 212, 223-6, 229-33, 238-40, 244-5, 247-9, 253-9, 261-3, 266-74, 276-7, 281-4, 291, 293, 300, 305-8, 310, 317, 321-4, 326-8, 331

Doherty, Johnnie, 252

Doherty, Mabel, 285

Doherty, Mary E., 253

Doherty, Matthew, 9, 244

Doherty, Michele, 244

Doherty, Officer Paul, 154

Doherty, Sabrina, 269

Doherty, Sergeant Kevin, 154

Doherty, Thomas F. III, 253

Doherty, Thomas F. Jr., 253

Doherty, Thomas F., 285, 295-6

Dolan, Captain Charles F. "Ted", 163-4

Dolan, Detective Sergeant Christopher J., 149-50

Dolan, Judge John J., 31-3, 109, 216

Dolan, Rosemary, 163

Dolan, Sergeant James J., 220

Dolan, Sue, 33

Dominican Academy, 299

Don Bosco, 38

Donohue, Sergeant Richard H. Jr., 227

Donovan, Assistant Clerk-Magistrate Denise M., 72

Donovan, Clerk-Magistrate Eric T., 71

Donovan, Clerk-Magistrate Michael J., 63

Donovan, Sergeant Denis, 207

Doolin, Judge Michael P., 86

Dooney & Bourke, 96

Dorchak, Attorney Christine A., 298-9

Dorchester Division, Boston Municipal Court, 38

Dornig, Clerk-Magistrate Laurie N., 70

Dortch-Okara, Chief Justice Barbara A., 42, 287

Doucette, Captain George, 324

Doucette, Officer Steve, 207

Douglas, Heather, 6
Douglas, Josh, 315
Douglas, Stephen, 279
Downes, First Assistant Clerk-Magistrate Terrence B., 72
Downing, 294
Downs, Kevin, 315
Doctor Phil, 124
Dragnet, 154
Driscoll, Captain Alan H., 166
Driscoll, Sue, 327
Drury, Attorney John L., 131
Dublin, 125, 265-6, 291, 305,
DuBois, Administrative Coordinator Catherine E., 70
Dubuc, Firefighter Brian, 236
Dudley District Court, 62
Dufort, John, 167
Dufort, Officer James F., 167
Duggan, Attorney Michael J., 131
Dukakis, Governor Michael S., 16, 27, 41-2, 46, 55, 62, 70, 107-8, 125, 127, 129, 177, 195, 320
Duke, 54
Dumont, Lieutenant Christopher J., 227
Dupiton, Lou, 315
Dundee, Angelo, 245
Dunkin' Donuts, 330
Dunkin', 263
Dunn, Jimmy, 51
Dunn, Judge Deborah A., 129
Dunn, Staff Sergeant James, 96
Dupont, Attorney Gerard J., 131
Dupuis, Judge Renee P., 129
Durfee High School, 11
Dushku, Eliza P., 186
Dyer, President Bob, 315

Eagan, Kevin, 250
Eames, Kim, RN, 117
East Boston Division, Boston Municipal Court, 64
Eberle, Sergeant David J., 207
Ebert, Rob, 315
Eckersley, Dennis, 262
Edelman, Julian, 310, 313

Edgartown District Court, 55
Edward R. Murrow Award, 209
Egan, Ambassador Richard J., 291
Egan, President Christopher F., 291
Egy, Detective Sergeant Dave C., 207
Ehlers, Adalyn M., (dedication), 85, 269, 271-2, 321
Ehlers, Christine E., RN, (dedication), 11, 20, 188-9, 192, 212, 238, 244, 246, 249-52, 255, 258-9, 262-4, 266, 269-70, 272, 303, 330
Ehlers, Daniel J., (dedication), 264-5, 269-70
Ehlers, Lucy A., (dedication), 85, 269-70, 272
Ehlers, Rose M., (dedication), 269-70,
Eighth Congressional District, 276
Eire Pub, 300
Eisenhower, President Dwight D., 47
Eisenstadt, Attorney David G., 131
Elizabeth Islands, 324
Elliott, Analyst Jennifer L., 226
Elliott, Detective Michael, 6, 225-6
Elliott, Judith A., RN, 226
Elliott, Superintendent Kyle M., 226
Ellis Island, 195
Ellis, 265
Ellis, ADA Patricia O., 214
Ellis, Deputy General Counsel Sarah W., 70
Ellsbury, Jacoby, 163
Ellsworth, Acting Chief Michael, 206
Emerald Square Mall, 87, 188-9, 198, 201, 217
Emerge, 128
Emond, Trooper Adam J., 205
England, 241
England, "Jumpin Joe", 315
Enos, Captain Robert A., (cover legend), 203-5,
Enos, Paula, 203
Environmental Police, 306
Errington, Sergeant Walter H. Jr., 205
Eruzione, Mike, 65
ESPN, 35, 286
Essex County, 50
Eufrazio, Joe, 315
Europe, 245
Eustis, Judge Richard, 122
Evans, Commissioner William B., 47, 51

Evans, Trooper Joseph G., 206-7
Ewell, Scott, 315
Extraordinary Chambers, Courts of Cambodia, 214
Eykel, Sergeant Glen R., 207

Fabiano, Assistant Clerk-Magistrate Mark, 72
Fagan, Chairman James H., 97
Faherty, Superintendent Robert, 194
Fall River District Court, 32, 35, 38, 84, 92, 122
Fall River Superior Court, 228
Fallon, Attorney Stephen J., 131
Falls Pond, 194
Falmouth District Court, 18, 19, 108
Falmouth Fishermen's Association, 316, 327
Faneuil Hall, 154
Faretra, Clerk-Magistrate Joseph R., 37, 64
Farkas, Mark, 123
Farrell, Chief Michael, 136
Farrell, First Assistant Clerk-Magistrate William G., 43, 72
Farrell, John, 62
Farrell's Café, 298
Fatality Review Working Group, 128
Fay, Lieutenant Martin, 206
FBI, 6, 166, 168, 195, 202, 206, 216-7
Federal Communications Commission, 100
Federal Courthouse, 168
Fee, Jimmy, 325
Fennessy, Attorney Robert H. Jr., 131
Fenton, Chief Justice John E. Jr., 130
Fenway Park, 23, 48, 64, 99, 163, 238-9, 254, 261
Ferg, Attorney Bruce E., 218
Fernandes Super Market, 113
Fernandes, Johnny, 317-8
Ferreira, Councilor Joseph C., 105, 204
Ferreira, Special Agent Lawrence S., 206
Ferringer, Intelligence Analyst Julie Flinn, 166
Ferris, Attorney Roger M., 102
Fever Pitch, 50
Ficco, Attorney Robert E., 131
Fidrych, Jessica, 260
Fidrych, Mark "The Bird", 260
FIGHTING IRISH, 320

Figueredo, Lieutenant George, 206
Filene's Basement, 250
Filippo Ristorante, 61, 64
Filosa, Attorney Philip F., 131
FIN AND TONIC, 320
Fine, Attorney Elliot, 131
Finigan, Judge Thomas L., 129
Finley, Charlie, 293
Finn (dog), 134
Finneran, Speaker Thomas M., 24
Finucane, Clerk-Magistrate Michael J., 70
Fiore, Attorney Jordan H. F., 131
FIRE ESCAPE, 320
FISH BANDIT, 326
Fisher, Karen, 6
Fishermen's View, 323
Fishman, Judge Kenneth J., 96, 129
Fisk, Carlton, 238
Fitbit, 53
Fitton, Captain Joseph E., 182
Fitzgerald, Ray, 295
Fitzpatrick, Director William, 207
Fitzpatrick, Trooper William R. Jr., 93-4
Fitzsimmons, Clerk-Magistrate John D., 71
Fitzy's Pub, 55
Five Guys, 45, 303
Flaherty, Clerk-Magistrate John E., 114-5
Flaherty, Councilor Michael F. Jr., 47, 187, 273
Flaherty, Judge Michael F. Sr., 129
Flanagan, District Attorney Newman A., 119, 281
Flanagan, First Assistant Clerk-Magistrate Paul A., 280
Flanagan, James, 281
Flanagan, John, 280-1
Flanagan, Kathy, RN, 281
Flanagan, Mark, 211-2
Flemmi, Stephen, 135
Flood, Lieutenant Gary, 207
Florida Keys, 3, 145, 229, 231, 303-4, 328
Florida State, 106,
FLUSH, 320
Flynn, Detective John P. "Jack", 11, 12, 146-8, 314

Flynn, Margaret, nee Brady, 11, 146
Flynn, Mayor Raymond L., (back cover plaudit), 47, 104-6, 237, 273,
Flynn, President Edward M., 105, 274
Flynn-Poppey, Attorney Elissa A., 131
Folan, Sergeant Bart, 207
Foley, Colonel Thomas J., 206
Forbes, Director Douglas P. Jr., 166, 263
Forbes, Firefighter Scott, 263
Ford LTD, 180
Fordham University, 309
Foreman, 265
Forry, Senator Linda Dorcena, 187, 277
Fort Apache, 200
Fort Myers Country Club, 200
Fort Stewart, 255
Foscaldo, Sergeant David, 206
Foster, Rick, 210
FOUR DIMES, 320
Foxborough Barracks, 93, 203, 215
Foxborough High School, 233
Foxborough Planning, Zoning & Conservation, 6
Foxborough Police Department, 206, 233
Foxborough Public Safety Building, 183
FOXBOROUGH PUBLIC SCHOOLS, 184
Foxborough Raceway, 260, 292-3
Foxx, Jimmy, 238
Fraga, Brian, 227
Framingham District Court, 46, 136, 138-9
Framingham Police, 144
France, 100, 240
Franco, Lieutenant James C., 166
Francomano, Attorney Patrick, 131
Franks, Chuck, 315
Frank, Congressman Barney, 281, *284*
Franklin Auto Body, 6, 261
Franklin Country Club, 301
Franklin Police, 124, 206
Frasier, Marsha, 138
Fratalia, Anne, 125
Fratalia, PO Stephen R., 125
Frazier, 265
Freitas, "Pistol Pete", 315

Frenje, Dr. Johan, 315
Friday, Sergeant Joe, 154
Friedman, Detective Ralph, 200
Friedman, Detective Sergeant Stu, 199, 200
Friedman, Dr. John, 321
Friend, Lieutenant Robert H., 206
Fu, 76
Fulton, EMT Michael, 263
Fund, Attorney Joan M., 131
Furcolo, Governor Foster, 212

G., Tony, 200
Gaffney, Attorney John T. Jr., 131
Gaffney, Attorney Kathleen M., 131
Galasso, Attorney Dale E., 131
Gallagher, Detective Charles, 206
Gallerani, Sergeant Scott, 207
Galway, 267, 305
Gambino, 267
Gamel, Special Agent John, 6
Gander International Airport, 161
Garden of Eden, 229
Gariepy, Officer Timothy P., 207
Garo, Attorney Victor J., 131
Garrison, Attorney Lee, 131
Garsh, Judge Susan E., 228
Garth, Judge Lance J., 129
Gassman, PO Andrew S., 83
Gautreau, Assistant Clerk Marcel W., 96
Gauvin-Fernandes, Clerk-Magistrate Pamela, 71
Gavigan, Colonel David W. Jr., 166
Gay, Attorney Thomas P., 131
Gay, Clerk-Magistrate John S., 71
Gay, Peter M., 6, 211
Gazzola, Sergeant Raymond, 205
Gehrig, Lou, 8, 317
General Motors, 147, 327
George, Lieutenant Michael, 206
Germani, Attorney Salvatore J., 131
Germani, Attorney Vincent M., 131
Germany, 91, 148, 157, 255
Ghiloni, Assistant Clerk-Magistrate Christopher, 72

GHOSTS OF PLYMOUTH, MASSACHUSETTS, 6, 280
Gibbons, Assistant Clerk M. Diane, 96
Gibbons, Attorney John P., 293
Gibbons, Marshall John, 47
Gibbs Lures, 315
Gibbs, Assistant Clerk-Magistrate Antonio, 72
Gibbs, Stan, 3, 315
Giblin, Attorney Thomas E., 110-11
Gibson, Bob, 240
Giggles Comedy Club, 50, 51
Gilgun, Judge Frederick V., 71
Gillan, Attorney Francis J. III, 131
Gillespie, Lieutenant Richard, 150
Gillette Stadium, 15, 44-5, 49, 85, 181, 184-5, 196, 224, 306
Gilligan, Judge Brian F., 129
Gillis, Commissioner John M., 286
Gilpin, Colonel Kerry A., 206
Gioia, Attorney Patrick M., 131
Giroux, Officer Robert L., 206
Glazer, Assistant Clerk-Magistrate Bruce, 38
Glennon, Jack, 305
Globe Magazine, 28, 74
Gobourne, Judge Franco J., 129
God, 11, 26, 48, 58, 106, 115, 128, 178, 203, 212, 239, 244, 294, 302, 324
Goings, Melissa, 279
Gold Medal Strategies, 4-6
Golden Dome, 26
Goldrick, Attorney Daniel E., 131
Gonsalves, Lieutenant Jose, 218
Gonsalves, Sergeant Jeffrey, 206
Goodale, Attorney Robert L., 131
Goodell, Commissioner Roger, 301
Goodrich, Allan, (cover legend)
Gookin, Lieutenant Frank M. Jr., 207
Gooley, Anne-Marie, 80, 81
Gordon, Attorney Nicholas A., 198
Gordon, Detective Sergeant Anthony M., 198-200
Gordon, Lisa C., 199
Gordon, Major Bruce P., 198-9
Gordon, Rena D., 198-9
Gore, Vice President Albert A., 160
Gormley, Attorney David J., 131

Gorton, Senator Slade, 325
Gorton's of Gloucester, 325
Gostkowski, Stephen, 224
Gotti, John, 267
Gould, Assistant Clerk-Magistrate Barbara, 72
Gould, Chief Michael P. Sr., 6, 190-1, 217-8
Gould, Lieutenant Michael P. Jr., 207
Gould, Sergeant David, 207
Gouveia, Bill, 6
Governor's Council to Address Sexual Assault & Domestic Violence, 128
Grabau, Assistant Clerk-Magistrate Olga, 72
Grace, Chief Michael A., 206
Graham, Renée, 210
Grant, Attorney Dale E., 131
Grant, Meme, 137
Grassia, Bill, 62-4, 235
Grateful Dead, 197
Gravina, "Paulie the Painter", 315
Gray, Diana, 6
Gray, Joe, 315
Greaney, Chief Justice John M., 41
Great Woods, 185, 196-7
Greater Attleboro Relay for Life, 210
Gremo, Kim, 74
Gremo, Pat, 74
Gremo, Tom, 74
Grenham, Lieutenant Colonel Thomas D., 206
GREY2K USA Worldwide, 298
Greyhound Hall of Fame, 6
Griffey, Ken Jr., 254
Griffey, Ken Sr., 254
Grim, Sergeant John, 207
Grimes, Detective Donald, 207
Grogan, Steve, 47, 286
Gronkowski, Rob, 15, 203, 225, 301
Gross, Attorney Frank J., 131
Gross, Commissioner William G., 206
Grossfeld, Stanley, 48, 316
Grosso, Liza, 270
Ground Zero, 161
Grousbeck, Wyc, 62
Grundy's Gym, 56, 244

Guildford Four, 241
Guilmette, Lieutenant Colonel Ronald J., 6
Guiney, Detective Brian, 235
Guinness, 10, 115, 164, 265, 267, 305
Gulf Hill, 12, 13, 320
Gulf of Mexico, 3
Gulfstream Park, 234
Guns N' Roses, 185
Guppy Lures, 315
Gursky, Kurt, 317
Gutwill, Detective Matthew, 144
Guy, Martin, 222
Guzman, Judge Margaret R., 129

Habeas Chorus, 99
Habeas Corpus, 98-9, 102
Haeffner, Matt, 325
Hague, First Assistant Clerk-Magistrate Sharon, 72
Hallandale Beach, 234
Halloran, Clerk-Magistrate Kenneth P., 70
Halpin, Administrator Bob, 121
Hampden County Housing Court, 41
Hampe, Attorney Kevin F., 131
Hannah, John, 49
Hannington, Attorney Glen, (cover legend), 43-6, 92, 223
Hannington, Louise L., 45
Hannington, Tevis L., 45
Hannon, PO Colleen, 83
Hanson Police, 37
Hanson's Drug Store, 97
Harbinger Development, 186
Harbour, Judge Robert G., 129
Harding, Lieutenant Herbert, 6, 206
Hardt, Gregory, 211
Hardt, Officer David, 211-2
Harnais, Judge Robert, 129
Harper, Jack, 210
Harrington, Sister Patricia, 239
Harriott, Judge James, 279
Hart, Clerk-Magistrate Donald P., 6, 187
Hart, Senator Jack, 277
Harvard, 91

Harwood, Speaker John B., 131
Havlicek, John, 106, 148, 242-4, 250
Haygood, Mike, 304
Hayhow, Attorney Van L., 131
Hayman, David, (cover legend)
Hazeldine, Detective Sergeant Jacklyn B., 207
Hazeldine, First Assistant Clerk-Magistrate Lesley J., 6, 74, 76, 81
Hazeldine, Officer James F., 74
Heagney, Captain Walter Jr., 151-2
Heagney, Chief Kyle P., 151-2
Healy, Attorney John M., 131
Healy, PO William P., 110
Hearon, Detective Sergeant Stephen, 207
Heartbreak Hill, 43-4
"Heaven Must Be Missing an Angel" 34
Hebb, Attorney John P., 166
Hebert, Joe, 260
Hebert, Sergeant Donald G., 205
Heckler, Congresswoman Margaret, 17
Heffernan, Judge Mary Elizabeth, 129
Heineken, 242
Heinsohn, Tom, 148, 242-4
Helmand Province, 226
Helms, Senator Jesse, 22
Henry, John W., 62
Here Comes the Boom, 50
Hernandez, Aaron, 34, 149, 225-8
Hernon, Judge Julieann, 129
Hess, Wayne, 315
Heuberger, Catherine, 6
Hibbert, Assistant Clerk-Magistrate Thomas Jr., 72
Hickey, Attorney John J. Jr., 98
Hickey, Dave, 125
Hickey, First Assistant Clerk Mary K., 96
Higgins, Chief Tom, 161
Highland Country Club, 17
Hill, Courtney Kennedy, 241-2
Hill, James, 6
Hill, Paul, 241-2
Hill, Ray, 293
Hill, Saoirse Roisin, 242
Himmel, Attorney George, 90

362

Hines, Lesley, 304
Hingham District Court, 60, 62, 66, 71-2, 127
History Channel, 241, 307
Hobin, Assistant Clerk-Magistrate Thomas J. Jr., 72
Hoffman, Attorney John J., 131
Hogan, Clerk-Magistrate Daniel J., 69
Hogan, Clerk-Magistrate Joseph M., 35, 70
Hogan, Clerk-Magistrate Michael F., 69
Hogan, Judge William T. Jr., 69
Holgerson, Attorney John L., 158
Holiday Inn, 126, 185, 205
Hollihan, 285
Holliston Police, 206
Hollywood, 268
Holmes, Lieutenant John W., 207
Homa, Amy, 320
Homa, John, 320
Honda Accord, 267
Hoover, President Herbert C., 285
Hopkins, Attorney Jo Anne, 88
Hopkins, Attorney Marybeth, 88
Horgan, Judge Thomas C., 129
Horgan, Officer Steve, 48-9
Horodas, Attorney Nicole Hannington, 45
Hostess Twinkies, 113
Hough, Bill, 325
Hourihan, Judge Neil A., 129
House Chamber, 287
House of Correction, 32, 39, 80, 102, 108, 154, 293
House of Representatives, 6, 24, 141, 286, 288
Hovey, Assistant Commissioner Dawson, 161
How to Beat a Speeding Ticket, 95
Howitt, Representative Steven S., 288
Hudson River, 161
Hughes, Clerk-Magistrate Kirsten L., 71
Hughes, Lisa A., 47, 209
Hunt, Attorney Jarvis, 131
Hunter, Torii, 48
Hurley, Bill, 315
Hurley, Cynthia, 127
Hurley, Judge Joseph P. III, 96, 122
Hurley, Judge Patrick J., 127, 319

Hurst, Bruce, 260
Hyannis Golf Course, 236
Hyannis Harbor Hawks, 235
Hyannis Mets, 235
Hyannisport Club, 149, 242

Iannella, Councilor Christopher A. Jr., 275
ICE, 144-5, 230
Igo Elementary School, 66, 67, 255-6
Igo, Vin, 42, 66, 287
In the Line of Duty: Hunt for Justice, 217
In the Name of the Father, 241
Indelicato, Carol A., 78, 80, 82
Indian, 168
Indie (dog), 318-9
International Criminal Tribunal, former Yugoslavia (Den Haag, Netherlands), 214
Iovieno, Attorney Thomas J., 55-6
Iran, 113
Iraq, 113, 255
Ireland, 3, 17, 24, 104, 119, 149, 163-4, 169, 203, 231, 240, 262, 265-6, 291, 300, 314
IRISH AYES, 319
Irish Club, 163-4
Irish Republican Army, 241
Irish Tenors, 162, 239
Islamorada, 144, 230, 328
"It Only Takes a Minute", 34
It's just the way it was, 153
Italy, 83, 87
Iwo Jima Memorial, 48
Iwo Jima, 48, 307

J. Crew, 87
J. Geils Band, 308
Jackson, Deputy Chief Robert, 136
Jackson, Deputy Chief Todd M., 207
Jackson, Joseph R., 70
Jackson, President Andrew, 167
Jacobi, Attorney John F. D. III, 131
Jacobs, Judge Susan L., 129
Jacoby, Jeff, 210
Jagger, Mick, 181

James H. Sullivan Courthouse, 107
James Montgomery Blues Band, 273
Jane Doe Inc., (copyright page), 128
Jarasitis, Judge Allen J., 129
Jeffers, Attorney Diane M., 293
Jeffries, Catherine, 119
Jeffries, Clerk-Magistrate Mark R., 119
Jenkins Hearing, 173-5,
Jenkinson, Bill, 315
Jennings, Sergeant Scott C., 219, 220
Jeopardy, 142
Jerry Springer Show, 94
Jesus Christ, 134, 297
Jethro (dog), 323
JFK Library, (cover legend), 6
J.J. Foley's Cafe, 23, 57
Joe Andruzzi Foundation, 49
Joe Tecce's, 61
John Havlicek Day, 250
John Joseph Moakley United States Courthouse, 278
Johnson Smith, Judge Emogene, (cover legend), 119, 120
Johnson, Chief legal Counsel Paul W., 20, 22
Johnson, Deputy Commissioner Neil, 42
Johnson, Janice P., 19, 100
Johnson, Kirby, 304
Jones, Attorney Stephen L., 131
Jones, Sam, 148
Joseph Case High School, 6
Josten's, 9
Joubert, Gary, 229
Joy, First Assistant Clerk-Magistrate Diane M., 72
Jubinville, Clerk-Magistrate Robert L., 46, 86, 222
Judicial Nominating Commission, 16, 18, 33, 99
Juicy Couture, 79
Julian, Judge John M., 129
Jury Commissioner's Office, 38

K Mart, 193
Kabat, Stacey, RN, 316
Kahalas, Attorney Howard M., 131
Kaiser, SAC Kenneth W., 195
Kane, Attorney Martin F. II, 92

Kane, Judge Robert J., 129
Kane, Peter, 213-4
Karam, Robert, 169
Karol, Representative Stephen J., 24
Keane, Lieutenant James J., 205
Kearney, Clerk-Magistrate Brian J. "Gruffy", 1, 6, 35, 116, 130, 133-145, 320, 327
Kearney, Detective William P., 133, 135
Kearney, Marguerite M., 141, 142
Kearney, Matthew J., 35, 139-41
Kearney, Michael, 142
Kearney, Officer Stephen, 133, 142
Kearney, Representative Patrick J., 3, 139, 140, 141, 315, 327
Kearney, Sergeant Maureen, 116, 133, 142, 320
Kearney, William P. Jr., 142
Keating, Anne, 223, 267
Keating, Congressman William R., 31, 47, 222-4, 305
Keating, Kristen, 82
Keegan, George, 315
Keegan, Joe, 315
Keegan, Sean, 315
Keenan, First Assistant Clerk-Magistrate Brendan T., 72
Kelleher, Chief Richard M., 207
Kelley, Assistant Clerk-Magistrate Robert J., 72
Kelley, Commander Thomas G., 47
Kelley, Judge Angel, 130
Kelley, Judge Michelle L., 3, 6, 25, 61, 73-78, 80-1, 98, 122, 145
Kelley, Madison A., 74
Kelley, Matthew T., 74
Kelley, Thomas P., 74
Kelly, Coach Brian, 30
Kelly, Jimmy, 315
Kelly, Paqui, 30
Kelly's Place, 268
Kelly's Roast Beef, 290
Kennedy Compound, 228, 241-2
Kennedy, Clerk-Magistrate John F., 71
Kennedy, Congressman Joseph P. II, 228, 240
Kennedy, Congressman Joseph P. III, 47, 227-8, 240
Kennedy, Councilor Terrence W., 289
Kennedy, Ethel, 241
Kennedy, General Robert F., 241-2, 280
Kennedy, Irene, 219, 220, 222-3

Kennedy, Joan, 240
Kennedy, John F. Jr., 240
Kennedy, President John F., 223, 228, 242, 280
Kennedy, Senator Edward M., (cover legend), 17, 240-1, 280
Kennedy, Thomas, 219
Kenney, Attorney Paul F., 131
Kenney, Attorney Paul V., 131
Kenney, Attorney Stephen J., 131
Keohan, First Assistant Clerk-Magistrate A. Daniel "Archie", 72
Kerr, First Assistant Clerk-Magistrate Cynthia J., 69, 75, 76, 78
Kessler, Larry, 210, 332
Key West, 144, 229, 231
Khoury, Dr. Charles P., 321
Kiley, Chief Terrell J., 33, 84
Killough, Lieutenant Scott W., 205
Kilroy, Deputy Chief Robert, 207
Kilroy, Officer Kerry, 206
Kimball, George, 56-7
King Philip Regional High School, 293
King Philip Regional School District, 6, 307
King, Dale, 210
King, Governor Edward J., 16, 18, 31, 36, 38, 69, 70, 71, 100, 112, 121, 129, 217, 225, 284
Kingsbury, Chief William Jr., 207
Kingston Police, 37
Kirby, Mike, 210
Kirby, Platoon Sergeant Lawrence F., 48
Kirk, Senator Paul G. Jr., 6, 288
Kirnon, Assistant Clerk-Magistrate Joseph A., 72
Kirrane, Detective Sergeant Thomas A., 206
Kiser, Officer Kory, 159
Kivlan, Attorney John P., 131
Kley, Paige, 6
Knights of Columbus, 21-2
KNOT RESPONSIBLE, 320
Koback, Attorney Ronald G., 131
Koban, Attorney Theodore J., 117
Kopelman, Judge David H., 129
Kosilek, Cheryl, 217
Kosilek, Michelle, (previously Robert) 217-9
Kowalski, Assistant Clerk-Magistrate John L., 72
Koza, Dave, 261
Krowski, Attorney Joseph F., 131

Kurtz, Dale L., 119
Khmer Rouge, 214

La Cosa Nostra, 122
Labonte, Deputy Chief George, 207
LaCasse, Donna, 83
LaCasse, Officer Kevin, 207
Lalancette, Officer Paul, 180
Lally, Diane, 236
Lally, Joseph, 236
Lamb, Brian, 123
Lamb, Officer William, 207
Lambirth, Chief W. David, 207
Lamonaco, Lieutenant Michael, 217
Lamonaco, Trooper II Philip J., 216-7
Landry, Assistant Clerk-Magistrate Harry, 38
Landry, Attorney Kevin P., 131
Landry, Jacqueline A., 77-80
Landry, Trooper Paul, (cover legend), 6, 215-17
Langelier, Clerk-Magistrate Daniel F., 70
Langer, Attorney Keith G., 131
Langley, Officer Walter P. Jr., 206
Lapinski, Toby, 325
LaRaia, "Mashpee Mike", 315
Laro, Supervisor Lillian, 288
Larry King Live, 168
Larson, Doug, 287
Launie, Attorney Robert N., 131
Lavery, Assistant Clerk-Magistrate William J., 72-3
Law & Order, 309
Law Day, (cover legend), 4, 47-53, 76, 105, 120, 136, 166, 186, 218, 225, 227, 240, 253, 277, 286, 308
Law, Ty, 49
Lawrence, J. M., 56
Lawton, Judge James R., 129
Lawton, Judge Mark E., 129
Lazarus, Manager Jodi B., 78-9
LBJ Internship, 223
Leach & Garner Company, 203
Leary, Judge Paul K., 122
Leavitt, Administrator Dana L., 38
Lebowitz, Becky, 25

Lechter, Attorney Stephen A., 109
LeClair, Arthur, 12, 13
LeClair, Donna, 13
Leco, Vice Chair Rick, 276
Leddy, First Assistant Clerk Philip F., 96
Ledgewood Apartments, 227
LeDuc, Assistant Clerk-Magistrate Stephen P., 72
Lee, Attorney John P., 131
Lee, Attorney Maureen A., 131
Lee, Darcy H., 6, 280
Lee, Judge Edward A., 212-4
Leedham, Attorney Thomas R. Jr., 97
Lefebvre, Sarah K., 206
Legal Sea Foods, 274
Lehigh, Scot, 210, 290
Lehr, Dick, 166
Lendino, "Timmy Tuna", 315
Lent, Cassidy, 6
Leo, Melissa, 217
Leo's Restaurant, 80
Leonard, Judge John B., 100-03
Leprechauns, 54
Levine, Dr. Lowell, 220
Lewis, Attorney James M., 131-2
Lewis, Jim, 142-3
Lewis, Representative Maryanne, 139, 141
Ligotti, Assistant Clerk-Magistrate Angelo J., 37, 62
Ligotti, Clerk-Magistrate Joseph A., 37, 62
Limerick, 267
Lincoln Downs, 292
Lincoln, President Abraham, 141, 279
Lindsey, Glenn, 315
Lindsey's Family Restaurant, 238
Linehan, President Bill, 277
Linskey, Superintendent in Chief Daniel P., 202
Linsky, Representative David P., 42
Lint, Attorney Bruce H., 132
Lint, Attorney Elizabeth Y., 132
Linton, David, 6, 31, 152, 170, 211, 223, 316
Linton, Sally A. Bruno, 6, 31, 122, 223, 302
Liotta, Leonardo, 63
Lisano, Clerk-Magistrate William A., 70

Lisi, SAC Vincent B., 206
LITTLE SISTER, 326
Littlefield, Manager Kathleen, 83
Littlefield, Sergeant Peter, 206
Livesey, Assistant Chief Glenn R., 307
Livesey, Chief Benjamin R. "Bob", 307
Livesey, Gary B., 307
Lloyd, Odin, 225, 228
Local 7 Ironworkers Hall, 277
LOCAL BUOY, 320
Locke, Galen, 327
Logan International Airport, 30, 160, 227, 240
Lombardi, Attorney Frank A., 132
Lombardi, Judge Leon J., 129
Lombardo, Francesca, 6
Lombardo, Vincent J., 67
Lombardo's, 67, 198
Lonborg, Dr. Jim, 62, 139
Lopez, Jennifer, 17
Lorincz, Attorney Paul F., 6, 132
Lorusso, Attorney Gerard C., 299
Los Angeles Lakers, 148
Loth, Renée, 210
Louison, Attorney Bradford N., 132
Lounsbury, Director Kathy, 6
Louro, Jeremy, 315
Lucchino, Larry, 62
Luciano's, 253
Luxembourg, 91
Lyle, Officer Norman E., 205
Lynch, Chief Thomas J., 206
Lynch, Congressman Stephen F., 276-8
Lynch, John, 241
Lynch, May, 266
Lynn District Court, 6, 38, 69
Lytle, "Wild Bill", 328

Mac (dog), 135,
MacDonald, Diana L., 66
MacDonald, Officer Jared P., 206
MacDougall, Ashley K., 78, 80, 177, 181
MacDougall, Officer Joseph R., 177

Machado, Frank, 325
MacKinnon, Bob "Bull", 315
MacNeill, Mark "Preacher", 315
Maco's Bait & Tackle, 315
Macy, Judge Joseph I., 129
Macy's, 138
Madden, Alexis K., 53
Madden, Attorney Margaret M., 132
Madden, Detective William A. II, 51-3, 56, 64, 69, 92, 95, 119, 319
Madden, William I., 53
Magnuson, Senator Warren G., 325
Magnuson-Stevens Act, 325
Maguire, Attorney Charles J. Jr., "Chip", 132
Maguire, Tom, 33
Mahan, First Assistant Clerk-Magistrate Beverly J., 72
Maher, Anna, 327
Maher, Paul J., 194-5, 300
Maher, Tommy, 300
Mahoney, First Assistant District Attorney Dennis C., 111
Mahoney, Tim, 30, 303
Maigret, Sergeant Raymond, 218
Maitland, Attorney Elizabeth, 132
Malley, Officer James R., 205
Malone, Attorney Gerard F., 106-7
Maloney, Assistant Clerk-Magistrate John D., 98
Maloney, Attorney Linda J., 132
Manchester, Clerk-Magistrate Daryl G., 70
Manchester, Wayne, 321
Manday, Mitch, 303
Mangiaratti, Attorney Robert S., 132
Manilow, Barry, 52-3
Mann, Doug, 144
Manni, Attorney John C., 132
Manning, Gerry, 236
Manning, Trooper David M., 176
Manoogian, Attorney David C., 33, 132
Mansfield Police Department, 164, 185, 196, 206, 218
Mantle, Mickey, 245
Marciano, Peter, 300-01
Marciano, Rocky, 300-01
Marie, Sister Bernard, 299
Marina Bay, (cover legend), 273

Marini, Judge Francis L., 129
Marinofsky, First Assistant Clerk-Magistrate George R., 136
Markey, Attorney Christopher M., 132
Markey, Judge John A., 129
Markey, Senator Edward J., 281, 283
Markey, Special Agent John, 216
Marks, Attorney Robert P., 132
Marlborough District Court, 136
Mars Bargainland, 67
Marshall, Chief Justice Margaret H., 129
Marshall's, 190
Marshfield Fair, 292, 295
Marsico, Officer Vito, 315
Marsico, Vinnie, 315
Martha's Vineyard, 324
Martin, Detective Sergeant Robert, 218
Martin, Speaker Joseph W. Jr., 17, 285
Martin, Vice President Sean, 186
Martinez, Pedro, 44
Marzilli, Chief Daniel T., 137-8
Mason, Attorney Charles R., 132
Mason, Colonel Christopher S., 206
Massachusetts Defenders Committee, 108, 158
Massachusetts DNA Registry, 222
Massachusetts General Hospital, 226
Massachusetts Maritime Academy, 140
Massachusetts State Police, 206
Massachusetts State Police Gang Unit, 165
Massachusetts State Police K-9 Unit, 219
Massachusetts State Police Medal of Honor, 227
Massachusetts State Police Museum & Learning Center, (cover legend)
Massachusetts State Police Truck Team, 178
Massachusetts State Racing Commission, 14, 290, 295-6
Massachusetts Striped Bass Association, 324
Massachusetts Supreme Judicial Court, 41, 42, 71, 109, 118, 127, 129, 173, 214, 221, 287,
Massasoit Greyhound Association, 296
Masters, Mary, 83
Mattapoisett Free Public Library, 6
Mattoli, Assistant Clerk-Magistrate Janet M., 72
Matzell, Shelby, 244, 246
Maxim, Henry, 6, 212
May, Kate, 141

May, Larry, 141
Mazeiko, Al, 315
McCabe, Clerk Francis P. "Frank", 6,
McCabe, Officer Neal, 144
McCabe, Patrick J., 163-4
McCafferty, Lieutenant Thomas, 207
McCallum, Judge Mary M., 129
McCallum, Judge Paul J., 129
McCann, Principal Brian, 6
McCann, Tony, 315
McCarthy, Attorney James P., 132
McCarthy, Jim, 292
McCarthy, Valerie, 276
McClure, Attorney Wesley A., 132
McConaghy, Captain Patrick J., 163
McCormick, Assistant Clerk-Magistrate Ann M., 37, 72
McCormick, Attorney Edward J. III, 89
McCourt, Frank, 267
McCoy, Joe "The Reel", 315
McCoy Stadium, 163, 259-261
McCue, Deputy Court Administrator Philip J., 27, 70
McCutcheon, Attorney Jill, 229
McDermott, Assistant Clerk James M., 96
McDermott, Attorney Frederick M., 132
McDermott, First Assistant Clerk-Magistrate Patricia F., 72
McDermott, John, 162, 239
McDermott, Sheriff Patrick W., (cover legend), 43, 96, 277,
McDonald, Captain Steven M., 220
McDonald, Judge John E. Jr., 64. 122
McDonald, Officer Joseph D., 95
McDonough, Clerk-Magistrate Keith E., 320
McDonough, Register Matthew J., 288
McEneaney, Administrator Michael J., 73
McEvoy, First Assistant Clerk-Magistrate William A. Jr., 72
McGahan, Attorney Michael T., 132
McGahan, Attorney Timothy J., 132
McGill University Dental School, 229
McGillicuddy, Principal Administrative Assistant Dana, 206
McGillvray, Sergeant John H., 206
McGilvray, Major Thomas R., 206
McGlone, Attorney John J. III, "Jack", 132
McGorty, Anna, 82

McGovern, Colonel Marian J., 165
McGovern, Congressman James P., 288
McGovern, Judge James J., 129
McGovern, Sergeant Stephen, 205
McGowan, Assistant Clerk-Magistrate Irene F., 72
McGowan, Chief Peter, 207
McGrath, Chief William R., 54
McGrath, Clerk-Magistrate John L., 70
McGrath, Detective Sergeant Barry, 207
McGruff the Crime Dog, 133
McHale, Deputy Superintendent Gerry, 273
McHale's Navy, 60
McHoul, Attorney Austin W., 132
MCI Cedar Junction, 220
MCI Framingham, 316
MCI Norfolk, 120
MCI Walpole, 220
McInness, Detective Mary, 206
McIntyre, Attorney John W., 132
McKay, Dan, 327
McKenna, Attorney James D., 130
McKenna, Captain Brian L., 203
McKenna, Sergeant Shane, 207
McKeon Park, 235
McKeon, Clerk-Magistrate Kathleen M., 78
McKeon, Colonel Richard D., 47
McKeon, Detective Kevin J., 207
McKeon, Sergeant Robert J., 206
McLaughlin, Attorney James M., 124
McLaughlin, Connie, 267
McLaughlin, Detective Sergeant Michael B., 144, 165
McLaughlin, Jim, 236
McLaughlin, Matt, 236
McLaughlin, Maureen, 236
McLeod, Clerk-Magistrate Duncan E., 70
McManus, Clerk Dennis P., 288
McMurray, Brooks, 162
McMurray, Jacki, 162
McMurray, Kaleigh, 162
McMurray, Special Agent Patrick W., 160-162
McMurray, Sue, 162
McNamara, Cathy, 256

McNamara, Gene, 256, 318
McNamara, Jason, 318
McNamara, John, 142
McQuade, Chief Richard K., 207
McRaven, Admiral William H., 47
McRoberts, Officer David, 207
McSharry, Greg, 315
McSweeney, Lieutenant David, 222
MDC, 149
Medeiros, Chief Bradford J., 166
Medicare, 45, 265, 302
Medway Police, 54, 207
Meehan, Congressman Martin T., 288
Meese, General Edwin III, 168
Megan, Chris, 325
Mello, Director Tammy, 128
Menard, "Taunton Teddy", 315
Menard-Parece, First Assistant Clerk-Magistrate Jody M., 72
Mendonsa, George A., 51
Mendonsa, Rita, 51
Mengele, Dr. Josef, 220
Menino, Mayor Thomas M., 62, 278
Menno, Judge James V., 89
Mercedes-Benz, 57, 267
Mercier-Locke, Attorney Carol, 132
Merrick, Chief Edward M. "Ned", 195
Merrick, Judge Brian R., 6, 195
Messier, Officer Robert P., 205
Messineo, Janet, 3, 324
Meyer, Lieutenant Ronald, 263
Michaels, Al, 65
Michelmore, Attorney John H., 132
Mick, Sergeant Hugh, 162-3
Middleborough Barracks, 205
Middleborough YMCA, 271
Middlesex Probate & Family Court, 38
Middleton, Rick, 62
Miliano, Clerk-Magistrate Richard P. "Dick", 70
Mill, Deputy Chief James A., 206
Miller, Sergeant Roger, 206
Millis Police Department, 98, 207
Mills, Samantha, 6, 285

Milton-Hoosic Club, 44
Minah, Officer Berryman P., 205
Minehan, Regional Administrative Justice Rosemary B., 42
Miss Attleboro Pageant, 21
Miss Massachusetts Pageant, 198
MIT, 32
Mittenzwei, Jim, 30, 303
Mittenzwei, Joanne, 30
Moakley, Congressman J. Joseph, 277, 279
Mohegan Sun, 199, 200, 322
Monac, Attorney Clifford A., 132
Monbouquette, Bill, 63, 235
Moniz, Judge Lawrence, 129
Monteiro, Sergeant Joseph I., 163
Montgomery, Clerk-Magistrate Keesler H., 70
Montgomery, James, 273
Monti, Captain Dave, 325
Mooney, Judge Toby S., 129
Mooney, Peter, 6
Moore, Robin, 106
Morani, George, 327
"More Than A Woman", 34
Morgan Magic, 262
Morgan, Dottie, 260-1
Morgan, Joe, 47, 260-262,
Morganelli, Mike, 323
Moriarty, Judge Paul F.X., 71
Moriarty, Sergeant Dermot P., 206
Morin's Restaurant, 38, 231
Morrison, Detective Patrick, 206
Morrison, Herb Jr., 310
Morrison, Herb Sr., 310
Morrissey, District Attorney Michael W., 224-5, 289
Morrissey, First Assistant Clerk-Magistrate Richard C. "Dick", 72
Morse, Detective Lieutenant Fred, 206
Morse, Jimmy, 293
Morse, Trooper Jason F., 207
Morse, Officer Peter J., 166
Morton Hospital, 11, 251-2
Moscow, Clerk-Magistrate Robert L., 125
Moscow, Dawn, 125
Moses, Attorney John M., 158-9

Moses, Detective James, 207
Most, Johnny, 242, 245-6
Moulton, Congressman Seth W., 288
Mount Rushmore, 244
Moynahan, Judge Ronald F., 129
Mrowka, Attorney Peter S., 132, 275
Mrs. Massachusetts, 198
Mt. Auburn Hospital, 227
Mucker the Trucker, 304
Muirhead, Judge MaryLou, 59
Mulcahy, Attorney Charles D., 132
Mulcahy, Cathy, 267
Mulkerrin, Sergeant Lynne F., 206
Mullaney, Kevin "Monger", 143
Muller, D. J., 324
Mulvee, Attorney John P. "Jack", 38
Muni-Tech, 194
Murphy, Attorney David G., 309
Murphy, Attorney Paul G., 132
Murphy, Attorney Peter F., 33, 132, 259
Murphy, Charlie, 320
Murphy, Clerk-Magistrate Kevin G., 38
Murphy, Clerk-Magistrate Sean P., 115-16
Murphy, Director Abby, 6
Murphy, Dr. Kevin R., 116
Murphy, Father Edward A., 103
Murphy, First Assistant Clerk-Magistrate Timothy F., 72
Murphy, Greg, 163, 275, 309-10
Murphy, Major Barney, 206
Murphy, Maureen, 236
Murphy, Meghan, 309
Murphy, Sergeant Elizabeth A., 116
Murphy, Sharon, 309
Murray, Attorney John T., 132
Murray, Lieutenant Governor Timothy P., 165
Murray, Marie, 315, 327
Murray, Patrick, 114
Murray, President Therese, 62
Murray, Russ, 295
Murray, Steven, 315
Muscato, Coach Val, 310
My Cousin Vinny, 249

Nadeau, Judge Gilbert J. Jr., 129
Nader, Ralph, 147
Nagle, Detective Timothy, 206
Nance, Jim, 106
Nantucket District Court, 6
Napper Tandy's, 125
NASCAR, 95
Nasson, Attorney Melissa, (copyright page)
Nasuti, Harvey, 301-2
Natick District Court, 6, 94, 130, 133, 136-8, 141
Natick Police, 137
National Anthem, 105, 218
National Baseball Hall of Fame, 6, 238
National Football League, 49
National Hockey League, 229
National Honor Society, 141
Naughton, Judge Harold P. Jr., 129
Nauticus Marina, 274
Navega, Attorney Stephen E., 132
Navy Cross, 307
Navy SEALs, 47, 300
Nazareth, 60
Nazi, 91, 115
NBA, 87, 104, 148-9, 242, 244
NBC's Meet the Press, 247
Neal, Lieutenant David, 207
Ned Devine's, 154
Ned Pepper Gang, 54
Nedder, Attorney Paula A., 132
Nelson, Assistant District Attorney Robert, 223
Nelson, Dave, 163
Nelson, Lori, 327
Nelson, Sergeant James, 206
Nesi, Anne, 212
Nesi, Judge Anthony R., 212
Nevens, Kenny, 315
New Bedford District Court, 113
New Bedford Police, 207
New Bedford School Committee, 14
New Bedford Superior Court, 218
New England Harness Raceway, 15

New England Heavyweight Champion, 56
New England Legal Foundation, 110
New England Mafia, 153
New England Patriots, 45, 58, 65, 198, 224-5, 286, 297, 301, 310, 313
New England Saltwater Fishing Show, 322
New England School of Law, 281, 299
New England Sports Stars for Ray Flynn, 106
New England Tea Men, 250
New Hampshire State Police, 180
New Hope, 128
New Jersey State Police, 216-7
New York City Firefighters, 49
New York City Transit Police, 199
New York Cosmos, 250
New York Giants, 211
New York Mets, 64
New York Rangers, 139
New York State Police Crime Lab, 220
New York Times, 211
New York Yankees, 260
Newman, Coach Stephen, 304
Newman, Paul, 292
Nguyen, Hiep "Henry", 315
Nicholas, Lieutenant Charles, 207
Nicholls, First Assistant Clerk-Magistrate Deborah A., 64
Nicholson, Dale, 325
Nicholson, Martin, 300
Nicky's Restaurant, 222, 306
Nike, 190
Nilan, Chris "Knuckles", 62
Ninety Nine Restaurant & Pub, 274
Ninth Bristol District, 107
Ninth Congressional District of Massachusetts, 31
Ninth Norfolk District, 110
Nixon Peabody LLP, 290
NO CLUE, 320
No Fluke Charters, 325
Noble, Sergeant Kevin W., Ph.D., 164-5
Nobrega, First Assistant Clerk-Magistrate David, 72
Noonan, Attorney Gerald J., 132
Noonan, Clerk-Magistrate Thomas J., 177-8
Noonan, Deputy Chief Richard H., 206

Norfolk County Bar Association, 3, 96
Norfolk County Commissioners, 286
Norfolk County District Attorney's Anti-Crime Council, 223
Norfolk County House of Correction, 293
Norfolk County Juvenile Court, 72
Norfolk County Probate & Family Court, 112
Norfolk County Prosecutor's Association, 167
Norfolk County Sheriff, 43, 207, 221, 224
Norfolk County Superior Court, 87, 127
Norfolk Police, 74, 95, 207
Norris, Dean, 217
North Attleborough Community Television, 6, 211
North Attleborough Police, 6, 121, 124, 149, 171, 178, 180, 188-90, 194, 199, 207, 213, 216-7, 225-6
Northbar Tackle, 315
Northeast Housing, 70
Northeastern University, 83
Norton Police, 167, 186, 207
Notre Dame, (cover legend), 29-30, 310
Nugent, Attorney Robert F. Jr., 132
Nunes, Attorney Richard A., 132
Nutmeg State, 199
NYPD, 164, 200

O'Boy, Attorney Francis M., 131
O'Brien, Assistant Clerk-Magistrate William, 72
O'Brien, Commissioner Francis W., 286
O'Brien, Councilor Edward M., 275-6
O'Brien, Officer Brad, 318
O'Brien, Officer Joe, 205
O'Brien, Officer Thomas P., 205
O'Brien, Treasurer Shannon, 275
O'Callahan, Sergeant Danny, 137
O'Connell, Assistant CPO Robert A., 113
O'Connell, Attorney William F., 132
O'Connell, Detective Robert, 224
O'Connor, Assistant Director David, 160
O'Dea, Judge Kevin J., 129
O'Donnell, Register William P., 42, 47, 96
O'Donnell, Trooper James, 207
O'Hara Hall, 310
O'Hara, Maureen, 247

O'Keefe, District Attorney Michael D., 203
O'Leary, Chief Edward T., 206
O'Leary, First Assistant Clerk-Magistrate Robert E., 38
O'Leary, Sergeant Timothy, 206
O'Malley, Judge Daniel W., 56-7, 220, 232
O'Neil, Clerk-Magistrate John C., 122-3
O'Neil, Detective Lieutenant Kevin P., 219
O'Neil, First Assistant Clerk-Magistrate Edward F. III, 38
O'Neil, Judge John H., 121-3
O'Neill, Chief Arthur M., 206
O'Neill, Judge James W., 129
O'Neill, Speaker Thomas P. "Tip" Jr., 103, 228
O'Reilly, Aiden, 24
O'Reilly, Ciara, 24
O'Reilly, Olive, 24
O'Reilly, Patricia, 24
O'Rourke, Attorney Paul, 86
O'Shaughnessy, Margaret Mary (see Heckler), 17
O'Shea, Judge Daniel J., 129
O'Toole, Clerk-Magistrate Philip B., 70
Oakland A's, 293
Obama, President Barack, 227, 280
Ocean Conservancy, 325
Ohio State, 106
Okun, Barry, 52, 248, 261, 312
Oliva, Nick, 261-2
Oliva's Market, 261-2
Oliveira, Clerk-Magistrate Roger J., 105-6
Oliveira, Maria, 105-6
Oliveira, Rogerio, 105-6
Oliver Ames High School, 310
Olson, Steve Ole, 6
On The Water, 3, 325
Ordway, Detective James, 137
Orlando, Kristen L., 77-8, 82, 309
Orleans District Court, 6, 195
Ortiz, David, 48
Ortiz, US Attorney Carmen M., (cover legend), 47, 202
Orzo Trattoria, 62
Osowick, George, 326-7
Ostrach, Judge Stephen S., 129
Otrando, Lieutenant John A., 205

Ottawa, 160-1
Otto, Officer Carl E., 205
Our Lady of Mount Carmel Church, 165
Oval Office, 285
Ovoian, Judge Robert S., 113-4
Owen, 160-1
Owens, Clerk-Magistrate Anthony S., 38
Oxford Creamery, 12

Padula, Attorney Peter E., 47, 117-9, 302
Padula, Detective Paul F., 206
Padula, Diane M., 118
Padula, John "The Master", 117-8, 301-2
Padula, Manager Paula J., 76-8
PAIN IN THE AFT, 320
Pakistan, 47
Palandjian, CEO Peter, 186
Palladini, Deputy Chief Michelle, 207
Palladini, Marissa, 81
Palm Beach Kennel Club, 142
Palmer, Detective Robert N., 205
Palminteri, Chazz, 268
Pan, Deanna, 212
Panchuk, Sergeant John, 207
Panek, Amy B., 42
Pantoliano, Joe, 268
Papa Gino's, 186
Pappas, Cindy, 320
Pappas, Sam, 320
Parker House, 252
Parkinson, Sergeant John P., 205
Pascucci, April, 6
Paterna, Clerk-Magistrate Salvatore, 27, 96
Patrick, Governor Deval L., 29, 62, 64, 66, 71-2, 111, 115, 122, 129-30, 136, 187, 222, 227, 290-1
Patriot Place, 303
Patterson, 265
Patterson, Detective Sergeant David A., 165-6
Patterson, Emily, 165
Patterson, Trooper Sheryl A., 165-6
Patton, General George S. Jr., 91
Paw Sox, 163

Pawtucket Police, 6, 163
Pawtucket Red Sox, 163, 210
Pawtucket Times, 210
Peabody, Governor Endicott H., 71, 129
Pearl Harbor, 177
Peck, Clerk-Magistrate Raymond S., 70
Pelusi, Attorney Anthony, R. Jr., 132
Pembroke Police, 37
Pender, Paul, 297
Penton, Trooper Jennifer J., (cover legend), 47
Pereira, George L., 166
Perenick, Clerk-Magistrate Charles H. "Charlie", 70
Perez, Tony, 238
Perino, Dana, 300
Perkoski, First Assistant Clerk-Magistrate James P., 33, 111-2, 216
Perot, Ross, 280
Perry Ellis, 87
Perry, Attorney Patricia M., 132
Perry, Paul, 308
Persian Gulf War, 164
Pesci, Joe, 249
Pesky, Johnny, 62, 64
Petersen, Deputy Chief Thomas J. Jr., 207
Peterson, Mike, 330
Petit, Mike, 50
Petition for Executive Clemency, 285
Petitt, Captain Mark, 320
Petracca, Tim "Hollywood", 315
Petralia, Assistant Clerk-Magistrate Ronald R., 72
Petrocelli, Rico, 62-3, 238
Petrowski, Attorney Thomas D., 132
Pfefferle, Lieutenant Frank, 207
Phantom Gourmet, 141
Philadelphia 76ers, 104
Phillips, Judge Gregory L., 129
Phipps, Attorney Bradley W., 132
Pickett, Special Agent Michael, 207
Pierce, Chief Justice Steven D., 42,
Pierce, Chief Richard J., 191, 202
Pino, Administrator Robert E., 222
Pitas, Lieutenant Stephen Jr., 205
Pizzi, Carol, 56, 253

Pizzi, Chief Alessandro, 6, 56, 83-4, 87, 222, 253, 261, 278
Pizzuto, Cathy, 267
Plainville Police, 181, 194, 207
Playzone, 270
Plum Island, 322
Plymouth County CPAC, 149, 198
Plymouth County House of Correction, 285
Plymouth County Juvenile Court, 72
Plymouth County Probate and Family Court, 89
Plymouth District Court, 77, 96
Plymouth Police, 37
Poirier, Representative Elizabeth A., 42
Polcari, John Jr., 169
Pomarole, Judge Michael J., 27
Pope John Paul II, 160
Porreca, Attorney Fiore, 132
Powell, Boog, 310-11
Powers, Holly, 100
Powers, John, 14-15
Powers, Judge Warren A., 99-100
Pozzessere, Clerk-Magistrate Maryann, 291
Presley, Elvis, 123
Prime, Assistant Clerk-Magistrate Noreen E., 72
Privitera Family Charitable Foundation, 63
Privitera, Attorney Philip J., 63
Prodouz, Bill "On the Grill", 80, 315, 327, 328
Proia, Captain David T., 159
Propp, Assistant Deputy Court Administrator Deborah L., 70
Prosser, Assistant Clerk-Magistrate Michael D., 72
Provi, 105
Providence College, 104
Pudolsky, Special Sheriff Gerald C., 220-1
Pugsley, Detective John R. "Jack", 156
Pugsley, Officer Jeffrey J., 156
Pugsley, Sergeant Arthur S., 156
Pulaski, General Casimir, 115
Pulitzer Prizes, 316
Puller, Attorney Alfred, 132
Purro, Gerry, 14, 293
Pye, Theresa, 306

Quale, Vice President Dan, 281, 283

Quarry, 265
Quebec, 161
Quencher Tavern, 237
Quigley, First Assistant Clerk-Magistrate Andrew P., 72
Quincy District Court, 55-6, 138, 225
Quincy Police, 183
Quinn, Assistant Clerk-Magistrate Thomas F., 72
Quinn, Assistant Dean John F., 107
Quinn, Brenda L., 100
Quinn, District Attorney Thomas M. III, 107, 227
Quinn, First Assistant Clerk-Magistrate Matthew R., 108
Quinn, Judge James M., 108-9, 158
Quinn, Judge Thomas M. Jr., 107, 122
Quintal, Attorney Kerri A., 132
Quintana, Carlos, 260

Radsken, Jill, 30
Rammel, Officer Natalie E., 206
Raposa, Chief Justice Phillip, 104
Rayburn House Office Building, 223
Raymond L. Flynn Marine Park, 186
Raynham Park, 36, 292, 296-8
Raynham Police, 36
Reagan, President Ronald W., 17, 168, 289
Reagan, Richard "Ripper", 296
Reali, Detective Sergeant Luigi, 217
RECESS, 127, 319
Record, Scott, 118
Red Rooster Bar & Grill, 305
Red Sox, 6, 9, 10, 23, 27-8, 47-8, 60, 62-4, 99, 107, 111, 163, 210, 225, 235-6, 239-40, 248, 253-4, 257, 261-2, 285, 292, 309-10, 312, 332
Red Top Sporting Goods, 315, 326, 329
Redd, Judge Edward R., 129
Reddington, Attorney Kevin J., 27, 65
Redfearn, Lieutenant James G., 203
REEL AMERICAN, 319
Regan Communications Group, 186, 273-4
Regan, Elizabeth, 274
Regan, George K. Jr., (cover legend & back cover plaudit), 186, 273-4
Regina, Sister Jane, 97
Reiley, Henry "Scoop", 210-11
Reilly, Chief John J., 124

Reilly, Lieutenant Jason C., 124
Reilly, Lieutenant Jody, 124
Reilly, Lieutenant, Philip J., 124
Reilly, Richard, 13
Reis, Wayne, 318
Revere Police, 183
Revolutionary War, 115
Reynolds, Patty, 166
RFK Human Rights Annual Golf Tournament, 149, 242
Rhinestone Cowboy, 49
Rhode Island Convention Center, 271, 322
Rhode Island House of Representatives, 6
Rhode Island State Police, 9, 56, 122, 216, 245
Rhode Island State Police Academy, 56, 245
Ricciardi, SAC Steven D., 153-4
Riccio, Attorney Nicholas, 234
Riccio, Barbara, 234
Riccio, Jack, 26, 234
Riccio, Pamela J., 234
Rice, Jim, 62, 260
Rich, Attorney Bruce G., 132
Rich, Attorney Daniel M., 131
Richards, Keith, 181
Richardson, Frank, 309
Richardson, Judge Maurice H., 27
Richardson, Rhondella D., 209
Riggieri, Paul, 74
Righetti, Dave, 260
Rimini Street, 110
River Shannon, 3
Rizos, Sergeant Byron L., 206
Roache, Assistant Clerk-Magistrate John, 72
Roadhouse Cafe, 232
Roake, Sergeant Kevin D., 95
Roberson, Special Agent John F. "Fred", 206
Robertson, Michael, 84-5
Robertson, Oscar, 106
Robichaud, Officer Marc, 207
Robinson, Attorney Frances, 86
Roche, Assistant Clerk Brian G., 96
Roche, Attorney John J., 132
Roche, Attorney Neil J., 132

Roche, Clerk-Magistrate James B., 168-9
Rochester Red Wings, 260
Rockett, Attorney Paul M., 132
Rodman Celebration for Kids, 52
Rodman Ford, 245
Rodman Ride for Kids, 52
Rodman, Donald E., 52, 245, 308
Rogers, Abby, 287
Rogers, Leader John H., 42, 138, 286-7, 320
Rojee, Officer John, 207
Rolling Stones, 181
Rollins, District Attorney Philip A., 18, 19
Roman, Attorney Brian D., 132
Romney, Governor Mitt, 38, 59, 70, 104, 110, 112, 114, 119, 122, 129, 136
Roper, Clerk-Magistrate George P., 72
Roque, Attorney Gerald W., 132
Rosata, Vinny 315
Rose, Attorney Dale E., 132
Rose, Officer Steve, 205
Rose, Officer Timothy J., 96
Roseland Ballroom, 147
Ross, Clerk-Magistrate Stephen I., 70
Rossetti, Joe, 320
Roster, Attorney Edward A., 251-2
Roster, Frank, 251
Rotary Club's Distinguished Service Award, 159, 226
Rotenberg, Judge Ernest I., 114
Rougeau, Attorney Julie A., 132
Roughsedge, Attorney Robert J., 132
Roy, Captain Jason, 207
Roy, Representative Jeffrey N., 132
Roy, Trooper Christopher, 206
Royal Ottawa Golf Club, 161
Rucker, Reggie, 59
Rull, Attorney John P., 132
Runyon, Damon, 292
Russell, Bill, 148-9, 242, 244
Russert, Tim, 247-8
Russo, Dave, 51
Ruth, Babe, 203, 317
Rutley, Attorney Jonathan C., 132
Ryan, Attorney Ralph, 132

Ryan, Clerk-Magistrate Robert L., 72
Ryan, Flo, 60
Ryan, Judge Paul E., 60
Ryan, Kristin M., 6
Ryan, Michael J., 60
Ryan, Nolan, 301
Ryan, Officer Pamela J., 60
Ryan, Officer Richard R., 207
Ryan, PO Diane M., 60
Ryshavy, Tom, 236

Sabitus, Jim, (cover legend)
Sabourin, Chief Roland D. Jr., 152
Sabra, Attorney Steven P., 132
Sabra, Judge Bernadette L., 129
Saipan, 307
Salmon, Clerk-Magistrate Raymond J. Sr., 70
Salmon, First Assistant Clerk-Magistrate Raymond J. Jr., 72
Salve Regina University, 105-6
Samarra, 255
Samis, Phil, 229
Sampson, Gary Lee, 149, 198
San Francisco Giants, 254
San Francisco Warriors, 87
Sanders, Thomas "Satch", 62, 148
Sanderson, Derek, 62, 250-1, 256
Sanderson, Jennifer, RN, 256
Sanderson, John, 256
Sanderson, Johnny, 256
Sandra C. Labaree Volunteer Values Award, 210
Sands, Natalie, 244
Santa Claus, 172, 177
Santarpio, Joia, 65
Santarpio's Pizza, 65
Santiago, Roberto, 258
Santos, Clerk Marc J., 96
Santos, Congressman George, 8
Sargent, Governor Francis W., 20, 27, 41, 64, 67, 70, 71, 114, 129, 130
Sargent, Judge Dennis P., 122
Sarmento, Sergeant Gary, 207
Sarrouf, Attorney Camille F., 132
Saturday Night Fever, 34

Saturday Night Live, 198
Saulnier, Detective Stephen, 207
Saurino, Attorney Joseph D, 59, 60
Saurino, Mary Ann, 59
Savage, Clerk-Magistrate Edward F. "Ted" Jr., 66
Schaefer Stadium, 211, 250
Schilling, Curt, 330
Schmidt, Attorney Richard P., 132
Schultz, Denise, 160
Scouras, Mickey, 306-7
Scouras, Pete, 306
Scully, Officer Brian, 66-7
Sea Crest Beach Hotel, 89
Seafood Marketing Steering Committee, 323
Seaport Hotel, 52
Seattle Mariners, 23, 254
Sebile, Patrick, 326
Seebeck, Detective Captain John S., 163
Seeberger, Tim, 271
Seery, Sergeant First Class Michael, 81
Segadelli, Attorney Drew J., 43, 320
Seguin, Lieutenant Richard W., 206
Selig, Commissioner Bud, 238
Semerjian, Chief Stephan H., 206
SEVEN MILES AFTER SUNDOWN, 3, 139, 255
Seven7 Jeans, 116
Sexton, Captain Paul, 315
Shane (dog), 219
Shanghai, 317
Shanley, Attorney Edward K. "Charlie", 131
Shanley, Terry, 131
Shannon, Assistant Clerk-Magistrate Paul W., 72
Shannon, General James M., 103
Shapiro, Deputy Court Administrator Ellen S., 70
Sharkansky, Judge Edward H., 129
Shaughnessy, Daniel, 238-9
Shaw, SAC Harold H., 206
SHE GOT THE HOUSE, 319
Shea Stadium, 163
Shea, Attorney Michael, 70
Shea, Detective Lieutenant Kevin P., 219
Shea, Second Assistant Clerk-Magistrate George L. Jr., 138

Sheehan, Lieutenant David C., 207
Sheerin, First Assistant Clerk-Magistrate James B. "JB", 113
Sheldon, Sergeant Leslie A., 171
Shepard, Officer Michael, 207
Sher, Assistant Clerk-Magistrate Michael, 72
Sherborn Police, 144, 165-6
Sherman, Casey, 6
Shields, Officer Paul, 206
Siddle, Kristen, 267
Silva, Attorney Richard J. Jr., 92
Silver Sulfadiazine, 165
Silvestri, Larry, 327-8
Silvestri, Sergeant Kevin, 207
Silvestri, Trooper First Class Randy S., 206
Silvia, Chief Carol A., 84
Silvia, Detective Captain Michael J., 174
Simard, Attorney Gordon O., 132
Simonelli, First Assistant Clerk-Magistrate Carmine M., 261, 308
Simpson, Officer John T., 206
Sing Sing, 315
Sippican Week, 271
Sister Mary Alice, 7
Siudut, Chief Edward F., 87
Sivonen, Ben, 315
Sivonen, Ron "Hollywood", 315
Skaar, Michelle, 6
Skelton, Harold, 315
Skurchak, Attorney John W. Jr., 132
Sloan, Attorney Victor T., 132
Smalley, Dan, 315
Smalley, Matt, 315
Smerlas, Fred, 202-3
Smith, Firefighter Jerry, 120
Smith, Officer Michael J., 207
Smith, Sergeant Jeffrey, 207
Smith, Thomas A., 166
Smolinsky, Sergeant David P., 207
Soares, Captain Charley, 3, 84, 325
Soffayer, Chief Christopher J., 207
Somerset Creamery, 94
Somerset Police, 105
Somerville District Court, 6, 25, 42, 61, 73, 92, 115,

Songin, Detective Timothy W., 207
Sonis, Fran, 267
Sousa, Attorney Henry J. Jr., "Joe", 132
Sousa, Attorney Stephanie A., 132
Sousa-Baranowski Correctional Center, 228
South Armagh, 163
South Bend, 29
South Boston Division, Boston Municipal Court, 114
South Bronx, 41st Precinct, 200
Southeast Housing Court, 62, 105, 119
Souza, Martin, 315
Soviet Union, 65
Spatcher, Attorney George I. Jr., 132
Spaulding Rehab, 59
Spaulding, Attorney Mandy L., 132
Spencer Gifts, 190
Spicer, Sergeant Richard H., 207
Spiewakowski, PO Stephen R., 83
Spillane Field, 44
Spillane, Attorney Florence M., 132
Spillane, Attorney Francis J., 132
Spirit of American Justice Award, 277
Spirit of Nursing Award, 251
Sport Fishing Expo, 324
Sports Huddle, 292
Sprague, Senator Jo Ann, 42
Sproul, Detective Joseph W., 205
Sragow, Judge Roanne, 129
Sroczinski, Paul, 315
St. Andrew the Apostle, 103
St. Anne, 59
St. Cyr, Assistant Clerk-Magistrate Gregory V., 72
St. Cyr, Judge John F., 67
St. James Gate, 265
St. John, Officer Pamela, 207
St. Louis Cardinals, 240
St. Mary's Grammar School, 97
St. Patrick's Day, 115, 149, 218, 239, 246, 277, 278
St. Patrick's Day Breakfast, 277-8
St. Paul's Elementary School, 299
Stan Gibbs Cape Cod Canal Fisherman's Classic, 3
Stanley Cup, 229, 250

Stanley, Bob, 64,
Stanton, Judge James M., 129
Stanziani, Clerk-Magistrate Doris A., 70
Stapleton, Clerk-Magistrate Donald M., 70
Stapleton, Judge John P., 222
Star Market, 99
State Ethics Commission Report, 188
State House Library of Massachusetts, 6
State Police Association of Massachusetts, 160
Steingold, Attorney Neil R., 132
Stenson, John, 300
Steve Newman Track, 304
Stevens, Judge David E., 71
Stevens, Senator Theodore F., 325
Stillman, Chief Richard B., 207
Stilwell, Fran, 267
Stockwell, Mark, 6, 210
Stoddart, Judge Douglas W., 136
Stoico, Katie, 81-2
Stone, Chief Charles H. Jr., 207
Stonebridge Marina, 320
Stonehill College, 104, 310
Stop & Shop, 126, 164, 203
Stork, Rob, 328
Stoughton Chamber of Commerce, 91
Stoughton District Court, 6, 56, 90
Strike Pro, 315
Striper Gear, 315
Stuart, Lieutenant J. Jeff, 206
Sturdy, Kerry, 240
Sturdy Memorial Hospital, 117, 263
Sturdy, Clerk-Magistrate Mark E., 111, 240
Suffolk Construction, 187
Suffolk County Superior Court, 104-5
Suffolk Downs, 292
Sullivan, Assistant Clerk Brendan P., 96
Sullivan, Clerk-Magistrate Brian V., 6, 38
Sullivan, Clerk-Magistrate Daniel J., 16, 46
Sullivan, Clerk-Magistrate James H., 16, 31, 33, 107, 111, 114
Sullivan, Judge James M., 77
Sullivan, Judge Mary Hogan, 69, 70
Sullivan, Judge Roger F., 129

Sullivan, Judge William F., (cover legend), 29
Sullivan, Mayor Joseph C., 288
Sullivan, Officer Paul, 206
Sullivan, Tim, 315
Sullivan, US Attorney Michael J., 288
Summers, Attorney AnDré D., 132
Summers, Trooper Thomas W., 217-8
Survivor, 253
Suter, Clerk William, 123
Sutter, Mayor C. Samuel, 132, 227
Suzie (dog), 10
Swain, Susan, 123
Swartz, Connor, 315
Swaylik, Dick, 320
Swaylik, Lesley, 320
Sweeney, Attorney Edward J. III, 132
Sweeney, Attorney Richard J., 96, 178
Sweeney, Steve, 50, 274
Swift, Governor Jane M., 27, 42, 46, 69-72, 77, 119, 129, 133, 141, 212
Swimsuit Competition, 21
Swindon, Supervisory Special Agent Kevin L., 206
Sylva, Assistant Clerk-Magistrate Elisabeth, 66
Syracuse Nationals, 104
Szwyd, "New Hampshire Bob", 315
Szymanski, Attorney Michael S., 132

Tabb, Chris, 167-8
Tackle Shop Triage, 329-30
Taggart, Officer Scot, 181
Tales from the City, 28, 74
Tampa Bay Buccaneers, 265
Tampa Bay Rowdies, 250
Tampa Bay, 309
Tampa Homecoming, 133
Tanous, Chief Justice's Executive Assistant Brenda, 70
Taunton Building Department, 285
Taunton Daily Gazette, 227
Taunton District Court, 36, 101, 103, 146, 174
Taunton Dog Track, 292, 294, 298
Taunton Police, 11, 146, 174
Tavares, 34
Tavares, Lieutenant Richard, 206

Tavares, Officer Ralph, 34
Tavares-Colicchio, Clerk-Magistrate Ann, 136
Teague, Clerk-Magistrate Edward B. III, 70
Teahan, Judge William W. Jr., 129
Ted 2, 51
Tedino, Councilor Carolyn J., 288
Tenth Norfolk District, 290
Terezakis, Anast, 315
Terezakis, Nick, 315
Terrell, 265
Terrio, Cindy, 30
Terrio, Ken, 30, 303
Terrio, Ralph, 30, 303
Terrio, Tallie, 30
Tex Barry's Coney Island Diner, 40
Texas Tech, 304
The ACCIDENTAL POPE, 106
The Baseball Encyclopedia, 238
The *Boston Globe* Library Collection at the Northeastern University Archives and Special Collections, 156
The Boston Globe, 3, 10, 30,48, 51, 56, 74, 210, 212, 238, 249, 260, 273, 273-4, 290, 295, 316
The Boston Sunday Globe, 123
The Bourne Review, 316
The Courts & You, 33
THE CURSE OF THE BAMBINO, 239
The Dubliner, 305
The Falmouth Enterprise, 325
The Fish Wrap Writer, 325
The Fisherman Statue, 331
The Fisherman, 325
The Hustler, 292
The Inn on Shipyard Park, 267
The Little Professor, 248
The Q-Tip, 43
The Quiet Man, 247
The Sun Chronicle, 3, 6, 25, 31, 33, 61, 107, 113, 152, 170, 195, 210-12, 289, 316, 332
The SUPREME COURT: A C-SPAN BOOK FEATURING THE JUSTICES IN THEIR OWN WORDS, 123
The Wooden Spoon, 303
There's Something About Mary, 50

They Were My Friends-JACK, BOB AND TED: My Life in and out of Politics, 280
Thibedeau, Sergeant John, 206
Thomas, Assistant Clerk-Magistrate Cynthia Vincent, 72
Thomas, Clerk-Magistrate Peter J., 113
Thomas, Judge Steven E., 129
Thompson, Attorney Bruce E., 132
Thrasher, Attorney James D., 132
Tiant, Luis, 62, 310, 312
Tiberi, Detective Sergeant Domenic J., 98
Times Square, 51
Timilty, Clerk Walter F., 96
Timilty, Councilor Kelly A., 275
Timilty, Senator James E., 202-4, 275
Timilty, Senator Joseph F., 275
Tingley, Chief Allen, 207
Tinian, 307
TJ Maxx, 190
Tobey Hospital, 116, 330
Tobin Bridge, 38
Tobin, Assistant Clerk-Magistrate Mark, 225
Tobin, Attorney A. Stephen, 132
Tobin, Clerk-Magistrate Arthur H., 225
Tobin, Governor Maurice J., 114-15
Tobin, Sergeant Bruce J., 225
Todd, Brenda Fiske, 68
Tomaiolo, Clerk-Magistrate Leonard F., 70
Tomasone, Clerk-Magistrate Robert A. "Ted", 6, 25, 37, 42, 61-5, 67, 73, 92, 114, 235, 275
Tomei, Marisa, 249
Tommy Hilfiger, 87
Toronto Maple Leafs, 229
Touchdown Jesus, 30
Touchstone Pictures, 112
TOWN DRUNK, 181
TPC Boston, 226
TPC Sawgrass, 226
Tracy, Attorney Cheryl A., 132
Tracy, Attorney Philip A. Jr., 132
Tracy, Officer Jerry, 54
Trahan, Congresswoman Lori A., 288
Travaglini, President Robert E., 62
Tringale, Assistant Clerk-Magistrate Robert C., 72
Triple Crown, 254

Troop, Director Toni K., 128
Trooper of the Year, 216
TROPHY WIFE, 320
Troy, First Assistant Clerk-Magistrate Paul F., 72
True Lies, 186
Trump, President Donald, 105, 274
Trupiano, Donna, 253
Trupiano, Jerry, 62, 64, 253-4
Tryon, Trooper Robert, 206
Tulsa Roughnecks, 250
Tuohy, Attorney John S., 132
Turcotte, Judge David T., 92
Turk, 251
Turkey, 113
Turner, Jim, 330
Turturro, Nicholas, 217
Tuttle, Attorney William R., 132
Tweedy, Attorney Talbot T., 132
Twelfth Norfolk District, 286
Twiss, Vice President Jeff, 6
Tworek, Dave, 328

US Coast Guard, 139
UCLA-University of Chelsea Logan Airport, 30
Uguccioni, Assistant Clerk Janice C., 96
Ukraine, 214
UMASS Boston, 160
Underhill, Paramedic John, 263
United Freedom Front, 216
United States Ambassador to Canada, 160
United States Ambassador to Ireland, 17, 291
United States Ambassador to Mexico, 22
United States Ambassador to New Zealand and Samoa, 105
United States Ambassador to the Holy See, 105
United States Attorney, 47, 202, 288
United States Capitol, 277, 325
United States Conference of Mayors, 104, 278
United States Congress, 17, 31, 103, 240
United States Constitution, 91
United States Customs, 184
United States Department of Justice, 285
United States District Court, 129-30, 278

United States Embassy, 160, 291
United States Immigration & Customs Enforcement, 184
United States Immigration Court, 121
United States Marine Corps Veteran, 52, 202, 323
United States Marines, 226, 245
United States Marshall Service, 168
United States Marshall, 47, 168
United States Navy SEALs, 300
United States Navy, 178
United States of America, (copyright page), 285, 299
United States Secret Service, 153, 160, 207
United States Senate, 42
United States Special Envoy for Northern Ireland, 240
United States Supreme Court, 81, 123
University of Cincinnati, 106
University of Florida, 225
University of Massachusetts Foundation, 46
University of Notre Dame, 29, 30
University of South Florida, 3, 9, 29, 30, 133, 250-1, 303
Unquiet Diplomacy, 162

V, Tony, 51
V. H. Blackinton & Co., Inc., 188
Valanzola, Attorney Edward W., 132
Valcourt, Clerk-Magistrate Ronald A., 35-6
Valentine, Bobby, 62
Vallee, Leader James E., 42, 290-1
Vallely, Attorney Sallie K., 132
Van Ness, Lieutenant Eric S., 207
Vargas, Detective Peter, 206
Varitek, Jason, 310, 312
Vaughan, Attorney Edward Foley, 132
Vaughan, Clerk-Magistrate Robin E., 71
Vaughn, Mo, 23, 27, 260
Vel's Restaurant, (cover legend)
Velino, Lieutenant Lawrence, 158
Venezuela, 83
Vennochi, Joan, 210
Vernon, Attorney William B., 132
Veterans Transition House, 306
Veterans Treatment Court, 69
Victory Distributors, Inc. v. Ayer Division of the District Court Department, 221

Viera, Clerk-Magistrate Roxana E., 70
Vietnam, 323
Vignone, Attorney Anthony M., 132
Vignone, Attorney Janet M., 132
Vignone, Attorney John P., 132
Vincent's Nightclub, 67
Viola, Frank, 254
VIRGINIA JOAN, 325
Vitale, Chief Robert P., 293
Vitale, Joanne M., 293
Vitale, Officer Steve M., 293
Vitale, Peter, 293
Vitale, Phil, 293-4
Vitali, Regional Administrative Justice Michael A., 129
Vitamin G, 265
Vito, Mona Lisa, 249
Viveiros, Clerk-Magistrate Carlton M., 62
Volk, Attorney Jan, 148
Volpe, Governor John A., 70, 113
Volterra, Attorney Max, 132

Wade, Attorney Victor, 125-6
Wagner, Attorney Andrea J., 132
Wagner, Judge Augustus F. Jr., 18
Wahlberg, Mark, 52
Wainwright, Attorney William M., 132
Wakefield, Tim, 62
Waldron, Officer Brian, 136
Walker, Bob, 304
Walmart, 256, 300
Walpole Police, 51-3, 55, 69, 92, 95, 119, 207, 219-20, 319
Walsh, Assistant Clerk-Magistrate Patrick T., 72
Walsh, Bill, 315
Walsh, District Attorney Paul F. Jr., 24, 103, 284
Walsh, Donny, 297
Walsh, Dr. Paul F., 14, 24, 284, 294, 296-7
Walsh, Judge Brian, 129
Walsh, Mayor Martin J., 186
Walsh, Vinny, 147-8
Walt Disney Pictures, 112
Walter Reed Hospital, 255
Wareham Gatemen, 44, 131

Wareham Police, 133-4, 144
Washington, President George, 8, 115
Wasserman, Assistant Clerk-Magistrate Nancy K., 72
Waxman, Kathryn, 6
Way Ho, 142
Wayne, John, 54, 247
WCOD FM, 320
WCVB, 6, 209-10
Webster, Mike, 315
Wedge, David M., (back cover plaudit), 211
Weeman, Sergeant Earl W., 206
Weilding, Attorney Douglas B., 132
Weinberg-Kraus, PO Gail, 83
Weiner, Judge Phillip L., 6, 214
Weir, "Breakin' Bob", 315
Weir, Lieutenant Patrick F., 207
Welch, Judge Joseph R., 55-6
Welcome, Larry, 315
Weld, Governor William F., 17-19, 22, 25, 36, 38, 42, 46, 56, 62, 70, 78, 89, 92, 99, 101, 104, 120, 122, 127, 129, 136, 168, 228, 274, 290
Werman, Officer Howie, 101
Werner, Attorney Joshua D., 132
West Roxbury Division, Boston Municipal Court, 115
West, President Ray, 324
Westborough District Court, 291
Weston State Police Barracks, 136
Whaling City, 109, 318
Wheaton College, 166
Whelan, Sergeant Timothy R., 206
White, Assistant Register Timothy H., 288
White, Assistant Special Agent in Charge Kevin R., 206
White, Jo Jo, 87
White, Judge Mary Dacey, 129
White, Mayor Kevin H., 115, 273
White, Sergeant Richard F., 206
Whitehurst, Kit, 303
Whitman Police, 37
Whitney, First Assistant Clerk-Magistrate Darryl S., 72
Whittemore, Katharine, 123
Who Wants to Be a Millionaire?, 57
Widmer, Ted, 2
Wiggins, Jermaine, 65

Williams, Chief Stephen T., 206
Williams, Dick, 310
Williams, Ted, 97, 221, 253
Williamson, Clerk-Magistrate Liza H., 70
Willis, Donnie "Hawkeye", 315
Willis, Rob, 315
Willowbend, 273-4
Wilner, First Assistant Clerk-Magistrate Arthur, 37, 72
Wilson, Attorney Sara Holmes, 132
Wilson, Attorney Tracy L., (cover legend), 43-4, 167
Wilson, Mookie, 64
Winn, Attorney Nancy Maloof, 132
Winslow, Judge Daniel B., 56, 110, 128, 287
Winston, 285
Wirth, Jonathan D., Dedication, 89, 259, 298
Wirth, Joseph D., Dedication, 269-71
Wirth, Kaitlin M., Dedication, 6, 20, 35, 89, 188-9, 192, 244, 246, 248-9, 255, 259, 262, 266-8, 270-1, 298, 309, 330
Wirth, Molly G., Dedication, 269-72
Witherell, Officer Donald L., 205
Witherell, Sergeant Brian J., 205
Witkin, Attorney Mark J., 292
Witkin, Attorney Roger, 86
Witkus, Lisa, 6
Wojnar, Chairman David E., 105
Wolloff, Joshua, 6
Wolves Den Sports Complex, 324
Woods Hole Golf Club, 296
Woodstock, 143, 197
Worcester District Court, 177
Worcester Telegram & Gazette, 325
Wordell, PO Jeffrey A., 110
World War II, 51, 115, 147, 177, 212, 307
Wrentham District Court, 3-4, 6-7, 23, 74, 88, 305
Wrentham Outlets, 79, 87,
Wrentham Police, 54, 78, 87, 150, 207, 224
Wu, Mayor Michelle, 281-2
Wynn, Attorney Paul F., 132
Wynn, Attorney Thomas J., 132

Xaverian Brothers High School, 90
Xifaras, Attorney Louis S., 104

Xifaras, Maxine, 104

Yale, 38, 136
Yankee Stadium, 8
Yastrzemski, Carl, 221, 254
Yastrzemski, Mike, 254
Yee, Attorney Frank A. Jr., 132
YES DEAR, 320
Youman, Attorney Alvin, 158
Yummy House, 182

Zaino III, Nick A., 51
Zandan, Jessica, 210
Zanello, Attorney Robert, 86
Zhejiang, 317
Ziter, Regional Coordinator Jill K., 70
Zolak, Scott, 49
Zoll, Chief Justice Samuel E., 27
Zwirblis, Attorney W. Alan, 158